Organizational Communication

Organizational Communication: Approaches and Processes

SEVENTH EDITION

Katherine Miller

Arizona State University

CENGAGE
Learning

Australia • Brazil • Japan • Korea • Mexico • Singapore • Spain • United Kingdom • United States

CENGAGE
Learning®

Organizational Communication: Approaches and Processes, Seventh Edition

Katherine Miller

Product Director: Monica Eckman

Senior Product Manager: Nicole Morinon

Content Developer: Larry Goldberg

Content Coordinator: Alicia Landsberg

Product Assistant: Colin Solan

Media Developer: Jessica Badiner

Marketing Development Manager: Kristin Davis

Production Management, and Composition: Manoj Kumar, MPS Limited

Manufacturing Planner: Doug Bertke

Rights Acquisitions Specialist: Ann Hoffman

Art Director: Carolyn Deacy, MPS Limited

Cover Designer: Ellen Pettengell

Cover image: T.J. Florian – Rainbow/Science Faction/Corbis

For product information and technology assistance, contact us at **Cengage Learning Customer & Sales Support, 1-800-354-9706**

For permission to use material from this text or product, submit all requests online at **www.cengage.com/permissions**

Further permissions questions can be e-mailed to **permissionrequest@cengage.com**

Library of Congress Control Number: 2013952132

Student Edition:
ISBN-13: 978-1-285-16420-5

ISBN-10: 1-285-16420-2

Cengage Learning
200 First Stamford Place, 4th Floor
Stamford, CT 06902
USA

Cengage Learning is a leading provider of customized learning solutions with office locations around the globe, including Singapore, the United Kingdom, Australia, Mexico, Brazil and Japan. Locate your local office at **international.cengage.com/region**.

Cengage Learning products are represented in Canada by Nelson Education, Ltd.

For your course and learning solutions, visit **www.cengage.com**.

Purchase any of our products at your local college store or at our preferred online store **www.cengagebrain.com**.

Instructors: Please visit **login.cengage.com** and log in to access instructor-specific resources.

Printed in the United States of America
1 2 3 4 5 6 7 17 16 15 14 13

About the Author

Dr. Katherine Miller is a leading scholar on processes of emotion and compassion in the workplace. She holds bachelor's and master's degrees in communication from Michigan State University, and a doctorate from the Annenberg School of Communication at the University of Southern California. She is currently a professor at Arizona State University and has also served on the faculties of Michigan State University, University of Kansas, and Texas A&M University. Dr. Miller is the author of four books and more than sixty journal articles and book chapters.

Brief Contents

Contents

Preface

As I have noted in the previous editions of this book, the "ages" of scholarly fields are notoriously hard to pinpoint. Most would agree, however, that organizational communication has been around for well over six decades. The infancy of the discipline was marked by struggles for survival and nurturance from other disciplines. The discipline's teenage years—the time when I was entering the field—saw a questioning of identity and fights for autonomy. Today, organizational communication has reached a maturity few would have envisioned in the middle of the twentieth century, and the field now encompasses a healthy eclecticism, in that a variety of theoretical approaches provides contrasting accounts of the ways in which communicating and organizing intersect. And this is definitely a good thing, for few would have predicted the changes that have occurred in our world—changes in politics, business, technology, values, the environment. We need a solid but dynamic understanding of organizational communication to cope with this complex and changing world.

This book attempts to reflect the eclectic maturity of the field of organizational communication. When I began writing the first edition of this book almost twenty years ago, my first conceptual decision was not to advocate a particular approach to the field. Instead, I tried to show that both traditional and contemporary perspectives provide potentially illuminating views of organizational communication processes.

For example, a critical theorist, an ethnographer, and a systems researcher may all look at a particular organizational communication phenomenon—say, socialization practices—and see very different things. A systems theorist might see a cybernetic system in which the goal of organizational assimilation is enhanced through a variety of structural and individual communication mechanisms. A cultural researcher might see socialization as a process through which the values and practices of an organizational culture are revealed to—and created by—individuals during organizational entry. A critical theorist might see socialization as a process through which individuals are drawn into hegemonic relationships that reinforce the traditional power structure of the organization.

All these views of the organizational socialization process are limited in that each obscures some aspects of organizational entry. But each view is also illuminating. Thus, early chapters of this book cover a gamut of academic approaches—from classical through human relations and human resources to systems, cultural, and critical—as lenses through which organizational communication can be viewed. The strengths and weaknesses of each approach are considered, but no particular approach is presented as inherently superior.

My next important choice in writing this book was deciding how to organize the voluminous research literature on organizational communication. At the time I started writing this book, most textbooks had taken a "levels" approach, considering in turn organizational communication at the individual, dyadic, group, and organizational levels. I find this approach frustrating both because there are some things that happen at multiple levels (for example, we make decisions alone, in dyads, and in groups) and because there are processes that are not easily linked to any of these levels. (For example, where does communication technology fit in? At what level do we consider emotion in the workplace?) Thus, the chapters in the second half of this textbook involve a consideration of organizational communication processes.

My goals in the "processes" portion of the book are fourfold. First, I want the processes considered to be up to date in reflecting current concerns of both organizational communication scholars and practitioners. Thus, in addition to looking at traditional concerns, such as decision making and conflict, this textbook highlights communication processes related to cultural and gender diversity, communication technology, organizational change, and emotional approaches to organizational communication. Second, I want to be as comprehensive as possible in describing relevant theory and research on each topic. Thus, each "process" chapter highlights both foundational and current research on organizational communication processes from the fields, including communication, management, industrial psychology, and sociology. Third, I want students to understand that each of these communication processes can be viewed through a variety of theoretical lenses, so I conclude each chapter with a section on the insights of the approaches considered in the first half of the book. Finally, I want readers to realize that organizational communication is a concern to individuals beyond the ivory towers of academia. Thus, I have included many real-world examples both in the discussion of each process and in pedagogical features.

ORGANIZATION OF THE TEXT

This textbook explores the world of organizational communication in terms of both scholarship and application. The majority of chapters consider either approaches that have shaped our beliefs about organizational communication practice and study (Chapters 2–6) or chapters that consider specific organizational communication processes (Chapters 7–13). The first two chapters on "approaches" (Chapters 2–3) both consider prescriptive approaches on how organizational communication should operate (Classical Approaches, Human Relations, and Human Resources Approaches), while the following three approaches chapters (Chapters 4–6) consider contemporary approaches regarding how we can best describe, understand, explain, and critique organizational communication (Systems and Cultural approaches, Constitutive Approaches, and Critical Approaches). When we move on to the "processes" chapters, we first consider enduring processes that have always characterized communication in organizations in Chapters 7 to 10 (Assimilation

Processes, Decision-Making Processes, Conflict Management Processes, and Change and Leadership Processes). Then, in Chapters 11 to 13, we look at emerging processes that have come into play in recent decades (Processes of Emotion in the Workplace, Organizational Diversity Processes, and Technological Processes). These chapters are bracketed by an introductory chapter (Chapter 1) and a concluding chapter (Chapter 14) that put these approaches and processes into context by considering specific challenges in today's world and the ways in which the study of organizational communication can help us deal with these challenges.

Those familiar with this textbook will note a number of changes from the sixth edition, which will enhance student understanding of organizational communication. One major change is a brand new chapter considering constitutive approaches (Chapter 5). Ideas regarding the communicative constitution of organization (CCO) have become increasingly important in our discipline in recent years, and I decided that these developments deserved a chapter-long consideration in this new edition. Chapter 6 has also been revised to consider feminist approaches as distinct from critical theory. In addition, all of the chapters have been updated to include current research and theory, leading to the addition of well over one hundred new references, with particular emphasis on current events and contemporary research conducted by communication scholars. The seventh edition of *Organizational Communication: Approaches and Processes* continues from the first six editions many features that are designed to develop students' abilities to integrate and apply the material. The seventh edition continues to include the "Spotlight on Scholarship" features, highlighting specific research that illustrates concepts considered in the chapter—six spotlights are new to this edition. I have retained other pedagogical features from earlier editions, including explicit links among the "approach" and "process" chapters, learning objectives at the beginning of each chapter, key concepts at the end of the chapters, tables and figures to illustrate key concepts, and case studies to apply conceptual material to real-life organizational communication situations. One of my favorite features of this textbook—the "Case in Point" feature that began in the fourth edition—continues in the seventh edition. One of the most fun tasks during this process of revising the textbook has been discovering and writing about current events that reflect a variety of concerns about organizational communication. There are many new "Case in Point" features in this revision, as well as some from the previous editions with which I couldn't part.

Like earlier editions, this seventh edition is accompanied by an Instructor's Manual, revised by Zachary Hart of Northern Kentucky University, which includes sample syllabi; paper assignments; key terms; chapter outlines; true/false, multiple choice, fill-in-the-blank, and essay test items; suggestions for effective use of the case studies; and helpful websites. The Instructor's Manual also includes "Case Study," "Spotlight on Scholarship," and "Case in Point" features from previous editions. This edition also offers predesigned Microsoft PowerPoint presentations, also created by Zachary Hart. These are available on the Instructor Companion Site, which also contains an electronic version of the Instructor's Manual and Cognero Computerized Testing.

ACKNOWLEDGMENTS

When you are asked to write a textbook, you don't realize the work that will be involved in writing subsequent editions of that textbook. It is challenging to maintain the focus of earlier editions and keep what is foundational yet also provide the needed updates, restructuring, and sprucing up necessary for new groups of students. However, the daunting task of revision can be made relatively painless through the efforts of a great support system. First, the team at Cengage Learning has been helpful throughout the process of revision.

The comments of a number of organizational communication scholars were instrumental in shaping the direction, content, and presentation of this textbook. These include colleagues around the country who commented on the revision project at various stages: Kathy Krone, University of Nebraska-Lincoln; Kurt Lindemann, San Diego State University; Irwin Mallin, Indiana University-Purdue University Fort Wayne; Michael Pagano, Fairfield University; Brian Richardson, University of North Texas; Matt Sanders, Utah State University; and Sandra Starnaman, Adams State University.

I am also grateful to organizational communication scholars for their ongoing research that is of such high quality and importance to real-world problems. As I was working on this revision, I found myself marveling at the development of our discipline's scholarship in a number of journals, but especially *Management Communication Quarterly*. New ideas for the "Case in Point" feature were often garnered from the "Organizational Communication in the News" Facebook page. And I'm happy that Owen Lynch and Zach Schaefer allowed me to adapt their paper (and Owen's experiences) for the Chapter 5 case study.

Finally, my most heartfelt thanks go to my friends and family for providing an environment in which writing this textbook was a pleasurable challenge. My daughter, Kalena Margaret Miller, was born while I was writing the first edition of this textbook. I'm amazed that she is now more than halfway through college—a young woman who continues to love learning and increasingly challenges my ideas with her own experiences and insights. She is a delight and an inspiration. Other family members—Jim, Mary, Barb, Ann, and a host of others—have provided great support and helpful suggestions. And my widespread friends—both real life and Facebook—consistently remind me of the wealth of experiences we all have as we navigate the complexities of organizational communication.

Katherine Miller

The Challenge of Organizational Communication

CHAPTER 1

AFTER READING THIS CHAPTER, YOU SHOULD ...

- Be able to describe how today's world is complicated by globalization, terrorism, climate change, and changing demographics.
- Understand the concept of "requisite variety" and appreciate the need for complex thinking to cope with complex situations.
- See ways in which we can complicate our thinking about organizations both by considering a variety of organizational forms and by viewing organizations that are often paradoxical and contradictory.
- Understand the distinction between a "transmission model" of communication and a "constitutive model" of communication.
- Be familiar with the seven conceptualizations of communication and the ways in which these domains of understanding can change our view of organizational communication.

In March 2013, Facebook reported having 1.11 billion users—approximately one out of seven people around the globe, and clearly a higher proportion in many parts of the world. As these billion-plus users contemplate the possibilities for establishing and updating their personal information on the site, they are met with a variety of possibilities for specifying relational status including single, married, engaged, in an open relationship, divorced, widowed, in a civil union, in a domestic partnership. In the midst of the list of options, one stands out as different from the rest—"it's complicated." That simple statement could be seen as defining much of our twenty-first-century world and our lives within that world. Our relationships are complicated. Our families are complicated. Our work is complicated. Our politics and government are complicated. Our global economy is complicated. Our connections with other nation-states are complicated. Our beliefs about ourselves are complicated.

Nowhere is this complexity more apparent than in a consideration of communication processes or in a consideration of organizations, institutions, and social groupings. There is little doubt that our organizational world is much more complicated than the world of 100 years ago (think of agriculture, increasing industrialization, and the birth of the assembly line) or the world of sixty years ago (think of moving to the suburbs, long-term employment, and *Father Knows Best)* or even twenty-five years ago (think of cross-functional work teams, the early years of the Internet, and the fracturing of the proverbial glass ceiling). Mark Penn (2007) contends that we have moved from the age of Ford, in which you could have a car in "any color, as long as it's black," to the age of Starbucks, in which the variety of beverages available is truly staggering. As advertising campaigns, in-store signs, and the person ordering in front of us constantly remind us, there are thousands of ways to customize a latte or a Frappuccino®. However, this is not to say that past time periods have not taught us a great deal about ways to understand the complexity of our world today or provided us with strategies for coping with the high levels of complexity that confront us. Indeed, on a daily basis, we as individuals, families, organizations, and societies find ways to live productively in this complicated world.

This textbook takes you on a journey of understanding into the complex world of organizational communication and the role of interacting individuals and groups within that world. This journey will involve trips to the past to consider how scholars and practitioners have historically approached issues relevant to organizational communication. It will also involve the consideration of a wide range of processes that make organizations complicated and that help us cope with that complexity. These include processes of socialization, decision making, conflict management, technology, emotion, and diversity.

In this first chapter, however, we will take an initial look at ways in which today's organizational world is complicated. This initial look will be a brief and partial one, but it will introduce some of the ways in which participants in twenty-first-century organizations are confronted with confounding and challenging problems. We will then consider strategies for thinking about the concepts of "organization" and "communication" that will assist us on our journey as we explore approaches and processes in the understanding of organizational communication.

OUR COMPLICATED WORLD

There are myriad ways we could illustrate the complexity of today's world, and as we work our way through this textbook, we will discuss many of the "complicated" issues that confront us. In the last chapter, we will look at how the landscape of organizational communication has changed in recent years and will continue to change in the future. In this chapter, however, we consider four aspects of our world that were barely on the radar several decades ago but that today dominate much of our thinking—and our news coverage. They are globalization, terrorism, climate change, and changing demographics.

Globalization

It has become a truism to state that we now live in a global economy and partici-pate in a global marketplace. As transportation and telecommunication systems improve, our world becomes ever more connected in economic, political, organiza-tional, and personal terms. As one analyst summarized, "welcome to the new global economy: One guy sneezes, and someone else gets a cold" (Bremmer, 2012). The emergence of a global economy was facilitated by key political changes, such as the end of the cold war and the development of the European Union, and it has included the emergence of a variety of institutions to help regulate the global economy, such as the World Trade Organization and the International Monetary Fund. The **globalization** movement has led to practices such as **outsourcing**, in which businesses move manufacturing and service centers to countries where labor is cheap. In a global economy, many organizations have a multinational or interna-tional presence, with employees of a single organization found in many locations worldwide. Furthermore, in a global economy, businesses are no longer centered in a few Western nations but are also spread among nations throughout the devel-oping world.

The complexity of these global interconnections became especially clear during the global recession that began in 2007. As one analytical website summarized: "A collapse of the US sub-prime mortgage market and the reversal of the housing boom in other industrialized economies … had a ripple effect around the world" ("Global Financial Crisis," 2009). Though the United States began to emerge from its recession in 2012 and 2013, European nations took a different tack in respond-ing to the crisis and continued to struggle during that period. And Bremmer (2012) notes that "the economy that should scare us the most right now is the Chinese one. The country is slowing down, and that's precisely because of the halting recovery and weakness in the U.S. and European systems, and the fact that the sputtering has been going on for some time."

Some commentators see globalization as a largely positive—and clearly unstoppable—development. For example, in *The World Is Flat* (2005), Thomas Friedman argues that the global economy offers exciting opportunities for entrepre-neurs with the requisite skills. However, many others argue that globalization can lead to problems such as domestic job loss, the exploitation of workers in third-world nations, and environmental problems. Indeed, some scholars have raised important questions about the extent to which models of capitalism developed in the United States should be exported to nations with very different governmental and cultural systems (e.g., Whitley, 2009).

It becomes clear from all sides of the debate that our new world involves com-plex interconnections between business, political, and cultural systems, and these interconnections make it difficult to fully understand the ramifications of both globalization systems and the proposed means for making globalization "work" effectively. Joseph Stiglitz, who critiques economic institutions associated with globalization in his 2002 book *Globalization and Its Discontents,* noted in 2006 that there is at least hope for dealing with these complex problems. He argues that "while globalization's critics are correct in saying it has been used to push a partic-ular set of values, this need not be so. Globalization does not have to be bad for the environment, increase inequality, weaken cultural diversity, and advance corporate interests at the expense of the well-being of ordinary citizens" (Stiglitz, 2006, p. xv). More recently, economist Dani Rodrick has argued that it may be necessary to scale back on the "hyperglobalization" that comes from deeply integrated economic systems in order to enhance the goals of national sovereignty and democratic politics.

The field of organizational communication can contribute a great deal to these debates about globalization. The challenges of globalization are not just economic—they also concern messages, relationships, and systems of understanding. Some of the questions that organizational communication scholars now consider in the area of globalization include:

- How can organizational members communicate effectively in the contracted time and space of global markets?
- How can communication be used to enhance understanding in the multicultural workplaces that are a crucial feature of our global economy?
- How can communication processes in business, government, and nongovernmental organizations be used to protect the rights of workers in the United States and abroad?
- How does "organizing" occur in the realm of the political and economic policy debates that are critical to the long-term direction of the global economy?
- How do corporations communicate about the balance between providing goods and services at a price preferred by consumers and providing a safe and economically secure workplace for their employees?

Terrorism

The terrorist attacks of September 11, 2001, changed the world in profound ways. In the years following 9/11, subsequent attacks in London, Madrid, Bali, India, and elsewhere—combined with frequent news stories about attacks that have been thwarted and individuals arrested for planning more attacks—make it clear that **terrorism** will be a watchword in our lives for many years to come. In recent years, terrorism once more hit home for U.S. citizens with the attack on the Libyan consulate in Benghazi on September 11, 2012, and the 2013 bombings at the finish line of the Boston Marathon. As Oliver (2007, p. 19) notes, "in the wake of the attacks on the World Trade Center and the Pentagon on 9/11, the conventional wisdom was that 'everything has changed.'" However, as Rosemary O'Kane (2007) points out in her book *Terrorism: A Short History of a Big Idea*, terrorists have been around for many centuries, and terrorism can be perpetrated by individuals, groups, nation-states, and regimes. She notes that terrorism is not a particular ideology but is a set of strategies that involves the use of unpredictable violence against individuals and thus creates ongoing fear and suspicion among large groups of people. The effectiveness of terrorism today can be enhanced both by the wide range of technological tools available to terrorists and by contemporary urban environments that have high concentrations of residents and mass transportation.

Case in Point: Can Tragedy Lead to Change?

On April 24, 2013, more than 900 garment workers were killed in a catastrophic building collapse at a factory in Bangladesh's Rana Plaza. It was the world's worst industrial disaster since the massive gas leak tragedy in Bhopal, India, in 1984. Greenwald and Hirsch (2013) note that the reaction to the factory collapse followed a typical pattern: "News article after news article focuses on finding the smoking gun, as if there were only one cause and as if minus that cause, those workers would be safe today. Or coverage treats these tragedies as natural disasters with a rush of charity before public attention turns to the next event."

Greenwald and Hirsch (2013), however, believe that the tragedy in Bangladesh should be used as an impetus to spur on communication about the global apparel industry. Because corporations outsource a great deal of the labor associated with producing clothing, the cost of apparel has fallen 39% since 1994. Some may see this as a worthy outcome of globalization, but Greenwald and Hirsch ask "to what extent is our demand for a $5

T-shirt or deep discounts on jeans responsible for disasters like this?" They compare the building collapse in Bangladesh to an industrial disaster of a century earlier—the Triangle Shirtwaist factory fire in New York City in 1911—and note that this fire (in which 146 were killed) has "become a stand-in for the terrible problems of an industrializing nation" and led to collective protests that eventually resulted in important safety codes, regulations, and labor law reforms. Though obviously many things have changed in 100 years, the processes of globalization have led to disturbing similarities: "Our clothes come from places like Rana, where the average work is, as in 1911, a young girl working in terrible conditions for starvation wages" (Greenwald & Hirsch, 2013). Though the issues are complex and implicate issues of economics, local government, and culture, we can only hope that horrible events like this can open up dialogue regarding the moral responsibility of consumers to support workers who toil in the global marketplace.

For individuals and organizations in the post-9/11 world, the implications of terrorism are everywhere but can be especially seen in two widespread areas: the **war on terror** and **homeland security**. Perhaps the most basic concern is for an understanding of how terrorist networks and terrorist organizations are constituted, operate, and grow (Stohl & Stohl, 2007, 2011). Such an understanding would involve a consideration of how terrorist organizations recruit and socialize their members, how terrorist cells make decisions and develop leadership, and how terrorist networks form interconnections through technology and interpersonal contact. But a consideration of the war on terror has also come to encompass military interventions, such as the wars in Afghanistan and Iraq. Thus, organizational communication scholars must also be cognizant of the complex communication processes involved in military actions and bureaucracy and the complexities of dealing with military personnel and their families during and after their service. The implications of the war on terror for organizational communication also include complex political negotiations with a wide range of government entities and the creation and dissemination of organizational rhetoric to connect institutional goals with public opinion. In the communication discipline, one important direction for research has been led by Steve Corman and his colleagues at the Center for Strategic Communication at Arizona State University. These scholars have considered the ways in which a narrative approach can be instrumental in under-standing issues including Islamist extremism (Halverson, Goodall & Corman, 2011), the war in Afghanistan (Corman, 2013), and counterterrorism and public diplomacy (Corman, Trethewey & Goodall, 2008).

Organizational communication scholars can also respond to the complexities of terrorism through a consideration of homeland security. When Brian Michael Jenkins of the RAND Corporation testified before the Homeland Security Subcommittee of the U.S. House of Representatives on January 30, 2007, he made it clear that home-land security is, at its heart, a problem of organizational communication. He notes:

> Homeland security is not a television show about mysterious government agencies, covert military units, or heroes with fantastic cell phones that summon F-16s. It is an ongoing construction project that builds upon philosophy and strategy to ensure effec-tive organization, establish rules and procedures, deploy new technology, and educate a vast army of federal agents, local police, part-time soldiers, private security guards, first responders, medical personnel, public health officials, and individual citizens. (Jenkins, 2007, p. 1)

For organizational communication scholars, then, critical questions revolve around how to develop communication systems to enhance border security, improve tracking of possible terrorist activities, and develop the ability of first-response organizations—police departments, fire departments, hospitals, military—to act quickly and appropriately in case of terrorist threats or attacks. But organi-zational communication scholars can go beyond this mandate to consider the role of the individual citizen as he or she encounters this organized effort of homeland security. At times, these questions will concern public relations and crisis communi-cation, as we consider ways in which homeland security issues can be best framed and conveyed to a wide range of people. At other times, these questions will involve how organizations can manage the daily operations of homeland security, such as airport security or the passport application process, in a way that conveys understanding for the frustrations of ordinary citizens. For example, the Spotlight on Scholarship included in Chapter 11 (Malvini Redden, 2013) highlights how standing in airport security lines heightens the emotions of today's travelers. At still other times, organizational communication scholars can contribute by enhanc-ing our understanding of high-level policy debates in which conflicts arise between the need for security and the preservation of civil liberties.

Thus, in terms of the war on terror and in terms of homeland security, our post-9/11 world illustrates the complexity of questions that confront organizational communication scholars and students. These questions include:

- How do terror networks organize, recruit, and socialize members and commu-nicate across time and space?
- What communication systems can and should be put into place to best ensure the security of our borders?
- How can we help prevent our fear of terror from becoming a fear of each other?
- How can we best deliberate policy and make decisions in the changed envi-ronment of our post-9/11 world?
- How can communication systems be designed to protect and enhance the well-being of individuals who serve as first responders in the war on terror?

Climate Change

Almost a decade ago, in his bestselling book *An Inconvenient Truth* (2006), Al Gore argues that humanity's role in **climate change** is an issue that can no longer be denied and must be addressed by governments, businesses, and individuals. Increasing attention has been drawn by scientific data about upward shifts in overall global temperature, rising sea levels, and extreme weather events. The vast majority of scientists now agree that recent changes in our climate—caused by the phenomenon known as global warming—can be attributed to the activities of individuals and organizations. Marlon, Leiserowitz, and Feinberg (2013) report that 97% of scientific papers on the topic of climate science stated a position that global warming is happening and is—at least in part—caused by human activities. The U.S. Environmental Protection Agency explains this in very basic terms:

> Our Earth is warming. Earth's average temperature has risen by 1.4°F over the past century, and is projected to rise another 2 to 11.5°F over the next hundred years. Small changes in the average temperature of the planet can translate to large and potentially dangerous shifts in climate and weather ... Humans are largely responsible for recent climate change. Over the past century, human activities have released large amounts of carbon dioxide and other greenhouse gases into the atmosphere ... Greenhouse gases act like a blanket around Earth, trapping energy in the atmosphere and causing it to warm. This phenomenon is called the greenhouse effect and is natural and necessary to support life on Earth. However, the buildup of greenhouse gases can change Earth's climate and result in dangerous effects to human health and welfare and to ecosystems. ("Climate Change," Environmental Protection Agency, 2013)

Scientists have already observed widespread effects from climate change. Sea levels are rising, glaciers are shrinking, and permafrost is melting. These changes in the natural environment lead to additional changes in plant and animal life, as growth patterns change in response to shifting environmental conditions. These changes are occurring on land and underwater, as climate change affects vast ecosystems and threatens the survival of some, such as coral reefs. Global warming also influences weather events, such as hurricanes, which gain strength over warmer ocean waters. But these changes are not necessarily consistent across the globe or even predictable. For example, the year 2012 included record winter cold in Europe, record spring heat in the United States, wildfires in Chile, massive flooding in Australia, extreme drought in the U.S. Southwest and parts of South America, torrential rains in China, and Superstorm Sandy in the eastern U.S. coast.

The role of organizational communication in climate change and global warming is widespread. Much of the human contribution to climate change can be traced to factors that began with the Industrial Revolution, such as our systems of energy production, factory manufacturing, and petroleum-fueled transportation. Thus, when searching for ways to reverse or at least slow the process of climate change, these industrial organizations play key roles. Organizational communication is also implicated in the debates about global warming and what to do about it. These debates are global ones because countries such as China and India are rapidly becoming increasingly industrialized, and there are arguments about nations' obligations to reduce greenhouse gases. In all countries, including the United States, debates about the balance between economic opportunity and environmental health are rife. These debates are further complicated by the gap between scientific and public perceptions regarding climate change. Though scientific opinions regarding climate change are nearly unanimous, almost 60% of the American public report that they either believe climate change is not caused by humans or unsure about the issue (Marlon et al., 2013). Thus, organizational communication is implicated in the representation of ideas about climate change to the general public.

Organizational communication is also important in dealing with many of the effects of global warming, such as the increased incidence of forest fires and extreme weather events. For example, Silverstein (2012) questions whether organizations such as public utilities have the decision-making capability and infrastructure needed to deal with serious disasters such as hurricanes. Finally, addressing global warming and climate change can open up opportunities for businesses that want to raise their level of environmental responsibility and sell themselves as **"green" companies** to consumers. Although there is debate about the extent to which "going green" is a move that businesses should take for the overriding goal of protecting the planet (Marcus & Fremeth, 2009) or only when it can affect the bottom line (Siegel, 2009), it is clear that an increasing number of organizational executives are making decisions about their businesses with environmental considerations in mind.

Thus, the field of organizational communication must be ready to deal with the complex questions that stem from climate change and global warming, including:

- How can organizations reinvent themselves to reduce or eliminate their contributions to global warming?
- How can government representatives engage in productive debate about ways nations can work together to influence climate change?
- How can entrepreneurs address the "greening of organizations" as an opportunity for both profit and social responsibility?
- As climate change increasingly affects local weather events and patterns, how should local, state, national, and international agencies coordinate their activities to cope with the human consequences of global warming?
- How do organizational and government representatives speak to various publics about ways in which energy policy and practices influence the environment?
- How can organizations effectively enhance awareness of the ways in which individuals can make a difference in influencing the process of climate change?

Changing Demographics

Compared to issues like globalization, terrorism, and climate change, the concept of **demographics** sounds pretty tame. Demographics refer to statistical descriptions of characteristics of a population, such as age, race, income, educational attainment, and so on. In one sense, these descriptions are simplistic, but they are also undeniably important. Demographics describe who we are in the most basic of terms and thus can have a foundational impact on how we communicate with each other, how we organize, and how we address critical problems in our social world as well as what those problems are in a given time and place.

The most typical way to think about demographics is to consider distributions of the characteristics of people and to look at those distributions in a comparative sense across either time or location. In the United States, the demographic trends are found through the national census completed each decade and through the tracking of other research centers. Consider a few recent trends, many drawn from results of the 2010 U.S. Census:

- The United States is anticipated to be a "majority minority" nation by 2050. This shift is driven especially by the growth in the Hispanic population, which has been steadily increasing through both immigration and reproduction patterns. By 2050, it is estimated that the Hispanic portion of the U.S. population will grow to as high as 29% ("A Milestone en Route to a Majority Minority," 2012).

- Married couples now constitute less than half of all American households, and only one fifth of households are the traditional image of married couples with children. This pattern marks a sharp contrast to the middle of the twentieth century—in 1950, 78% of households included married couples and 43% of households were traditional nuclear families ("Married Couples Are No Longer a Majority," 2011). Interestingly, though, U.S. household size has grown because of the increase in multigenerational households ("Census 2010: Household Size Trends," 2011).

- The rural U.S. population is now the lowest it has ever been—16% now compared to 72% a century ago. In contrast, a third of Americans live in cities and over half of Americans live in suburbs. The fastest-growing places in America are small cities in the suburbs of large metro areas in the Sunbelt region ("Rural U.S. population lowest in history," 2011).

- In 1930, 5.4% of the U.S. population was 65 years or older; by 2007, the number more than doubled to 12.6% of the population. It is anticipated that by the year 2050, more than 20% of the U.S. population will be 65 or older ("Statistics on Aging," Administration on Aging, 2007).

In terms of sheer description, then, the United States is a dramatically different place than it was in decades past, and these different descriptors of who we are, where we live, who we live with, and how long we live lead to dramatically different experiences as we encounter organizations and communicate in them. For example, consider the issue of age. Scholars often divide populations into **generational cohorts** that indicate similarities in birth year and associated similarities in experience (Schuman & Scott, 1989). Thus, my mother's experiences as a member of the "World War II Cohort" are very different from mine as a member of the "Late Baby Boomer Cohort" or my daughter's as a member of the "Millennial Cohort." In terms of work experience, members of the World War II Cohort are known for dependability, long-term employment, and relationships with organized labor. Members of my cohort are known for their ambition but also their cynicism. Members of my daughter's generation are coming to be known as technologically savvy but also a bit spoiled in the ways of work. Clearly, a similar demographic analysis could be applied to ethnicity, family structure, social class, or household location.

Case in Point: 400 Million People

The demographic trends presented in this chapter have highlighted patterns within the U.S. population. However, given the trends in globalization also considered within this chapter, it is critical to consider these trends in comparison with demographic developments around the world. For many years, large populations in areas of the world, such as China, Japan, and Singapore, fueled a huge economic expansion in East Asia. However, this pattern is clearly changing. As Joel Kotkin, author of The Next Hundred Million: America in 2050 (2010b), points out, "With a fertility rate 50 percent higher than Russia, Germany, or Japan, and well above that of China, Italy, Singapore, South Korea, and virtually all of Eastern Europe, the United States has become an outlier among its traditional competitors, all of whose populations are stagnant and seem destined to eventually decline" (Kotkin, 2010a). Indeed, it is estimated that the U.S. population will reach 400 million by the year 2050, and the key employment demographic group aged 15 to 64 will increase by 42% in the United States, while this age segment in China and Japan will decline by 10% and 44%, respectively.

These shifts pose important organizational and political challenges across the globe. For nations with an increasing proportion of older citizens, it will be crucial to find ways to take care of older citizens, and this need is likely to influence many sectors of the economies in these countries. For example, Kotkin notes that "lacking a developed social-security system, China's rapid aging will start cutting deep into the country's savings and per capital income rates" (2010a). For the United States, the challenge will be to generate jobs for a growing number of working-age citizens—a particularly daunting task when considering the high unemployment rates seen during the recent United States and global recession. However, Kotkin believes that another demographic trend—immigration to the United States—will be instrumental in addressing this problem. Increasingly, new residents in the United States are starting small businesses in basic industries, such as construction, manufacturing, agriculture, and energy, and it is these small businesses—more than megacorporations—that will be engines of employment. "Expanding our basic industries, and focusing on the necessary skills training for those laboring in them, will provide new opportunities" (Kotkin, 2010a) needed in the workplaces of tomorrow.

But changing demographics do not just influence the organizational experience of individuals. They also create new challenges for organizational communication. Changing demographics result in multicultural workplaces, in workers with increasing responsibilities to aging family members, in workers with longer commutes, and in workers who telecommute. Changing demographics also pose the challenge of treating individuals from different ethnic backgrounds, races, ages, genders, disabilities, and sexual orientations in ways that respect these differences and create opportunities for meeting both individual and organizational goals. Thus, questions confronting organizational communication scholars as they consider these demographic shifts include:

- How can we communicate with members of a culturally diverse workforce in ways that respect difference and help achieve organizational and individual goals?
- How do members of the "sandwich generation" cope with the stresses of work and family concerns?

- What are the various communication patterns and needs of individuals from different age groups?
- How can we use communication technology to design virtual workplaces for employees in a variety of locations?
- How do we make the tough decisions regarding the roles of institutions and government in supporting an aging America?
- What role does communication play in assuring a level playing field for individuals with disabilities?

From this brief consideration of several newsworthy facets of the twenty-first century, it is clear that we live in a complex world and that organizational communication can play a pivotal role in addressing these complexities. It is important, though, to consider the ways in which our thinking about organizational communication can best facilitate our ability to make a difference in today's world. One important theorist who can help us in this is a scholar named Karl Weick, who we will encounter later in this book. Weick has a lot to say about how we organize and make sense of organizing through ongoing interaction. At this point, though, it is helpful to consider one concept that Weick emphasizes: **requisite variety**. This concept suggests that successful organizations and groups need to be as "complicated" as the problems that confront them. For example, the organizational structure of a small catering service can probably be relatively simple. However, if that small catering service grows into a large restaurant or an even larger food service organization, the structure needed for decision making, payroll, customer service, training, and myriad other functions must become increasingly complex. The organization must be as complicated as the problem.

The same principle holds for our consideration of how we should see "organizational communication" as a means for approaching the challenges of today's world. We have talked about issues such as globalization, terrorism, climate change, and changing demographics as just a few of the complexities that must be dealt with through organizational communication. Thus, if we see these problems as complicated, we must also complicate our thinking about organizations and complicate our thinking about communication.

Complicating Our Thinking about Organizations

The first way of complicating our thinking about organizational communication is to complicate our thinking about organizations. In the first edition of this book (Miller, 1995), I defined organization as including five critical features—namely, the existence of a social collectivity, organizational and individual goals, coordinating activity, organizational structure, and the embedding of the organization within an environment of other organizations. These critical features still hold today, but in complicating our thinking about organizations, it is important to stretch our understanding of each of these concepts. For example, when we think about the idea of "structure," we need to consider more than basic hierarchical structure or even more complex team structures. We also need to consider structures based on collective and communal relationships, structures that eschew hierarchy in favor of flat organizational forms, and structures that cross boundaries of time and space.

When we think about the concept of "goals," we need to move far beyond the economic goals that are often assumed in discussions of the "bottom line." The goals that drive many organizations and individuals today involve changing the world in big and small ways or perhaps simply concern about "connection" itself.

When we work to stretch our thinking in these ways, we see that there are many examples of organizational types in today's world that were not often considered in past decades. To take a basic example, we often think about "businesses"—entities that are designed to make money—as the epitome of organizations, but scholars are now increasingly interested in communication processes in nonprofit organizations (see, e.g., Koschmann, 2012). For both profit and nonprofit organizations, more and more organizations can be characterized as service organizations rather than manufacturing organizations. In areas around the globe, nongovernmental organizations (NGOs) are especially important in coordinating processes of change in first- and third-world nations. It is increasingly common for individuals with similar needs and goals to come together in organizations known as cooperatives (co-ops) that are often motivated by a concern for democracy, social justice, and environmental and global responsibility. Furthermore, with advances in computer and communication technology, organizations often do without the brick-and-mortar physical location and operate as virtual organizations. It is also critical to stretch our thinking to understand that the features of an "organization" are also relevant for the consideration of social organizations, such as fraternities and sororities, or even families or groups of friends who are coordinating around valued goals and tasks.

Complicating Our Thinking about Communication

It is also important for us to complicate our thinking about communication if we are to deal with the complicated world that confronts us. Early models of communication were highly simplistic, arguing that communication could be conceptualized with a model such as the S-M-C-R model, in which a Source transmits a Message through a Channel to a Receiver. In the organizational context, this could be seen as a supervisor (source) asking for volunteers to work on the weekend (message) through an e-mail (channel) sent to all her employees (receivers). Even when a "feedback loop" is added to this model (e.g., responses to the e-mail), it is clear that it fails to encompass the varying ways we need to think about communication. Communication is not just about sending simple messages to one or more receivers. Communication is also about the intricate networks through which computers link us to others. Moreover, communication is about the creation of meaning systems in families and cultures; understanding a market segment to enhance persuasion and increase sales; and the multiple ways information must flow to provide aid when a natural disaster strikes. It is about framing information about a possible threat so the public is warned but not panicked. Communication is about coming to an understanding within a community about issues that both unite and divide.

Robert Craig (1999) proposed a model of communication theory that helps sort out these various aspects of communication. First, he contrasts a **transmission model of communication** with a **constitutive model of communication**. In a transmission model, communication is a way of moving information from sources to receivers, similar to the S-M-C-R model. In a constitutive model, communication is seen as a "process that produces and reproduces shared meaning" (Craig, 1999, p. 125). We will consider the ways in which the notion of "constitution" has been applied in detail to organizational communication processes in Chapter 5. Craig suggests that the simple distinction between transmission and constitution is not particularly helpful, though, when considering broader theoretical approaches to communication. For one thing, he argues that it is not really a fair fight, as the transmission model is usually just presented as something easy to knock down. But Craig also believes that the transmission model can be useful to consider in some cases. For example, when the goal is to get evacuation information to residents in the path of a hurricane, the effective transmission of information is a lot more important than the creation of shared meaning. However, Craig doesn't think we should stop at the simple choice between a transmission model and a constitutive model. Instead, he suggests we complicate our thinking.

Craig argues that we should recast the constitutive model of communication as a metamodel—an overarching way of thinking about communication. That is, if we see the constitutive model as a "model of models," it is possible to constitute communication in a wide variety of ways. These different ways of constituting communication can provide different avenues for the development of theory and research. But more important for our purposes here, various ways of constituting communication can help us deal with the practical challenges that individuals face in organizations today. That is, there will be times when it is important to think about communication as a way of getting information from one person to another. There will be other times when it is important to think about communication as shared dialogue and a way to enhance understanding about self and others. There will be other times when communication is best seen as a means of persuasion and motivation. Thus, Craig's metamodel of communication can help us meet the practical challenges of today's organizational world.

Craig proposed seven **domains of communication theory**—seven different ways of thinking about how communication works in the world. These are presented in Table 1.1, and they range from the notion of communication as information processing (the cybernetic model) to communication as the experience of otherness and dialogue (the phenomenological model). Table 1.1 also considers how each way of thinking about communication might be put into play in the organizational context. It should be clear that these various approaches to communication allow us to answer—and, perhaps more important, to ask—very different questions about how organizations and people work in today's complex society.

In summary, then, our world is becoming increasingly complex, and the intricate situations that arise with globalization, terrorism, climate change, and changing demographics require multifaceted approaches to understanding. Indeed, even without these issues, life in organizations is complex enough! Thus, it is critical to complicate our thinking and discussion about "organization" and "communication" in ways advocated by scholars such as Tretheway and Ashcraft (2004) and Craig (1999). In the final pages of this chapter, we will look ahead to the remainder of the book to consider how these ideas about organization and communication will be brought to bear on traditional and contemporary approaches to the study of organizational communication and on a wide range of organizational communication processes.

Table 1.1 | Approaches to the Concept of Communication

	Communication Theorized As:	Possible Use in the Organizational Context:
Rhetorical	The practical art of discourse	Considering the communication strategies of organizational leaders during times of crisis
Semiotic	Intersubjective mediation by signs	Studying the ways that organizations create and sustain identity through corporate symbolism
Phenomenological	Experience of otherness; Dialogue	Using dialogue to mediate conflict between two employees
Cybernetic	Information processing	Finding optimal ways to set up a communication network system for employees who telecommute
Sociopsychological	Expression, interaction, and influence	Using knowledge about personality and interaction style to improve conflict management programs
Sociocultural	(Re)production of social order	Looking at the intersection of organizational, national, and ethnic cultures in multinational organizations
Critical	Discursive reflection	Confronting the issue of sexual harassment in the workplace through programs designed to shift beliefs about gender and power

Portions adapted from R. T. Craig (1999). Communication theory as a field. *Communication Theory, 9,* 119–161.

LOOKING AHEAD

Chapters 2 and 3 will take us back to consider several "founding perspectives" that have influenced the study of organizational communication. These approaches originated in other academic fields (e.g., sociology, psychology, management) and in business and industry and provide the foundation on which the field of organizational communication stands. Several aspects of these founding approaches are important to note. First, although these schools of thought provide the historical backdrop for our study of organizational communication, they are not "dead" subjects. Indeed, the influence of these approaches is widely seen in organizations today, and our discussion of them will consider both their historic and current significance. Second, these approaches are largely prescriptive in nature. That is, these theorists were primarily interested in prescribing how organizations should run rather than describing or explaining how they actually do run. Chapter 2 will take us back to the early part of the twentieth century to explore classical and bureaucratic approaches to the understanding of organizational communication. In Chapter 3, we will move to the middle and later years of the twentieth century to consider two related approaches: human relations and human resources. In human relations approaches, the spotlight is on individual needs; in human resources approaches, it is on the role of employees as valued contributors to organizational functioning. In Chapters 4 through 6 of this textbook, we will consider more contemporary ways of viewing organizations that shift the focus in several ways. First, these contemporary approaches constitute ways to understand and explain organizational communication. In contrast to founding approaches, they are not prescriptive theories but are theories that can be used to enhance our understanding of any organization, be it guided by classical, human relations, or human resources practitioners. Second, these approaches are primarily used by scholars rather than practitioners, although, of course, there are important pragmatic implications that stem from all these approaches. Third, all of these approaches continue to exert substantial influence today in terms of how organizational communication is studied. An organizational communication scholar would find research stemming from all of these approaches in current academic journals.

Chapter 4 will consider two metaphors that guided the study of organizational communication during much of the latter part of the twentieth century and continue to exert influence today. The first of these, the systems approach, looks at organizations as complex interactions of systems components and processes. The second, the cultural approach, considers organizations as emergent entities of values, norms, stories, behaviors, and artifacts. In Chapter 5, we will look at a set of ideas that hold great currency in today's study of organizational communication— the notion that organizations are constituted through communication. Finally, in Chapter 6 we will turn to critical and feminist approaches that emphasize various aspects of organizational power and control and aspire to the emancipation of marginalized voices within the organizational context.

In the second half of this textbook, we will move our focus from approaches that inform our understanding of organizational communication to the specific processes to which these approaches have been applied. What do I mean by process? Simply, it is something that happens in an organization. Organizations are marked by constant activity. People learn about new jobs, make decisions, deal with conflict, cope with customers, program computers, form alliances, institute change, and cope with differences. All these communication processes have been the focus of organizational communication scholars, and the last half of this book will consider our knowledge about what happens in these processes, how it happens, and why it happens.

The first four chapters that consider organizational communication processes can be seen as "enduring" processes because they consider things that have probably been happening in organizations for as long as organizations have existed.

In Chapter 7, we will look at assimilation—or the processes through which individuals attach to—and detach from—organizations. Chapter 8 investigates how communication influences organizational decision making and knowledge management, and Chapter 9 presents theories and research on the role of communication in organizational conflict. Then, in Chapter 10, we look at change in organizations and the leadership processes that are often crucial in terms of both change and stability.

Finally, in the last four chapters of this textbook, we will consider some of the organizational communication processes that have emerged in the last twenty to thirty years as the workplace has changed and evolved. These "emerging" processes in organizational communication certainly existed in past organizations, but current developments in the workplace have brought these issues to the forefront, and they increasingly demand the attention of both organizational practitioners and researchers. In Chapter 11, we will look at a fundamental shift in the way we have come to view organizations and the people in them. This is the shift from assuming organizations are always "rational" and "logical" to acknowledging the role of emotion in organizational life. In Chapter 12, we discuss the phenomenon of diversity in the workplace, considering the ways in which various aspects of diversity—race, culture, gender, age, sexual orientation, and others—affect communication in the workplace. In Chapter 13, we examine communication technology in the workplace and how technology has shifted the way we work and think about work. Finally, in Chapter 14, we conclude in much the same way we began—by considering trends that are changing the landscape of organizations.

DISCUSSION QUESTIONS

1. How have organizations that you work in or have dealings with been affected by issues such as globalization, terrorism, climate change, and changing demographics? How do these issues have different effects on different people and different kinds of organizations?

2. Consider how airports deal with homeland security. What organizational communication processes have changed as a result of the threat of terrorism? Do you think airports and airlines have dealt effectively with these changes? Why or why not?

3. What kinds of organizational structures and processes stem from globalization? Why are these new structures and processes necessary? How do they enhance—or detract from—the quality of life for individuals working in or with the organizations?

4. How would each of the communication domains considered in this chapter approach the organizational issues that arose in the aftermath of events such as the BP oil spill, the Boston Marathon bombings, or tornadoes that often strike the midsection of the United States? How do these different lenses help us understand the complexity of organizational communication processes?

KEY CONCEPTS

globalization
outsourcing
terrorism
war on terror
homeland security

climate change
"green" companies
demographics
generational cohorts
requisite variety

transmission model of
  communication
constitutive model of
  communication
domains of communication theory

Classical Approaches

CHAPTER 2

AFTER READING THIS CHAPTER, YOU SHOULD ...

- Understand the ways in which a machine metaphor provides insight into organizational communication.
- Appreciate the historical context of the early years of the twentieth century when classical approaches to organizing were proposed.
- Be familiar with Henri Fayol's Theory of Classical Management, especially his principles of management regarding structure, power, reward, and attitude.
- Know how Max Weber's Theory of Bureaucracy corresponds to Fayol's and be able to discuss the forms of authority that Weber sees as existing in organizations and bureaucracies.
- Be able to describe the key aspects of Frederick Taylor's Theory of Scientific Management and explain how his ideas responded to the concerns about industry in his time.
- Understand how communication processes are influenced by the Theory of Classical Management and be able to recognize principles of classical organizing in contemporary organizations.

Before the Industrial Revolution in the nineteenth century, most work was conducted by individuals or in small groups. Goods were created by individual artisans, by families, or in small "cottage industries" in which skilled workers accomplished large tasks from start to finish. For example, consider a shoemaker during the eighteenth century. A cobbler during this time period would put together a shoe from tanned leather to finished product (and perhaps tan the leather too). Clearly, this is a different type of organizational process from today's shoe factory.

With the advent of the Industrial Revolution in the late nineteenth century, common methods of producing goods began to change. Instead of cottage industries, increased mechanization and industrialization led to the organization of larger groups of people in factory and assembly-line settings. Scholars and consultants in the early twentieth century tried to make sense of these new organizational forms and to provide business and industry with advice about how best to organize in light of these new developments. A number of theories gained prominence during this period. Three of the more important ones are Henri Fayol's Theory of Classical Management, Max Weber's Theory of Bureaucracy, and Frederick Taylor's Theory of Scientific Management. Before we consider the details of each theory, let us consider what they have in common—the belief that organizations should be modeled after machines.

THE MACHINE METAPHOR

The Industrial Revolution had profound impacts on how people worked and even on how they thought about work. The world was moving from an agrarian society (centered around farming) to an industrial society. It is not surprising, then, that a **machine metaphor** is central to classical organizational theories.

The notion of a metaphor in organizational theorizing suggests that we can learn something about organizations by considering a disparate object that an organization resembles (Morgan, 1986, 1997). For example, we might contend that "an organization is like a loaf of bread" in that it must have people (flour), communication (water that holds the flour together), and goals (yeast that makes the dough rise). Although this particular metaphor is somewhat whimsical, any metaphor can be helpful in pointing out aspects of organizational functioning that we might not otherwise notice. Metaphors can also de-emphasize aspects of an organization. That is, a metaphor is a partial view of an organization that will both reveal and obscure important aspects of organizing.

As noted, classical theorists share a dedication to the machine metaphor. What does this metaphor suggest about organizations? What can we learn by considering the ways in which organizations are like machines? We will consider many detailed answers to these questions when we look at the theories of Fayol, Weber, and Taylor, which share the machine metaphor.

One aspect of the machine metaphor is the importance of *specialization*. Think about a machine like a car engine. Every part of the engine has a specific function. For example, the carburetor or fuel injector is responsible for producing the proper mixture of gasoline and air. The spark plug is then responsible for igniting the explosion that drives the piston. Thus, the fuel injector and spark plug play special-ized roles—both of which are necessary for the proper operation of the combustion engine. When we see organizations as machines, we see the same kind of specializa-tion. For example, think about a sandwich shop in which one worker is responsible for slicing the bread, a second is responsible for meats and cheeses, a third is responsible for vegetables and condiments, and a fourth is responsible for bagging and ringing up the order. This specialization of tasks—sometimes called division of labor—illustrates one way in which organizational functioning can be seen as machine-like.

A second aspect of the machine metaphor is *standardization*, which includes the related notion of *replaceability*. Machines are designed in such a way that the parts in one machine are the same as those in a similar machine and hence can be easily replaced. For example, if the belt in your vacuum cleaner snapped, you could easily buy a new one that would fit perfectly. When conceptualizing organizations as machines, the same principle holds for the human "parts" that work in the orga-nization. That is, if a worker on an assembly line quits, a machine-like organization can easily replace that worker. The individuals who labor in the organization are seen as the cogs of the machine, and those cogs are standardized and interchangeable.

Finally, machines are *predictable*. There are rules that govern the way a machine is built and how it operates. When it breaks, a finite number of things might be wrong, and if we carefully and rationally think through the problem, we should be able to fix the machine. A quick perusal of any appliance's operating manual illustrates this principle. An organization conceived as a machine has the same qualities. It runs according to specific rules and standards, and if the organization is dysfunctional, it can be fixed by a rational consideration of the manner in which the rules and standards are being applied or misapplied.

Thus, looking at organizations through the lens of a machine metaphor points out the ways in which organizations are specialized, standardized, and predictable. These aspects do not exhaust the insights we might gain about organizations by thinking of them as machines. Furthermore, it should be very clear that, in many ways, organizations are not like machines. I will note the weaknesses of the machine metaphor later in this chapter and in subsequent chapters.

However, at the turn of the twentieth century, when industrialization was gaining a foothold, theorists generally looked at organizational functioning through this mechanistic lens. The next three sections of this chapter present the theorists who were the most prominent proponents of this trend: Henri Fayol, Max Weber, and Frederick Taylor.

HENRI FAYOL'S THEORY OF CLASSICAL MANAGEMENT

Henri Fayol, described by Koontz and O'Donnell (1976) as the "father of modern operational-management theory," was a French industrialist who lived in the late nineteenth and early twentieth centuries. His major work appeared in French in the early twentieth century and was translated into English several decades later (Fayol, 1949). Two aspects of Fayol's theory that have been particularly influential are his consideration of the *elements of management* and his consideration of the *principles of management*. Both of these components concern the managerial function of organizing. The **elements of management** deal with what managers should do, and the **principles of management** deal with how managers should enact these elements.

Elements of Management

Fayol proposes five fundamental elements of management—the *what* of managerial work. The first of these elements is *planning*, which involves looking to the future to determine the best way to attain organizational goals. Fayol (1949) believes that "[t]he plan of action facilitates the utilization of the firm's resources and the choice of best methods for attaining the objective" (p. 50). His second element of managing is *organizing*. Fayol looks at this element in terms of the arrangement of human resources (employees) and the evaluation of those employees. The third element Fayol emphasizes is the *command* element of management. This is the element through which managers set tasks for employees in order to meet organizational goals. The fourth element of management is *coordination*. It is through this element that "the separate activities of an organization must be harmonized into a single whole" (Miner, 1982, p. 365). The final element of classical management is *control*, which involves the comparison between goals and activities to ensure that the organization is functioning in the manner planned.

It is interesting to note that Fayol does not include communication as one of his elements of management. However, with the possible exception of the planning element, it is difficult to imagine the performance of these elements without communication. That is, the organizing, command, coordination, and control elements of classical management theory all require communication between management and workers. Thus, communication can be seen as an implicit part of Fayol's elements of management.

Principles of Management

In addition to discussing the *what* of management through a consideration of the elements, Fayol provides prescriptions regarding *how* management can best function. Although these principles of management are often presented as a simple checklist, let us group them into four sets, each of which deals with a different aspect of how an organization should be managed.

Principles of Organizational Structure

Many of Fayol's principles of management concern how the parts of an organization should be put together. Six principles deal specifically with organizational structure:

- **Scalar chain:** An organization should be arranged in a strict vertical hierarchy and that communication should be largely limited to this vertical flow (i.e., move up and down the organizational chart).
- **Unity of command:** An employee should receive orders regarding a particular task from only one supervisor.
- **Unity of direction:** Activities having similar goals should be placed under a single supervisor.
- **Division of labor:** Work can best be accomplished if employees are assigned to a limited number of specialized tasks.
- **Order:** There should be an appointed place for each employee and task within the organization.
- **Span of control:** Managers will be most effective if they have control of a limited number of employees. Fayol generally suggests a limit of twenty to thirty employees for first-level managers and six employees for higher-level managers.

Taken together, these six principles of management propose an organization that is highly structured and hierarchical. The organization is divided into functional divisions (division of labor, unity of direction, and order principles). Within these divisions, managers command a specific number of employees (span of

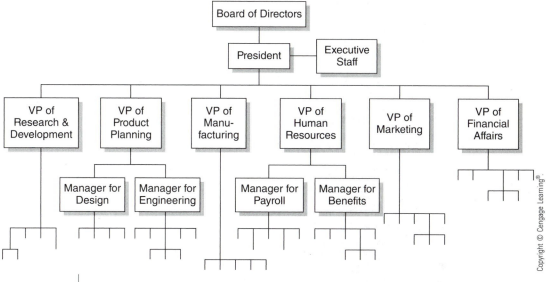

Figure 2.1 | Organizational Chart for Classical Organization

control principle), and each employee has only one supervisor (unity of command principle). Throughout the organization, communication flows through vertical and highly structured channels (scalar chain principle). The type of organizational structure advocated by Fayol is illustrated in Figure 2.1.

One caveat is in order with regard to the structural principles proposed by Fayol. In general, Fayol advocated strict adherence to vertical communication flow within the hierarchical structure presented in Figure 2.1 However, he also recognized that horizontal communication across the **hierarchy** could sometimes facilitate organizational functioning. Thus, he proposed a structural "gangplank" (sometimes called Fayol's bridge) that would horizontally link employees at the same hierarchical level. Fayol proposed that such a link should be used only when authorized by a manager at the next highest level but should be used whenever such communication would aid in the accomplishment of organizational goals. "It is an error to depart needlessly from the line of authority, but it is an even greater one to keep to it when detriment to the business ensues" (Fayol, 1949, p. 36).

Principles of Organizational Power   The next three principles of management all deal with power relationships within the organization. These principles are:

- **Centralization:** Organizations will be most effective when central management has control over decision-making and employee activities. However, Fayol believed that contingency factors such as firm size and the personal characteristics of the managers and employees could influence the optimal level of **centralization** (Miner, 1982).
- **Authority and responsibility:** Managers should hold authority that derives from both their position in the organization and their personal characteristics

(such as intelligence and experience). However, this principle also holds that responsibility must accompany authority in equal measure.

- **Discipline:** All organizational members should be obedient to the rules of the organization and to the managers who enforce them.

These three principles describe Fayol's prescribed power structure for optimal organizational functioning. Fayol suggests that power should be relatively centralized in the managers, who hold both authority over and responsibility to the employees. The employees within this power structure should then submit to the rules and orders of the managers.

Principles of Organizational Reward   The third set of principles concerns Fayol's suggestions regarding appropriate rewards in organizations:

- **Remuneration of personnel:** Employees should be rewarded for their work with appropriate salaries and benefits. Kreps (1990) notes that "[t]his principle is based on the notion that organization members' primary motivation is financial and that work performance is dependent on the amount of remuneration they receive from the organization" (p. 69).
- **Equity:** In remuneration (as well as in all organizational behavior), employees should be treated justly.
- **Tenure stability:** The organization should guarantee sufficient time on the job for employees to achieve maximum performance. Fayol (1949) also notes that too much tenure stability could be counterproductive.

Thus, Fayol's principles of management suggest that employees are rewarded within the organization by the knowledge that their jobs are relatively secure and by the fair application of monetary rewards.

Principles of Organizational Attitude   Finally, Fayol sets forth three principles that consider the proper feelings and attitudes of organizational employees:

- **Subordination of individual interest to general interest:** An organization can be effective only when the interests of the whole take precedence over the interests of individuals. Thus, individuals must always consider organizational goals first.
- **Initiative:** Managers should value and direct an employee's efforts to work in the best interest of the organization.
- **Esprit de corps:** This principle proposes—in the spirit of the Three Musketeers' "all for one and one for all" cry—that there should be no dissension in the organizational ranks.

Summary of Fayol's Theory

Ultimately, Fayol paints a picture of how an organization should be run. According to his principles of management, an effective organization is highly structured, and each individual knows where he or she fits. Clear structures facilitate the functioning of the organization, and clear rules deal with these structures. Employees are

Case in Point: Are There Limits to Rewards?

In the fall of 2008, many huge financial firms in the United States and elsewhere were on the brink of collapse. Perhaps because they were seen as too big to fail, many were saved by congressional action that established the Troubled Asset Relief Program to bail them out of their fiscal miseries. Following these actions, an office of "Pay Czar" was created in order to prevent Wall Street firms from dispensing giant bonuses to executives and other employees.

A year later, in the fall of 2009, the bonuses were again being paid at firms up and down Wall Street, and there was huge anger from government officials (President Obama said, "I'd like to think that people would feel a little remorse and feel embarrassed and would not get million-dollar or multimillion-dollar bonuses") and throughout the American public. But this outrage seemed to have little effect on those dolling out and receiving the bonuses. As Daniel Gross expresses, "Shame? Self-awareness? Remorse? Come on, these are bankers we're talking about" (Gross, 2009).

Gross argues that this disconnect between the general public and Wall Street can be attributed to the vastly different reward cultures that dominate different kinds of organizations. "Just as Tiger Woods was placed on this earth to whack the dickens out of dimpled balls, Wall Streeters were placed on this planet to dispense and receive bonuses" (Gross, 2009). Although it may seem outrageous to most of working America, these bonuses are viewed as part of the expected compensation package for Wall Street bankers, thus comporting well with Fayol's notion of rewarding workers with appropriate salaries and benefits. This situation illustrates, though, that the evaluation of what is "appropriate" can be very specific to the organizational system in which the rewards are being distributed. As Daniel Gross concludes about rewards for bankers, "We will continue to be shocked by the level of bonuses—and Wall Street will continue to be shocked that we're shocked."

rewarded through the equitable distribution of monetary rewards and are encouraged to labor strictly for the goals of the organization rather than for their own individual interests.

Let me emphasize again that Fayol's theory is a **prescriptive theory** rather than descriptive or explanatory. In fact, relatively strong evidence demonstrates that this theory does not adequately describe or explain the ways in which organizations actually function (see Miner, 1982, for a review of empirical research results). To take one example, Fayol proposes that the elements of management are planning, organizing, commanding, coordinating, and controlling. However, in a classic study of what managers actually do, Mintzberg (1973) found ten work roles that had little to do with these functions. Instead, Mintzberg's roles included a number of interpersonal, informational, and decisional functions. However, in spite of the weakness of Fayol's theory as an explanatory or descriptive mechanism, the **Theory of Classical Management** has had a huge impact on how management is taught in schools and evaluated in the business world.

MAX WEBER'S THEORY OF BUREAUCRACY

The second classical management theory we will consider was developed by Max Weber, a German sociologist, who lived in the same time period as Fayol. His ideas were introduced to the United States in English translations at approximately the same time as Fayol's (Weber, 1946, 1947). However, Weber is a very different kind of theorist from Fayol. Whereas Fayol provides prescriptions to managers about how organizations should be run, Weber takes a more scholarly approach. Weber's **Theory of Bureaucracy** has been termed an "ideal type" theory. An **ideal type theory** does not advocate a particular organizational form as best but rather lays out the features of an abstract—or idealized—organization of a given type. Thus, in his Theory of Bureaucracy, Weber enumerates the characteristics of a particular form of organization: the bureaucracy. Although skeptical about some of the tenets of bureaucracy, Weber believed that bureaucratic organizations would eventually dominate in society because of their technical superiority (Clegg, 1990).

Weber's Theory of Bureaucracy cannot be as easily divided into elements and principles as Fayol's can. However, six facets of bureaucracy permeate Weber's writing on the topic. Three of these are familiar from our discussion of Fayol. First, Weber believes that a bureaucracy should be operated through a *clearly defined hierarchy*. Second, Weber sees bureaucracy as characterized by *division of labor*. Third, he believes that bureaucracies are characterized by the *centralization* of decision making and power. Because these notions are very similar to elements of Fayol's Theory of Classical Management, I will not consider them in detail here. However, three other aspects of Weber's Theory of Bureaucracy were not emphasized in Fayol's theory.

In addition to the categories of hierarchy, division of labor, and centralization, Weber emphasizes that bureaucracies are relatively **closed systems**. That is, to the extent possible, a bureaucracy will shut itself off from influences of the outside environment because environmental interruptions could hamper its smooth functioning. Thompson (1967) extends this idea by proposing that organizations have "technical cores" that must be buffered from the environment through structural or communicative means. For example, in a physician's office, the technical core is the interaction between physician and patient in the examining room. This technical core is buffered from environmental interruption by receptionists, rules about appointments, and medical personnel who monitor the flow of patients.

Weber's Theory of Bureaucracy also emphasizes the *importance of rules* for organizational functioning. Weber believes that rules should be rationally established and that there should be a rule for all possible contingencies in the organization. Furthermore, he believes that these rules should be codified in written form.

Perhaps the most important aspect of Weber's Theory of Bureaucracy, though, is the attention he gives to the *functioning of authority*. Weber sees bureaucracies as working through a system of authority, power, and discipline. He postulates that such authority is based on one of three possible grounds:

- *Traditional authority* (sometimes called legitimate authority) is power based on long-standing beliefs about who should have control and is often vested in particular positions within an organizational hierarchy. For example, the queen of England has **traditional authority** that is based on age-old traditions within British society. Similarly, in some organizations, the president or head of the board of directors may have power based on a tradition of authority rather than on actual abilities, actions, or behaviors.

- *Charismatic authority* is power based on an individual's personality and ability to attract and interact with followers. This kind of authority is highly unstable, as followers may become disenchanted with the leader's charismatic qualities. **Charismatic authority** can be seen in the operation of many cult organizations in which a single individual draws in followers and demands obedience through the power of his or her personality. Political figures such as Barack Obama or Sarah Palin and business leaders such as the late Steve Jobs have also been described as having charismatic qualities.

- *Rational-legal authority* is power based on the rational application of rules developed through a reliance on information and expertise. With **rational-legal authority**, power rests not in the individual but rather in the expertise and rationality that have created a system of rules and norms. As Weber (1968) notes, "Every single bearer of powers of command is legitimated by the system of rational norms, and his [*sic*] power is legitimate insofar as it corresponds with the norm. Obedience is thus given to the norms rather than to the person" (p. 954).

Although Weber believes that all three types of authority (traditional, charismatic, and rational-legal) exist singly and in combination in organizations, he sees rational-legal authority as the type of power that dominates in the bureaucratic system. Traditional power and charismatic power rely on the position or the individual holding the position to define authority. Rational-legal power relies instead on rationality, expertise, norms, and rules. Thus, rational-legal power is far more impersonal than either traditional or charismatic authority. It is this reliance on rationality and impersonal norms that led Weber to advocate rational-legal authority as the basis of bureaucratic functioning.

In summary, Weber's theory concerns the ideal type features of the organizational form known as bureaucracy. He proposed that a bureaucracy is a closed system driven by rational-legal authority. Within this system, there is a strict reliance on rules, division of labor, and a clearly established hierarchy in which power is centralized. The result is a highly impersonal organization in which rationality is the guiding force and individuality is discouraged. As Miner (1982) summarizes: "Bureaucratic systems dominate through knowledge, and this fact gives them their rationality. The result is a climate of formal impersonality without hatred or passion and hence without affection or enthusiasm" (p. 391).

FREDERICK TAYLOR'S THEORY OF SCIENTIFIC MANAGEMENT

The third and final classical theory we consider in this chapter is one developed by Frederick Taylor in the early twentieth century. Taylor was a U.S. businessman, and like Fayol, his goal was to provide prescriptions for how organizations could be better run. However, in contrast to Fayol's theory, Taylor concentrates on the micro level of organizational functioning. That is, Taylor is not concerned with organizational structure but with the relationship between manager and employee and the control of the individual at work. First, we will discuss why Taylor developed his Theory of Scientific Management and then we will consider the detailed components of his system.

Impetus for the Theory of Scientific Management

Taylor developed his **Theory of Scientific Management** because he was frustrated with typical industry operations at the turn of the century. Several issues concerned him. First, most tasks in organizations were learned by newcomers watching more experienced workers at a particular job. Of course, this apprenticeship system would be effective only when the more experienced workers were doing the job in an efficient and effective manner. Thus, Taylor believed that learning tasks in this way could lead to work of uneven quality in the organization.

A second concern involved the manner in which individuals were rewarded for their work. At the turn of the century, piecework pay was the typical organizational reward system. That is, a bricklayer might be paid a penny for every five bricks he could lay. If he laid one hundred bricks an hour, he would be paid twenty cents for that hour's work. Taylor was not concerned with the piecework pay system in and of itself. Rather, he was concerned with what could happen if a particularly efficient worker came on the job. For example, a group of workers might have established a norm of laying one hundred bricks per hour. A new worker might come on the job and lay two hundred bricks an hour (and hence earn forty cents rather than twenty cents). A manager observing this productive behavior might conclude that everyone should be laying two hundred bricks per hour and "bust the rate" down to a penny per ten bricks rather than a penny per five bricks. More productive workers thus became known as "rate busters" because managers would often lower piecework pay as a result of their productivity.

Of course, workers wanted to avoid having the piecework pay scale lowered. Therefore, a group of workers would often pressure each other to keep rate busting to a minimum. If productivity were kept down, wages would stay up. Taylor observed this social pressure to keep productivity down and wages up and labeled it "systematic soldiering." Thus, Taylor looked at organizational functioning and saw two impediments to optimal productivity. The first impediment was the *uneven work* that resulted from job training through custom and tradition. The second impediment was the **systematic soldiering** that resulted from rate busting and the system of piecework pay. To deal with these problems, Taylor developed his system of scientific management.

Components of Scientific Management

Taylor detailed his system in a book titled *The Principles of Scientific Management* (Taylor, 1911). In this book, he explains how his system has been successful in a number of organizations. For example, Taylor discusses the usefulness of scientific management at Bethlehem Steel Corporation. His system vastly improved the efficiency of this plant—the amount of material shoveled per day increased from sixteen tons to fifty-nine tons.

Like Weber's Theory of Bureaucracy, there are a variety of ways that Taylor's system can be broken down. In this section, we will consider four major tenets.

First, *there is one best way to do every job.* This tenet directly attacks the old system of learning through custom in which individual job skills were passed down from generation to generation. Instead, Taylor believes that the one best way to do every job can best be determined through **time and motion studies.** Thus, a critical aspect of implementing his system is determining the most time-efficient way to accomplish the task at hand. For example, Taylor might analyze a dozen different methods of bricklaying to determine which method is the most efficient. That "one best way" would then be taught to all workers.

The second and third tenets of Taylor's system involve the importance of a proper fit between worker and job. His second principle requires the *proper selection of workers* for the job, and his third principle considers the importance of *training workers* in the manner suggested by time and motion studies. Taylor believes that workers should be scientifically selected and trained for each job and that only "first-class workers" should be retained. An inefficient bricklayer who was better suited to hauling dirt should be shifted to that job. If no "proper job" could be found for the inefficient bricklayer, the worker should be fired.

Fourth, Taylor believes that there is an *inherent difference between management and workers.* According to Taylor, organizational managers are best-suited for thinking, planning, and administrative tasks. In contrast, organizational workers are best-suited for laboring. He therefore advocates a strict **division of labor** in which workers perform physical labor that is planned and directed by management.

Thus, Taylor's system of scientific management is one in which scientific methods are used to determine the best way to do each job. After this best way is

Case in Point: Systematic Surgery

A century ago, Taylor advocated systematic analysis through time and motion studies to find the best way to do menial tasks, such as hauling pig iron and laying bricks. It is intuitively clear that relatively simple jobs like this can be systematized to find more efficient ways to get the work done. But can this kind of approach work in the twenty-first century in such complex tasks as medicine and surgery?

Atul Gawande, a well-known surgeon and author, argues in his book *The Checklist Manifesto* (2009) that the answer to this question is a resounding yes. Gawande contends that the field of medicine has become so complex that it is difficult for an individual physician to know everything that needs to be known or even to perform tasks in ways that are consistently safe, correct, and reliable. Gawande turns to experts in fields that include architecture and aviation and finds that quality is enhanced by

reliance on a very simple tool: the checklist. He then reviews studies in medical settings and finds that there have been dramatic drops in infection and death from implementing a simple list of procedures that reminds medical personnel to do such simple things as wash hands, check that the surgery is taking place on the correct person and the correct body part, and establish that the proper instruments are being used.

Gawande knows that many surgeons might resist the use of a checklist as demeaning; indeed, he resisted the procedure himself. But he argues that the evidence is compelling and that lives are on the line. Using a checklist provides a way to systematize operations so simple things aren't missed. Furthermore, the use of standard procedures enhances teamwork and communication by making sure that everyone in the operating is working from the same page—a checklist.

determined, workers are scientifically selected for their jobs and trained in the methods deemed most appropriate by time and motion studies. The organization functions by maintaining a strict distinction between workers and managers: Workers are responsible for physical labor, and managers are responsible for thinking and organizing.

Taylor believed that this system effectively corrected the past problems of organizational functioning. The problem of *uneven work* would be eliminated by instituting the scientific investigation of work procedures through time and motion studies. The problem of *systematic soldiering* would be combated in two ways. First, although the scientific management system does not reject the practice of piecework pay, Taylor proposes that the piece rate should be based on minimum standards set through time and motion studies. Because these piece rates would be scientifically determined rather than capriciously set, management would not be free to bust the rate. Second, the social pressure of systematic soldiering would be diluted by selecting specific workers for specific jobs. This selection process would often break up original work groups and hence eliminate the social interaction that sometimes led to systematic soldiering.

Taylor's theory and methods fell into some disrepute in the later part of his life when he faced opposition from unions and became known as the "enemy of the working man." Although it is possible to read some of his writings as supporting laborers (for example, he discusses the importance of cooperation and harmony), it is also true that a great deal of his work indicates a low regard for the typical worker. Consider the following example:

> Now one of the very first requirements for a man who is fit to handle pig iron as a regular occupation is that he shall be so stupid and phlegmatic that he more nearly resembles in his mental make-up the ox than any other type.... He is so stupid that the word "percentage" has no meaning to him, and he must consequently be trained by a man more intelligent than himself into the habit of working in accordance with the laws of this science before he can be successful. (Taylor, 1911, p. 59)

Whether we consider Taylor a friend or an enemy of laborers, it is clear that his work has had a substantial impact on the way organizations function. Even in the twenty-first century, many organizations attempt to enhance efficiency through the scientific study of work processes. In combination with Fayol's and Weber's theories, Taylor's ideas give us a clear picture of organizational functioning in the classical mode. The next section of this chapter looks specifically at communication processes within organizations modeled after these classical standards.

COMMUNICATION IN CLASSICAL APPROACHES

It should be clear from our exploration of the work of Fayol, Weber, and Taylor that these theorists saw organizations through the lens of a machine metaphor. As I noted earlier, organizations run in a mechanistic manner will rely on the principles of standardization, specialization, and predictability in order to operate. In the theories we have considered thus far, these general principles are represented by the more specific ideas of organizational structure (such as span of control, scalar chain, hierarchy, division of labor), power (such as primacy of rational-legal

Spotlight on Scholarship: Scientific Management—The Internet Update

It is clear that in organizations ruled by "Taylorism" in the early years of the twentieth century, somebody was always watching the workers. Time and motion studies were being conducted to determine the best way to do various jobs, the bosses were on the lookout for laborers who might be engaged in dangerous systematic soldiering behaviors, and control systems were in effect to be sure that all workers were putting enough effort into accomplishing the goals of the organization. But those were the old days, right?

Scott D'Urso suggests that the old days may not have changed much, as he observed in his article "Who's Watching Us at Work?" D'Urso points out that issues of surveillance and monitoring are just as prevalent now—perhaps even more prevalent—than they were one hundred years ago. There are several reasons for this trend. First, technology in the workplace (especially computer technology) not only gives employees new opportunities for avoiding work and doing social tasks on the job but also gives employers a new way of monitoring the extent to which this kind of activity is taking place. Furthermore, new concerns in the post-9/11 world make issues of electronic monitoring and surveillance in the workplace even more salient. And as D'Urso points out, "[although this type of government activity seems to go against rights guaranteed to the citizens of this nation, a cursory examination of the U.S. [C]onstitution reveals no explicit 'right to privacy,' despite the fact that this basic right is often thought to apply to nearly every aspect of civic life" (D'Urso, 2006, p. 282).

D'Urso begins his examination of this topic by considering the extent to which electronic monitoring occurs in the workplace. Consider just a few of the facts he raises:

- Almost 80% of major U.S. firms conduct surveillance on their employees. Half of them monitor phone calls either by listening or recording.
- Fifty-five percent of U.S. companies participating in a large survey in 2005 noted that they retain and review e-mail. This was an increase from 47% in 2001.
- In a survey, 90% of employees admitted that some of their e-mail at work is personal in nature. And in a separate survey, employees noted that they knew content on their computer was being tracked (23%) or were unsure of company policy on surveillance (40%).

Given the growing prevalence of electronic monitoring and surveillance on the contemporary organizational landscape, D'Urso argues that it is important for research to model the ways in which these practices might influence such outcomes as communication privacy, organizational control, organizational fairness, job performance, workplace satisfaction, and workplace communication. He proposes a model that considers issues such as the types of communication technologies used; organizational factors such as centralization, size, and climate; and policy factors. He hopes that his model will spur research into the ways in which we are still being watched as we move further into the twenty-first century.

D'Urso, S. C. (2006). Who's watching us at work? Toward a Structural-perceptual model of electronic monitoring and surveillance in organizations. *Communication Theory, 16*, 281–303.

power, importance of authority), work design (such as specialization and scientific design of jobs), and attitude (such as subordination of individual interest to organizational goals). It is no surprise that *communication processes* take on particular characteristics in these machine-like organizations. What is communication like in the organizations of Fayol, Weber, and Taylor? To answer this question, let us

Table 2.1 | Communication in Classical Organizations

Content of Communication	Task
Direction of communication flow	Vertical (downward)
Mode/channel of communication	Usually written
Style of communication	Formal

consider several aspects of communication, including (1) the content of communication, (2) the direction of communication flow, (3) the mode or **channel of communication**, and (4) the style of communication. These are summarized in Table 2.1.

Content of Communication

In the classical theories we have considered, there are certain things that should be talked about and certain things that should not be talked about within the organization.

For example, consider Fayol's principle of "subordination of individual interest to general interest." This principle suggests that employees should focus on the goals of the organization, not on their own individual needs and desires. It would follow from this principle, then, that communication within the organization should be focused on task-related topics.

In classical organizations, communication about task is very narrowly focused. For example, Farace, Monge, and Russell (1977) talk about three kinds of communication that often flow in organizational settings: **task-related communication,** **innovation-related communication** (communication about new ideas), and **maintenance-related communication** (communication on social topics that maintains human relationships). Clearly, social communication would be strongly discouraged in the organizations represented by classical theories. Such communication would be counterproductive to the achievement of organizational goals. However, it is interesting to note that innovation-related communication would also be discouraged in these organizations—at least for the vast majority of employees. Consider a worker in an insurance company run according to Taylor's Theory of Scientific Management. This worker would not be encouraged to talk with coworkers about better ways to process insurance forms, as it is assumed that the best way has already been determined scientifically and that the worker is not capable of improving on these ideas. Thus, both social and innovation communication are discouraged in classically run organizations. The content of communication in these organizations is restricted to work-related issues.

Direction of Communication Flow

A second way to characterize communication in the classical theories is to consider how messages are routed through the organizational system. There are a number of possible directions in which communication can flow. For example, communication can flow vertically up and down the organizational chart, with supervisors talking to subordinates and vice versa. Communication can flow horizontally, with employees at the same level of the organization talking to each other. Or communication can be free-flowing, in which all organizational members are encouraged to talk with all other members.

In the classical theories of Fayol, Weber, and Taylor, the most important route for communication is the **vertical flow of information** along the scalar chain of the organizational hierarchy. Furthermore, in these classical theories, the vast majority of communication in the organization flows *downward* in the form of orders, rules, and directives. There is little feedback that moves upward from lower-level employees to higher-level management. (However, Fayol's gangplank allows the possibility of some horizontal communication.) The likelihood of horizontal and free-flowing communication does increase at higher levels of the organization as the tasks taken on tend to involve more planning and coordination. However, horizontal and free-flowing communication is the exception within classical theories. The rule for communication is the flow of information downward from managers to employees.

Channel of Communication

In addition to content and direction, a variety of channels can facilitate communication flow. To name just a few, information can be communicated through face-to-face channels, through written channels, or through a variety of mediated channels, including the telephone or computer. Although all these modes of communication are possible within an organization run according to classical theories, it is likely that the *written* mode of communication is the most prevalent.

Several principles of classical theory point to the importance of written communication. Weber is most explicit about this issue in advocating the importance of rules and the importance of codifying them in written form. Taylor and Fayol also seem to favor written communication. For example, the notion of having one best way to do every job in scientific management lends itself to the production of written employee handbooks and instructions. For Fayol, the principle of order advocating a specified place for all employees and tasks in the organization would also suggest the importance of written instructions and guidelines. In short, because classical theories emphasize the permanence of rules and procedures for efficient organizational functioning, these organizations will probably also rely heavily on written communication in the form of employee handbooks, instructions, mission statements, rules, and performance evaluations.

Style of Communication

Finally, we can consider the **style of communication** that might be found in the organizations of these classical theorists. We have already noted that communication will tend to be top-down, written, and task-related. It is also likely that the tone or style of that communication will be highly *formal*. For example, forms of address will often be distant rather than familiar (for example, Mr. and Ms. rather than first names). Titles will be used (such as supervisor, secretary, or administrative assistant) to separate managers from other employees. The vocabulary chosen for messages will avoid slang and colloquial terms, opting instead for highly standard language. The formality of communication style in a classical organization might also be seen in nonverbal communication, such as dress styles, where suits and ties or uniforms will be favored over more casual or individualized forms of attire. In short, the bureaucratic and professionalized climate of these organizations will often lead to formal—some might say sterile—styles of communication.

CLASSICAL MANAGEMENT IN ORGANIZATIONS TODAY

The theorists we have talked about in this chapter—Fayol, Weber, and Taylor—have all been dead for many years. These men created their theories in the early twentieth century with the organizations of that period in mind. This could lead us to question whether these theories are totally outdated. Are classical theories of management only relevant for newly industrialized factories, or are these theories still applicable in today's world?

The answer to this question is clear. An examination of the vast majority of present-day organizations reveals the prevalence of classical management thought. For example, consider the process of registering for the organizational communication class in which you are currently enrolled. This registration process undoubtedly involved many of the principles discussed in this chapter, including rules for who can take a class and when, standardized procedures for signing up for the class, paperwork that may provide you with documentation of registration, and so on. Even today's typical online registration system could not proceed without highly systematized operations; indeed, standardization and systematic processing is especially important in designing the programs that allow technology to play a role in such a process.

If you go to a fast-food restaurant for lunch today, you will also see the principles of classical theorists at work. These organizations have determined the one best way to make a hamburger, and that procedure is followed religiously. There is also one best way to greet and serve customers—pity the poor counterperson who forgets to ask if you want fries with your order.

In short, your daily activities reveal the widespread use of classical principles in today's organizations. Let us consider two specific ways in which the tenets of classical management are still in popular use today.

Classical Structure in Today's Organizations

As we have noted, the structure advocated by classical theorists is one in which there is a well-defined division of labor and a strict hierarchy. In today's organizations, such a structure is most clearly represented by military organizations. The notions of scalar chain, unity of command, and span of control are the basis of organizing in the military, for without the checks and balances provided by hierarchy and rules, an individual could cause great harm by making an uninformed decision. Sadly, in recent years, concerns about sexual assault in military organizations (see, e.g., Cloud, 2013) point to the ways in which rigid chains of command can be ineffective in addressing the very human problems of organizational members. These classical structures can also be seen in a great many manufacturing and service organizations in which various departments are responsible for specific tasks and in which these functional units are linked through a hierarchical and formalized organizational chart. In these settings, the core task is highly repetitive and routine, promoting the use of mechanistic principles. And even in nonprofit organizations, there is a press toward being as efficient as possible so that donated money is spent with as little waste as possible (Quinn, 2006).

Classical Job Design and Rewards in Today's Organizations

Classical theorists, especially Taylor, advocate the scientific design of jobs, the routinization of those jobs, and the fitting of the employee to his or her optimal task. Although we would be hard-pressed to find an organization that uses scientific management to the extent proposed by Taylor, we do see many of his principles used in today's organizations. For example, consider an organization that is trying to computerize its system for dealing with accounts payable and accounts receivable. Such an organization will attempt to find the most efficient way to accomplish these tasks. Designers will look for the simplest system that reduces the number of keystrokes necessary for inputting information and keeps mistakes to a minimum.

In today's organizations—especially with the technological advances in the last few decades and the advent of robotic technology—we are often looking for the one best way to accomplish tasks. Organizations today also often follow Taylor's ideas about fitting the job to the individual, especially in terms of the match between the job and the psychological profile of an employee. For example, Lawler and Finegold (2000) argue for the importance of "individualizing the organization" in a way that accounts for personal differences in employee abilities, needs, and desires in the workplace. However, in today's workplace, the idea of matching individuals to work involves much more than the specific components of the task. Kalleberg (2008) argues that there are five important factors that can lead to "mismatches" in the twenty-first-century workplace—skills and qualifications, geographical location, time preferences, inadequate earnings, and work/family conflicts. When there is a mismatch in any of these areas, the results may include dissatisfaction, turnover, or poor performance.

Contemporary organizations also continue to be concerned with the role of financial rewards in the motivation of organizational members. Money will probably always be a critical factor in both recruiting employees and rewarding them, and commentators today debate about the extent to which various pay structures are worth it for the bottom line of a company. For example, as highlighted in the "Case in Point" earlier in this chapter, there has been great debate in recent years about bonuses paid to professionals in the financial sector and about the huge payouts received by many chief executive officers (CEOs) in a variety of industries. In 1994, CEO compensation was 142 times the compensation of the average worker. By 2011, CEOs made 380 times the average worker ("CEO Pay," 2012). However, it can be argued that CEOs of contemporary organizations earn the extra money because they are managing much larger firms, taking more risks, and making decisions that touch a wide range of employees and the public (Foroohar, 2007). Unfortunately, recent studies have suggested that there isn't a clear link between CEO compensation and performance (Davidson, 2013).

SUMMARY

In this chapter, we have explored several classical organizational theories, all of which use a machine metaphor in which organizations are conceptualized as highly standardized, specialized, and predictable. The first theory we considered was Henri Fayol's Theory of Classical Management, which proposes that managing consists of the elements of planning, commanding, coordinating, controlling, and organizing. Fayol also proposes a number of principles to guide the structure, power relationships, reward system, and attitudes within an organization.

The second theory we considered was Max Weber's Theory of Bureaucracy. This theory has many features in common with Fayol's theory but in addition emphasizes the closed nature of bureaucracy, the importance of organizational rules, and the predominance of rational-legal authority in bureaucratic functioning.

We then considered Frederick Taylor's Theory of Scientific Management, a microscopic theory that considers relationships between management and workers and the manner in which jobs should be designed. In Taylor's system, jobs should be designed through time and motion studies, and organizations should be based on a strict division between workers and managers, in which workers provide the physical labor and managers provide the mental planning of the work.

We then considered the nature of communication in organizations designed along classical lines. Communication in these organizations is characterized as primarily top-down, formal, task-related, and written. Finally, we looked at the existence of classical management principles in organizations today, exploring how both structure and job design in today's organizations often reflect the ideas expounded many years ago by classical theorists.

DISCUSSION QUESTIONS

1. What aspects of a classical approach to organizing are revealed by the machine metaphor? What aspects are concealed or obscured? Are there other metaphors for organization and communication that could shed more light on how classical theorists thought about organizational communication?

2. What are areas of similarity and difference among the three major theorists considered in this chapter? Are the ideas of Fayol, Weber, and Taylor still relevant for today's organizations? Why or why not?

3. Thinking ahead to ideas beyond classical approaches to organizing, what are your major critiques of these ideas? How do you think the theories presented in this chapter misrepresent the nature of both people and organizations?

KEY CONCEPTS

machine metaphor
prescriptive theory
Theory of Classical Management
elements of management
principles of management
Theory of Bureaucracy
ideal type theory
hierarchy

division of labor
centralization
closed systems
traditional authority
charismatic authority
rational-legal authority
Theory of Scientific Management
systematic soldiering

time and motion studies
task-related communication
innovation-related communication
maintenance-related
    communication
vertical flow of information
channels of communication
style of communication

CASE STUDY | **The Creamy Creations Takeover**

THE SHOPPE

Creamy Creations Ice Cream Shoppe is a small and popular ice cream parlor in a midsized southern city. In 2007, Creamy Creations had been open for almost two years and was gathering a loyal clientele of families and students from the local community college. Creamy Creations specialized in fancy, individualized ice cream confections. Customers would order their base ice cream (or frozen yogurt) plus the toppings they wanted to make their own "creamy creation." The toppings ranged from the typical (such as hot fudge, marshmallows, nuts, fruit syrups, and crushed candy bars) to the exotic (mango fruit chutney, chocolate-covered hazelnuts, and crystallized ginger). Each creamy creation was made start to finish by one of the high school or college students working behind the marble counter. Many customers had a favorite "creamy creator" and would wait for that person to be available to make a special sundae.

In the first eighteen months of the existence of Creamy Creations, it was owned by Bob Peterson, a local retiree who had started the business after thirty years in the military. However, after a year and a half of successful operations, Bob's wife talked him into selling the ice cream business "while it's hot" and buying a motor home to tour the country. Bob sold Creamy Creations to Burger Barn, a local fast-food chain that wanted to expand into other types of food service establishments.

THE TAKEOVER

When Burger Barn took over operations at Creamy Creations, management was pleased with what it saw. Creamy Creations had a solid customer base and had been making a modest profit almost since it opened. Customers spoke highly of the quality product and the friendly atmosphere. As a result, repeat business was high. Not surprisingly, though, Burger Barn thought that Creamy Creations could do even better. Burger Barn had built its reputation on high-quality food served in an efficient and friendly manner. When Burger Barn executives looked at Creamy Creations, they were pleased with the food quality and the friendliness but disturbed by the lack of efficiency. Customers would often have to wait ten minutes before placing an order and would typically wait another ten minutes for the order to be filled. This wait seemed excessive to Burger Barn executives, especially when they looked to the new FroYo frozen yogurt place down the street that was making a lot of money based on an entirely self-serve system.

After observing operations for several weeks, the Burger Barn managers decided that the best way to improve operations at Creamy Creations was to strike a happy medium between the previous Creamy Creations model and the FroYo operations by instituting three workstations behind the counter. Customers would first order their base ice cream at the "scoop station" and then move on to the worker at the "topping station" to have their sundae completed. Finally, the customer would move to the "pay station" to order drinks and have the bill rung up. Because workers were already trained in all facets of the Creamy Creations operation, they could shift easily from station to station. Burger Barn executives reasoned that this would keep them from being bored with their work and help maintain a high level of flexibility for scheduling.

THE AFTERMATH

After six months of operations under the Burger Barn umbrella, Creamy Creations was doing reasonably well. Profits were slightly higher than they had been before the takeover, although not as high as Burger Barn executives would have liked. Employee turnover had increased substantially, but Burger Barn executives did not see this as a troubling problem because there was a large labor market in the community capable of this type of unskilled work. Creamy Creations was still doing a brisk business, although there were many more customers getting their orders to go and fewer using the restaurant as a local gathering place. When watching operations, Burger Barn executives were pleased that customers were served more quickly than before, although there was sometimes a bottleneck of customers at the toppings station because this operation was more complex than activities at either the scooping station or the pay station.

CASE STUDY | **The Creamy Creations Takeover** *continued*

Burger Barn executives considered splitting the toppings station into two separate work areas ("syrup station" and "finishing touches") to further improve efficiency and avoid delays in customer service. They also considered eliminating some of the more bizarre topping options because these toppings were very expensive, were rarely ordered, and tended to clutter up the work area and slow down operations.

All in all, the executives were pleased with the progress made in their acquisition. It was becoming clear that with the recent changes, Creamy Creations had the potential to become a profitable member of the Burger Barn family. They even thought of opening more Creamy Creations in surrounding communities.

CASE ANALYSIS QUESTIONS

1. The Burger Barn executives see a rosy future ahead for Creamy Creations. Do you see any reasons why they should not be so optimistic? Have these executives indeed reached a happy medium between customization and self-serve?

2. How are the principles of classical management reflected in what has happened at Creamy Creations? Which tenets of Fayol's Theory of Classical Management, Weber's Theory of Bureaucracy, and Taylor's Theory of Scientific Management are in evidence? How have the advantages and disadvantages of the classical approach been played out at this business?

3. If you were called in as a communication consultant by Burger Barn executives, what kind of information would you gather in making an assessment about the likely future of Creamy Creations? What would you predict your findings might be, and how would these findings influence your recommendations to Burger Barn executives?

Human Relations and Human Resources Approaches

CHAPTER 3

AFTER READING THIS CHAPTER, YOU SHOULD ...

- Know about the Hawthorne Studies and how they proved to be a springboard for the human relations approach.
- Be familiar with Abraham Maslow's Hierarchy of Needs Theory and Douglas McGregor's Theory X and Theory Y as exemplars of the human relations approach.
- Understand the ways in which the human relations approach was empirically inadequate and misused and how these problems led to the human resources approach.
- Be able to explain how the Managerial Grid and System IV management describe aspects of human resources management.
- Be able to describe typical communication patterns in classical, human relations, and human resources organizations.
- Appreciate the challenges of instituting human resources principles into today's organizations.

As you discovered in Chapter 2, management theory in the early part of the twentieth century was marked by an allegiance to a machine metaphor and a search for ways to increase efficiency and productivity through systems of structure, power, compensation, and attitude. Indeed, many principles of classical management are still widely used today. However, it should be clear from our consideration of Fayol, Weber, and Taylor that certain aspects of organizational communication are conspicuously absent from classical theories. For example, these theorists pay little attention to the individual needs of employees, to nonfinancial rewards in the workplace, or to the prevalence of social interaction in organizations. These theorists were also uninterested in how employees could contribute to meeting organizational goals through knowledge, ideas, and discussion—the only valued contribution was that of physical labor. Issues such as these drove the thinking of the theorists we will consider in this chapter—scholars and practitioners who represent the *human relations* and **human resources approaches** to organizational communication. In this chapter, we will consider these two approaches that began almost ninety years ago and still influence values and practices today. We will first consider the human relations approach that emphasizes the importance of human needs in the workplace. We will then consider developments from this early movement—the human resources approach—that concentrate on the contributions of all employees in reaching organizational goals. In discussing each approach, we will consider the historical and scholarly context that led to the approach and representative theorists within the approach. We will then consider ways in which the human relations and human resources approaches influence communication in organizations and the ways in which these approaches are exemplified in today's organizations.

THE HUMAN RELATIONS APPROACH

From Classical Theory to Human Relations: The Hawthorne Studies

From 1924 to 1933, a number of research investigations were conducted at the Western Electric Company's Hawthorne plant in Illinois that have become collectively known as the **Hawthorne studies**. All but the first of these were conducted by a research team led by Elton Mayo of Harvard University (Roethlisberger & Dickson, 1939). Mayo and his research team were initially interested in how changes in the work environment would affect the productivity of factory workers. These research interests were quite consistent with the prevailing theories of classical management, especially Frederick Taylor's Theory of Scientific Management. That is, like Taylor and other supporters of scientific management, the research team at the Hawthorne plant attempted to discover aspects of the task environment that would maximize worker output and hence improve organizational efficiency. Four major phases marked the Hawthorne studies: the illumination studies, the relay assembly test room studies, the interview program, and the bank wiring room studies.

The Illumination Studies   The illumination studies (conducted before the entry of Mayo and his research team) were designed to determine the influence of lighting level on worker productivity. In these studies, two groups of workers were isolated. For one group (the control group), lighting was held constant. For the second (experimental) group, lighting was systematically raised and lowered. To the surprise of the researchers, there was no significant difference between the productivity of the control group and the experimental group. Indeed, except when workers were laboring in near darkness, productivity tended to go up in both groups under all conditions. It was at this point that Mayo's research team entered the scene to further investigate these counterintuitive findings.

The Relay Assembly Test Room Studies   To better understand the productivity increases they saw in the illumination studies, Mayo and his team of researchers isolated a group of six women who assembled telephone relay systems. A number of changes were then introduced to this group, including incentive plans, rest pauses, temperature, humidity, work hours, and refreshments. All changes were discussed with the workers ahead of time, and detailed records of productivity were kept as these changes in the work environment were instituted. Productivity went up in a wide variety of situations. After more than a year of study, the researchers concluded that "social satisfactions arising out of human association in work were more important determinants of work behavior in general and output in particular than were any of the physical and economic aspects of the work situation to which the attention had originally been limited" (Carey, 1967, p. 404). Because productivity remained high under a wide range of conditions, Mayo and his colleagues believed the results could be best explained by the influence of the social group on productivity and the extra attention paid by the managers to the six workers in the group.

The Interview Program   The unusual findings for the relay assembly test room group led Mayo and his colleagues to conduct a series of interviews with thousands of employees at the Hawthorne plant. Although the goal of these interviews was to learn more about the impact of working conditions on productivity, the interviewers found workers more interested in talking about their feelings and attitudes. Pugh and Hickson (1989) note that "[t]he major finding of this stage of the inquiry was that many problems of worker-management cooperation were the results of the emotionally based attitudes of the workers rather than of the objective difficulties of the situation" (p. 174).

The Bank Wiring Room Studies   A final series of investigations involved naturalistic (nonexperimental) observation of a group of men in the bank wiring room. Observations revealed that the men developed norms regarding the proper level of productivity and exerted social pressure on each other to maintain that level. Slow workers were pressured to speed up, and speedy workers were pressured to slow down. This social pressure (similar to the notion of systematic soldiering discussed in Chapter 2) existed in opposition to the organization's formal goals regarding productivity contained in production targets and incentive schedules. Mayo and his colleagues concluded that the social group's influence on worker behavior exceeded the leverage exerted by the formal organizational power structure.

Explanations of Findings in the Hawthorne Studies   A number of explanations can be offered to account for the findings of the Hawthorne studies. For example, productivity increases were often associated with changes in the work environment, such as work hours, temperature, lighting, and breaks. In the relay assembly test room studies, productivity also increased when pay incentives were offered to workers. Both of these explanations are consistent with classical approaches to organizing, and both were rejected by the investigating team at the Hawthorne plant.

Mayo and his colleagues instead turned to explanations that revolved around the social and emotional needs of workers. First, these researchers concluded that worker output increased as a direct result of the attention paid to workers by the researchers. This phenomenon—whereby mere attention to individuals causes changes in behavior—has come to be known as the **Hawthorne effect**. A second explanation proposed by the Hawthorne researchers is that worker output was increased through the working of informal *social factors*. Recall that the women in the relay assembly test room were separated from other factory workers during the experiment. Mayo and his colleagues concluded that these six women formed a tightly knit group and that social interaction in this group served to increase productivity. This explanation was enhanced through the observation of social pressure in the bank wiring room and the comments of the workers during interviews. Finally, the researchers believed that *management style* could account for some of the observed productivity changes. This conclusion was based on the impact of open communication between workers and managers in the relay assembly test room portion of the studies.

Were Mayo and his colleagues correct in their conclusions that productivity increases should be attributed to social factors, management style, and the Hawthorne effect? Subsequent analyses of the data from the Hawthorne studies clearly suggest that they were not (see, e.g., Carey, 1967; Franke & Kaul, 1978). Indeed, these re-analyses suggest that more traditional explanations, such as incentives, pressure from management, and worker selection, are better explanations for the Hawthorne findings. However, the questionable value of these findings and interpretations does not diminish the fact that at the time—and for many years after—it was *widely believed* that the results of the Hawthorne studies could be best explained as a function of social factors and the satisfaction of the human needs of workers. These interpretations had a substantial impact on the thinking of organizational scholars in the 1930s. Because of these studies, theorists, researchers, and practitioners began to turn away from the mechanistic views of classical theories and instead consider the possibility that human needs and social interaction played an important role in organizational functioning. As Pugh and Hickson (1989) conclude: "Taken as a whole, the significance of the Hawthorne investigation was in 'discovering' the informal organization which, it is now realized, exists in all organizations" (p. 175).

Thus, although the Hawthorne studies may have been lacking in scientific value and interpretive rigor, the sociological impact of the investigations cannot be underestimated. The Hawthorne investigations served as a springboard, moving organizational theorists from classical theories to human relations approaches. These studies also began to highlight the role of communication, especially informal and group communication, in organizational functioning. The next two sections of this chapter present two representative theorists from the human relations movement: Abraham Maslow and Douglas McGregor.

Maslow's Hierarchy of Needs Theory

Abraham Maslow developed his **Hierarchy of Needs** Theory over a period of many years as a general theory of human motivation (Maslow, 1943, 1954). However, he and others have applied this theory extensively to organizational behavior, and it serves as a prototype of a human relations approach to organizing and management.

Maslow proposes that humans are motivated by a number of basic needs. The five types of needs that are consistently presented in his writing are described next—the first three types are often referred to as lower-order needs and the final two as higher-order needs.

1. **Physiological needs:** These are the needs of the human body, including the need for food, water, sleep, and sensory gratification. In the organizational context, these needs can be most clearly satisfied through the provision of a living wage that allows individuals to buy adequate food and clothing, and through physical working conditions that do not violate the physical requirements of the human body.

2. **Safety needs:** Safety needs include the desire to be free from danger and environmental threats. In the organizational context, these needs can, again, be satisfied through wages that allow employees to procure shelter against the elements and through working conditions that are protective and healthy.

3. **Affiliation needs:** This set of needs—sometimes referred to as "belonging needs" or "love needs"—refers to the necessity of giving and receiving human affection and regard. These needs can be satisfied in the organization through the establishment of social relationships with coworkers and managers.

4. **Esteem needs:** Esteem needs refer to the desire of individuals to feel a sense of achievement and accomplishment. Esteem needs can be divided into external esteem—achieved through public recognition and attention—and internal esteem—achieved through a sense of accomplishment, confidence, and achievement. In the organizational context, external esteem needs can be met by compensation and reward structures. Internal esteem needs can be met by the provision of challenging jobs that provide employees with the opportunity to achieve and excel.

5. **Need for self-actualization:** Maslow characterizes this need as the desire to "become more and more what one is, to become everything that one is capable of becoming" (1943, p. 382). In the words of Army recruitment ads, the need to self-actualize is trying to "be all that you can be." Clearly, this need will take different forms for different people. However, it is likely that an organization can facilitate the satisfaction of this need through the provision of jobs that allow an individual to exercise responsibility and creativity in the workplace.

Maslow proposed that these five types of needs are arranged in a **hierarchy of prepotency.** The notion of prepotency suggests that lower-level needs must be satisfied before an individual can move on to higher-level needs. For example, an individual will not attempt to satisfy affiliation needs until needs for physiological functioning and safety have been provided for. Thus, in the organizational context, social relationships on the job will not be satisfying if the organization has not provided adequate wages and working conditions.

Although there has been mixed support about its empirical accuracy (see, e.g., Kamalanabhan, Uma & Vasanthi, 1999; Miner, 1980), Maslow's Hierarchy of Needs Theory is critical in its provision of a clear example of human relations principles and their possible application to the organizational context. Maslow's

Case in Point: Satisfying Higher-Order Needs by Satisfying Lower-Order Needs

Maslow's Hierarchy of Needs is organized in a "Hierarchy of Prepotency" in which lower-order needs—such as food and shelter—must be satisfied before higher-order needs—such as esteem and self-actualization—can be considered. The ruminations of an American farmer who gave up a lucrative and secure job for the chancy and sometimes unpleasant life of farming both supports and refutes this idea. As Lisa Kerschner writes: "Sweaty, dirty, hot, and tired. Those are the words that describe how I feel on a typical July day.... Oh, and then there are gnats and biting flies.... It's times like these that I've wondered, Why on earth am I doing this?" (Kerschner, 2008, p. 17).

In one sense, Kerschner's labor of love refutes Maslow's ideas about human need fulfillment. After all, she is deriving great satisfaction from a job that depends on the weather, back-breaking work over long hours, and the vagaries of the marketplace. Furthermore, as she notes, "farmers are not always looked upon very highly" (Kerschner, 2008). However, her explanation for why she derives such satisfaction from such work is a testament to an understanding of Maslow's ideas. She argues: "It is often said that the three most basic needs are shelter, water, and food. Growing food, then, may be one of man's highest callings. We all need to eat, and most of our food comes from farms. I get a great sense of satisfaction knowing that my farming life is feeding people." In other words, as Kerschner helps others satisfy their most basic desire for sustenance, she is able to feel great about herself—perhaps even self-actualize—as she realizes her critical role in this process.

concentration on the satisfaction of human needs—especially the higher-order needs of esteem and self-actualization—reflects the shift in organizational theorizing that began when the Hawthorne researchers "discovered" the importance of social interaction and managerial attention in the workplace.

McGregor's Theory X and Theory Y

The second exemplar of the human relations movement that we will consider is Douglas McGregor's **Theory X** and **Theory Y** (McGregor, 1960). McGregor was a professor at Massachusetts Institute of Technology and one of the strongest advocates of the human relations movement. Theory X and Theory Y represent the divergent assumptions that managers can hold about organizational functioning. As you will see in the following list of propositions and beliefs, Theory X is representative of a manager influenced by the most negative aspects of classical management theories. In contrast, a Theory Y manager is one who adheres to the precepts of the human relations movement.

McGregor (1957, p. 23) spells out three propositions of the typical Theory X manager. These propositions argue that management is responsible for organizing money, material, and people for economic ends; that people must be controlled and motivated to fit organizational needs; and that without intervention and direction, people would be passive or resistant to the achievement of organizational needs. McGregor's Theory X postulates (McGregor, 1957, p. 23) about human nature are even more straightforward:

1. The average man is by nature indolent—he works as little as possible.
2. He lacks ambition, dislikes responsibility, and prefers to be led.
3. He is inherently self-centered and indifferent to organizational needs.
4. He is by nature resistant to change.
5. He is gullible, not very bright, and the ready dupe of the charlatan and the demagogue.

McGregor asserts that these beliefs are widely held by managers but are incorrect. He believes that managers should conceptualize workers as motivated by the higher-order needs in Maslow's hierarchy and as capable of independent achievement in the workplace. These managerial assumptions are represented in McGregor's presentation of Theory Y (McGregor, 1960, pp. 47–48):

1. The expenditure of physical and mental effort in work is as natural as play or rest.
2. External control and the threat of punishment are not the only means for bringing about effort toward organizational objectives. Man will exercise self-direction and self-control in the service of objectives to which he is committed.
3. Commitment to objectives is a function of the rewards associated with their achievement. The most significant of such rewards, such as the satisfaction of ego and self-actualization needs, can be direct products of efforts directed toward organizational objectives.
4. The average human being learns under proper conditions not only to accept but also to seek responsibility.
5. The capacity to exercise a relatively high degree of imagination, ingenuity, and creativity in the solution of organizational problems is widely, not narrowly, distributed in the population.
6. Under the conditions of modern industrial life, the intellectual potentialities of the average human being are only partially utilized.

Thus, a Theory X manager assumes that a strong and forceful hand is essential for harnessing the efforts of basically unmotivated workers. In contrast, a Theory Y manager assumes that workers are highly motivated to satisfy achievement and self-actualization needs and that the job of the manager is to bring out the natural tendencies of these intelligent and motivated workers. Not surprisingly, McGregor advocates the use of Theory Y management. He believes that behaviors stemming from these managerial assumptions (such as management by objectives and participation in decision making) would lead to a more satisfied and more productive workforce.

McGregor's thinking—like Maslow's Hierarchy of Needs Theory—emphasizes a conceptualization of employees as individuals characterized by needs for attention, social interaction, and individual achievement. Employees in human relations theories are motivated not only by financial gain but also by the desire to satisfy these higher-order needs. Indeed, in comparison to the machine metaphor of classical theorists, the metaphor that could aptly be applied to the human relations approach

✳ Spotlight on Scholarship: Communicating Like a Theory Y Leader

More than half a century ago, McGregor introduced the idea that a supervisor's assumptions about workers could make a big difference in the organizational context. McGregor believed that managers who hold Theory Y assumptions are much more successful in motivating workers toward high performance than Theory X managers. McGregor—and other human relations theorists—believed that leaders' assumptions would lead to different ways of behaving toward subordinates and that these different ways of behavior would influence worker satisfaction and eventual workplace performance.

Although there has been some evidence that Theory X and Theory Y assumptions influence leadership behaviors and the beliefs and attitudes of subordinates, there has been surprisingly little research that looks at what is presumably one of the most important intervening variables in this human relations process: the communication style of managers. It makes sense that if the assumptions of leaders are going to matter in the organizational context, this difference will occur because the leaders are communicating in contrasting ways with their subordinates.

In 2008, Kevin Sager took on this intuitively logical—but under-investigated—idea in a survey study that asked organizational managers about both their assumptions regarding workers and the workplace and the typical style they use in communicating with subordinates. Sager considered six different communicator style variables: the extent to which a manager is dominant, supportive, anxious, closed, nonverbally expressive, and impression-leaving (either positive or negative). He then correlated responses on these style measures with measures of Theory X and Theory Y managerial assumptions.

Sager's results were not especially surprising, but they provide good support for the idea that the way a manager thinks about employees and the workplace can have a systematic effect on the way that manager communicates with employees. Specifically, Theory X managers were more likely to use a "dominant" style of arguing and asserting control over subordinates in the workplace. In contrast, Theory Y managers were more likely to be supportive and nonverbally expressive and less likely to be anxious in their workplace communication patterns. For both Theory X and Theory Y managers, strongly held assumptions were correlated with communication patterns that are likely to leave an impression—presumably, positive for Theory Y managers and negative for Theory X managers—on their employees.

These results are consistent with fifty years of thinking about management assumptions and support the idea that these assumptions will lead to very different communication patterns. As Sager concludes, "the warm style profile of the Theory Y superior may serve to reinforce subordinates' sense of worth and enhance their sense of relatedness to others.... The cold style profile of the Theory X superior, on the other hand, may function to heighten subordinates' sense of interpersonal distance between self and other" (Sager, 2008, p. 309). And to take the reasoning one step further, managers with "warm" or "cold" profiles could strongly influence the attitudes, behavior, and mental health of those working for them.

Sager, K. L. (2008). An exploratory study of the relationships between theory X/Y assumptions and superior communicator style. *Management Communication Quarterly*, 22, 288–312.

---

is the **family metaphor.** Using this metaphor emphasizes the notion of relationships as central to our understanding of organizational functioning. Just as a machine thrives on precision and regularity, a family thrives when needs are fulfilled and opportunities are provided for self-actualization. However, it should be noted that there are still distinctions among members of a family. Parents in a family—like management in a human relations organization—are held responsible for providing opportunities through which children's needs can be fulfilled and talents can be nurtured. And children in a family—like workers in a human relations organization—are often limited in terms of the power and influence they wield within the family unit.

Thus, human relations theorists share an allegiance to principles that highlight human needs and the satisfaction of those needs through interaction with others in the workplace and through the choices managers make about motivating and rewarding employees. Indeed, in moving from the classical theorists of the early twentieth century to human relations theorists of the mid-twentieth century, we shift from a belief that "workers work" to a belief that "workers feel." However, there was yet another movement afoot following the human relations movement. This was a consideration of how workers can contribute to the workplace not only through just "working" or "feeling" but also through thinking and participating in many aspects of organizational functioning. This approach—the human resources approach—is considered next.

THE HUMAN RESOURCES APPROACH

The approach to organizational communication we will look at in this section builds on the contributions of classical and human relationships theorists and adds an important twist. The *human resources approach* acknowledges contributions of classical and, especially, human relations approaches to organizing. Human resources theorists recognize that individuals in organizations have feelings that must be considered and also recognize that individual labor is an important ingredient for meeting organizational goals. What human resources theorists add to the mix is an emphasis on the cognitive contributions employees make with their thoughts and ideas. In this section, we first consider a few of the factors that led organizational theorists and practitioners from classical and human relations principles to the ideas at the center of the human resources approach to management and organizations. We then discuss two theories that provide early statements of some fundamental aspects of the human resources approach to organizing: Robert Blake and Jane Mouton's Managerial/Leadership Grid and Rensis Likert's System IV.

Impetus for the Human Resources Approach

The Hawthorne studies served as a springboard that moved thinking about organizations from the classical school to the human relations school. Was there a similar watershed event that provoked disillusionment with the human relations school and led to the human resources approach? Not really. No single study or incident induced dissatisfaction with the ideas of human relations theorists—indeed, these views are still widely held today. However, in the 1950s, 1960s, and 1970s, there was a growing feeling that models of employee needs were insufficient for describing, explaining, and managing the complexities of organizational life. In particular, there was concern about whether human relations principles really worked and whether they could be misused by organizational practitioners.

Do Human Relations Principles Work?   The principles of human relations theories are certainly intuitively appealing. We would like to believe that by assuming good things about employees, by treating them well with enriched and challenging jobs, and by fulfilling their needs for esteem and self-actualization, we could generate a climate in which worker satisfaction and productivity will flourish. However appealing, though, there is evidence that many of the ideas of human relations theorists simply do not hold up when put to the empirical test. This is true at the level of the individual study and theory, as there is limited support for the conclusions of the Hawthorne studies or for the specific theoretical propositions of scholars like Maslow and McGregor. In addition, this lack of support can also be seen when we consider the general principles on which the human relations movement rests.

At its most basic level, the human relations approach posits that higher-order needs can be satisfied through job design, management style, and other organizational factors. When these higher-order needs are satisfied, employees should be happier. When employees are happier, they should be more productive. This general pattern is depicted in Figure 3.1.

Let us now consider the various links in this human relations model. The first link is between aspects of the work environment and the satisfaction of higher-order needs. Evidence has shown that various job characteristics can serve as motivational factors, although aspects of the job that motivate may vary considerably by person and situation. Thus, this link of the human relations model seems to hold up. Evidence has also shown that job satisfaction will be the next step in the progression (e.g., Muchinsky, 1977). It is the third link in the model connecting job satisfaction and performance that is sometimes seen as problematic. It would *seem* to be obvious that employees who are more satisfied will also be more productive. However, years of research stemming from the human relations movement have failed to provide robust support for this connection (see, e.g., Brief, 1998; Cote, 1999). Why aren't satisfied employees also more productive employees? Perhaps other motivations for hard work, such as financial reward or threat of punishment, take precedence over satisfaction. Furthermore, recent research has suggested that the relationship between satisfaction and performance might depend on other factors, such as whether an organization values individual outcomes over collective outcomes (Ng, Sorensen & Yim, 2009). Whatever the reason, it is clear that "humans are complicated, choice-making animals whose decisions about the amount of effort they should spend on any particular activity are based on a myriad of personal considerations" (Conrad, 1985, p. 118).

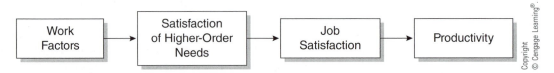

Figure 3.1 | Flowchart of Human Relations Principles

Misuse of Human Relations Principles   Another factor that steered many to the human resources approach was the extent to which tenets of the human relations movement could be used in a superficial or manipulative way in organizations. For example, a manager who holds Theory X assumptions (e.g., that employees are inherently lazy and stupid) might adopt some superficial Theory Y behaviors in an effort to gain more control over the workforce. For example, the manager might ask for employees' opinions about an issue without having any intention of taking those opinions into account during decision making. Because this "pseudo-participation" is not based on a solid foundation of human relations principles, it is likely that it would backfire and be an ineffective organizational strategy. It is also likely that this manipulative use of human relations ideas would fail to satisfy worker needs.

Miles (1965) first highlighted this problem many years ago in his article "Human Relations or Human Resources." When Miles asked practicing managers about their *behaviors,* the managers reported a number of activities that would be endorsed by human relations theorists, such as participation in decision making and supportive and open communication. However, the *beliefs* of these managers did not match these behaviors. The managers did not think employees had sufficient abilities and talents to make high-quality decisions or to work independently. Miles's study—as suggested by the title of his article—highlights the difference between *human relations* and *human resources.* Both human relations and human resources managers might advocate the same kind of organizational behavior—but for very different reasons.

Consider the issue of participation. A human relations manager would institute participation to satisfy employee needs for affiliation and esteem and hope that this need satisfaction would lead to higher levels of productivity. In contrast, a human resources manager would institute participation to take advantage of the innovative ideas held by subordinates. In other words, this manager sees employees as human resources that can be accessed to enhance the functioning of the organization and satisfy the needs of the individuals. It is also likely that the form of participation would distinguish a human relations manager from a human resources manager. A human relations manager might see a suggestion box or a weekly staff meeting as sufficient for meeting relevant employee needs. In contrast, a human resources manager would want to institute a form of participation that could fully tap the ideas and skills of organizational members.

Although Miles first raised this issue many years ago, organizational scholars continue to be concerned about the ways in which those in power in organizations might misuse participative programs. For example, Wendt (1998) describes a "paradox of participation" which includes "the team worker who constantly participates and contributes to problem solving but who, in the final analysis, has no control over the decision-making process becomes frustrated by a paradoxical dimension of empowered organizing" (p. 359). Wendt further argues that "small tokens of recognition (the quality coffee cup) and freedom (jeans day) are strategic organizational symbols that may add somewhat to the quality of work life but do little to foster control and autonomy" (p. 359). In short, for a human resources approach to be truly empowering, it requires more than surface changes in communication patterns. It requires fundamental changes in assumptions about organizational functioning and fundamental

Case in Point: Slashing Emergency Room Waiting Times

Many of us have been there—sitting on hard plastic chairs in the waiting area of a hospital, hoping that you will finally get in to see the doctors and nurses and have your health emergency addressed. You've probably thought that there must be more efficient and effective ways to run an emergency room and provide care to people who are ill or who have experienced trauma. The employees at Parkland Hospital in Dallas, Texas, thought so, and they started working in 2007 to streamline the admissions process. Their process of working through this problem is a clear reflection of what can happen when human resources principles are put into practice (Gordon, 2007).

In April 2007, a committee was formed to improve the emergency room (ER) at Parkland by looking at issues such as patient transportation, bed turnaround times, discharge predictions, and the process through which medical orders are issued. Before this committee was formed, three outside consultants had failed to have an impact, but in the two months after the problems were directly addressed by employees, Parkland had saved more than 2,000

hours of patient care. How did this happen? Some of the changes have been as simple as moving x-ray services to a location closer to the emergency room. Others include more complex systemic changes. But it was critical that the people making the changes were those working in the hospital every day and who understood the challenges confronting the ER.

Three years later, Parkland Hospital was still working on the problem of ER wait time (Jacobson, 2010). The average time elapsed between arrival at the hospital and evaluation by a physician is down to less than an hour, a number that pleased hospital administrators. But there are also new challenges brought on by the lagging economy and overworked health care system, as the public hospital continues to have more ER visits than the system can handle. Indeed, although the initial wait to see a physician has been shortened, the wait for patients who eventually land in a hospital bed is almost nine hours, as the hospital works at peak capacity. Thus, even with the work of highly skilled "human resources," there are sometimes economic and organizational limits on what can be accomplished.

changes in organizational structure and interaction. Indeed, a study of high involvement work practices finds evidence that involvement will not lead to changes in performance unless employees believe they can make a difference through proactive behaviors that are supported by the organizational system (Butts, Vendenberg, Dejoy, Schaffer & Wilson, 2009).

There are several theories that illustrate this fundamental shift from human relations to human resources. We will consider two particularly influential theories: Blake and Mouton's Managerial Grid and Likert's System IV.

Blake and Mouton's Managerial Grid

Robert Blake and Jane Mouton developed their *Managerial Grid* (now called the *Leadership Grid* and referred to in this chapter as the Managerial/Leadership Grid) as a tool for training managers in leadership styles that would enhance organizational efficiency and effectiveness and stimulate the satisfaction and creativity of individual workers (Blake & McCanse, 1991; Blake & Mouton, 1964). They began with the assumption that leaders will be most effective when they exhibit both *concern for people* and *concern for production,* thus combining the interests of classical management (concern for production) and human relations (concern for people).

Blake and Mouton formed a grid in which concern for people and concern for production were gauged from low to high (see Figure 3.2). Both of these dimensions were numbered from 1 to 9. Any manager could then be placed on this grid, depending on his or her levels of concern. Although a manager could be placed on any portion of this grid, Blake and Mouton distinguished five prototypical management styles.

The first prototypical management style—*impoverished management*—is characterized by a low concern for people and a low concern for production (1,1 on the Managerial/Leadership Grid). Such a manager cares little for either the goals of the organization or the people in it and would do the minimum necessary to get by. The second prototypical management style—*country club management* (1,9 on the Managerial/Leadership Grid)—is characterized by high concern for people and low concern for production. This kind of manager would concentrate efforts on the establishment of a pleasant workplace with friendly and comfortable human relations. The third prototypical management style—*authority-compliance* (9,1 on the Managerial/Leadership Grid)—is characterized by high concern for production and low concern for people. This manager—like those of scientific and classical management—would endeavor to arrange all components of the workplace, including people, in order to maximize efficiency and attain goals. There would be little

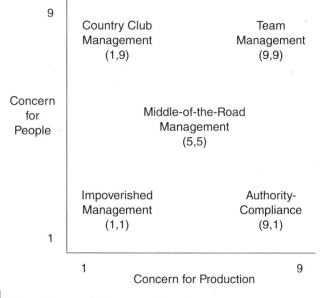

Figure 3.2 | The Managerial/Leadership Grid

The Leadership Grid® figure from Leadership Dilemmas-Grid Solutions by Robert R. Blake and Anne Adams McCanse (formerly the Managerial Grid by Robert R. Blake and Jane S. Mouton). Houston: Gulf Publishing Company, Copyright 1991 by Grid International, Inc.

concern for human needs. The fourth prototypical management style—*team management* (9,9 on the Managerial/Leadership Grid)—is characterized by high concern for both production and people. This type of manager believes that the best way to achieve organizational goals is through the interdependent action of committed, talented, and satisfied individuals. Thus, this manager tries to maximize both productivity goals and employee needs. Finally, *middle-of-the-road management* (5,5 on the Managerial/Leadership Grid) describes a manager who attempts to balance concern for people and production without going too far for either goal. The watchword of such a manager would probably be "compromise." Not surprisingly, Blake and Mouton believe that all managers within an organization should adopt a team management approach because such an approach would maximize concern for both production and people.

Likert's System IV

Blake and Mouton's Managerial/Leadership Grid concentrates on how a manager can combine the values of the human relations school and the classical school into a leadership style that will maximize the potential of human resources within the organization. The second theorist we consider here works to specify the details of the organizational form that will incorporate the ideals of the human resources movement. **Rensis Likert** was the founder and longtime director of the Institute for Social Research at the University of Michigan. His work has been influential in a variety of academic fields. The contributions we will now discuss stem primarily from two of his books: *New Patterns of Management* (1961) and *The Human Organization* (1967).

Likert theorizes that there are a number of forms an organization can take and that these various forms are more or less effective in satisfying organizational and individual goals. He concentrates attention on the explication of four organizational forms, labeled **System I to System IV**. Likert believes that these four system types can be clearly differentiated in terms of motivational factors, communication, decision making, goal setting, control, influence structure, and performance:

- Likert's System I—called the *exploitive authoritative organization*—is characterized by motivation through threats and fear, downward and inaccurate communication, top-level decision making, the giving of orders, and top-level control. The exploitive authoritative organization includes all the worst features of classical and scientific management.
- Likert's System II is called the *benevolent authoritative organization*. This organizational type is characterized by motivation through economic and ego rewards, limited communication, decision making at the top, goal setting through orders and comments, and top-level control. It is in many ways similar to a System I organization but does not incorporate the explicit goal of exploiting workers. However, the management style in this organization is still authoritative because the managers believe that this style is "best for the workers."
- System III—the *consultative organization*—differs markedly from Systems I and II. In this organizational type, decisions are still made at the top and

control still rests primarily at the upper levels of the hierarchy. However, before decisions are made, employees are consulted, and their views are taken into consideration. Goals are set after discussion, and there is a high level of communication moving both up and down the hierarchy.

- System IV—a *participative organization*—provides a sharp contrast to the other system types. In a System IV organization, decision making is performed by every organizational member, and goals are set by complete work groups. Control is exercised at all levels of the organization, and communication is extensive, including upward, downward, and horizontal interaction. The contributions of all organizational members are strongly valued, and employees are rewarded through the satisfaction of a wide variety of needs.

These four system types, then, represent the move from the worst that scientific and classical management has to offer (System I) to an organizational type that values and encourages the contributions of all organizational members (System IV). Likert believes that a human resources organization (System IV) is more than just managerial attitudes. Rather, he advocates structural changes and practices that enhance the participation of individuals and the performance of the organization.

These two theorists provide a good initial look at human resources principles as they were developed in the mid-twentieth century. In some ways, these principles hark back to classical approaches because organizational effectiveness and productivity are again benchmarks of success. In other ways, the human resources approach is merely an extension of the human relations framework, as higher-order human needs for challenge and self-actualization are fulfilled through organizational activities. However, the human resources approach is distinct from both of the other approaches in two ways. First, it aspires to maximize *both* organizational productivity and individual need satisfaction. Second, in order to optimize both goals, the human resources approach emphasizes the contributions that employee ideas can make to organizational functioning. We will now consider ways in which both the human relations and human resources approaches are reflected in organizational communication goals and practices. These issues are summarized in Table 3.1.

Table 3.1 | Communication in Classical, Human Relations, and Human Resources Organizations

	Classical Approach	Human Relations Approach	Human Resources Approach
Communication Content	Task	Task and social	Task, social, and innovation
Communication Direction	Vertical (downward)	Vertical and horizontal	All directions, team-based
Communication Channel	Usually written	Often face-to-face	All channels
Communication Style	Formal	Informal	Both but especially informal

COMMUNICATION IN HUMAN RELATIONS AND HUMAN RESOURCES ORGANIZATIONS

Content of Communication

In Chapter 2, we introduced the typology of Farace, Monge, and Russell (1977) that considered various types of communication in organizations. We noted that organizations following a classical model will emphasize task communication. However, as we consider human relations and human resources approaches, we see the other two types of communication content come into play. In human relations organizations, task-related communication still exists, but it is accompanied by communication that attempted to maintain the quality of human relationships within the organization—*maintenance communication.* And when we consider interaction in human resources organizations, the third type of communication in the Farace, Monge, and Russell typology comes to the forefront. This is *innovation communication,* which is interaction about how the job can be done better, new products the organization could produce, different ways of structuring the organization, and so on. Because the human resources approach to organizing places a premium on input from employees, the innovation content of communication is critical.

Direction of Communication Flow

In classical organizations, communication flows in a predominantly downward direction, as directives flow from management to workers. A human relations approach does not eliminate this need for vertical information flow but instead adds an emphasis on *horizontal* communication. As discussed earlier in this chapter, human relations theorists believe that an important aspect of need satisfaction is communication among employees, so interaction that flows horizontally among employees is just as important as downward communication in the accomplishment of organizational goals. In a human resources organization, the goal is to encourage the flow of ideas from all locations throughout the organization. Thus, in the simplest sense, communication in this organizational approach will include all directional flows—downward, upward, horizontal, and diagonal. More specifically, this multidirectional communication flow often takes place in *team-based* settings in human resources organizations. That is, rather than restricting communication flow to the hierarchy of the organization (whatever the direction), a human resources organization will often reconfigure the organizational chart to optimize the flow of new ideas.

Channel of Communication

As you saw in Chapter 2, organizations run in a classical style are dominated by written communication because a strong value is placed on permanence. In the human relations approach, in contrast, face-to-face communication takes center stage. This channel of interaction allows for more immediate feedback and more consideration of nonverbal cues. Thus, face-to-face communication is more appropriate for addressing the human needs emphasized in the human relations approach. In a human resources organization, it is unlikely that any particular channel of communication will be favored over others. Human resources theorists desire to maximize the productivity of the organization through the intelligent use of human resources. Sometimes, these resources can be best used through face-to-face contact in meetings. Sometimes, the situation calls for written memos or e-mail. Thus, some scholars have suggested that effective managers will work to *match* the communication channel to the task at hand (Trevino, Lengel & Daft, 1987). For example, these researchers believe that tasks with a high level of uncertainty require a communication channel that is relatively "rich" (e.g., face-to-face interaction), whereas tasks with a low level of uncertainty require a communication channel that is relatively "lean" (e.g., written communication).

Style of Communication

I noted in Chapter 2 that classical organizations emphasize formal communication, as standards of professionalism and bureaucratic decorum hold sway. In contrast, a human relations organization is likely to want to break down the status differential between managers and employees as a means of satisfying social needs. Thus, it is likely that informal communication—with less emphasis on titles, formal business attire, and bureaucratized language—will be emphasized. However, human resources organizations have the dual goals of enhancing organizational effectiveness and fulfilling human needs. On the needs side of the equation, an informal style is most likely to satisfy needs for affiliation. On the organizational effectiveness side, an informal style will also probably serve better than a formal one because employees will probably feel more comfortable contributing in a relatively informal manner. However, a human resources manager would certainly not eschew the use of a formal style if it were the most appropriate for the task at hand.

HUMAN RELATIONS AND HUMAN RESOURCES ORGANIZATIONS TODAY

Human relations theories were proposed as a reaction to classical management systems and to evidence that meeting human needs is a critical aspect of organizational performance. The basic impetus of these ideas has certainly carried over the decades to today's organizations. For example, the influence of human relations ideas can clearly be seen in the general attitude of management toward employees. It would be difficult indeed to find managers today who would characterize their subordinates as interchangeable cogs whose needs play no role in organizational decisions. For example, if a manufacturing organization needed to shut down a factory, management would be likely to consider both economic issues and human factors, such as the needs of workers and their families for severance pay and job placement or retraining programs. Furthermore, human relations principles can be seen in today's organizations in the area of job design. In many of today's organizations, an effort is made to enrich jobs by designing tasks that will satisfy some of the higher-order needs of workers through jobs that increase autonomy, variety, and task significance.

In general, though, it is the principles of human resources theorists that are most often reflected in today's organizations. Indeed, many of the ideas of early human resources theorists have been transformed in light of the contingencies facing today's organizations. Theoretically, two of the most important developments in this area are the consideration of organizations as learning systems and the development of systems of knowledge management. Peter Senge and his colleagues (Senge, 1990; Senge, Roberts, Ross, Smith & Kleiner, 1994) have made a distinction between *learning organizations* and those that could be seen as having "learning disabilities." **Learning organizations** are organizations that emphasize mental flexibility, team learning, a shared vision, complex thinking, and personal mastery. It is proposed that learning organizations can be promoted through participation and dialogue in the workplace. Scholars interested in **knowledge management** (see DeLong, 2004; Heaton & Taylor, 2002) see the organization as embodying a cycle of knowledge creation, development, and application.

Both of these approaches, then, have further developed the notion that effective organizations are those that can harness the cognitive abilities of their employees, and, indeed, these ideas developed from the kernel of the human resources approach are seen by many as the ideal way to run contemporary organizations. In the final sections of this chapter, we will look at how these abstract principles are often embodied in the practice of organizational life. We will first consider the question of what constitutes human resources management in today's organizations and then discuss how these programs can be instituted to enhance their effectiveness.

The *What* of Human Resources Programs

A number of organizational programs exemplify the use of human resources principles in today's organizations. These programs all emphasize **team management** and the importance of **employee involvement** in ensuring product or service quality and organizational productivity. Cotton (1993) defines employee involvement as "a participative process that uses the entire capacity of workers, designed to encourage employee commitment to organizational success" (p. 3). The goal is generally one of creating a "knowledge-enabled organization" (Tobin, 1998) in which the collective knowledge of workers facilitates high performance (Fisher & Duncan, 1998).

Although specific programs of team management and employee involvement vary widely in terms of the specifics of human resources management, they all share the basic principle of trying to structure the organization in ways that maximize the contribution of employees, both individually and collectively. Pfeffer (1998) labels this important principle as "putting people first" in his book *The Human Equation* (see also Pfeffer & Veiga, 1999, for a summary). This book—based on both anecdotal evidence and social scientific research—highlights seven practices of successful organizations that serve as a useful summary of *what* is done in organizations today that follow human resources principles. These practices are presented in Table 3.2. As this table illustrates, the *what* of a successful human resources program includes many nuts-and-bolts issues regarding compensation, employment security, and organizational structure. This table also highlights the critical role of communication processes, both in terms of information sharing and teamwork and

Table 3.2	Pfeffer's Seven Practices of Successful Organizations

Practice	Description
Employment security	Job security demonstrates a commitment to employees and develops employees who understand the organization.
Selective hiring	Employees who are a good fit for the organization—in terms of skills, abilities, and other attributes—will stay with the organization and enhance organizational performance.
Self-managed teams and decentralization	Teams will permit employees to pool information and create better solutions as well as enhance worker control over work processes.
Comparatively high and contingent compensation	Contingent compensation connects performance outcomes with critical rewards.
Extensive training	Frontline employees need training to identify workplace problems and contribute to innovative solutions.
Reduction of status differences	By reducing both symbolic (e.g., language and labels) and substantive (e.g., pay) inequities, all employees will feel more valued.
Sharing information	Employees can only contribute if they have adequate information about their own jobs and about the performance of the organization as a whole.

Table developed from Pfeffer, J. (1998), *The human equation: Building profits by putting people first.* Boston: Harvard Business School Press, and from Pfeffer, J. & Veiga, J. F. (1999). Putting people first for organizational success. *Academy of Management Executive*, 13(2), 37–48.

in terms of the communicative processes through which training occurs and status differentials are reduced.

The *How* of Human Resources Programs

There are clearly ways in which the principles of the human resources approach can be put into play in today's organizations. However, both our everyday experience and social scientific research suggest that these programs often *don't work*. As Jassawalla and Sashittal (1999) note with regard to collaborative teams, "[although they are formed with great optimism, few are managed for success." The chance of failure with human resources efforts can also be seen in specific programs. For example, total quality management (TQM), was extremely popular in the closing decades of the twentieth century. However, Choi and Behling (1997) provide extensive evidence regarding the failures of TQM, including surveys of executives who do not believe TQM has enhanced competitiveness, programs that have been discontinued because of failure to produce results, and award-winning TQM programs that have stumbled. In the twenty-first century, there are fewer approaches to human resources management that have become widespread trends. Instead, practitioners now tend to recognize the possible benefits and pitfalls of various management systems and look for ideas about more specific processes (e.g., managing global teams, virtual teams, or entrepreneurial teams). Whatever specific system is used, however, the literature points to a number of ways to enhance the possibility for program success. Although the following list is admittedly brief, it highlights some of the issues that should be taken into account when instituting the major change required by most human resources programs.

- **Know when team-based management is appropriate:** Many scholars and consultants suggest that there are times when team-based organizations will be particularly effective (Forrester & Drexler, 1999). For example, work that cuts across functional lines, a diverse and complex organizational environment, a rapidly changing workplace in which innovation is critical—all these factors suggest a need for team-based management.

- **Consider the attitudes of top management:** Although human resources programs involve the empowerment of workers throughout the organization, the impetus for change and the responsibility for dealing with change still often rest with top management.

- **Deal with cynicism about change:** Employees are often dismayed by the prospect of yet another "program of the month" at their organization. Reichers, Wanous, and Austin (1997) recommend that cynicism about organizational change can be minimized by keeping people involved in plans, by seeing change from the employees' perspective and providing opportunities to vent, by rewarding supervisors for effective communication, and by minimizing surprises. (See also the discussion of organizational change processes in Chapter 10.)

Case in Point: From the Golf Course to the Gym

The human relations approach puts a high value on social relationships because it is assumed that these relationships will make workers happy and that worker satisfaction will translate to productivity. For human resources theorists, however, the reason for valuing relationships shifts. For those advocating this approach, relationships can be seen as valuable resources for new information, for networking, and for business growth.

In the past, these relationships were nurtured around the water cooler, on the golf course, or perhaps at the legendary three-martini lunch. However, David Tao (2013) notes that in recent years "the gym has quietly grown as a new center for business, where aspiring partners in commerce can work off stress while making connections that follow them right back to the office." Tao notes that there is a special kind of camaraderie that develops during workouts: "If I trust someone to spot me when I've got a few hundred pounds hovering above my chest, chances are I'm bullish on them replying to my e-mails on time." Further, organizations see important benefits to creating relationships in fitness contexts. The three-martini lunch may have helped develop business contacts, but it was clearly detrimental to employee health. If those relationships are nurtured during a spin class or participating in a Tough Mudder, the result could be reduced health care costs for the organization and the benefits that accrue from the ability of exercise to enhance creativity and abstract thinking (Barron & Barron, 2012). In short, "it's a win-win that has employees getting more active and all sorts of companies teaming up with health and wellness entrepreneurs" (Tao, 2013).

- **Facilitate the translation process:** Every new program in an organization will require a new language to be learned. For example, in the days of Total Quality Management, employees had to understand terms such as "just in time," "Pareto chart," and "statistical methods quality indicators." Programmatic changes in the organization can be accomplished only if members understand the terminology of the program (Fairhurst & Wendt, 1993) and if managers frame the change in a way that helps members enact their roles in the organization in viable and effective ways (Fairhurst, 1993).

SUMMARY

In this chapter, we looked at two related approaches to the study and practice of organizational communication: the human relations approach and the human resources approach. The human relations approach was inspired, in large part, by the Hawthorne studies, which pointed scholars and practitioners toward the importance of human needs and the consideration of management practice and job design to meet those needs. The human relations approach was illustrated by Maslow's Hierarchy of Needs Theory and McGregor's contrast between Theory X and Theory Y assumptions. However, there was often limited support for human relations theories, and the principles of human relations were often instituted in half-hearted and manipulative ways. The human resources movement that emerged from these frustrations emphasizes the need to maximize both organizational productivity and individual employee satisfaction through the intelligent use of human resources. Human resources ideas were illustrated through the models of Blake and Mouton (the Managerial/Leadership Grid) and Rensis Likert (System IV).

We then examined the nature of communication in human relations and human resources organizations by considering factors of communication content, direction, channels, and style. Finally, we considered ways in which human relations and, especially, human resources principles are utilized in today's organizations. We discussed the *what* of human resources management by looking at both specific programs and general principles for "putting people first." We concluded with some ideas about *how* human resources programs can be instituted.

DISCUSSION QUESTIONS

1. A great deal of research has discredited many of the findings from the Hawthorne studies. Given this research, why were the Hawthorne studies influential when they were conducted? Are they still influential today? Why or why not?

2. In jobs you have had, what aspects of the workplace did you find particularly satisfying? What role did managers have in making the organization a satisfying place? How do your experiences, then, fit in with the ideas of Abraham Maslow and Douglas McGregor?

3. In Chapter 2, we noted that the classical approach follows a machine metaphor, and in this chapter, we associated human relations theorists with a family metaphor. What metaphor would you use to describe the human resources approach? What are the strengths and weaknesses of the metaphor you propose?

4. Is the human resources approach more appropriate for some kinds of jobs and organizations than others? Why or why not? Can human resources principles be adapted for a variety of workplaces?

KEY CONCEPTS

human relations approach	Theory X	learning organizations
Hawthorne studies	Theory Y	knowledge management
Hawthorne effect	human resources approach	team management
Hierarchy of needs	managerial/leadership grid	employee involvement
hierarchy of prepotency	Rensis Likert	
family metaphor	System I to System IV	

CASE STUDY | ## Teamwork at Marshall's Processing Plant

Marshall's is a large plant in the midwestern United States that processes corn into the fructose syrup used in many soft drinks. Marshall's is a continuous processing plant, running 24 hours a day, 365 days a year. There are two major components of the plant. In the wet mill, where 75 employees work, the corn is soaked. Then, the soaked corn moves on to the refinery (employing eighty employees), where the soggy corn is processed into fructose syrup. Marshall's is a computerized state-of-the-art plant, and much of the work in the wet mill and refinery consists of monitoring, maintenance, cleanup, and troubleshooting. There are also 30 staff members who work in the office and in various other support positions. All the employees except the support staff work 12-hour shifts.

Three years ago, Marshall's instituted a "team management" system to enhance productivity in the plant and improve worker morale. The program included two types of teams. First, work teams met on a weekly basis to consider ways of improving the work process within their own portion of the plant. In addition, the plant-wide "Marshall Team" met on a monthly basis to consider decisions about issues facing the plant as a whole, such as benefit and compensation plans, company policies, and capital equipment purchases. Each work team elected one member to serve on the Marshall Team. Management at Marshall's regarded the teams as "consultative" bodies. That is, management used team suggestions as input but retained the right to make final decisions about all plant operations.

For the first three years of the team program, the same set of people participated heavily in team meetings, and the same people tended to get elected to the

Marshall Team. These go-getters took their roles very seriously and liked having a voice in company decisions. However, management at Marshall's was becoming concerned about the people who did not participate in the team program. After evaluating the problem for a while, management decided that it was a complicated issue and that there were three kinds of employees who were not participating in the team program.

First, one group of employees complained that the program led to too many meetings and had a lot of extra busywork. This group was epitomized by Kenny Suh. Kenny was a hard worker and was well-respected at the plant, but he was also a no-nonsense kind of person. When asked about participating in work teams and the Marshall Team, he said: "I don't have time to sit around and shoot the breeze. When I'm on the job, I want to be working, not just chitchatting and passing the time."

A second set of workers resented the fact that they had to deal with so much of their own work situation. These employees believed that management was not providing enough input and was counting on the work teams to figure everything out. For example, consider Bill Berning. Bill had lived near the Marshall's plant all his life and liked working there because the pay was good. However, he saw his job simply as a way to earn money that he could spend on the great love of his life: motorcycles. When management started asking him to do more and more on the job, he just clammed up. After all, he argued, management was getting paid to make the decisions, not him.

Finally, a third set of employees refused to participate because they did not think their input would be

CASE STUDY | Teamwork at Marshall's Processing Plant *continued*

listened to. In many ways, this was the group that most disturbed higher management because many of these people had participated in team activities in the past. Natalie Nelson was a prime example. When the team management system was instituted, Natalie was very active in her area's work team and was even elected to the Marshall Team several times. However, after a couple of years, she stopped participating. When asked, Natalie said: "I thought that the team idea was great at first, but then I realized that management is just going to do what it wants regardless of what we say. I can live with autocratic managers—I just don't want them to make me wake up early for a team meeting and then ignore what I have to say. If the teams are just window-dressing, it's not worth it to me."

Marshall's wants to have a team management system that really works, and they know that they need to get more participation in order to have this happen. However, they've now realized that the problem is more complex than they realized at first. You have been called in as a consultant to help them fix their program. What kind of suggestions will you make?

CASE ANALYSIS QUESTIONS

1. Do the original goals of the team management system used at Marshall's comport more with the philosophy of human relations or human resources management? How would the theorists discussed in this chapter (Maslow, McGregor, Likert, and Blake and Mouton) analyze the current situation at Marshall's?

2. Employees identified three reasons for not participating in the program at Marshall's. How would you deal with each of these problems? Is it possible (or desirable) to satisfy all groups of employees and achieve full participation? Would human relations and human resources theorists have different ideas about the importance of these various reasons for not participating in the team management system?

3. What changes would you make in the team management system at Marshall's that would increase participation? What changes would you make to enhance the effective use of human resources at Marshall's? How would you institute these changes and communicate them to employees?

4 | # Systems and Cultural Approaches

AFTER READING THIS CHAPTER, YOU SHOULD ...

- Recognize the differences among a machine metaphor, a systems metaphor, and a cultural metaphor for describing organizational processes.
- Be able to explain systems components, systems processes, and systems properties and illustrate these ideas with organizational communication examples.
- Understand the value of studying communication networks at various levels of analysis.
- Appreciate Weick's theory of organizing as an important way to "make sense" of the workings of organizational communication.
- Know about how the cultural metaphor for understanding organizations was first developed as a prescriptive model for improving organizational performance and be able to describe the weaknesses of this prescriptive approach.
- Appreciate ways of describing organizational cultures as complicated, emergent, unitary, and ambiguous.

Back in Chapter 2, we considered classical and scientific management approaches to organizational communication theory and found that these theories are based on a mechanistic metaphor. That is, classical theorists thought that organizations could be best understood by comparing them to machines that are predictable and comprised of replaceable parts. The human relations and human resources approaches we considered in Chapter 3 objected to this model because of the way it conceptualized workers—as individuals who should be considered as laborers without feeling or thought. However, in addition to these concerns about employee treatment and involvement, many theorists also continue to find the machine metaphor to be an unsatisfying model for explanation and understanding because organizations—to a large extent, at least—do not behave in predictable and machinelike ways. In later parts of the twentieth century, two new metaphors gained ascendency as ways to understand organizational processes. The first of these, the **systems metaphor,** views organizations not as self-contained and self-sufficient machines but as complex organisms that must interact with their environment to survive. The second, the *cultural* metaphor, takes an anthropological approach in understanding organizations as sites of interlinked beliefs, values, behaviors, and artifacts.

In this chapter, we explore both of these metaphorical approaches to the understanding of organizational communication. We first consider the systems approach by considering some basic systems concepts and the ways in which these ideas have held sway in the study of communication networks and *sensemaking* in organizations. We then consider the cultural approach by exploring both prescriptive and descriptive ways in which practitioners and scholars have approached organizational cultures.

THE SYSTEMS METAPHOR AND SYSTEMS CONCEPTS

Systems theory did not originate in the study of organizations but rather in the fields of biology and engineering. One of the key founders of the systems movement was Ludwig von Bertalanffy, a theoretical biologist who was interested in the study of "living systems" within his own academic field. However, von Bertalanffy was also concerned with the extent to which intellectual disciplines were isolated from one another, and he argued that systems concepts could be applied to a large number of fields in both the natural and social sciences (von Bertalanffy, 1968). The study of systems was eagerly adopted by organizational theorists such as Katz and Kahn (1978) who took an open systems approach to organizational behavior and Farace, Monge, and Russell (1977) in the field of communication. In short, the 1960s and 1970s were marked by extensive attention to the systems metaphor as a way of understanding the processes of organizational behavior and communication.

Though there is substantial variety in the details presented about systems theory across various scholars, almost all systems theories embrace certain aspects of the systems metaphor. In the following sections, we consider a number of concepts that are endorsed by a wide range of systems theories. We first look at what systems are made of—system components. We then consider how systems work—system processes. Finally, we discuss the unique characteristics that arise from these components and processes—system properties.

System Components

At its most basic level, a system is an assemblage of parts, or components. In a biological system, these parts include cells and organs. In an organizational system, these components are the people and departments that make up the organization. We could also think about the larger society as a system. In this case, the parts would be the organizations and institutions that make up the society. Regardless of what particular system we look at, the first task of a systems theorist is to identify the relevant components that comprise the system. After the components of the system have been identified, it is interesting to look at how these parts are arranged and how they work. Three concepts characterize system components: hierarchical ordering, interdependence, and permeability.

Hierarchical Ordering   A system is not simply an undifferentiated set of parts thrown together. To the contrary, system components are arranged in highly complex ways that involve subsystems and supersystems—a hierarchical ordering. If you think about your body as a system, you can observe this hierarchy. Your body is composed of a number of subsystems—the cardiovascular system, the digestive system, the neurological system, and so forth. In turn, these systems are also made up of subsystems—for example, the cardiovascular system includes the heart, lungs, and blood vessels. We could take this even further with a consideration of organ components, cells, and so on.

The same hierarchical ordering can be seen when considering the organization as a system. For example, let us look at a hospital as an organizational system. A hospital consists of a number of departmental subsystems, including surgical units, recovery units, the emergency room, laboratories, and offices. These subsystems, in turn, are composed of smaller work groups and individuals. We could also move in the other direction and see that the hospital is part of a larger supersystem—the health care industry. This supersystem would include organizations such as hospitals, clinics, insurance companies, and pharmaceutical companies.

Interdependence   A second concept that characterizes system components is **interdependence**. The notion of interdependence implies that the functioning of one component of a system relies on other components of the system. Think again about the human body. The brain needs a constant supply of blood in order to function, but this supply would not be possible if it were not for the heart's pumping action. In turn, the heart relies on the lungs to bring in the oxygen that fuels the blood. Both the heart and the lungs rely on the brain for the neurological signals that facilitate functioning. In short, the body is a highly interdependent system in which the breakdown of one component would lead to breakdowns in other components and in the system as a whole.

As a system, an organization is also highly interdependent. For example, in our hospital, the surgical units could not function effectively without laboratories to provide important test results. The laboratories rely on the purchasing department for supplies, such as test tubes and chemicals. Many hospital units depend on the personnel and business offices to deal with the paperwork of compensation and insurance. Thus, no component within the hospital can function effectively without active assistance from other system parts. At levels higher than the individual organization, interdependence can be seen by considering the complex relationships among organizations within a given business sector or in related sectors. This interdependence is particularly apparent in today's highly connected global economy (Browning and Shetler, 2000).

Permeability   A third characteristic of system components is that they have **permeable boundaries** that allow information and materials to flow in and out. The degree of permeability varies from system to system; some are relatively closed, whereas others are extremely open. However, all biological and social systems require some degree of permeability to survive. Permeability refers both to the system as a whole—which must be open to its environment—and to the components within the system. For example, the human body must be open to its environment in order to take in the air, food, and water necessary for survival. The components of the human body must also be permeable to allow the flow of materials among organs and organ systems. In our hospital, we can also observe both system and component permeability. The hospital must be open to its larger environment so patients, information, and resources can move into and out of the organization. Similarly, hospital units must be open to each other to facilitate the flow of people, information, and materials.

System Processes

Let's now look at how these hierarchical, interdependent, and permeable components function in a system. At the most basic level, systems are characterized by *input-throughput-output* processes (Farace, Monge & Russell, 1977). That is, a system "inputs" materials or information from the environment through its permeable boundaries. The system then works on these inputs with some kind of transformational process; this is "throughput." Finally, the system returns the transformed "output" to the environment. For example, an insurance claims adjuster must gather information about relevant damages, make decisions based on insurance coverage, and then output that information (and, hopefully, a check!) to the policyholder.

Two kinds of processes characterize input-throughput-output operations. The first of these—the process of *exchange*—is apparent in both input and output activities. That is, both the input of materials and information and the output of transformed materials and information require a process of exchange with the environment outside the system. Obviously, this process of exchange is intimately related to the permeability of system boundaries. Some organizations have highly permeable boundaries to facilitate the exchange process, whereas others are relatively closed.

A second type of process—*feedback*—is critical to the throughput portion of organizational functioning. Feedback is information that helps to facilitate the interdependent functioning of system components. Two types of feedback are important to system functioning. The first of these is variously referred to as *negative* feedback, *corrective* feedback, or **deviation-reducing** feedback. This kind of feedback helps to maintain steady system functioning. For example, suppose that a restaurant supervisor notices that one of the waiters is telling patrons about yesterday's specials instead of today's specials. The supervisor might inform the waiter about his error so he can change his message to the diners. This is corrective feedback that serves to keep organizational functioning on a steady course.

A second type of feedback is known as *positive, growth,* or **deviation-amplifying** feedback (see Maruyama, 1963). This is information that serves to change system functioning through growth and development. For example, our restaurant supervisor might notice that increasingly more patrons are highly linked to social media outlets. Our supervisor, then, might suggest to higher management that the restaurant take advantage of this trend by establishing an online presence through Facebook and Twitter and offering Groupon coupons. This kind of feedback serves to change the entire system rather than maintain it in a steady state.

System Properties

Now we will consider system properties that emerge from the interaction of these components and processes. Four properties are particularly relevant: holism, equifinality, negative entropy, and requisite variety.

Holism   The property of **holism** suggests that a system is more than the sum of its parts. Systems have this property because of the interdependent nature of their components and the information that flows through **feedback and exchange processes**. For example, imagine that five individuals are asked to solve an organizational problem. These individuals may come up with many interesting and innovative ideas while sitting alone in their respective offices. However, if these five people are placed in an interdependent system, it is likely that many more and different problem-solving ideas will emerge from their interaction.

Equifinality   The system property of **equifinality** states that "a system can reach the same final state from differing initial conditions and by a variety of paths" (Katz & Kahn, 1978, p. 30). This, again, is a result of the interdependent operation of system components. Because the components of the system are integrated in highly complex ways, a variety of means exist to reach any system goal.

The notion of equifinality becomes particularly important in today's complex organizational world. For example, *Rework*, a book by Internet entrepreneurs Jason Fried and David Heinemeier Hansson (2010), argues that there are many ways to reach success in today's business world that defy the typical rules of management textbooks. For example, Fried suggests that success can be gained by ignoring standard practices such as strategic planning, staff meetings, and typical promotion standards (Summers, 2010).

Negative Entropy   Entropy is the tendency of closed systems to run down. For example, if a body is totally closed to its environment (and receives no food, water, or oxygen), it will quickly deteriorate. Open systems, however, are characterized by negative entropy, or the ability to sustain themselves and grow. **Negative entropy** is possible because of the flow of information and materials between the environment and the system. For example, U.S. auto companies in the 1960s were relatively closed to their environment, ignoring information about world conditions and consumer preferences. If the auto companies had remained closed, they would have deteriorated and gone out of business. It was only through the intake of information from the environment that the automakers were able to survive. In the first decade of the twenty-first century, U.S. auto companies again seemed to be ignoring conditions outside of their own walls (building huge SUVs while other automakers concentrated on fuel-efficient hybrids), and by the end of the decade, governmental bailouts were needed to keep several U.S. companies in business. This is the principle of negative entropy in action—a system's success and very survival depends on active exchange with the system's environment.

Requisite Variety   A final system property again deals with the relationship between a system and its environment. The property of **requisite variety** states that the internal workings of the system must be as diverse and complicated as the environment in which it is embedded. This "matching complexity" allows the organization—or team or group within the organization—to deal with information and problems in the environment. Morgan (1997, p. 113) argues that this "is not just an abstract concept.... If a team or unit is unable to recognize, absorb, and deal with the variations in its environment, it is unlikely to evolve and survive." For example, consider the contrast between two political campaign organizations. In one campaign, the candidate is running unopposed. In the second campaign, a bitter battle is being waged between a Republican, a Democrat, and a third-party candidate. The first campaign organization could be relatively small and simple because the political environment of an unopposed campaign is uncomplicated. However, the second campaign organization would need more complex subsystems to monitor, evaluate, and react to the quickly changing politics that surround a hotly contested three-person race.

To summarize, when we look at an organization as a system, we see it as a collection of system components that are hierarchically arranged, interdependent, and permeable to each other and the environment. The organizational system is characterized by input-throughput-output processes that require exchange with the environment and positive and negative system feedback. Because of the openness and interdependence of organizational systems, they are characterized by the properties of holism, equifinality, requisite variety, and negative entropy. These basics of the systems approach are summarized in Table 4.1.

Table 4.1 | Summary of Systems Basics

System Components	Principle
Hierarchically ordered	A system consists of smaller subsystems and is embedded within larger supersystems.
Interdependent	System components depend on each other for effective functioning.
Permeable	A system is open to its environment, and system components are open to each other.

Input-Throughput-Output Processes	Principle
Exchange processes	Input and output processes require exchange between the system and the environment. Throughput processes require exchange among system components.
Feedback processes	System control is maintained through feedback. Corrective (negative) feedback serves to keep a system on a steady course. Growth (positive) feedback serves to transform or change a system.

System Properties	Principle
Holism	Because of component interdependence, a system is more than the sum of its parts.
Equifinality	Because of component interdependence, there are multiple paths to any system outcome.
Negative entropy	Because of system openness, a system has the ability to avoid deterioration and thrive.
Requisite variety	Because of system openness, a system should maintain the internal complexity necessary to cope with external complexity.

SYSTEMS APPROACHES TO ORGANIZATIONAL COMMUNICATION

As noted earlier in this chapter, a great many theories relevant to organizational communication have been based on systems concepts. In this section, we look at two examples that emphasize different aspects of systems theory and principles. The first of these is especially relevant to the ideas of system components and the processes associated with those components: the study of communication networks. The second deals more with some of the emergent properties of organizational systems that occur during interaction: Karl Weick's ideas about communication and sensemaking.

Communication Networks

One of the hallmarks of systems theory is the denotation of the interconnections among system components and the arrangement of those components into subsystems and supersystems. When the components of systems are people and social groups, the "mapping" of relationships among people becomes crucially important. Monge and Eisenberg (1987) differentiate between positional tradition of studying communication networks and the relational tradition. Typifying the positional tradition is the formal organizational chart that defines the prescribed flow of communication within an organization (see McPhee & Poole, 2001, for more on formal structure and hierarchy in organizational communication research). However, Monge and Eisenberg note that the formal chart is often a poor reflection of the actual system of communicative relationships. Thus, the relational tradition considers the actual communication relationships that emerge through the activity of the organizational system.

Properties of Networks   Put as simply as possible, a network consists of a system of links among components (e.g., individuals, work groups, organizations). There are a number of ways we can characterize a network as a whole, including network content, network mode, and network density. *Network content* refers to the stuff that is flowing through the linkages in the network. For example, material can flow through a network as can many types of information or even intangibles such as affection or influence. It is also possible to consider "semantic networks"—the ways in which words and ideas are linked within text. *Network mode* refers to the communication medium through which network linkages are maintained. Early research often differentiated between written and face-to-face modes, although the advent of communication technologies has increased the number of possible network modes dramatically. For example, with wireless connections we can see connections across entire campuses, neighborhoods, and cities, or we can look at the ways in which hyperlinks connect information on the Internet (e.g., Shumate, 2012). Third, the network as a whole can be characterized in terms of its *density*. A highly dense network is one in which there are many interconnections among network members, whereas a less dense network is more loosely interconnected. Finally, the network can be considered in terms of its *level of analysis*. Intraorganizational networks will look at connections among individuals within a given organization, whereas interorganizational networks will consider links among many organizations (see Eisenberg et al., 1985). In a global and complex society, interorganizational networks—of businesses, governments, and nongovernmental organizations—become particularly important (see, e.g., Atouba & Shumate, 2010; Doerfel & Taylor, 2004).

Properties of Network Links It is also possible to characterize the connections that link members of a network together. There are many ways to consider network links (see Monge & Contractor, 2001, p. 442), but three of the most often used identifiers involve the properties of strength, symmetry, and multiplexity. Link **strength** has been defined in a variety of ways. For example, a strong link might be one in which there is a great deal of communication flowing between two people, one that has endured over a long period of time, or one in which the exchange is deemed important by network participants. The **symmetry** of a communication link refers to whether the two nodes involved in the link have the same kind of relationship with each other. For example, the supervisor/subordinate relationship is asymmetrical, whereas the coworker relationship is symmetrical. Last, the **multiplexity** of a link refers to the number of different kinds of content that flow through a particular link. Two organizations that share material resources, information, and personnel would be said to have a multiplex link.

Network Roles Each "node" within a network can be described in a variety of ways (e.g., how central the node is in the network; see Monge & Contractor, 2001, p. 443). However, one of the most interesting ways to consider the individual actors in a communication network is to consider network roles. **Network roles** define the ways in which individuals are connected with each other. Consider the hypothetical network represented in Figure 4.1. By looking at this diagram, it is clear that individuals are connected in very different ways within the network. For example, compare the connections of Mike, Tomas, and Ernest. Mike doesn't talk to anyone in the network, and he would be characterized as an *isolate*. Tomas talks to a number of highly interconnected individuals (Dan, Yun-Mi, Natalie, and Stefan), and all these people would be characterized as *group members*. Within this group, Dan serves as a *bridge* to individuals outside of the group. Finally, Ernest talks to two people who have radically different connections within the network, and he would be characterized as a *liaison*.

Explanatory Mechanisms Finally, a systems consideration of communication network is enhanced when researchers do more than just describe the features of the network and delve into the reasons that the network develops and is maintained. Monge and Contractor (2003; see also Shumate & Contractor, 2013) describe a number of theoretical mechanisms that can be used to explain the emergence and evolution of communication networks. For example, a group of activist organizations might come together in order to enhance their own *self-interests* or the possibility of *collective action*. A group of employees who work together in the same office might develop a tight friendship network based on *proximity* or the *homophily* of shared interests. Departments within a complex organization are often linked because of *dependency* relationships or the need to *exchange* information or resources. In short, it is critical to consider the theoretical mechanisms behind

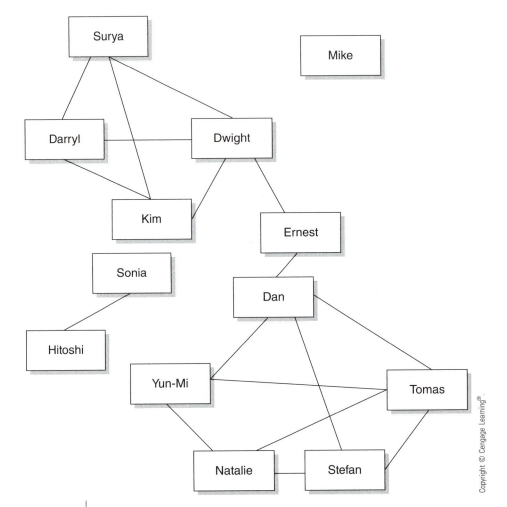

Figure 4.1 | A Hypothetical Communication Network

various types of communication networks. It is also critically important to consider processes of change and evolution within network systems (Monge, Heiss, & Margolin, 2008). For example, Shumate, Fulk, and Monge (2005) found that an interorganizational (and international) network of organizations coping with the HIV-AIDS crisis changed substantially over a period of eight years.

Karl Weick's Theory of Organizing

Karl Weick's scholarship—in particular, his books *The Social Psychology of Organizing* (1979) and *Sensemaking in Organizations* (1995)—has had a profound impact on organizational theory, especially in the area of organizational communication. These include evolutionary theory, information theory, and general systems theory (see Kreps, 1990). Weick defines the process of organizing as "the resolving of equivocality in an enacted environment by means of interlocked behaviors embedded in conditionally related processes" (Weick, 1969, p. 91). This is a rather dense and complex definition. Let's try to clarify it through a look at its critical components.

Central to Weick's theory of organizing is the idea that organizations exist in an environment. Weick is clear, though, that this environment is not merely a physical environment but is an *information environment*. Furthermore, the information environment of an organization does not exist "out there" in an objective manner. Rather, individuals create the environment that confronts them through the process of **enactment**. The process of enactment suggests that different organizational members will imbue information inputs with different meanings and hence create different information environments. As Weick (1995) explains, "There is not some kind of monolithic, singular, fixed environment that exists detached from and external to people. Instead, people are very much a part of their own environments." For example, if you and a coworker were both asked to "see the boss as soon as possible," you might imbue the situation with very different meanings, depending on your past experiences, goals, personalities, and so on.

In Weick's model, the major goal of organizing is the reduction of equivocality in the information environment. **Equivocality** is the unpredictability that is inherent in the information environment of an organization. In an equivocal information environment, there are many interpretations that could be used for a particular event. For example, in the "go see the boss" example, an individual might be able to attach many logical (and probably many illogical!) explanations for the requested meeting. According to Weick, reducing equivocality—or making sense—is central to the process of organizing. Some organizations are likely to be generally predictable. However, for organizations in highly competitive or quickly changing business environments or for any organization during a time of crisis, equivocality is likely to be high.

How, then, is sense made in these equivocal information environments? Weick proposes that organizational members use *assembly rules* and *communication cycles*. Assembly rules are procedures (sometimes called recipes) that can guide organizational members in set patterns of **sensemaking**. For example, a personnel director might always ask applicants for a résumé in a particular form in order to simplify the information environment. Assembly rules are particularly useful for sensemaking when the information environment is not especially equivocal. However, when equivocality in the environment is high and there are many possible explanations for an event, organizational members engage in communication cycles. Through communication cycles, organizational members introduce and react to ideas that help to make sense of the equivocal environment. The selected assembly rules and communication cycles will sometimes be effective in reducing equivocality in the information environment and will sometimes be ineffective. When sensemaking is effective, Weick proposes a *retention* process in which rules and cycles are saved for future organizational use. Rules and cycles can be retained in the form of *causal maps* that are used to make sense of future equivocality in the information environment.

Weick's model of organizing is obviously highly complex and abstract. At the risk of oversimplifying his ideas, let's look at an organizational communication situation that exemplifies some of them. In a study of a midwestern hospital, Miller,

Case in Point: Making Sense of My Money

When we think about organizational sensemaking, we often consider the ways in which interpersonal communication with those around us reduces confusion about organizational events. However, the Internet connects us in ways that can both heighten our distress over equivocality and provide us with important new sources for understanding and support.

Andrew Herrmann made this point in his study of stockholders in cyberspace (2007). In recent years, more and more individuals have started investing in the stock market, and media outlets with information about various options for investing have flourished. If your head has ever started spinning while watching the multiple crawls and popups on CNBC or similar financial cable networks, you understand

that there is a lot of information out there, and it would be fair to characterize much of the financial data as highly equivocal.

How is an individual to make sense of this huge influx of information? Hermann suggests that many people turn to discussion boards and chat rooms on the Web for help, and he analyzed one message board (discussing Warren Buffett's Berkshire Hathaway, Inc., on the Motley Fool website) to demonstrate this. The messages show individuals drawing on a wide array of media sources—and, especially, each other—to make sense of complicated financial data. Herrmann does not know if individuals' bank accounts were enriched, but it appears that their equivocality was reduced.

Joseph, and Apker (2000) looked at a group of nurses who were coping with major changes in the health care environment. The hospital where they worked was encountering increased competition within the new managed care payment environment and hence decided to develop a new system emphasizing interdisciplinary health care. The nurses in the study were designated as "care coordinators" but were given little guidance about what this new role would entail. The nurses in this situation were placed in a highly equivocal situation; they had to make sense of new roles that could be interpreted in a wide variety of ways. The Miller et al. (2000) interviews with these nurses suggest that some relied on simple assembly rules (e.g., I'll just assume that "care coordinator" is the same thing as "discharge planner"). Other nurses—perhaps the more successful ones in the long run—relied instead on intense interaction with each other and with others in the hospital environment to craft and make sense of their new organizational roles. This example illustrates both the importance of sensemaking and the selection of various communication strategies for making sense in an equivocal organizational environment.

This presentation has, of course, oversimplified Weick's model and has left out a number of his innovative ideas about the processes through which organizational members make sense of their environments. However, even from this cursory look, it should be clear that Weick's theory of organizing emphasizes a number of relevant systems theory concepts. The notions of environment and permeability are critical to his theory, as is the concept of system component interdependence. The sensemaking process proposed by Weick also highlights the concept of requisite variety. That is, simple decision rules and structures can be used in sensemaking when equivocality is low, but more complex communication cycles and systems are needed to make sense of highly uncertain information environments.

In the first half of this chapter, we have reviewed the systems approach to the study of organizational communication, a dominant metaphor during the later years of the twentieth century that is still important to scholars today. We explored a number of basic concepts relevant to this metaphor, including the nature of system components, the nature of system processes, and the properties that emerge from the conceptualization of organizations as interdependent and open sets of interacting components. We then considered two schools of thought that illustrate the systems metaphor at work—communication networks and Weick's theory of sensemaking. In the second half of this chapter, we will take up a second dominant metaphor that has held sway in thinking about organizations in recent decades—organizational culture.

THE CULTURAL METAPHOR

What is a culture? When we think about the culture of a nation, many things come to mind. Consider U.S. culture, for example. We might think about some of the values that many Americans hold: freedom, independence, hard work, or achievement. We might think about some of the symbols of U.S. culture: the stars and stripes, the bald eagle, baseball, and apple pie. We might think about the rites and rituals of Americans: Fourth of July picnics, blowout wedding receptions, or Super Bowl parties. We might think about the daily life of Americans: early mornings on the family farm, ninety-minute commutes on the Los Angeles freeways, or long days balancing the demands of work and family. But, of course, the notion of American culture is not always straightforward and uncontested. Especially in our post-9/11 world, there are debates about what it means to be American both within our own borders and as a part of the interdependent global world, and there are many political and social clashes that pit various subcultures of America against each other. In short, when thinking about U.S. culture, we think about a complicated patchwork of values, symbols, and behaviors that define the term *America* in various ways for various people.

In using a cultural metaphor for the investigation of an organization, we are again looking for the qualities that make an organization what it is. What makes Google different from Apple? What makes McDonald's different from Burger King? What makes the University of Texas different from Texas A&M University? What makes the Delta Gamma house on your campus different from Alpha Chi Omega's? As Pacanowsky and O'Donnell-Trujillo (1983) note, "Each organization has its own way of doing what it does and its own way of talking about what it is doing" (p. 128). To discover these ways of doing and ways of talking is to investigate organizational culture. In the following sections, we consider two different ways of thinking about culture. The first—originating in the popular business press over three decades ago—looks at culture as something an organization *has*. According to this approach, having the right kind of culture can make or break an organization. The second approach considers culture as something an organization *is*.

Prescriptive Approaches to Culture

During the last part of the twentieth century, organizational scholars and practitioners became fascinated with the concept of "organizational culture." The metaphor of culture clearly resonated with both academics and practitioners—it simply made sense to see organizations as complex arenas of stories and values rather than as entirely rational institutions. It is not surprising that culture quickly became a part of everyday talk in carpools and around water coolers. As Eisenberg and Riley (2001, p. 292) point out, "organizational discourse was soon peppered with such statements as 'The culture here won't allow us to ...' or 'Our culture is very intense—we work hard and play harder.'"

The early popularity and widespread use of cultural terminology can be traced back to two popular books published in the early 1980s. These books are *Corporate Cultures: The Rites and Rituals of Corporate Life* by Terrence Deal and Allen Kennedy (1982) and *In Search of Excellence: Lessons from America's Best-Run Companies* by Tom Peters and Robert Waterman (1982). Both books propose that successful companies can be identified in terms of their cultures.

Deal and Kennedy's "Strong Cultures"   Deal and Kennedy (1982) argue that business success can be enhanced through the development of a "strong" culture. If an organization has the components of a strong culture, it will be a better place for individuals to work and will improve individual and organizational performance. Deal and Kennedy identify four key components of a strong culture:

1. Values are the beliefs and visions that members hold for an organization. For example, 3M Corporation espouses a value for innovation, whereas Prudential Insurance represents a value of stability.
2. Heroes are the individuals who come to exemplify an organization's values. These heroes become known through the stories and myths of an organization. For example, Bill Gates exemplifies entrepreneurship and philanthropy through his work at Microsoft and the foundation he directs with his wife, Melinda.
3. Rites and rituals are the ceremonies through which an organization celebrates its values. An organization that values innovation may develop a ritualistic way of rewarding the new ideas of employees. In other organizations, rites and rituals might include a company picnic or an awards banquet for outstanding employees.
4. Finally, the cultural network is the communication system through which cultural values are instituted and reinforced. The cultural network could consist of both formal organizational channels, such as newsletters, and the informal interactions of employees.

Peters and Waterman's "Excellent Cultures"   A second book that made a big impact on the business community in the 1980s is *In Search of Excellence* by Peters and Waterman (1982). Like Deal and Kennedy, Peters and Waterman were attempting to identify aspects of organizational culture that were prevalent in high-performing companies. They studied sixty-two organizations deemed **excellent**

cultures by employees and organizational experts. They then identified "themes" that characterized the cultures of these organizations. These themes are presented in Table 4.2. As this table indicates, the themes emphasize the importance of people (e.g., "close relations to the customer" and "productivity through people") and downplay bureaucratic structure and values (e.g., "autonomy and entrepreneurship" and "simple form, lean staff").

Both *Corporate Cultures* and *In Search of Excellence* had an enormous impact on organizational practice. These books emphasize the importance of organizational intangibles, such as values and heroes, and signal a move away from strictly rational models of organizing. However, the books were not as widely embraced by the academic community, primarily because they provide prescriptions for managerial practice rather than descriptions or explanations of organizational life. For example, Deal and Kennedy's book argues that a strong culture held by all employees is the only route to success in the business world. Similarly, individuals reading Peters and Waterman's book would conclude that excellence could be best achieved through the themes laid out in Table 4.2. Indeed, some scholars later called this approach "value engineering" because it espouses the belief that "effective cultural leaders could create 'strong' cultures, built around their own values" (Martin & Frost, 1996, p. 602).

It is important to stress that the values prescribed in this view of culture are, in large part, ones that can—and do—make positive contributions to organizational performance and to the work lives of organizational members. For example, there

Table 4.2 | Peters and Waterman's Themes for Excellent Organizations

Theme	Description
1. A bias for action	Excellent organizations react quickly and do not spend excess time planning and analyzing.
2. Close relations to the customer	Excellent organizations gear decisions and actions to the needs of customers.
3. Autonomy and entrepreneurship	Excellent organizations encourage employees to take risks in the development of new ideas.
4. Productivity through people	Excellent organizations encourage positive and respectful relationships among management and employees.
5. Hands-on, value-driven	Excellent organizations have employees and managers who share the same core value of productivity and performance.
6. Stick to the knitting	Excellent organizations stay focused on what they do best and avoid radical diversification.
7. Simple form, lean staff	Excellent organizations avoid complex structures and divisions of labor.
8. Simultaneous loose-tight properties	Excellent organizations exhibit both unity of purpose and the diversity necessary for innovation.

is little doubt that customer service organizations will be more successful if they gear decisions and actions to customer needs (Theme 2 from Table 4.2). However, these **prescriptive approaches to culture** also fall short in two important respects. First, it is naive to assume that there is a single cultural formula for achieving organizational success. For example, although a "bias for action" may have proven effective for the organizations studied by Peters and Waterman, there are certainly times when a more contemplative approach to organizing would be appropriate. Second, these prescriptive approaches treat culture as a *thing* that an organization *has*. This objectification of culture is risky because when we objectify culture, we de-emphasize the complex processes through which organizational culture is created and sustained.

Because of these problems, most scholars who adopt a cultural approach to the study of organizations avoid the prescriptive tack taken by these writers. Instead, cultural researchers seek to describe and understand the complex ways in which organizational culture is developed and maintained. The next section considers these alternative approaches to culture.

Descriptive and Explanatory Approaches to Culture

Today, most scholars interested in organizational culture eschew the simple prescriptive approaches discussed above. Rather than seeing culture as a *thing* that can and should be *managed*, these researchers see culture as the emerging and sometimes fragmented values, practices, narratives, and artifacts that make a particular organization what it is. Putnam (1983) introduced this interpretive approach in the communication discipline, noting that this approach requires a consideration of "the way individuals make sense of their world through their communicative behaviors" (p. 31). Although this chapter cannot fully explore the multitude of positions taken by those trying to describe and understand organizational culture (see, especially, Eisenberg & Riley, 2001; Martin, 1992, 2002), four issues highlight the distinction between prescriptive approaches to culture and the approaches taken by most cultural scholars today: culture is complicated; culture is emergent; culture is not unitary; and culture is often ambiguous.

Organizational Cultures Are Complicated   The complexity of organizational culture is demonstrated by the wide variety of markers that scholars use to investigate it. We will consider just a few. Beyer and Trice (1987) argue that an organization's culture is revealed through its rites, and they differentiate among rites of passage, rites of degradation, rites of enhancement, rites of renewal, rites of conflict reduction, and rites of integration. Dandridge (1986) looks at organizational ceremonies as indicators of culture. Quinn and McGrath (1985) focus on the roles of values and belief systems in the transformation of organizational cultures. Smith and Eisenberg (1987) consider the metaphors of employees and management in a study of the culture at Disneyland. Boje (1991) and Meyer (1995) contend that culture can be best revealed through the stories that organizational members tell. Schall (1983) and Morley and Shockley-Zalabak (1991; Shockley-Zalabak & Morley, 1994) investigate communication rules in the development of culture. Even organizational hallway talk can be a lens for viewing culture (Gronn, 1983).

Edgar Schein (1992) argues that these various markers of can be seen as the outer layer of an organizational culture "onion." He sees these markers as artifacts and behaviors that are the most visible manifestation of culture. The middle layer of Schein's model consists of individual and group values. Though Schein cautions that "the difficulty is figuring out what the artifacts mean, how they interrelate, what deeper patterns, if any, they reflect" (1985, p. 15), he also notes that the values held by members of an organization often—though not always—are manifest in outward behavior. The core levels of culture in this model are basic assumptions—paradigmatic ideas that might serve to either unit or divide an organizational culture. As an example of how these levels of culture interact, members of an organization might hold an underlying *assumption* that change is good. This underlying assumption might generate *values* for innovation and outward *behaviors* and *artifacts* such as a relaxed and creative atmosphere, bonuses for new ideas, and suggestion boxes throughout the office.

Organizational Cultures Are Emergent   A second point of agreement among most organizational culture scholars is the notion that cultures are socially created through the interaction of organizational members. This idea is central to a communication focus on culture in which culture is not merely transmitted through communication but also in which communication is "constitutive of culture" (Eisenberg & Riley, 2001, p. 294). Pacanowsky and O'Donnell-Trujillo (1983) took this emergent approach into the cultural realm in their work on "Organizational Communication as Cultural Performance," arguing that a study of organizational culture should concentrate on the communication processes through which culture is created. They further argue that these communication processes can be best conceptualized as "performances" that are interactional, contextual, episodic, and improvisational.

Cultural performances are interactional in that they require the participation of multiple organizational members. Cultural performances are contextual in that they are embedded in organizational situations and organizational history. Cultural performances are episodic in that they are distinct events in organizational life. Finally, cultural performances are improvisational because there are no scripts that guide organizational members. By pointing to the importance of "cultural performance," Pacanowsky and O'Donnell-Trujillo highlight the communicative processes through which organizational cultures emerge and shift over time.

Organizational Cultures Are Not Unitary   Most organizational culture researchers agree that it is impossible to characterize an organization as having a single culture. Rather, most scholars agree that organizations are characterized by a multitude of **organizational subcultures** that "may co-exist in harmony, conflict, or indifference to each other" (Frost, Moore, Louis, Lundberg &c Martin, 1991, p. 8). Martin (2002) highlights this aspect of culture in her discussion of a differentiation approach, in which inconsistencies among cultural views are expected and often seen as desirable.

But where are these various subcultures found in an organization, and how do they work? Louis (1985) addresses these questions in her consideration of the sites of culture and cultural penetration. Louis first argues that there are a number of sites where culture might develop in an organization, including a "vertical slice" (e.g., a division), a "horizontal slice" (e.g., a particular hierarchical level), or a specific work group. Martin (2002) also points out that subcultures might emerge around networks of personal contacts or demographic similarity. These cultural sites all "serve as breeding grounds ... for the emergence of shared meaning" (Louis, 1985, p. 79). Thus, a wide range of subcultures could spring up at various sites in a single organization. For example, Marschall (2002) conducted a study of a software development firm and found that skilled workers in the Internet economy created their own occupational community. This community—although perhaps divided by geography—shared work practices, ideas about what was important in the workplace, and even adopted a distinct language and vocabulary.

One additional consideration of the nonunitary nature of organizational culture is that various subcultures within an organization may represent important differences in power and in interests (see, e.g., Alvesson, 1993). In other words, not only can the subcultures of the corporate boardroom and the assembly line be described as different, but these differences also point to fundamental schisms in power and ideology in the organization. For example, at your own university, the student population might have a distinct subculture that is quite different from those of faculty or staff (see Kramer & Berman, 2001). However, it is likely that the values espoused through the student culture hold less sway than those espoused by faculty or administrators.

Organizational Cultures Are Often Ambiguous   Finally, scholars of organizational culture recognize that there is not always a clear picture of the organization's culture—or even of its various subcultures. There may be multiple manifestations of culture that are difficult to interpret. Martin (2002) discusses this approach to culture as the fragmentation perspective and argues that fragmentation studies will

Case in Point: Searching the Internet for Cultural Values

The web search engine giant Google is among the largest corporations in the world, and it has a huge impact on both daily life and the health of the global financial system. Ted Leonsis (2010) points out that Google's success may be based on more than just an incredible business model and savvy decision making. Leonsis argues that Google is "a prime example of ... a double-bottom line company—an organization that measures its success by both its fiscal results and its positive impact on humanity" (p. 16). The first bottom line is the one we all know about—profits—and Google is clearly no slouch in this area. But Google also considers a second bottom line in the higher calling reflected in its motto ("Don't be evil") and in its goal to make information universally accessible.

These two bottom lines that form the core assumptions of Google's culture permeate into behaviors including a 2010 decision to flout China's censorship laws, using a herd of sheep to trim the lawn at corporate headquarters, switching names with Topeka, Kansas, for a day, and an organizational setting that provides supportive services for employees. Leonsis notes that some of these behaviors don't make sense on the surface—"by refusing to participate in Chinese censorship, the company imperiled billions of dollars in future profit" (2010, p. 16). The other side of the coin, however, is the second bottom line of pro-social values. Google "protected its status as a happy company at peace with its values—and happy companies are more, not less, likely to continue being successful" (Leonsis, 2010, p. 16).

Spotlight on Scholarship: Building Systems and Cultures of Compassion

Understanding organizations as systems and cultures suggests that organizations matter as collectives and that organizational systems and cultures can develop various collective capabilities—perhaps the capability to be profitable or the capability to be creative. Jacoba M. Lilius and her colleagues drew on these ideas in proposing the notion that organizations can be seen as systems and cultures with the collective capability for compassion. These scholars began with the important observation that "suffering is an inevitable, ubiquitous, yet often overlooked, aspect of organizational life" (Lilius, Worline, Dutton, Kanov, & Maitlis, 2011, p. 874) and argued that it is important to expand our understanding of compassion from a focus on the individual to a focus on the collective capacity of organizations to respond in compassionate ways when suffering occurs.

Lilius's research team explored this idea through an interview study of Midwest Billing, a unit of a larger health care system involved in the reimbursement process for physicians. They initially concluded that this unit did exhibit a capability for compassion—there were expressions of compassion on numerous occasions, there was little evidence of compassion fatigue, and compassion was just seen as the way things were done at Midwest Billing. The scholars then turned to the question of how this collective capacity was developed and maintained—in other words, how did Midwest Billing become and remain a unit in which compassion was the norm? Their answers have clear implications for the way we understand organizations as both cultures and as systems.

Consistent with ideas of organizational culture that link ongoing communicative performances with values and norms, Lilius and her colleagues identified seven "everyday practices" as the foundation for compassion capability at Midwest Billing: acknowledging the contributions of unit members, addressing problems directly in a straightforward manner, bounded play in which employees could engage in fun activities but be aware of the need to focus on work, celebrating important events in individuals' lives, collective decision making about both work and social issues, proactive help-offering, and orienting new members to the people and tasks of the organization.

These seven everyday practices were argued to come together in creating two "relational conditions" critical to engendering the unit's collective capacity for compassion. In line with systems approaches to organizations, these conditions suggest the important roles of connections among individuals and systemic boundaries. Lilius et al. argue that the first relational condition required for compassion capability is high-quality connections that include positive regard, mutuality, and flexibility. This system of high-quality connections enabled Midwest Billing workers to notice when others were in need of compassion, to identify with the group, and to honestly discuss resources available for compassionate response. The second relational condition, a dynamic boundary-permeability norm, helped employees to understand and manage the intersection between home and work and thus recognize and respond appropriately to the need for compassion.

Lilius and her colleagues, then, suggest that compassion is not just a feeling that individuals have for each other. Rather, given the right conditions, organizations can be systems and cultures in which compassion is valued and likely to occur—places like Midwest Billing in which "If there's somebody having a hard time with their house, or their family, or financially or anything, word just spreads and we all just pull together and help each other out" (Lilius et al., p. 874).

Lilius, J. M.; Worline, M. C.; Dutton, J. E.; Kanov, J. M.; Maitlis, S. (2011). Understanding compassion capability. *Human Relations*, *64*, 873–899.

see an ambiguous culture as "a normal, salient, and inescapable part of organizational functioning in the contemporary world" (p. 105).

This notion that culture is oftentimes ambiguous and hard to pin down is particularly important when considering organizations that are rapidly changing. Many scholars argue that we now live in a postmodern world that is multifaceted, fragmented, fast-moving, and difficult to understand (see, e.g., Holstem & Gubnum, 2000). In such an environment, it is not surprising that organizational culture might also be in a state of flux. For example, Risberg (1999) analyzed the culture of a Swedish manufacturing company that had just been acquired. Risberg noted that "a post-acquisition process cannot be understood in one clear way. There are ambiguities in interpretation of situations and statements. These ambiguities illustrate the multiple realities within the organization and during the post-acquisition process" (p. 177). These ambiguities can be particularly challenging for individuals as they try to forge their own identities within these reconfigured organizational cultures (Pepper & Larson, 2006).

In summary, current organizational culture scholars take an approach to culture that seeks to understand the ways in which communication and interaction create a unique sense of place in an organization. These scholars look for the complex web of values, behaviors, stories, rules, and metaphors that comprise an organization's culture, acknowledging that culture is socially created through the communicative performances of organizational members. These scholars also look for the similarities and differences among various subcultures that exist simultaneously in any organization and acknowledge that culture is often ambiguous and in a state of flux.

SUMMARY

This chapter has presented approaches that view organizations and communication through two metaphoric lenses that help us appreciate the complexity of organizational communication. We first considered the systems metaphor that emphasizes issues such as connectivity, interdependence, and sensemaking. We then looked at the cultural metaphor both in terms of the prescriptions through which the concept was popularized and through the more nuanced considerations of culture as complicated and socially constructed through the communicative interaction of organizational members. These descriptive and explanatory views of culture also emphasize concepts of fragmentation and ambiguity. These metaphorical looks at organization move us in important ways away from the classical, human relations, and human resources approaches considered in earlier chapter toward contemporary ideas that continue to drive organizational scholarship today.

DISCUSSION QUESTIONS

1. How do the concepts of "organizational systems" and "organizational cultures" move us away from the practice-based ideas advocated by classical, human relations, and human resources approaches? Would it be possible to describe an organization run through the principles of classical, human relations, or human resources approaches using a systems or cultural lens?

2. What aspects of the systems metaphor are highlighted in a network approach to organizational communication? What aspects are highlighted in a sensemaking approach?

3. Why is "organizational culture" such a powerful concept for both practicing managers and those who want to have insight into organizational functioning? In what ways does this metaphor for organizing provide a better (or at least different) lens for looking at organizations than other metaphors we've considered in this book?

4. Think about an organization you know well. This could be a workplace, a church, or perhaps the school you attend. How could a network approach help you better understand relationships in this organization? What would you look for in developing a cultural profile of this organization? How would these approaches help you develop a more comprehensive understanding of this organization?

KEY CONCEPTS

systems metaphor
interdependence
permeable boundaries
feedback and exchange processes
deviation-reducing feedback
deviation-amplifying feedback
holism
equifinality
negative entropy

requisite variety
enactment of information environment
equivocality
strength
symmetry
multiplexity
sensemaking
network properties

link properties
network roles
prescriptive approaches to culture
descriptive approach to culture
markers of organizational culture
cultural performances
organizational subcultures
cultural fragmentation

CASE STUDY   The Cultural Tale of Two Shuttles

The first space shuttle flight occurred on February 18, 1977, with the launch of Enterprise. It was a proud day for NASA and the beginning of a new age in space exploration. Less than nine years later, on January 28, 1986, the nation was stunned when the space shuttle Challenger disintegrated seventy-three seconds after launch. All seven crew members perished. The technical explanation for this disaster was the "O-ring" problem—a crucial shuttle component was compromised by the cold weather on that launch day. Subsequently, people spoke out against the launch because of worries about the O-ring problem. However, there were pressures to launch and a belief in the infallibility of the decision-making process. Thus, voices speaking against the launch were silenced.

During the late 1980s and 1990s, there were a plethora of studies considering the Challenger disaster, and many pointed to organizational factors at

NASA as crucial contributing factors leading to the launch decision (McCurdy, 1992). For example, in 1990, the U.S. government issued the "Augustine Report" on the future of the U.S. space program (U.S. Advisory Committee, 1990). This report was built largely on the premise that organizational culture directly contributes to organizational performance. The report notes that "[t]he most fundamental ingredient of a successful space program ... is the culture or work environment in which it is conducted" (U.S. Advisory Committee, p. 16). This committee also worked from the assumption that the culture at an organization like NASA needs to be fundamentally different from that at many organizations. NASA works with the most complex of technologies, and the stakes are incredibly high. As McCurdy notes, "[e]rrors that might be forgotten in other government programs can produce in NASA a myopic space

CASE STUDY | **The Cultural Tale of Two Shuttles** *continued*

telescope or an exploding space shuttle" (McCurdy, 1992, p. 190). Given these assumptions, the report pointed to many specific aspects of organizational culture at NASA and made recommendations regarding cultural beliefs and assumptions that should characterize a successful space program. These include the beliefs that:

- The success of a mission should take precedence over cost and deadlines. Mission success is more important than the role of any individual or group.
- Space flight requires open communication in which individuals are encouraged to report on problems or anomalies. Issues need to be put on the table for consideration.
- The space program cannot succeed in an environment where avoiding failure is seen as an important goal. Instead, the risky nature of the operation must be acknowledged.
- The space program should not get spread too thinly by working simultaneously on different projects, such as flight, research and development, and design. "Either operations dominates to the detriment of research and development, or employees working on new projects neglect operations" (McCurdy, 1992, p. 190).

NASA seemed to be following these cultural guidelines in the 1990s. The first post-Challenger mission took place on September 29, 1988, with the launch of Discovery. The one hundredth shuttle mission occurred on October 11, 2000. However, as we all know, there was yet another tale of shuttle disaster to be written. On February 1, 2003, the space shuttle Columbia disintegrated during reentry. Pieces of the shuttle fell over eastern Texas, and all seven crew members died. The sense of déjà vu was mournful and unavoidable. And the reports dissecting this disaster came quickly.

Of course, a different technical problem led to the Columbia disaster. In this case, a piece of foam fell off the shuttle during launch and ripped a hole in its left wing. During reentry, this mishap allowed superheated gases to enter the wing interior, and the wing frame melted. But were the underlying cultural traits that led to the Columbia disaster similar to the ones

that doomed Challenger? Sadly, the Columbia Accident Investigation Board concluded that the cultural themes of the two tales were much the same. Indeed, "[t]he board's final report said that NASA had done little to improve shuttle safety since it lost the shuttle Challenger in 1986" ("Concerns Raised That Changes in NASA Won't Last," 2003). This report listed specific cultural traits that contributed to the Columbia disaster, including:

- Reliance on past success as a substitute for sound engineering practices
- Organizational barriers that prevented effective communication of critical safety information and stifled professional differences of opinion
- The evolution of an informal chain of command of decision making that operated outside the organization's rules

So, had NASA gained any insight at all from the Challenger disaster? Had the organization learned from it but just fallen back into its old questionable cultural habits? The chairman of the investigation board, Harold Gehman Jr., thought that backsliding might have occurred. He noted, "Over a period of a year or two, the natural tendency of all bureaucracy, not just NASA, to migrate away from that diligent attitude is a great concern to the board because the history of NASA indicates that they have done it before" ("Concerns Raised," 2003).

Perhaps the most poignant comment during this time came from Jonathan Clark, a NASA flight surgeon whose wife, Laurel Clark, died in the Columbia disaster: "I wasn't here during the Challenger disaster but I certainly talked to a lot of people who were. And, yes, there were similarities, as Diane Vaughn pointed out earlier in her book [The Challenger Launch Decision, 1996]. You could almost erase the O-Ring problem and put in the tile shedding and put 'Columbia' instead of 'Challenger'" ("Columbia Spouse: Report a Prescription for Change," 2003).

Fourteen brave Americans lost. The separate tales of two destroyed space shuttles linked by one organizational culture. The first post-Columbia launch occurred on July 25, 2005, and the final shuttle was launched on July 8, 2011. As NASA looks back on this important period of its history and moves forward

CASE STUDY | **The Cultural Tale of Two Shuttles** *continued*

that it heeds Jonathan Clark's advice: "I think we are really going to have to look very carefully at what lessons we didn't learn from Challenger and make sure we absolutely learn them this time" ("Columbia Spouse," 2003).

CASE ANALYSIS QUESTIONS

1. What factors in NASA's culture contributed to the Challenger and Columbia shuttle disasters? Is it possible to identify specific cultural markers, performances, and values that were critical?

2. Cultural change was obviously difficult at NASA. Can you think of specific things that could have been done to make cultural changes more lasting or more effective?

3. How could Karl Weick's model of organizing be brought to bear on these disasters? Can you identify patterns of sensemaking that actors used in coping with equivocality? Did these sensemaking patterns contribute to what happened at NASA?

CHAPTER 5

Constitutive Approaches

AFTER READING THIS CHAPTER, YOU SHOULD ...

- Recognize the weaknesses of a container metaphor for the organization and the ways in which criticisms of this metaphor led theorists to consider the communicative constitution of organizations (CCO).
- Understand how basic concepts of the CCO approach are grounded in social constructionist theorizing.
- Be familiar with structuration theory and the ideas of discourse and Discourse as relevant to CCO concepts.
- Be able to describe the nature of *text* and *conversation*, understand the recursive relationship between these concepts, and explain how these concepts become scaled up in the process of organizing.
- Appreciate the possibility that texts can *do things* in organizations.
- Describe each of *The Four Flows* of organizational communication—membership negotiation, self-structuring, activity coordination, and institutional positioning—and understand how these flows are relevant to the constitution process.

In the last four chapters, we have encountered many metaphorical ways to look at organizations. Classical theorists see organizations as machines, while human relations theorists prefer to think of organizations as families. More recently, theorists have conceptualized organizations as systems of interconnected nodes and relationships or as cultures where behaviors and artifacts are reflections of agreed-upon or contested values and assumptions. These metaphors are extremely helpful in highlighting various aspects of organizational communication for our consideration—a machine metaphor points us to the underlying regularity of many processes, for example, or a systems metaphor draws our attention to the complexity of interlocking flows of interaction. What all of these metaphors share, to a greater or lesser extent, is a conceptualization of the organization as a *container* within which communication occurs. The nature of the communication processes might vary greatly within the container, but for these approaches the organization is seen largely as a thing that holds communication processes and that influences the nature of those processes. For instance, the communication "contained" in a human resources organization is likely to encourage the expression of new ideas and value employee contributions to organizational goals.

In recent years, many organizational communication scholars have objected to this **container metaphor**. This dissatisfaction started with Ruth Smith more than twenty years ago (1992) and has been taken up by theorists and researchers who are interested in moving beyond this metaphorical framework to consider ways in which organizations are produced through communication and ways in which organization and communication produce each other. Taylor, Cooren, Giroux, and Robichaud (1996) describe this move:

> We are not saying there is no organization, just that it is not an objective "thing." That it must be born and re-created in the equivocal interpretations that are intrinsic to communication does not make it less real—just not "real" in the material sense. (p. 5)

In this chapter, we will consider this important movement toward a *constitutive* view of organization and communication. We will first highlight the basic framework of these approaches and connect them to several larger theoretical schools of thought. We will then discuss two specific constitutive approaches that have their home in the discipline of organizational communication: the *Montreal School* developed by James Taylor, Francois Cooren and their colleagues and *The Four Flows* approach developed by Robert McPhee and his colleagues. We will then consider ways in which these constitutive approaches open up new questions for scholars interested in the study of organizational communication.

COMMUNICATIVE CONSTITUTION OF ORGANIZATIONS

As we discussed back in Chapter 1 when we considered ways to complicate our thinking about communication, it is often important to move beyond ideas about communication as simply transmitting information—and related ideas about the organization as the container in which that information is transmitted—to consider the ways in which communication processes create and recreate systems of meaning and understanding. This shift in how we understand the social world is often called a *social constructionist position* (e.g., Berger & Luckmann, 1967) and it argues that reality (and an organization, for instance, as part of that reality) is not an objective thing but is, instead, an intersubjective construction created through communication. In a social constructionist approach, "we create our social world through our words and other symbols, and through our behaviors" (Leeds-Hurwitz, 1992, p. 133). For example, a social constructionist would argue that the idea of "bureaucracy" should not be seen as an objective concept with established and unwavering meaning but should be understood as an idea that has developed over years of communication processes. Further, this social construction of bureaucracy is ongoing in our daily encounters with, for example, interminable lines, unreadable forms, and automated phone systems.

Within organizational communication, this position has come to be known as the **communicative constitution of organization**—often abbreviated CCO. CCO scholars reject seeing the organization as a thing or as a container that bounds communication processes. Instead, CCO theorists try to understand the complicated processes through which our interactions create, re-create, and change organizations. In moving to this emphasis on communication as a constitutive process, we start to appreciate the importance of organizing—the verb—rather than organization—the noun (Weick, 1979).

There are a number of theoretical schools of thought that have been important to the development of the CCO position in addition to general ideas regarding **social constructionism**. One social theorist who has been influential with many CCO scholars is Anthony Giddens, whose **structuration theory** (1984; see Poole & McPhee, 2005, for summary relevant to organizational communication) contains key ideas relevant to constitutive approaches. Structuration theory posits that the social world is generated through the **agency** of active participants. The idea of agency suggests that there is a possibility that people can "act otherwise" in a situation. There are rules and resources (what Giddens calls **structures**) that agents draw on while they interact in the social world, but these structures can also be changed during the course of interaction.

Consider, for example, an everyday activity like shopping for food. When you enter a grocery store, there are rules that guide how you are to behave. Some of these might be very explicit (you need to pay; you should only go in the express line if you have a certain number of items) and others are more implicit (you should exchange pleasantries with workers and other shoppers, but not much beyond that). These structures thus *constrain* our behavior by giving us specific directions about how to act. However, there are also ways in which the *agency* of actors within the grocery store can resist or oppose the structures. A clerk might invite you into the express line even if you have sixteen items rather than fifteen or fewer. You might open up a personal conversation with another person in line. Through this agency, it is possible that the structures can be changed, either for the time being or into the future. Thus, we are producing and reproducing the structures that enable and constrain our behavior. This is the notion of **duality of structure**, and it resonates with many of the ideas of CCO scholars.

A second area of theory with strong implications for CCO theorists is work on the concept of *discourse*. Scholars interested in discourse have very diverse ideas about the concept—indeed, Alvesson and Kärreman (2000) claim that the concept can be accused of "standing for everything, and thus nothing" (p. 1128). However, many theorists make a distinction between "little-d discourse" and "big-D Discourse." In this distinction, "discourse … refers to the study of talk and text and social practices and Discourses as general and enduring systems of thought" (Fairhurst & Putnam, 2004, p. 7). That is, we could say that "compassion" is a Discourse that holds sway for many human service workers—compassion is an enduring system of thought. However, the way a social worker talks with a client or the way a nurse treats a patient are ways in which the ideas of "compassion" might be instantiated in the ongoing discourse of a human service organization. Fairhurst and Putnam (2004) further distinguish among several approaches to studying organizational discourse. Some scholars take an approach in which the organization is seen as an object with particular discursive features. That is, we could see the hospital in which the nurse works as an object that dictates particular kinds of small-d discourse. In contrast, some scholars take a "becoming" approach in which discourse creates organizing and organizations. This is similar to a social constructionist position in which the ongoing interaction in the health care setting is seen as creating the hospital. Finally, some scholars take a "grounded in action" approach that highlights the continual production and reproduction of social systems through discourse. This is similar to the notion of the recursive relationship between agency and structure for structuration theorists. CCO scholars are most clearly influenced by the second two approaches, as the first is similar to the container metaphor typically rejected by these researchers.

These are just two of a number of foundational ideas relevant to organizational communication scholars taking a CCO approach. Though we've only considered the most cursory aspects of these foundations, several patterns should be clear. First, we are moving to a strong emphasis on communication as central to any understanding of organizing: "a force present within communication creates, calls into being, or otherwise produces organization" (Bisel, 2010, p. 125). Second, these ideas highlight the reciprocal and recursive relationship between ongoing interaction at the micro level (i.e., the action of agents or discourse) and systems of meaning at the macro level (i.e., structures or Discourse). In the next two sections, we will consider two schools of thought generated by organizational communication scholars that serve as influential exemplars of CCO theory and research. We will first look at The Montreal School and then consider The Four Flows of organizational communication.

THE MONTREAL SCHOOL

The Montreal School of CCO theorizing refers to a growing body of work emanating initially from scholars at the University of Montreal, including James Taylor, François Cooren, and their colleagues (e.g., Cooren, 2000; Taylor et al., 1996; Taylor & Van Every, 2000). These scholars have drawn on "a dizzying number of linguistic, interpretive, and critical theories" (Bisel, 2010, p. 226) to draw together a still-growing framework about the ways in which communication constitutes organizing. We'll just consider a few of their myriad ideas here.

Text and Conversation

The heart of the Montreal School's CCO approach is the concept of "co-orientation"—the process through which people coordinate activity through interaction. Montreal School scholars see co-orientation as achieved through the interlinked ideas of conversation and text. In this CCO approach, **conversation** refers to ongoing interaction among individuals facilitated by language. In contrast, **text** refers to substance or meaning and can take many forms—an understanding of a particular interaction, a memo, a mission statement, a value for formality, and the like. Texts influence the co-orientation process that occurs during conversation; for example, the goals expressed in an organizational mission statement could well influence what how interaction occurs during a strategy meeting. However, the texts are also created through conversation; that is, a new set of action items might emerge from that strategy meeting. Thus, text and conversation work recursively: "Text is the product of conversational process, but it is also its raw material and principal occupation. Together, then, conversation and text form a self-organizing loop" (Taylor & Van Every, 2000, pp. 210–211).

These ideas about text and conversation are similar to some of the concepts we encountered earlier in this chapter when talking about structuration theory and about the notions of **discourse and Discourse**. All of these ideas get at some of the most basic principles regarding the communicative constitution of organization—that conversation (or interaction, or discourse) draws on systems of meaning such as texts (or structures, or Discourse) and also creates and recreates those systems in an ongoing way and over time. As you sit in a classroom, the conversation that occurs draws on all sorts of texts. For example, your conversation is guided by the syllabus, by this textbook, by norms about how professors and students should interact in a classroom, perhaps by values in play at your specific college or university. We should never forget, however, that these texts have been created over time through conversation and that we have agency to influence those texts in meaningful ways. This is the reason that interaction in one class never quite feels the same as interaction in another—the relationship between text and conversation plays out differently in every situation.

Constitution as "Scaling Up"

The co-orientation processes involved in the interplay between text and conversation form the core of the Montreal School's approach to CCO. However, these scholars also provide important insights into how this core relationship is part of larger processes of organizing. Understanding this process begins with the concept of *distanciation*, the notion that the meaning created in the relationship between text and conversation can be codified (for example, in physical books or computer software) and thus make a difference in situations beyond the initial interaction. Kuhn (2012) notes that "Montreal School thinking builds on this claim about distanciation in advocating a 'scaling up' approach to organizational emergence" (p. 552). Taylor and his colleagues (1996) describe this process as a series of steps—**degrees of separation**—through which the original intent of a speaker is embedded in conversation and then distanced from that conversation—scaled up—through its transformation into text. These ideas about degrees of separation are illustrated in Table 5.1.

We can think about this entire process by considering Alana, Brian, and Kevin—three high school friends who love music. In the general course of talk among friends, they discover their shared passion and decide to get together and play. Over time, they develop new ways of understanding each other, create their own musical style, start playing for friends and eventually in public venues, and label themselves "KabKids" based on their initials. They post their videos on YouTube, get a lot of followers, and eventually start making and recording music for money. Their CDs are moving, they are hot sellers on iTunes, and they start touring—first locally, then nationally, then around the world. Within a few years, KabKids is consistently trending on Twitter and a critic hails the "KabKid sound" as an important new direction in the industry.

This may be an unusual story—not everyone has this kind of success—but it is one that makes sense to us and illustrates the ideas of the Montreal School. Organizing here begins with conversation—interaction among Kevin, Alana, and Brian—but that conversation draws on all sorts of texts (common language; ideas about

Table 5.1	Degrees of Separation in the Scaling Up Process
First Degree of Separation	The intent of the speaker is embedded in conversation. (Patrick, a worker at an urban nonprofit, suggests a new way to connect homeless individuals with job opportunities.)
Second Degree of Separation	The conversation is given a narrative representation. (Heather tells others about the ideas Patrick shared with her.)
Third Degree of Separation	The text is transcribed into a more permanent form. (A written plan is developed based on Patrick's ideas.)
Fourth Degree of Separation	A specialized language is developed that is used in subsequent texts and conversations. (Specific terminology is created for components of Patrick's plans so others in the city center can share in the planning.)
Fifth Degree of Separation	The texts and conversations are transformed into material and physical frames. (Procedure manuals are created and kiosks are built in strategic locations.)
Sixth Degree of Separation	The standardized form is disseminated to a broader public. (The new system is shared with nonprofits in other urban areas.)

Adapted from Miller (2002). Based on pp. 24–25 of Taylor et al., 1996.

popular culture, music theory, and technique). Their conversations then become textualized in a variety of forms—their own songs, on the Internet, formal publicity, and word-of-mouth about the KabKids. These texts then become more and more separated from those initial conversations—scaled up—and in turn influence other ongoing conversations. So, perhaps, a few years later, when another trio of high school kids gets together to play music, they will draw on these various "KabKids" texts in their own interaction.

Current Directions

Scholars working with ideas from the Montreal School have been very active in pursuing research projects that explore aspects of the co-orientation process and in considering the theoretical implications of many of their ideas. Much of the research connected to the Montreal School has involved detailed analysis of the everyday conversations that contribute to the constitution of organization process. For example, Chaput, Brummans, and Cooren (2011) recently examined a debate regarding the constitution of a new political party in Quebec to highlight ways in which identification processes unfolded.

Scholars have also developed the theoretical trajectory of the Montreal School. We'll just consider a few of these ideas here. François Cooren has written extensively about the ways in which nonhuman parts of organizations (e.g., computers, memos, signs) function to "do things" in organizations—that is, he argues regarding the extent to which *texts have agency* (Cooren, 2004). Through the processes of distanciation described earlier, texts often become separated from their authors—we don't remember, for example, who wrote a certain memo or when a sign was

Case in Point: The Textual Power of Emoticons

Though it is likely that people have used typescript to indicate emotion for many decades—if not centuries—the modern emoticon was born in 1982 when a Carnegie Mellon University computer scientist named Scott Fahlman suggested using the three character sequence of :-) to denote a smiling face (☺). Since then, the use of emoticons has proliferated. A Web search will unearth sites giving instructions for how to imbed hundreds of different emoticons into your e-mails or Facebook chat messages.

We may think that we have control over these emoticons. We decide when to embed them in a conversation, with whom, and with what goal in mind. But Montreal School theorists would remind us that as we use these emoticons in conversation they become text and develop meaning that may not be connected with our original intent. The emoticon, as text, has agency and can do things on its own.

Such is the case with the popular "winky face" emoticon created by a semicolon followed by a parenthesis. 😉 This emoticon is very popular on social media sites and in texting, and using emoticons is also par for the course these days in business communication: A majority of both men and women say they use emoticons in communicating with colleagues. However, the winky face might have textual agency that sends the wrong message. A recent survey found that 71 percent of women and 90 percent of men believed that receiving a winky face in an e-mail indicated the possibility of romance or a first date ("Office Romances," 2012). This might be OK with you, as another recent study found that almost 85 percent of workers between 18 and 29 indicated that they would have a romantic relationship with a coworker. However, it is also possible that your use of this particular emoticon in conversation means nothing of the sort. So, "if you're not in the market for an office hook-up, lay off the emoticons" ("Office Romances," 2012)—you may not appreciate the textual agency that they develop.

put up in the hallway. He believes that understanding the ways in which texts can "make a difference" will enhance our appreciation for the complexity of organizational constitution. Further down this road of textual agency, Cooren (2010) also considers the process of **ventriloquism** in organizational communication. This idea suggests that one agent in an organization can do the speaking for other agents, just like a ventriloquist and a dummy. That is, a person could post an anonymous comment on a company website and let that comment do the talking. However, there are times when these texts take on a life of their—have agency, that is—and might come back and speak for others in various ways. As Cooren (2010) notes, "whether we like it or not, the [texts] we produce in interactions make us do things (in which case we are the dummie while they are our ventriloquist) as much as we make them do things (in which case, they are our dummies while we are the ventriloquist)" (p.135).

In sum, then, the Montreal School has developed an approach to the communicative constitution of organization that is grounded in very basic processes of interaction and considers the ways in which these conversations become textualized and scaled up into organizations and institutions. By considering this **scaling up process**, these scholars also open up the possibility that texts have agency apart from the humans who have created them through conversation. In the next section of this chapter, we'll consider an alternative approach to CCO that takes a somewhat more macroscopic look at the constitution process.

Spotlight on Scholarship: Constituting Collaboration

One of the hallmarks of the communicative constitution of organizations (CCO) approach is the rejection of the container metaphor for understanding processes of organizing. Organizations are not containers that hold various communication processes, but rather are ongoing accomplishments of interaction. Nowhere is the inappropriateness of a container more apparent than in the consideration of interorganizational collaborations (IOCs)—groups of organizations and their representatives that organize to address problems or issues and accomplish things that couldn't be done through individual action. For example, IOCs might work to address the complicated problems of homelessness in a large city or the challenges of enhancing access to medical care in rural areas. However, these "uncontained" collaborations often include people and organizations with widely divergent goals and operating procedures. Thus, "one of the biggest challenges facing IOCs is the sheer diversity that exists across partner organizations as they try to develop productive relationships toward some form of cooperation" (Koschmann, 2013, p. 62). Matthew Koschmann addressed these challenges by considering the processes through which one IOC—a group he called City Partners—developed a sense of collective identity that contributed to its legitimacy and its ability to address important community problems in a midsize southwestern community.

To understand the collective identity of City Partners, Koschmann drew on many concepts developed by CCO scholars—particularly the Montreal School. For example, he used the notions of text and conversation discussed in this chapter and looked at the intertextual struggles of City Partners as members interacted and struggled with the identity that would move it forward after the influential founder of the IOC retired. One important concept Koschmann used to understand collective identity was the process of distanciation through which "localized interactions" enlarged "their effect beyond situated conversations" (Koschmann, 2013, p. 66). The concept of an authoritative text (Kuhn, 2008)

informed Koschmann's analysis. As he explains, "an authoritative text is more than just a formal mission statement ... it is a broader concept that emphasizes relations of power and legitimacy, clarifies roles and responsibilities, and provides an overall sense of what an organization is" (Koschmann, 2013, p. 68).

Through months of field observation and many interviews at a pivotal point in the development of City Partners, Koschmann documented the ways in which ongoing interaction among IOC members gained traction as the collaboration grappled with their collective identity. For example, Koschmann saw "seeds of constitution" sown in the development of annual awards for the ICO founder. Perhaps the most interesting example of the communicative constitution of collective identity at City Partners, however, started at a planning meeting when the current director commented that "maybe we could think of our work as sort of like keeping an eye on the dashboard of a car" (Koschmann, 2013, p. 78). This casual reference spawned ongoing references about the "dashboard thing" and related comments about "moving the needle," making sure the "tank was full," and so on. Soon members of the ICO forgot that the metaphor began with the comments of the current director—that is, it became distanciated—and gained the power to shape subsequent interactions and efforts at City Partners. That is, the idea of a community dashboard became an authoritative text that was a critical defining aspect of collective identity for the ICO. Koschmann argues that this case study is important not only for understanding the ways in which interorganizational groups define themselves but also in appreciating the process through which organizations are communicatively constituted: "what we might think of as momentary communication practices and language use can, in some circumstances, gain stability, as in the case of the community dashboard" (Koschmann, 2013, p. 83).

Koschmann, M.A.. (2013). The communicative constitution of collective identity in interorganizational collaboration. Management. *Communication Quarterly, 27,* 61–89.

THE FOUR FLOWS

A second influential CCO approach was developed by Robert McPhee and his colleagues (McPhee & Iverson, 2009; McPhee & Zaug, 2000). The theorizing in the Four Flow school is "explicitly structurationist in arguing for the constitutive force of communication in organizing" (Kuhn, 2012, p. 558) and argues that we can understand the communicative constitution of organization by appreciating the types of communication flows that happen during the process of organizing. Four Flow theorists differ from Montreal School theorists in several ways. First, as we saw in previous sections, Montreal School scholars concentrate to a large extent on the "micro" processes of constitution—the ways in which specific conversations take place and eventually get "scaled up." Four Flow scholars don't examine this process explicitly and instead begin at a somewhat higher level to consider the communication flows as they intersect and constitute organization. Second, Four Flow theorists look more explicitly at the *functions* of communication flows in constituting organizations. That is, "these four communication flows encompass what are typically seen as internal and external matters that, taken together, perform essential organizational functions" (Kuhn, 2012, p. 558). In looking at the idea of functions, Four Flow theorists consider more of the content of communication during the constitution process and what specific flows need to occur in order for organizing to take place. These theorists see themselves as contributing to the ongoing question of "how large-scale, purposefully-controlled organizations are constituted" (McPhee & Zaug, 2000, para 1). We will now consider the specific flows presented by these theorists.

Membership Negotiation

The first of The Four Flows is communication relevant for *membership negotiation*. This flow makes clear the point that organizations are communicatively constituted through people who bring the organization into existence and enter and exit over time. However, as McPhee and Iverson (2009) note, "membership is often not a simple yes-or-no or once-and-for-all issue" (p. 63), so the communication processes of membership negotiation are varied and continuous. We will deal with many of these issues in more detail in Chapter 7 when we consider processes of organizational socialization, but a few aspects of this flow can be highlighted here.

First, one crucial aspect of the membership negotiation flow is the idea of crossing some various boundaries; not necessarily the explicit boundaries of an organizational container, but boundaries of knowledge, legitimacy, and connection that can separate organizational members from others. For example, Texas A&M University is known for many traditions that exemplify what it means to be an Aggie. The saying in Aggieland that "from the outside you can't understand it, from the inside you can't explain it" shows the important boundary of knowledge that is negotiated during membership processes. The communication involved in negotiating membership boundaries might include asking questions and sharing information—at Texas A&M, learning from current students, for example. It might involve storytelling, introductions, and initiation events—like the "Fish

Camp" orientation that many freshman attend the summer before starting school at Texas A&M. And most of all, this membership negotiation communication includes simple immersion in the ongoing interaction of the organization—classes, football games, dorm life, and so on. But the membership negotiation flow is about more than organizational entry, as communication processes continuously serve to shift and change membership status, perhaps through organizational exit or perhaps through changing senses of connection to the organization. At Texas A&M University, another typical claim is: "Once an Aggie, always an Aggie." This may be true in some senses, but the membership negotiation flow would suggest that the nature of that "Aggieness" may change in substantial ways over time.

Self-Structuring

The second flow of *self-structuring* considers processes that serve to design the organization, provide guidance about resource allocation, institute policies and procedures, and create rules about how work is accomplished. McPhee and Zaug note that the **self-structuring flow** is what "distinguishes organizations from groupings such and lunch mobs or mere neighborhoods" (para 27) and provide a lengthy list of types of communication that is part of this second constituting flow:

> Examples of communication like this are easy to give—if anything, they are stereotypical of organizational communication. Official documents such as charters, organization charts, policy and procedure manuals; decision-making and planning forums; orders, directives, and the more casual announcements that often substitute for them; processes of employee evaluation and feedback; budgeting, accounting, and other formalized control processes … Self-structuring communication includes any process that serves to steer the organization or part of it. (McPhee & Zaug, 2000, para 28)

This second flow, then, provides norms, standards, and rules for getting work done in organizations. Though communication in this flow can often be ongoing (scheduling meetings, discussing new procedures, providing feedback), this flow also includes communication that is very often saved in more permanent forms such as legal documents, policy procedures, and ongoing and repetitive schedules and plans. Thus, communication in the self-structuring flow can often substitute for ongoing interaction between members of an organization—everyone knows how things are supposed to proceed, so there's no need to talk about it. For example, teachers at an elementary school might know that there is always a staff meeting on Friday morning, that there are exacting standards for filling out report cards, and that specific content relevant to grade-level curriculum requirements needs to be included in ongoing lesson plans. Thus, these are all aspects of interaction that don't need to be spoken about because they are codified in the self-structuring flow that has constituted these aspects of the organization.

Activity Coordination

When we think of particular organizations, we typically connect those organizations to one or more goals or purposes. A utility company is in the business of providing power and other resources to the businesses and residents of a community. Habitat for Humanity achieves its purpose of providing affordable housing by partnering with families and communities in building homes. Ford Motor Company is in the business of manufacturing and selling cars and trucks. The college or university you attend probably has interlinked missions of teaching, research, and service. To some extent, the question of how these goals and purposes are reached is answered by the self-structuring flow we considered earlier—that is, there are standards, rules, and procedures that relate to the how electricity moves through the grid, how homes are built through the partnership process, how parts are procured and become part of the production process, or how professors create syllabi or apply for research grants. However, achieving (or at least trying to achieve) the purposes of an organization requires more than what is included in this self-structuring flow, because "such structural directions can never be complete or completely relevant, are never completely understood, and are frequently amended in an informal patchwork of adjustments" (McPhee & Zaug, 2000, para 32). Thus, ongoing communication is necessary for processes of collaboration and ongoing work accomplishment—this is the third communication flow of *activity coordination*.

The **activity coordination flow** refers to the ongoing interaction that is necessary to get work done in an organization. This flow highlights the idea of interdependence that we considered when talking about systems theory—that is, various actors in an organization depend on each other to accomplish things and thus must communicate in order to coordinate activities. Sometimes this is an essential aspect of task accomplishment; for example, a surgeon needs to communicate with the surgical nurse regarding the required instrument, with the anesthesiologist regarding ongoing sedation needs, with the assisting physician about coordinating surgical activities. There are other times when the activity coordination flow is brought into play when communication from the self-structuring flow doesn't provide enough guidance (or provides the wrong guidance) regarding ongoing activities of the organization. For instance, when you call the passenger service line of an airline, there are a lot of things that can be accomplished via communication processes that have already been self-structured: you can confirm a reservation, check on flight arrival times, get a seat assignment. However, there are times when what you need isn't "self-structured" into the system—perhaps there has been a death in the family and you need to talk with someone about options for travel, or perhaps you had an unusual problem on a flight that needs to be addressed. In these cases, the automated options aren't enough and you need to talk to a representative, and this interaction is part of the activity coordination flow.

It should also be noted that communication within this flow—like communication in the other four flows—is not always successful or effective, and the communication may not even be in line with the stated goals of powerful actors in the organization. As McPhee and Zaug note (2000, para 35) "members can coordinate on how not to do work, or coordination may be in abeyance as members seek power over one another or external advantage for themselves from the system." Thus, the existence of the activity coordination flow doesn't suggest that everyone in the organization has the same goals or that any particular set of purposes are accomplished. Instead, this flow suggests that organizations are in a very basic

Case in Point: The Four Flows—Vatican Style

As we consider about the role of communication in constituting organization, we often think about organizations in their early phases of development. However, the constitution process is ongoing, and even the most established organizations are continually characterized by the change and development associated with the four flows of communication. This was recently made clear in one of the oldest existing organizations—the Catholic Church and its seat of power in the Vatican.

During the last months of the papacy of Pope Benedict XVI (before his resignation marked a membership negotiation flow that hadn't been seen in centuries), the Vatican was rocked by a scandal when the pontiff's personal correspondence was leaked by his butler. Space doesn't permit a full airing of the events (see "Pope Benedict XVI's Leaked Documents" 2013), but suffice to say that in the midst of normal course of getting things done for the Pope (activity coordination flow), the butler absconded with documents that laid bare the politics involved in many Vatican policies and procedures (self-structuring flow) and again shifted public perception about an institution already dealing with mounting criticisms relating to sexual abuse, the place of women in the church, and a number of other social and moral issues (institutional positioning flow). So even if St. Peter was the rock on which the Catholic Church was built, it is clear that the rock is not unmoving. It still shifts and changes with The Four Flows of communicative constitution.

way constituted by ongoing and interdependent communication through which individual activity is coordinated.

Institutional Positioning

The three communication flows we have considered so far deal primarily with the members of a focal organization as they coordinate activity, membership and structure internal organizational policies and procedures. However, organizations interact within larger systems. To consider one of our organizational examples from the last section, Ford Motor Company must deal with suppliers, comply with a host of government regulations, advertise and market to a wide range of customers, and compete with other car manufacturers. These processes exist at the macro level of interorganizational communication and involve a wide range of activities. Four Flow theorists have labeled this communication as *institutional positioning*.

Communication within the **institutional positioning flow** involves a number of different types of interaction. For example, communication in this flow requires establishing relationships with other entities in the environment and establishing ways that information and other resources can move among relevant organizations. For example, organizations might have departments that are charged with material procurement, with collecting on accounts, with marketing the product, or with the legal complications that can arise in complying with government regulations. All of these specific communication processes can be seen as part of the institutional positioning flow as they involve the ways in which relationships are set up and maintained with other organizations and the ongoing communication that flows within these relationships. Beyond this, however, the institutional flow often involves issues of **organizational identity** as a particular organization tries to establish itself as a viable partner or create and maintain an image that will help it successfully position itself with other organizations in the larger environment or with the public. For example, in March 2013, the Livestrong Foundation responded to ongoing concerns about Lance Armstrong's use of performance enhancing drugs by changing its logo from one highlighting "Livestrong: Lance Armstrong Foundation" to "Livestrong isn't about one person. It's about the millions of people facing cancer who need support as they face the toughest battle of their lives" ("Armstrong Lanced," 2013). This is an example of the a purposeful shift of identity in the institutional positioning flow.

Thus, Four Flow theorists argue that understanding the communicative constitution of organization requires the consideration of four divergent descriptions of communication processes. As McPhee and Zaug (2000, para 42) summarize:

> The first recounts the struggle of individuals to master or influence their member roles, statuses, and relations to the organization. The second articulates how organizational leaders design, implement, and suffer problems with decision and control mechanisms. The third focuses on members engaging in interdependent work or deviating from pure collaborate engagement. The fourth describes the organization as a partner, often anthropomorphized, in exchange and other social relations with other organizations.

The Four Flows (depicted in Figure 5.1) are seen as necessary conditions for organization. Further, their relationship with organization is seen as reciprocal—the organization that is constituted through these flows continues to influence ongoing interaction within the flows. This is similar to the relationship between text and conversation in the Montreal School. Further, The Four Flows will often influence each other—as when, for example, there are self-structured policies for membership negotiation or the needs of institutional positioning require a particular pattern of activity coordination. As McPhee and Zaug (2000, para 44) argue, "a constituted organization is not just a set of flows, but a complex relationship of them."

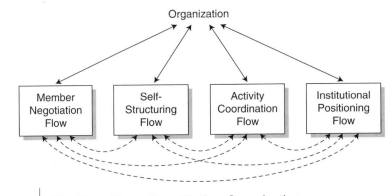

Figure 5.1 | The Four Flows Constituting Organization

Adapted from arguments of McPhee and Zaug (2000)

SUMMARY AND CHALLENGES FOR CONSTITUTIVE APPROACHES

As the field of organizational communication moved into the twenty-first century, one of the most dominant shifts in thinking was a movement away from thinking of communication as something that "happens in" and is "shaped by" the organization. This mode of thinking had been dominant for many decades and is represented in much of the thinking we've reviewed in earlier chapters. For example, tables presented in Chapters 2 and 3 of this book are emblematic of this approach in exploring how communication is viewed in classical, human relations, and human resources organizations. That is, we are seeing each type of organization as a particular kind of container—one that will shape the content and flow of communication within it in predictable ways. Indeed, we still often think about organizations this way, as it makes sense and comports with much of our everyday experience.

The scholarship we've considered in this chapter, however, represents an important move away from this way of thinking. Influenced by foundational positions such as social constructionism, discourse analysis, and structuration theory, scholars in this emerging approach consider the ways in which communication constitutes organizing. CCO theorists are interested in the ways in which interaction shapes and reshapes the emerging organization. These theorists also emphasize the recursive nature of this process by also studying the ways in which interaction is constrained by organizational texts and structures. We examined the two schools of CCO thought that have had the most influence in organizational communication. First, we looked at the Montreal School and its ideas about the ways in which co-orientation occurs in the process of conversation and then scales up into various forms of texts. We considered the ways in which these texts become distanced from the conversation and can be seen as exercising agency on their own. We then turned to the more macro approach of The Four Flows of communication constitution.

Researchers taking this approach argue that organizing is constituted by four specific flows: membership negotiation, self-structuring, activity coordination, and institutional positioning.

These approaches have had great influence on the field of organizational communication. Indeed, even scholars who do not explicitly use the ideas of the Montreal School or The Four Flows would likely agree with the most basic concepts presented in this chapter—that organizations are constituted through communication and that there are problems regarding organizations as mere containers that hold various communication processes. However, there are also challenges associated with the CCO approach.

First, because the emphasis of CCO scholars is on communication and interaction, there is a natural tendency to think primarily about symbolic issues in the organization. That makes it easy to downplay some very real aspects of organizational life—these are issues of **materiality** and include concerns with objects such as buildings and furniture or with the bodies we inhabit. That is, it is one thing to say that we socially construct our organizational world. However, it is also true that organizing is influenced by the physical site in which it occurs, by the extent to which infrastructures are able to provide energy and transport material, and by the ways in which our bodies are implicated in a variety of work processes. Scholars such as Ashcraft, Kuhn, and Cooren (2009) explicitly address this issue in their call to "materialize" organizational communication and not concentrate exclusively on the social and symbolic aspects of organizing.

A second critique of CCO approaches is that as scholars work to describe and understand the interactional creation of organization and the flows that constitute organizing, they sometimes put less emphasis on the "wider structures ... of relational power within which ongoing political processes and practices are necessarily embedded" (Reed, 2010). This criticism argues that CCO researchers may miss larger issues of power and control because they are interested in more basic processes of the ways in which microscopic interactional processes create and recreate organizational texts and communication flows. Putnam and Nicotera (2010) respond to this critique by saying that "power and domination are exercised through communication" and thus these concepts are part of the larger CCO project though not always explicitly emphasized. However, concepts of power and control are indeed pervasive in organizational life—hence, we will turn to these ideas in Chapter 6, our final chapter to discuss approaches to organizational communication.

DISCUSSION QUESTIONS

1. How do the approaches considered in this chapter move away from the container metaphor of organization? Does this shift make sense to you? How does it comport with the ways in which we talk about organizations in our daily lives? Are there ways we can reconcile these two modes of thought by considering the container as a helpful social construction?

2. How are the Montreal School's ideas of text and conversation related to structuration theory, discourse approaches to organizing, and the general social constructionist movement? What are the most central concepts that unite these various positions? How does the theorizing of the Montreal School move beyond these ideas?

3. Do you think The Four Flows are all necessary conditions for an organization to exist? Do you think they are sufficient conditions? Can you think of an example of an organization that exists *without* one of the four flows? Can you think of an example when the four flows are present, but you *wouldn't* call it an organization?

KEY CONCEPTS

container metaphor
communicative constitution of
   organization (CCO)
social constructionism
structuration theory
structures
agency

constraint
duality of structure
discourse and Discourse
conversation
text
scaling up process
degrees of separation

ventriloquism
member negotiation flow
self-structuring flow
activity coordination flow
institutional positioning flow
organizational identity
materiality

CASE STUDY | ## A Drop in the Bucket

Unlike most of the case studies in this textbook, this one is a true story. It is a story that I first heard through an academic paper written by Owen Lynch and Zach Schaefer (Lynch & Schaefer, 2012), and it recounts the events of several years earlier when Owen was working as a teacher at a private preparatory school while he was in his PhD program. Owen and Zach describe a series of tumultuous meetings that occur over a several month period at the high school and relate them to the larger ideas of this chapter—the interplay of conversation and text and how organizations are constituted through flows of communication. In the space available here, I won't be able to do justice to all the complexities of this case and will just highlight a few crucial scenes. But let's start with an understanding of the setting—a place Lynch and Schaefer call "The Prep."

> The Prep was founded on a picturesque deeply wooded 400-acre property just on the outskirts of a small southwestern city. The school was a boarding community where faculty, their families and the students all learned, worshipped, ate and lived together on the same campus. The Prep was founded on the ideals of social and environmental progressivism with a motto of developing the entire student: spiritually, academically, and athletically. The experiment was a success and The Prep is now considered one of the top academic prep schools in the nation. A large part of this academic success comes from the small informal classes and the engaged learning philosophy but most of all the close relationship between students and teachers. (Lynch & Schaeffer, 2012)

Sounds idyllic, right? Unfortunately, times change and The Prep changed, too. By the time Owen worked there as a teacher, 70% of the students were day students, the city had grown up around the school, and the economy and a series of bad investment decisions had led to a serious fiscal crisis. To deal with these issues, The Prep brought in a new Headmaster, hired a new chief financial officer (CFO), and convened a "benefits review committee" that included members of the Board of Trustees, community members, school administrators, and one faculty representative—Owen. The committee met a number of times, discussing topics including school history and culture, relationships to donors, comparisons of The Prep with other high-quality preparatory schools, hiring practices, and benefits issues such as how much should be contributed to 401K packages. The discussions were wide-ranging, but for the sake of this case, we'll settle in on one particular issue raised during a meeting several weeks into the ongoing work of the benefits review committee.

At this meeting, the topic under discussion was tuition waivers for the children of faculty and staff.

Owen suspected coming into the meeting that this issue would be contentious, and he was right. As the discussion ensued, two camps emerged. On one side were faculty members who wanted to maintain the tuition waiver. These individuals argued that the tuition waiver was part of the school's history and culture and that many faculty and staff chose to work at The Prep in part because they were "investing in their children's future." During a meeting break, Owen asked the CFO, "Was not every person here promised the dependent tuition waiver when they were hired? I know I was." The head of the high school produced letters from teachers pleading that the benefit not be cut and examples of job offers teachers had turned down because they were counting on the tuition waiver at The Prep.

On the other side of this argument were members of the Board of Trustees and the CFO. One trustee pointed out that the tuition waiver was not a "formal policy" and that sometimes difficult decisions needed to be made in the name of fiscal responsibility. Another argued that "the policy is not equitable to the faculty members who do not have dependents," and the CFO brushed off concerns about faculty leaving by saying that "a little turnover is healthy." The CFO then followed up on the issue of affordability by noting that the children of many teachers and staff could qualify for financial aid. The conversation became extremely heated as the two sides confronted each other on a variety of issues. Before they came to blows, though, the head of the committee called the session to a close, noting that it had been a "productive meeting" and that "we will not reach a consensus on this topic in this room." After requesting further feedback from faculty, the meeting was adjourned.

The opportunity to gather that feedback occurred at a meeting of the entire faculty designed as an "informative town hall" to review the work of the committee. The CFO presented the case for the reductions to the staff benefits package—including the elimination of the tuition benefit—using facts and figures to demonstrate the scope of the crisis. He was making a clear argument that something needed to be done if The Prep were to successfully weather the storm, and that the "something" needed to include sacrifice on the part of the faculty. He also noted, however, that many faculty and staff children would

CASE STUDY | **A Drop in the Bucket** *continued*

be eligible for financial aid and would hence still be able to attend The Prep as their parents desired. The discussion that followed clearly indicated that many members of the faculty were not buying the CFO's logic. In the midst of the discussion, the head of the middle school raised her hand and asked a question: "In the big scheme of things, how much money would be saved by cutting the tuition benefit as many of the staff and teachers' kids would receive financial aid?" The CFO responded: "In the big scheme of things, it is only a drop in the bucket." At that comment, shock, indignation, and heated discussion ensued.

So we have examined two crucial scenes in the drama of The Prep and its fiscal crisis; one scene a committee meeting, the other a faculty meeting. The final scenes of this case took place across a wide swath of locations at The Prep, including the mail room, the parking lot, bathrooms, and offices. In these scenes, the starring role was played by a photocopy of a bucket into which a single drop is about to fall. The artist who created this rendering was a mystery, but its meaning was clear, and Owen recounts that the image spread quickly: "It was posted in clever places all over the school, on the wall of the faculty lounge, on the door of the stall in the men's bathroom next to the CFO's office. I personally observed a teacher who, finding the bucket picture in his box, laughed, and then, as he walked past the new headmaster's car, put it under the wiper like a ticket." In short, the bucket could not be avoided.

We could go further in recounting events at The Prep. There followed yet more discussion and another concluding meeting of the benefits review committee. Eventually a compromise was reached in which tuition benefits would be cut for future hires but maintained for current faculty and staff. In short, there were more conversations, but the enduring text of the case is clear: A bucket that speaks for itself.

CASE ANALYSIS QUESTIONS

1. How can we understand the history of The Prep and the meetings described in this case in terms of The Four Flows that constitute organization? Which flows are highlighted in this description? Which flows have most strongly influenced the change that has occurred at The Prep? How have flows such as membership negotiation and self-structuring influenced institutional positioning?

2. This case describes a number of specific interaction episodes. Can these episodes be understood as conversation in the terminology of the Montreal School? What texts are drawn on during these conversations? Do different participants draw on different texts? Do other interactants in the conversation accept the authority of the texts that are drawn on?

3. What are the implications of the bucket drawing in terms of textual agency? Relatedly, how can we understand events in this case using the concept of ventriloquism? Can we see either the bucket drawing or Owen as a dummy who speaks for others in the organization? If so, whom is being spoken for, and what are the implications of anonymous author in the case of the bucket?

Critical and Feminist Approaches

CHAPTER 6

AFTER READING THIS CHAPTER, YOU SHOULD ...

- Understand the distinctions between critical and feminist approaches and the other approaches we have thus far considered.
- Appreciate the centrality of power to the critical approach and be able to describe how power is represented through the modes and means of production and through organizational discourse.
- Be familiar with the critical concepts of ideology, hegemony, emancipation, and resistance and be able to describe how these concepts fit together for critical theorists.
- Be able to describe how the theory of concertive control represents important concepts to critical scholars.
- Appreciate the argument for framing feminist organizational communication as an outgrowth of the larger feminist movement rather than as an offshoot of critical theory.
- Understand patriarchy and the ways in which organizations are constituted in a gendered way.
- Be able to distinguish among various forms of feminist activism.
- Appreciate the contribution to the feminist project of scholarship regarding sexual harassment, women-led organizations, and disciplined bodies.

We have gone down a long road in the previous four chapters in learning about various approaches to the study of organizational communication. We began with classical approaches that conceptualize organizations as machines and emphasize rationality and efficiency. We next considered human relations and human resources approaches, which, respectively, emphasize the needs of employees and the contributions those employees could make to organizational functioning. We then looked at two more recent approaches to organizational communication, conceptualizing organizations first as systems and then as cultures. Finally, in Chapter 5, we moved away from the container metaphor implied by many of these approaches and learned about contemporary scholars who investigate the communicative constitution of organization. As we traveled along this road, we highlighted the differences among these approaches. Indeed, these approaches to organizational study *are* quite distinct. However, common threads underlie all of them.

The first of these underlying threads involves the political frame of reference used to understand the organization. Burrell and Morgan (1979) distinguish among unitary, pluralist, and radical frames of reference. In the **unitary frame of reference**, emphasis is placed on common organizational goals. Conflict is seen as rare and negative, and power is the natural prerogative of management. In the **pluralist frame of reference**, the organization consists of many groups with divergent interests. Conflict is seen positively, as "an inherent and ineradicable characteristic of organizational affairs" (Morgan, 1997, p. 202). Finally, in the **radical frame of reference**, the organization is viewed "as a battleground where rival forces (e.g., management and unions) strive for the achievement of largely incompatible ends" (Morgan, 1997, p. 202). Conflict and power are seen as reflections of larger class struggles in society.

The approaches to organizational communication we have considered so far have used unitary or pluralist frames of reference. For example, classical approaches clearly adopt a unitary frame of reference. This is true to a lesser extent of human relations and human resources approaches. Systems and cultural approaches tend to take pluralist approaches by considering the management of divergent subgroup interests. The CCO approach is harder to categorize in this scheme, but it would largely not be seen as using a radical frame of reference to understand organizational communication processes.

A second underlying thread involves the role of the theorist in approaching organizational life. For classical, human relations, and human resources approaches, the role of the theorist is typically one of finding effective techniques for organizing. For scholars taking systems, cultural, and CCO approaches, the role of the theorist is to *understand* or *explain* organizational communication phenomena, though the form of understanding or explanation can take very different forms, depending on the approach. None of these theorists, however, would be likely to step in and attempt to *change* the organization in their roles as theorists. As Bernstein (1976) notes, "while the theorist may be passionately interested in the fate and quality of social and political life, he [sic] must bracket this practical interest in his [sic] pursuit of theory" (p. 173).

The approaches we consider in this chapter take a turn away from these commonalities. Specifically, both *critical approaches* and *feminist approaches* adopt a radical frame of reference by considering organizations as *sites of domination*. Furthermore, these approaches see theory as a force that can emancipate individuals from these dominating organizational forces or consider how employees resist organizational dominance. Thus, the theorist takes an activist role in instigating and encouraging organizational transformation. We first look at historical and contemporary framing assumptions that are used by most critical theorists and consider an example of critical theorizing in organizational communication. We then consider the ways in which feminist approaches to organizational communication are related to, although clearly distinct from, critical approaches, and we look at several examples of contemporary work that takes a feminist approach to organizational communication.

CRITICAL APPROACHES

Although the roots of critical scholarship can be traced to a variety of influential thinkers, including Georg Hegel and Max Weber (see Miller, 2005, for review), some of the most important roots of critical theory in organizational communication can be found in the work of Karl Marx. Marx, a German intellectual of the nineteenth century, examined the relationship between owners and workers in a capitalist society and theorized that there was an inherent imbalance in this relationship and that eventually workers would rise up in revolt against the capitalist system. Marx believed that "critique" would lead to revolution because it would reveal fundamental truths about the human social condition. He noted that "what we have to accomplish at this time is all the more clear: relentless criticism of all existing conditions, relentless in the sense that the criticism is not afraid of its findings and just as little afraid of the conflict with the powers that be" (Marx, 1967, p. 212).

Marx's political influence has been, of course, widespread. Theoretically, his thoughts have also shaped the work of theorists taking a critical approach to social research. Perhaps the most widely known of these are researchers from the Frankfurt School of critical theory. Scholars aligned with the Frankfurt School pursued social and political critiques that would lead to "the development of normative alternatives which might enable humans to transcend their unhappy situation through critical thought and action" (Huspek, 1997, p. 266).

It would be impossible to provide a thorough review of the various strands of critical theory (see Alvesson & Deetz, 1996; Morrow, 1994; Mumby, 2000). At the risk of oversimplifying, however, critical theorists tend to agree on the following: First, critical theorists believe that certain societal structures and processes lead to fundamental imbalances of power. Second, these imbalances of power lead to alienation and oppression for certain social classes and groups. Third, the role of the critical theorist is to explore and uncover these imbalances and bring them to the attention of the oppressed group. Emancipation is then possible, either through direct political action, individual resistance, or awareness of the oppressed individuals. In the next few sections of this chapter, we will unpack this explanation of critical theory by considering several key concepts: power, ideology, hegemony, emancipation, and resistance.

The Pervasiveness of Power

No concept is as important as *power* for the critical theorist. As Mumby (2001, p. 585) argues, critical theorists see power as "a defining, ubiquitous feature of organizational life." The concept of power is typically equated with the related constructs of control and domination (Pierce & Dougherty, 2002), and these ideas are central to all critical theories. In exploring the concept of power, it is useful to examine three approaches to the topic outlined by Conrad and Ryan (1985). The *traditional approach* considers power to be a relatively stable entity that people or groups possess. Researchers adopting a traditional approach ask questions about the factors that lead to organizational power and the impact of power on outcomes such as job satisfaction and performance. These scholars often equate power with control over resources or with hierarchical status in the organization (Hardy & Clegg, 1996). The *symbological approach* (see also Mumby, 2001, for related discussion of the *interpretive approach)* views power as a product of communicative interactions and relationships. Researchers taking this approach are interested in how communication constitutes understandings of power through socially constructed organizational relationships (Mumby, 2001, p. 594).

The third approach to power—the **radical-critical approach**—is most germane to the theorists considered in this chapter. In this approach, the theorist is concerned with the "deep structures" that produce and reproduce relationships in organizational life. Furthermore, these theorists contend that there are inherent contradictions between the "surface structure" and the deep structure of power that must be explored. The role of the radical-critical theorist, then, is to explore the ways in which economic, social, and communicative relationships produce and maintain organizational power relationships.

What, precisely, are the structures that serve to shape power relationships in the organization? Morgan (1997) explored fourteen sources of power within the organizational setting, as presented in Table 6.1. This table presents just a sampling of the sources of power in the organization; others could probably be added. As Hardy and Clegg (1996) note, "All resource lists are infinite, however, since different phenomena become resources in different contexts" (p. 626). This table is instructive, however, in pointing out the wide range of power sources that can be drawn on in the organization. Some of these sources of power are relatively overt and tend to be the focus of traditional theorists. These include, for example, formal authority, control of scarce resources, and control of knowledge and information. Other

---

Table 6.1 | Sources of Power in Organizations

The following are among the most important sources of power:

- Formal authority
- Control of scarce resources
- Use of organizational structure, rules, and regulations
- Control of decision processes
- Control of knowledge and information
- Control of boundaries
- Ability to cope with uncertainty
- Control of technology
- Interpersonal alliances, networks, and control of "informal organization"
- Control of counterorganizations
- Symbolism and the management of meaning
- Gender and the management of gender relationships
- Structural factors that define the stage of action
- The power one already has

These sources of power provide organizational members with a variety of means for enhancing their interests and resolving or perpetuating organizational conflict.

Used by permission of Sage Publications, Inc., from Morgan, G. (1986), *Images of Organization*, 2d, Beverly Hills, CA: Sage.

sources of power, however, are less obvious to the casual observer; these covert and unobtrusive forms of power in organizations tend to be the focus of critical theorists. We will now consider two sources of power in more detail. The first of these—control of **modes and means of production**—is associated most clearly with the Marxist tradition of critical theory. The second—control of **organizational discourse**—highlights concerns most typically associated with critical theorists in the communication discipline.

Control of Modes and Means of Production Classic Marxist theory examines the ways in which capitalist owners have control over the modes and means of production in the workplace (see Clegg & Dunkerley, 1980). The modes and means of production constitute the *substructure* of society—its economic and production base. The term *modes of production* refers to the economic conditions that underlie the production process. For example, Marx argues that the capitalist mode of production is based on owners expropriating surplus labor from workers and that this creates conflict between workers and owners. However, owners and workers in a capitalist system are not necessarily aware of this process. As Deetz and Mumby (1990) explain:

> To Marx, the surplus value of labor was hidden from both workers and capitalists. The capitalist would understand the realization of profit as coming from the investment in the plant and equipment, with the amount of profit determined by market conditions rather than by unpaid labor. The worker being paid a wage would not be in a position to determine the portion of the value of the product that was a result of his or her labor and hence could not recognize unpaid labor. (p. 20)

The term *means of production* refers to actual work processes—how products are made and services rendered. According to Deetz and Mumby (1990), "In Marx's view, industrialization brought with it dehumanization and alienation from work and work products ... the division of labor, the treatment of labor as a commodity, and the separation of the individual from his or her product produced a fragmented, lost person, estranged from his or her own production activities" (p. 20). This controlling aspect of means of production has been further elaborated by Braverman (1974), who argues that as the workplace becomes more technologically sophisticated, workers become "deskilled" and alienated from their work. For example, assembly-line production leads to highly specialized, fragmented, and monotonous jobs. Retail and service jobs often involve repeating the same simple tasks over and over again. Office work often has similar characteristics, as computer software programs often break down jobs and take autonomy and freedom away from individuals. Telemarketers are provided specialized scripts they must follow, and data-entry workers can have their jobs broken down to the individual keystroke.

But what is the outcome of this monotonous and fragmented work? Surber (1998, p. 77) explains: "Anyone who has worked for an hourly wage at some repetitive and mechanical task will realize not only how one's own physical activity can come to appear alien but also how easily she or he can be replaced by another person willing to do the same work." In short, when owners and managers have control over workplace processes and technologies (the means of production), critical theorists believe the result will be an alienated and oppressed workforce. Alienation can occur through the repetitive and boring jobs created by technology; oppression can occur as workers are replaced or limited in advancement by robotics or other technical achievements. Furthermore, the mechanization of the workplace allows management to constantly monitor the behavior of workers. Think, for instance, of how many times you hear the phrase "this call may be monitored for quality-control purposes" when calling an organization for sales or service help. This kind of surveillance is one more example of how management maintains its domination over employees (see D'Urso, 2006, in Chapter 2, "Spotlight on Scholarship").

Control of Organizational Discourse   Critical scholars in the communication field argue that power relationships are produced and reproduced through organizational discourse (Mumby, 1988, 1993). Like some cultural researchers and the CCO theorists we considered in the last chapter, these scholars believe that organizational reality is socially constructed through communicative interaction.

However, critical researchers go further by explicitly arguing that the reality created through discourse is the site of domination. Mumby (1989), for instance, plays off Geertz's (1973) definition of culture as "webs of significance." Mumby (1989) comments:

> If we extend Geertz's own web metaphor a little further it might be suggested how power relations are fundamentally structured into all social relations. After all, a spider's web is not simply an intricately constructed and beautiful product of nature; it is itself a site of struggle. The very existence of the web structures and instantiates a particular kind of power relationship between the spider and its prey. (p. 292)

There are a number of ways in which organizational discourse can be seen as creating and re-creating power structures in the workplace. For example, the use in our culture of particular phrases to describe work can be seen as reinforcing dominant power structures. Clair (1996) examined the ways in which the phrase "real job" (as in "when are you going to get a real job?") serves a political function by implying that the kind of jobs held by college students (e.g., waiting tables, retail clerking) are not as important as other types of employment. Thus, this phrase—and the meanings that surround it—serves to define power relationships in the workplace.

Mumby (1987, 1993) extends this view by looking at how organizational narratives (i.e., stories) can function in power-laden ways in the organization. Mumby (1987) argues that "narratives provide members with accounts of organizing. Such accounts potentially legitimate dominant forms of organizational reality and lead to discursive closure in the sense of restricting the interpretations and meanings that can be attached to organizational activity" (p. 113). Thus, the stories people tell make sense of the organization in a way that often supports the dominant organizational coalition. Mumby (1987), for example, analyzes a famous, often-told IBM story in which a lowly security worker refuses to let the company president into a restricted area without the proper identification. Mumby argues that although this story is held up as showing the strength of the little people, it also serves to strengthen the dominant coalition by highlighting the importance of bureaucratic rules and regulations.

In a third example of the power of discourse, Zoller (2003) argues that entire industries can be influenced by the discursive constructions found in regulatory materials. She considers the discourse of the Occupational Safety and Health Administration (OSHA), arguing that OSHA standards act to establish control by defining occupational injury and illness in particular ways—ways that support the power of management. For example, Zoller notes that the terms *cumulative stress disorder* and *repetitive strain injuries* are being replaced in OSHA standards by the term *upper extremity musculoskeletal disorder* because the latter term does not imply that the workplace caused the physical problem.

Ideology and Hegemony

In the last section, we explored how the economic structure of the workplace and organizational discourse can serve as instruments of domination and control. What are the outcomes of these control structures and processes? Critical theorists argue that these processes of control will lead to a shaping of ideology and to hegemony. Let's define these concepts and talk about how they fit into the models of critical theorists.

Ideology refers to "the taken-for-granted assumptions about reality that influence perceptions of situations and events" (Deetz & Kersten, 1983, p. 162). This definition has several important facets. First, ideology refers to more than a set of attitudes or beliefs. Rather, ideology "structures our thoughts and controls our interpretations of reality" (Eisenberg & Goodall, 1997, p. 153). As Therborn (1980, p. 18) argues, ideology shapes our understanding about what *exists,* what is *good,* and what is *possible.* Second, ideology involves assumptions that are rarely questioned or scrutinized. Deetz and Kersten (1983) provide an example of this in considering our ideological beliefs about organizational structure. As they note, "most people assume that organizational hierarchy is a necessary and useful arrangement. When a person encounters superior-subordinate situations, he or she views them as normal, acceptable, and unproblematic" (p. 162). Third, by shaping our view of the world, an ideology can also influence our behaviors. As Bernstein (1976) observes, "The *power* of ideologies is related to the way in which they are used to justify and legitimize actions" (p. 108).

For critical theorists, however, ideology is not a neutral concept but is intimately tied to systems of power and domination (Mumby, 1989). This leads us to the concept of **hegemony**, originally developed by Gramsci (1971). Hegemony refers to a process in which a dominant group leads another group to accept subordination as the norm (Hall, 1985). It is "manufactured consent" (Habermas, 1971), in which employees willingly adopt and reinforce hierarchical power structures. As Mumby (2001, p. 587) argues, "Hegemony does not refer to simple domination, but rather involves attempts by various groups to articulate meaning systems that are actively taken up by other groups." Hegemonic control is typically accomplished by shaping ideology in such a way that the controlled group accepts and actively participates in the control process. For example, most organizational members accept the legitimacy of rules and may actively participate in formulating them. However, these rules serve as a source of managerial control over organizational

Case in Point: Power of the Pretty

As this chapter points out, there are many sources of power in organizations: formal authority, technology, decision making, gender, to name just a few. One factor that is rarely mentioned in discussions of organizational power is attractiveness, but appearance clearly has an effect on organizational outcomes. As Dahlia Lithwick (2010) has recently pointed out, the way a person looks influences a wide range of life events: "College students tell surveyors they'd rather have a spouse who is an embezzler, drug user, or a shoplifter than one who is obese. The less attractive you are in America, the more likely you are to receive a longer prison sentence, a lower damage award, a lower salary, and poorer performance reviews" (Lithwick, 2010, p. 20). Indeed, recent alleged cases of "beauty bias" include Hooters firing servers for being too heavy and Abercrombie & Fitch examining photos of sales associates to check for issues such as weight gain and acne (Lithwick, 2010).

Legal scholar Deborah Rhode believes that such discrimination should be illegal. In her book, *The Beauty Bias*, Rhode makes the case that employment bias toward attractive men and women is widespread and should be banned like discrimination based on sex, age, ethnicity, disability, and religion. Perhaps she is right. But as we examine this argument, we also need to consider the notion of hegemony introduced in this chapter. Clearly, the existence of huge industries supporting cosmetic surgery and beauty treatments suggests that many, if not most, Americans are complicit in valuing beauty more than other characteristics. Or as Lithwick summarizes, "[A]ppearance bias is a massive societal problem with tangible economic costs that most of us—perhaps especially women—perpetuate each time we buy a diet pill.... [T]he law won't stop us from discriminating against the overweight, the aging, and the imperfect, so long as it's the quality we all hate most in ourselves" (Lithwick, 2010, p. 20).

members. This is an example of hegemonic control, in which the subjugated group becomes complicit in the control process.

For the critical theorist, then, social structures and processes allow the dominant class to shape organizational ideology. The result of this ideological monopoly is a hegemonic relationship in which one group is controlled by another through coercion, acceptance, or even active participation. What is to be done about these social imbalances? For critical theorists, the next step is emancipation of the oppressed group. For participants in these organizational structures, the next step might be activities of resistance. These two concepts are discussed next.

Emancipation

The ultimate goal of the critical model is **emancipation**, or "the liberation of people from unnecessarily restrictive traditions, ideologies, assumptions, power relations, identity formations, and so forth, that inhibit or distort opportunities for autonomy, clarification of genuine needs and wants, and thus greater and lasting satisfaction" (Alvesson & Willmott, 1992, p. 435). Although some critical theorists in the Marxist tradition advocate overt political action and "bloody revolution" (see Burrell & Morgan, 1979), most see emancipation as a process of emerging awareness and communicative action on the part of the oppressed.

Habermas (1971) has compared the role of the critical theorist in the emancipation process to the role of the psychoanalyst. A psychoanalyst's job is to help a client break down resistances and gain a deep level of self-understanding. As Bernstein (1976) notes, "The success of therapy ultimately depends not on the analyst's understanding of the patient, but on the extent to which the patient by his [*sic*] own self-reflection can appropriate this analytic understanding and dissolve his [*sic*] own resistances" (p. 201). By analogy, the role of the critical theorist is to reveal the social structures and processes that have led to ideological hegemony. When alienated people are able to consider their condition critically, emancipation will be possible. For organizational communication theorists, then, it is important to find ways that people can participate in free and open communication about power and control in the organizations where they work. In discussing such structures, Deetz (2005, p. 99) argues that "minimally, forums would be available for discussion and decision making, and no individual or group would be excluded arbitrarily from the opportunity to participate."

Resistance

We have now talked extensively about how power and control are exercised in organizational settings—the concept of **resistance** considers how workers can exert counterpressure on this exercise of power and control. Mumby (2005, p. 21) notes that scholarship in organizational communication has been moving in this direction for a number of years: "While early critical studies focused almost exclusively on organizational processes of control and domination, more recently the pendulum has swung more toward a focus or perhaps even a celebration of—possibilities for employee resistance." However, Mumby argues that these ideas shouldn't be seen in an "either/or" way and are better conceptualized as intimately linked in organizational communication processes. He illustrates this with a Malaysian proverb: "When the great lord passes, the wise peasant bows deeply and silently farts" (Mumby, 2005, p. 20). Domination (the bow) and resistance (the silent fart) are intimately linked in processes of organizational communication.

Resistance is sometimes seen in collective and organized processes such as unionization, strikes, boycotts, and large-scale social movements. For example, protestors at the World Trade Organization meeting held in Seattle in 1999 are often credited with stopping a multilateral economic agreement that protestors believed was contrary to the interests of workers (Ganesh, Zoller & Cheney, 2005). But organizational communication scholars are more often interested in resistance undertaken by the individual. For example, Murphy (1998) considered ways in which flight attendants would go along with the rules of the airline in public (e.g., serving pilots beverages before takeoff) but communicate their resistance to the rules through the "hidden transcripts" (Scott, 1990) of backstage and ironic forms of communication (e.g., joking with pilots about their "hydration" needs). Bell and Forbes (1994) documented how office workers sometimes decorate their cubicles with cartoons that signal resistance (e.g., cartoons reading "I have PMS and a handgun ... Any questions?" or "When I woke up this morning, I had one nerve left, and damned if you ain't got on it!").

Research from communication scholars points to the complexity of resistance processes that have sprung from changing organizational forms and evolving technologies. For example, Gossett and Kilker (2006) considered the phenomenon of "counterinstitutional websites" in a study of RadioShackSucks.biz. On this website, many members of the Radio Shack community (employees, past employees, customers) shared their dissatisfaction with Radio Shack management and policies, vented frustrations, and suggested actions that could be used as more active-resistance strategies. For example, posters to the website facetiously suggested things that should *not* be done after quitting a job at the company: "I have decided NOT to remove every price tag in the store on MY last day ... nor will I break off the key in the cage padlock" (Gossett & Kilker, 2006, p. 77). Thus, Internet technology provided a forum for widespread and anonymous organizational resistance.

In sum, the underlying assumptions of critical approaches provide a view that is both sobering and hopeful. The view is sobering because it highlights the many ways that individuals can be controlled and dominated in organizational settings. The view is hopeful because its ultimate aim is the emancipation of oppressed groups through critical reflection and action and because avenues of resistance are revealed that provide insight into the tension inherent in workplace domination processes. This coexistence of critique and hope also permeates more specific critical theories that have been used extensively in organizational communication. We'll consider one of these—concertive control theory—next.

A Theory of Concertive Control

In Chapter 3, we noted the increasing prevalence of team-based structures within today's organizations. Following human resources principles, these team-based structures are intended to distribute participation and accountability throughout the organization and facilitate a more democratic organizational form. But do team-based organizational structures actually fulfill these democratic ideals? This is the question addressed by an important theory in organizational communication—the theory of **concertive control** (see Miller, 2005, for a review of the theory). This theory, which originated with the work of James Barker, George Cheney, and Phil Tompkins, attempts to explain how power relationships can be transformed in an era of team-based and "alternative form" organizations. Three concepts are particularly important to an understanding of this theory: *control, identification,* and *discipline.*

Control   Concertive control theorists (Barker, 1993, 1999; Barker & Cheney, 1994) begin with organizational strategies of control originally enumerated by Edwards (1981). Edwards identified three broad strategies for exerting control in the modern organization. **Simple control** involves the direct and authoritarian exertion of control in the workplace. **Technological control** involves control exerted through technological workplace processes such as assembly lines or computer programs. *Bureaucratic control* is based on the power of hierarchical structure and the rational-legal rules (Weber, 1968) that emanate from the bureaucratic structure. These three forms of control have long exemplified typical forms of power in organizations. However, some theorists propose that in team-based organizations, a new form of control has emerged—*concertive control*. Daniels, Spiker, and Papa (1997, p. 196) define concertive control systems as those in which

> the locus of control in an organization shifts from management to workers, who collaborate to create rules and norms that govern their behavior. The role of top management in this process is to provide a value-based corporate vision that "team members use to infer parameters and premises (norms and rules) that guide their day-to-day action." (Barker, 1993, p. 413)

Identification   The second key concept for understanding concertive control systems is **identification**. Identification refers to "the perception of oneness with or belongingness to [a collective], where the individual *defines* him or herself in terms of the [collective] in which he or she is a member" (Mael & Ashforth, 1992, p. 104). Thus, when an individual identifies with an organization or a work group, that individual takes on the concerns of the organization or group and accepts those concerns as his or her own. Within a concertive control system, an individual identifies with the values of the organization or work group and hence will act in accordance with those values even in the absence of simple, technological, or bureaucratic control.

Discipline   A final concept important for understanding the theory of concertive control is *discipline*. Barker and Cheney (1994) draw on the work of Foucault (1976) in seeing discipline as embedded within the "discursive formations" of a social group. That is, through communicative interaction, work groups develop techniques to reward and punish behavior that conforms with or deviates from the values identified as important by the work group. These disciplinary techniques might include direct criticism, the use of silence, social pressure, or a host of other interaction strategies. What is important to note is that although the values being upheld may emanate from management, the discipline is meted out by the work group. Thus, a concertive control system is established in which workers identify with organizational values and then discipline behavior in accordance with those norms.

These various aspects of a concertive control system come together in an organization analyzed by Barker (1993; Barker & Cheney, 1994). This organization was moving from a traditional hierarchical model to a team-based organizational system. Barker describes how team members came to identify with values developed by management (e.g., quality, on-time shipment, team responsibility) and then disciplined team members who were not behaving in accordance with those values. Indeed, Barker notes that, ironically, the discipline enacted by the teams was often more powerful, more difficult to resist, and less obvious than similar discipline enacted in a bureaucratic control system. Consider, for example, the comments of "Danny," describing how his team dealt with problems of punctuality:

> Well we had some disciplinary thing, you know. We had a few certain people who didn't show up on time and made a habit of coming in late. So the team got together and kinda set some guidelines and we told them, you know, "If you come in late the third time and you don't wanna do anything to correct it, you're gone." That was a team decision that this was a guideline that we were gonna follow. (Barker, 1993, p. 426)

✳ Spotlight on Scholarship: Patriarchy in Public and Private Life

Critical approaches to organizational communication point to the power of ideology—deep-seated beliefs about the world and how it should work. Feminist approaches argue that the very constitution of organizations is characterized by the ideology of **patriarchy**. For many years, this ideological framework of patriarchy has been reflected in assumptions about men and women in the workplace and the relationship between the public sphere of work and the private sphere. A recent study by Sarah J. Tracy and Kendra Dyanne Rivera point to ways in which scripts about men's and women's roles at home and at work have both shifted and remained relatively impervious to change in recent years.

Tracy and Rivera (2010) interviewed thirteen male executives about the relationship between work and home and the roles of men and women in these life spheres. The voices of male executives have rarely been heard in this type of research but are undoubtedly important. As Tracy and Rivera argue, "Because male executive gatekeepers play a pivotal role in shaping organizational policy, culture, and practice, it is important to hear what they have to say" (2010, p. 4). The men interviewed, aged thirty to forty-nine, were all married and had children. Seven of them had wives who did not work for pay outside of the home. The researchers analyzed transcripts of the interviews, looking at both what these men said about work and home and how they said it.

This research revealed a number of fascinating findings regarding the ideology of work and home life among male executives. When asked about their abstract attitudes regarding gender equity, respondents noted that work–home balance was an issue for both men and women and that home life should take precedence over work concerns. However, these abstract attitudes were not reflected when these men talked about their own lives and families. Indeed, Tracy and Rivera note that "when we asked participants about their own practices as well as their specific hopes for their children's futures, a different story emerged" (2010, p. 15).

This alternate story is one in which women have a "choice" about working (ignoring the many women who need an income to support themselves and their families) and in which navigating the challenges of work and home is the responsibility of the woman (not her spouse or the organization). These male executives looked at their own home lives and used these personal experiences as templates for organizational policy. For example, Nathaniel looked at his own family life with a stay-at-home wife and preschooler and stated that it was unreasonable to expect "the working person to be home by a given time ... because of the dynamics of the day-to-day working environment" (Tracy & Rivera, 2010, p. 18). Furthermore, these male executives looked to the future with a similar vision for work and home life—they saw specific career options for their sons, but "when speaking of their daughters, interviewees often focused on their daughter's family life" (Tracy & Rivera, 2010, p. 21).

Tracy and Rivera (2010) came away from their study somewhat discouraged about this enduring ideology about the roles of men and women in the workplace. After all, the beliefs of organizational leaders can have a strong impact on the organizational culture and on specific policies. However, they also express some hope for the future. The men they interviewed were interested in the topic and willing to engage the issue. Furthermore, in considering the manner in which ideas were communicated, Tracy and Rivera found that respondents often had increased rates of pauses and verbal fillers such as "ums" and "ahs" when talking about the complex relationship between work and home. The researchers believe "that the number of disfluencies and talk repairs in the data are not just signs of embarrassment or political correctness but also signify that executives' viewpoints on these issues are in a state of flux" (Tracy & Rivera, 2010, p. 31). Thus, although the ideology of sexism was still apparent in these executives' talk, there were also "flickers of transformation" (Tracy & Rivera, 2010, p. 3).

Tracy, S. J. & Rivera, K. D. (2010). Endorsing equity and applauding stay-at-home moms: How male voices on work-life reveal aversive sexism and flickers of transformation. *Management Communication Quarterly, 24*, 3–43.

In summary, the theory of concertive control argues that power is embedded in a system of identification and discipline. Workers identify with the values and norms of management and then use these values as a basis for making workplace decisions and for disciplining other members of the work team. Even in a workplace designed with democratic and participatory ideals (or with the culture of a family or team—see Casey, 1999), the ideology of management is upheld through the everyday practices of organization members.

FEMINIST APPROACHES

In past editions of this textbook, the discussion of feminist approaches in organizational communication was framed as a subset of critical approaches. That is, I positioned gender as one source of power in the organization that could implicate the issues of ideology, hegemony, emancipation, and resistance that we've encountered here. This is a comfortable way to position feminist scholarship, as it draws on familiar terms and can find a comfortable academic home. However, Karen Ashcraft (2005) argues that this positioning is problematic: "In this light, feminist scholarship looks like a subsidiary branch of critical organization inquiry, narrow in scope compared with the broader emancipatory agenda of the critical project" (p. 143). She notes that this is only one of several ways to recount the development of feminist organizational communication scholarship.

Another way of narrating this story is to turn to early research on the different experiences of men and women in the workplace. During the late decades of the twentieth century, both public and academic attention turned to such issues, including the notion of a "glass ceiling" that prevented women from moving up in the management hierarchy (Morrison & Von Glinow, 1990), the idea that when women rise to higher ranks they are seen as "tokens" (Kanter, 1977), and arguments that men and women have very different communication patterns (Tannen, 1994) that implicate distinctive styles of leadership (Natalle, 1996). These ideas were often seen as problematic, however, because they suggest a model of gender that is binary—either male or female—and that oversimplifies both historical and ongoing communication processes. Second, this research often treated all women as having the same set of problems, and because studies most often involved women who were white, middle-class, heterosexual, and professional, a wide swath of women (e.g., women of color, working class women, lesbians) were ignored or misrepresented. Third, this research tended to see gender issues as interpersonal and psychological issues that occurred within a neutral organization. We discussed critiques of the container metaphor in Chapter 5, and these critiques are especially important when considering issues of gender, as the metaphor suggests that there is nothing problematic about the ways in which the organization has been constituted (Acker, 1990) and instead places the blame on individuals.

In contract to these two ways of situating feminist organizational communication (either as a subset of critical approaches or in terms of the distinct experiences of men and women within a neutral organization), Ashcraft emphasizes the links of feminist organizational communication scholarship with the larger feminist movement. This movement emphasizes **activism** and an intellectual framework that sees issues of

feminism and organizing within a constitutive framework. Ashcraft believes that feminist scholarship in organizational communication resonates with this emphasis and "reflects an entrenched commitment to do more than talk within the walls of an ivory tower; it embodies the desire for tangible forms of justice that enhance the lives of real people" (2005, p. 145).

Let's consider first the intellectual framework in this account of feminist organizational communication. This approach begins with the basic ideas that organizations—in their traditional and bureaucratic forms—are inherently patriarchal (see, e.g., Ferguson, 1984). For example, Buzzanell (1994) argues that traditional views of organizational communication highlight the importance of individualism, cause-and-effect thinking, and autonomy. In such a bureaucratic workplace, the most valued commodities are the stereotypical male characteristics of logic, aggressiveness, and competitiveness. In contrast, stereotypical female characteristics—such as emotion, empathy, intuition, connectedness, and cooperation—are likely to be downplayed in organizational life. Feminist scholars also argue that the concepts used to understand organizational life (such as rationality and hierarchy) tend to be male-biased (see, e.g., Mumby & Putnam, 1992) and that the very structure of language is patriarchal (see, e.g., Penelope, 1990). These ideas all point to an overall pattern in which the organization is constituted in gendered ways, and this point is foundational for feminist organizational scholars. Ashcraft (2005) provides more detail by enumerating a number of key theoretical assumptions shared by scholars who take a feminist approach to organizational communication research. These include (see Ashcraft, 2005, pp. 153–155):

- The belief that gender is a primary way in which identity and power relations are configured.
- The belief that work is a key site where gender identity and power relations are organized.
- A belief that dominant systems of gender privilege men and masculinity relative to women and femininity, although these systems are not rigid or neatly drawn.
- A belief that gender, power, and organization are continuously created and changed in ongoing everyday life and that communication is the process through which this is accomplished.
- A belief that, in addition to the centrality of communication, material conditions are also critical for an understanding of gender, organization, and power.

These are some of the important intellectual commitments of those who take a feminist approach to organizational communication. However, in emphasizing the roots of this approach in the larger feminist movement, it is important to also consider issues regarding the social world beyond academia and the variety of paths feminist activism can take. Within this focus on activism, there are a variety of views regarding what should be done (see Buzzanell, 1994; Mumby, 1996). For example, *liberal feminists* believe that remedies for female subordination should come from within the system and that women should work to gain their fair share of control in institutions currently run by men. Other feminists balk at this approach, arguing that it only serves to support the patriarchal nature of society. *Radical*

Case in Point: Using the F Word

In recent years, the word *feminist* has fallen into disrepute. As Anna Quindlen (2003) states in a column entitled "Still Needing the F Word," people see the word feminist as inappropriate, offensive, or simply off-putting. In part, this reputation can be attributed to commentators who see feminists as activists for an unwanted agenda ("femi-nazis"). However, this current disregard for feminism also stems from the belief that we are now in an era in which all the battles have been won. As Quindlen states, "[Conventional wisdom has it that we've moved on to a postfeminist era, which is meant to suggest that the issues have been settled, the inequities addressed, and all is right with the world" (p. 74).

However, recent research suggests that feminists have not progressed as far as they would like (e.g.,

pay inequity remains a major problem, and women still struggle against sexual harassment in the workplace) and may even have taken a few steps backward. For example, Quindlen argues that although women in the past felt pressured to be the perfect housewife and mother, women today strive to be models of perfection in the workplace while maintaining the same old pressures at home. In *The Second Shift* (1993), Arlie Hochschild argues that women still do the majority of domestic work even while taking on enhanced responsibility at work. In other words, says Quindlen, "[W]omen have won the right to do as much as men do. They just haven't won the right to do as little as men do" (p. 74).

feminists believe that emancipation for women can occur only through the destruction of male-dominated institutions or through the total separation of women from these institutions. Other feminists argue for more symbolic courses of action. *Standpoint feminists* work to enhance the opportunity for a variety of marginalized voices to be heard within societal dialogue, and *postmodern feminists* attempt to "deconstruct" male-dominated meaning systems in order to highlight women's perspectives. Ashcraft (2000) argued for a hybrid form of feminism that she calls *pluralist feminism*. Ashcraft's research suggests that even in feminist organizations, there are pragmatic contingencies that constrain an idealistic view of feminism. In developing pluralist feminism, scholars could become "responsive to the needs of organizations that seek social change yet cannot fully embrace antibureaucratic, countercapitalist ideals and practices" (Ashcraft, 2000, p. 381).

Feminist scholarship within organizational communication research is expanding rapidly. Some researchers consider specific practices that illustrate the gendered nature of organizations; for example, Norander and Harter (2012) described the ways in which women in an nongovernmental organization (NGO) worked for their own version of political action by concentrating on long-term networking and relationships. Others have examined the intersections of gender with race and class in organizational life (e.g., Parker, 2003). Recently, D'Enbeau and Buzzanell (2011) considered the ways in which workers at a feminist popular culture magazine balanced their commitment to feminist ideology with the challenges of the marketplace. Still others have investigated whether there are communicative differences between traditional bureaucratic organizations and woman-controlled and nonhierarchical organizations (e.g., Buzzanell et al., 1997). We will briefly consider three areas of study to provide a sampling of feminist scholarship in organizational communication.

Sexual Harassment

Because of its ongoing presence in the workplace, the issue of **sexual harassment** is an important strand of research for feminist scholars. Scholars who began looking at sexual harassment as a communication phenomenon in the 1990s emphasized the crucial point that harassment is an expression of power, not of sexuality. "It is the antithesis of intimacy, self-knowledge and growth" (Taylor & Conrad, 1992, p. 414). Further, research has revealed that men and women see sexual harassment very differently because of contrasting experiences with power and fear (Dougherty, 1999) and different socialization regarding masculinity and femininity (Scarduzio & Geist-Martin, 2010). For example, Dougherty (2001) found that behaviors such as sexual joking and innuendo that women viewed as harassment were seen by men as a way to release tension from their stressful jobs.

One representative investigation of sexual harassment in the feminist tradition (Clair, 1993) examined the narratives of women talking about their experiences in the workplace. Clair examined the "framing devices" women used in the telling of these harassment stories. For example, a woman could frame her story as "simple misunderstanding," or she could trivialize the event. The framing devices examined and their definitions are presented in Table 6.2. Clair argued that the frames used by women often served to reinforce the dominant ideology—an example of the concept of *hegemony* we discussed earlier in this chapter. That is, viewing sexual harassment as "a harmless joke" or "mere flirting" or "the way things are" are ways of normalizing and even supporting the patriarchal underpinnings of the workplace.

Table 6.2 | Framing Devices on Sexual Harassment Narratives

Framing Device	Explanation
Accepting dominant interests	Sexual harassment accepted or justified as a less important problem than other managerial concerns
Simple misunderstanding	Sexual harassment accepted or justified as "mere flirting"
Reification	Sexual harassment accepted or justified as "the way things are"
Trivialization	Sexual harassment accepted or justified as "a harmless joke"
Denotative hesitancy	Sexually harassing encounter not defined by the term sexual harassment
Public/private expression—public/private domain	Sexual harassment described as part of private—rather than public—life or described using private forms of expression (e.g., embarrassment, fear)

Based on Clair, R. P. (1993b). The use of framing devices to sequester organizational narratives: Hegemony and harassment. *Communication Monographs, 60,* 113–136.

Discourse at Women-Led Businesses

Many feminist scholars argue that life can be different in an organization that exemplifies feminist values such as cooperation, emotion, and support. Paige Edley (2000) examined this assumption in her study of a woman-owned interior design firm that employed mainly women (the only men were part-time delivery and warehouse workers). One of her major findings was that although everyone in the organization "talked the talk" of a cooperative and flexible workplace (e.g., one in which family concerns were taken seriously), the owner of the business often did not "walk that talk." Instead, the owner often publicly derided those who took too much time off for family concerns or kept those individuals from key work assignments. Second, although Edley found that communication in this organization was often marked by emotion and conflict, such interaction was often labeled as simply the way women talk. Edley (2000, p. 293) reports that "conversations were filled with references to women as cranky and moody and blaming nonverbal expressions of anger on PMS [premenstrual syndrome]." By blaming their anger and emotional outbursts on "the way women are," workers in this organization could downplay the importance of conflict in the organization. Thus, Edley found that, in many ways, the women in this organization played into the sexual stereotypes of women. This sounds, in many ways, like a very negative construction of women within this woman's organization. However, Edley argues that there were rewards for the women, as they saw themselves as working in an ideal workplace in which they could speak and act as women.

Another study of a woman-led business was conducted by Tracy Everbach (2007) who looked at the culture of the first newspaper in the United States to have an all-women management team. Everbach found that the workplace had more family-friendly policies, more openness in communication, and more egalitarian decision-making. But workers also reported that the atmosphere had become more gossipy and catty, and some believed that assertive reporting behaviors were encouraged. Interestingly, the content of the newspaper changed very little—Everbach suggests that the news becomes "masculinized even when reported by women" (Everbach, 2007, p. 481).

Disciplined Bodies

Finally, the research of Angela Trethewey (1999, 2000, 2001; Trethewey, Scott & LeGreco, 2006) has examined how the organizational context—as well as society and culture in general—serves to discipline women in terms of bodily display. For example, she reviews research that has considered the ideal body for white, middle-class women. These bodies have a particular size and shape that must be maintained through diet and exercise regimes. These bodies must pay careful attention to nonverbal movement—walking, sitting, and gesturing in particular ways. These bodies must be displayed with makeup and clothing that exhibit the appropriate level of femininity. And these bodies can become particularly problematic when they age in ways that don't comport to societal ideals.

Trethewey argues that women are faced with a conundrum in the workplace: Although a "professional body" is strong and competent, such a body might contradict the nurturing and soft body of traditional femininity. How are women to manage this dilemma? Trethewey's interviews with a wide range of professional women provided several answers to this question. First, women clearly saw a professional body as a fit body that symbolized discipline and endurance. Second, women believed they needed to control their nonverbal displays in a way that communicated strength—but that was nonthreatening. For example, one of Trethewey's respondents said, "We still need to have that firm handshake, but don't overdo it" (Trethewey, 2000, p. 119). Finally, women talked about the need to control and discipline the female body's tendency to "leak out through unruly clothing, menstrual bleeding, pregnancy, or emotional displays" (Trethewey, 2000, p. 20). Such a leaking body calls attention to the feminine and private nature of a woman's body in a public context that values control.

SUMMARY

At the beginning of this chapter, we noted two threads that underlie classical, human relations, human resources, systems, cultural and constitutive approaches to organizational communication: (1) Organizations consist of unitary or pluralist systems of control, and (2) the organizational theorist's job is to understand and explain. The critical and feminist approaches we considered in this chapter have questioned these basic assumptions. We first looked at critical approaches and examined important concepts such as power, ideology, hegemony, and resistance and considered concertive control theory as an example of a critical theory developed by organizational communication scholars. We then moved on to feminist approaches and argued that these approaches can best be seen as an extension of the larger feminist movement rather than a subset of critical theory. We concluded by considering three strains of research that exemplify contemporary feminist organizational communication scholarship.

DISCUSSION QUESTIONS

1. Many abstract concepts are important to critical work in organizational communication. How do these concepts fit together? For example, how is ideology related to hegemony? How is power related to discourse? How is emancipation related to resistance?

2. Think about how the terminology used in an organization or the stories told in an organization contribute to power imbalances. What are ways of fighting against these imbalances?

3. If you are a woman, do the studies of feminist organizing described in this chapter ring true for you? Do you have other stories about the challenges of being a woman in a patriarchal organization? If you are a man, are these studies revealing to you? Do you think men suffer from similar constraints in the workplace?

KEY CONCEPTS

unitary frame of reference
pluralist frame of reference
radical frame of reference
radical-critical approach

organizational sources of power
modes and means of production
workplace alienation and
    oppression

organizational discourse
ideology
hegemony
emancipation

resistance
simple control
technological control
concertive control

identification
discipline
feminism
patriarchy

activism
sexual harassment

CASE STUDY | **Talking Turkey**

Brandon and Gabriella Houston were both home from college for Thanksgiving weekend. Brandon, a senior, attended a state university about ninety miles from home. Gabriella, a sophomore, attended a small college in a neighboring state. Both were home for the first time during the school year and were spending some time catching up. As they lounged in the living room watching football, the smell of roast turkey wafted through the house, and assorted relatives milled around munching on celery sticks and green olives.

Brandon and Gabriella's parents contributed the lion's share of their children's college expenses, footing the bill for tuition and the majority of room and board. However, both Brandon and Gabriella had to pitch in a small portion of the housing tab and cover any incidental expenses they might incur. Thus, both held part-time jobs while going to school. Brandon worked twenty hours per week at the Baxter Company, a small manufacturing firm that assembled corrugated boxes. It was boring but dependable work and paid slightly better than minimum wage. Gabriella worked for Personal Greetings, a small company that specialized in personalized party greetings, including singing telegrams and "strip-o-grams." Gabriella worked eight to ten jobs per week (each job lasted about an hour) and earned $25 per job plus tips. Brandon was mortified when he heard what Gabriella was doing to earn her college money. "Gabs, I can't believe you're taking off your clothes for money! Does Mom know what you're doing?"

"Well, not exactly, but I don't think she'd mind. Mom and Dad are pretty liberal about these things, and I don't actually take off all my clothes. It's really pretty innocent—just some entertainment for people who like to have a good time. Unlike you, brother dear. Besides," Gabriella added, "I make great money. I usually pull in over $400 a week for about ten hours of work. Can you say the same?"

"The money isn't the point. And neither is being liberal or conservative, for that matter. The point is

that you're being exploited. You may be making $400 a week, but you can bet that Personal Greetings is making a lot more than that. And they're making it off your body. How can you be a woman in this day and age and allow people to do this to you—isn't this the very thing that feminists have been fighting against for years?"

"Well, maybe the feminists are wrong about this," Gabriella replied. "It seems to me that everyone is benefiting from this situation. I make great money and can support myself while I get an education and move on to something else in my life. The company is highly successful and can keep paying people like me a good wage. And the customers are getting a service that they're eager to pay for. Who loses? If you want to see someone being exploited, you should just look at yourself, Brandon."

"What do you mean? I'm doing good honest work. I may not be paid a lot, but at least I'm keeping my clothes on!"

"Yeah, I'm stripped of my clothes, and you're just stripped of your dignity," Gabriella retorted while Brandon stared back in disbelief. "The Baxter Company is making money hand over fist, and they've got you working for minimum wage. They set your hours, they give you boring work to do, they control when you can take a break, and who you can talk to on the job. And you just shuffle along and pick up your paycheck and feel good because you're doing 'honest work.' Maybe your kind of job is the American way, but I'd rather wiggle my butt for a living and have a lot of free time to study and have some fun!"

Gabriella and Brandon's mother stood at the doorway. "I think dinner's ready, kids. We've got turkey, cornbread dressing, cranberry sauce, green bean casserole, corn, and three kinds of pie. I don't think anyone will go hungry today!"

Brandon led the way past his mother into the dining room. As he left, he turned back for one last parting shot. "Sounds great, Mom, and I'll take an extra

CASE STUDY | **Talking Turkey** *continued*

portion of dressing. Given Gaby's current line of work, I don't think she'll be wanting any."

CASE ANALYSIS QUESTIONS

1. How would you evaluate the argument between Brandon and Gabriella? Are either or both of them being exploited? If so, how?
2. How does this discussion illustrate the concepts of power, ideology, and hegemony?
3. What oppressive structures of organization and communication are in evidence in the jobs held by Brandon and Gabriella? Do either Gabriella or Brandon participate in a system of concertive control?
4. Does a feminist approach serve to shed any additional light on the job held by Gabriella? Would different types of feminist theory reach different conclusions about the nature of her job?
5. How would a critical theorist work to achieve emancipation for Brandon and Gabriella? Would either of them want to be emancipated? How could either Brandon or Gabriella exercise resistance in their work?

Socialization Processes

CHAPTER 7

AFTER READING THIS CHAPTER, YOU SHOULD ...

- Appreciate the importance of understanding processes of organizational socialization and exit.
- Know the three major phases of organizational socialization—anticipatory socialization, encounter, and metamorphosis—and know which critical communication processes are active in each phase.
- Be familiar with the types of information typically learned during socialization and understand the processes (such as information seeking) through which this information can be gained.
- Understand the functions of an employment interview and the different roles that the interviewer and interviewee play.
- Be able to explain the processes through which roles are developed and negotiated over time in organizational settings.
- Appreciate the increasing influence of communication technologies at all stages of the organizational socialization process.
- Understand the implications of demographic and cultural changes for organizational exit and retirement and be familiar with how exit often happens in organizations.

In times past, people would often work for one organization throughout their entire life. Perhaps it was a family business, a farm, or a corporation that nurtured long-term relationships with employees. However, in the United States today, the odds are that you will work for several or many organizations in your lifetime. Our society has become increasingly mobile, and people switch jobs and even careers with great frequency. With all these organizational "comings and goings," it becomes useful to understand the processes through which individuals and organizations adapt to each other.

Fred Jablin and his colleagues use the term **assimilation** to refer to "those ongoing behavioral and cognitive processes by which individuals join, become integrated into, and exit organizations" (Jablin & Krone, 1987, p. 712). Assimilation is a dual process. On the one hand, the organization is trying to influence the adaptation of individuals through formal and informal **socialization** processes. For example, socialization occurs when an individual learns about the requirements of the job or decides that dressing formally will help him fit into the organizational culture. In contrast, an employee may try to change some aspect of the organization to better suit her needs, abilities, or desires. This type of change happens through the process of **individualization**. Individualization might occur, for example, if a new employee develops an improved strategy for collecting payments on overdue accounts or if a group of new employees starts a new tradition of going out for beers on Friday after work. These two processes—socialization and individualization—play out over time as an individual encounters and becomes part of an organization.

In this chapter, we consider the role of communication in organizational assimilation. Because most of the research concentrates on socialization, our attention will focus on these processes, although we will not ignore the ways in which an individual is active in a variety of entry and role development activities. In the next few pages, we first look at models that lay out the stages and the content of socialization. Then, for the largest share of the chapter, we look at some key communication processes that occur during socialization. We first consider the dynamics of the **employment interview**. Then, we look at how individuals entering organizations obtain information through formal and informal channels. Next, we consider the ongoing "role development" processes that characterize a person's continuing adaptation to the organization. Finally, we look at communication processes during **organizational exit** and retirement.

MODELS OF ORGANIZATIONAL SOCIALIZATION

The processes through which individuals adapt to organizational life are complicated (see Kramer, 2010, for a comprehensive review of organizational socialization research). These processes develop over a great span of time and involve many organizational members and activities. Thus, a number of scholars have attempted to better understand organizational socialization by developing theories that model portions of the socialization process. We consider two aspects of socialization in the following sections. We first look at how socialization unfolds over time and then we consider what is "learned" during the assimilation process.

Phases of Socialization

When an employee joins an organization, adaptation is not automatic and immediate. Rather, adjusting to organizational life takes place gradually. Scholars considering this process often divide socialization into three phases. Of course, these phases are not cut-and-dried across people or time. Indeed, the socialization process is undoubtedly marked by "turning points" in which individuals become more (or less) connected to the organization (Bulks & Bach, 1989). These turning points will be different for each individual and may include events such as promotions, changes in job responsibility, or perhaps a new boss or coworker who changes the atmosphere in the workplace. In this sense, then, socialization is a process that may have many ups and downs and sometimes may not seem to follow a distinct pattern. However, despite the individual nature of the socialization process, the consideration of phases has proven to be a useful tool for studying many of the processes

Table 7.1 | Stages of the Socialization Process

Stage	Description
Anticipatory socialization	Socialization that occurs before entry into the organization. Encompasses both socialization to an occupation and socialization to an organization.
Encounter	Sensemaking stage that occurs when a new employee enters the organization. The newcomer must let go of old roles and values in adapting to the expectations of the new organization.
Metamorphosis	The state reached at the "completion" of the socialization process. The new employee is now accepted as an organizational insider.

that individuals experience as they enter organizations. In this section, then, we will consider three such phases: **anticipatory socialization, encounter,** and **metamorphosis.** These phases are summarized in Table 7.1.

Anticipatory Socialization Anticipatory socialization refers to socialization processes that occur before an individual actually enters an organization (Van Maanen, 1975). There are several aspects to anticipatory socialization: learning about work in general, learning about a particular occupation, and learning about a particular organization.

In a very basic sense, we grow up learning about what "work" means. This knowledge can come from a variety of sources. Children might learn about the nature of work through participating in household chores or completing school assignments (Bowes & Goodnow, 1996). For an eight-year-old, a parent's or teacher's order to "get your work done" has a great deal of meaning, and recent public debates about appropriate levels of homework suggest that some believe this socialization into the rigors of work may come too quickly. The meaning of work is also developed through part-time employment during the teen years (Barling, Rogers & Kelloway, 1995), through interactions with friends (Levine & Hoffner, 2006), and through media contact. Indeed, as we discussed in Chapter 6, Clair (1996) argues that by the time an individual in the United States reaches college, the notion of having a "real job" has taken on a very specific meaning imbued with the values of a capitalist economy.

Anticipatory socialization also involves ideas about the nature of specific careers and occupations, a process scholars call "vocational anticipatory socialization" (Myers, Jahn, Gaillard, & Stoltzfus, 2011). Before even starting school, many children have an answer to the question "What do you want to be when you grow up?" One girl might dream about being a veterinarian because she loves her dog so much; a boy might want to be a police officer because of what he has seen on television. These ideas about particular careers can stem from a variety of sources, especially family members and the media (Hoffner, Levine & Toohey, 2008), vary a great deal across cultures (Berkelaar, Buzzanell, Kisselburgh, Tan & Shen, 2012), and are often highly idealized and inaccurate. However, it is clear that ideas about possible occupations begin early in life. As the child grows up, he or she learns more about what it means to work in a particular field. Our vet-to-be, for instance, might read books about working with animals or visit the local small-animal clinic. When she goes to college and vet school, she learns even more about her chosen occupation. Thus, from childhood onward, she is being socialized into an occupational role.

The third portion of anticipatory socialization involves learning about a particular organization. For example, many college graduates go through the ritual of interviewing with prospective employers through the campus placement center and investigate possible job sites through the Internet. Consider a college senior contemplating work with CompuStuff, a computer software company. Before even signing up for an interview, she is likely to learn a great deal about CompuStuff through its website, through social media such as Facebook and Twitter, and through media coverage of CompuStuff. Information obtained in this way might include objective characteristics such as the company's structure, goals, and financial position and public impressions of the company. Then, through the interviewing process, she enhances her understanding of CompuStuff by learning more about what it might be like to work for CompuStuff—job responsibilities, salary, what other employees might be like. Before setting foot on company grounds, she is able to anticipate details of her possible work life at CompuStuff.

Encounter   The second phase of socialization occurs at the organizational "point of entry," when a new employee first encounters life on the job. Louis (1980) describes the encounter experience as one of change, contrast, and surprise, and she argues that the newcomer must work to make sense of the new organizational culture. In order to interpret life in the new organization, the newcomer relies on predispositions, past experiences, and the interpretations of others. There are times when an individual might already know a great deal about the organization. For example, Gibson and Papa (2000) found that entering blue-collar workers in a company town already knew a great deal about the organization from family members and others in the community—for these individuals, entry was a "relatively effortless absorption of organizational values, beliefs, and understandings" (Gibson & Papa, 2000, p. 84). For most people entering a new organization, however, the encounter phase of socialization can cause a great deal of stress for the newcomer. Thus, the encounter phase encompasses learning about a new organization and role and letting go of old values, expectations, and behaviors.

The encounter phase can involve a wide variety of formal and informal communication processes. These include organizationally designed orientation programs (Van Maanen & Schein, 1979) and formal and informal mentoring (Zey, 1991). When organizational programs and systems are well-designed and work toward investing the newcomer in the company's goals and culture, they can be successful in enhancing commitment and reducing turnover (Allen, 2006). For example, Stephens and Dailey recently found that orientation programs can be very effective in enhancing the extent to which new employees identify with the organization— particularly if the new employee had previous experiences and knowledge to draw on. In addition to organizational programs, the encounter phase involves extensive information-seeking on the part of the employee (Miller & Jabin, 1991). We will

Spotlight on Scholarship: Organizational Entry as a Laughing Matter

We've all been there. Those awkward times on a new job when we're not sure what's going on. We may giggle nervously at things to cover our discomfort. We may wonder if others are laughing at us or laughing with us. Or we might be grateful that others joke about how difficult their own first days on the job were. In short, the period of organizational entrance is filled with stress and ambiguity, and humor can play an important role in helping us understand the new job and our connection to others in the organization. Sarah N. Heiss and Heather J. Carmack recently explored the often understudied role of humor in organizational life in considering the ways in which both newcomers and veterans use humor to make sense of organizational entry experiences.

As Heiss and Carmack note, "the hiring of new organizational members is a form of organizational change that brings challenges for both the new and veteran members of the organization" (Heiss & Carmack, 2012, p. 108). Humor can be helpful in managing uncertainty and in relieving stress, but it can also heighten anxiety if newcomers don't get the humor that is often based on shared understandings and past experiences. The researchers explored these issues through a study of a vocational counseling center that involved both participant observation of work interactions and interviews with organizational members. Through their investigation, they found that humor was instrumental in the entrance process in three important ways.

First, humor was often used to communicate job expectations in indirect ways. For example, the director of the center noted that "Teasing is a way

to say 'you're doing something wrong' without just saying it" (Heiss & Carmack, 2012, p. 116). Newcomers might have appreciated more direct instruction about tasks, but humor was often seen as more socially appropriate. Second, humor was used to inculcate newcomers with the values of the organizational culture. One frequently observed event was joking about late arrival at staff meetings. If employees were tardy, they might be met with a comment like "glad you made it" and subsequent chuckling. The authors note that "these discursive rituals let employees know that their tardiness did not go unnoticed. Additionally, these rituals reify the organizational values for veterans" (Heiss & Carmack, 2012, p. 120).

Finally, humor served to communicate organizational affiliation. Humor was sometimes used as way to select appropriate employees and the appreciation of one's sense of humor often seen as a mark that an employee really belonged to the workgroup. For example, one employee recounted a day he returned from time off for a health problem to encounter a large poster with messages both supportive and teasing: "And I know they took shots at me, but their intentions—I interpreted it was good. I was really part of the group" (Heiss & Carmack, 2012, p. 124). Humor as a mark of affiliation is often a double-edged sword, however. For just as humor can indicate you are part of the group, there are often times when you know that you're not in on the joke. And that's no laughing matter.

Heiss, S. N., & Carmack, H. J. (2012). Knock, knock; who's there? Making sense of organizational entrance through humor. *Management Communication Quarterly, 26*, 106–132.

deal more extensively with the proactive role of the individual in the encounter phase later in this chapter.

Metamorphosis   The final stage of the socialization process occurs when the new employee has made the transition from outsider to insider. "During this stage the recruit begins to become an accepted, participating member of the organization by learning new behaviors and attitudes and/or modifying existing ones" (Jablin & Krone, 1987, p. 713). This is not to suggest, however, that the relationship between the individual and the organization is static at this point because there is always some measure of flux and uncertainty in employees' understandings of organizational roles and culture. Furthermore, even long-established members of an organization must deal with the ongoing processes of new employees becoming part of the organization (Gallagher & Sias, 2009).

This flux within the **metamorphosis stage** is demonstrated in work by Michael Kramer (e.g., Kramer, 1993) analyzing the process of adjusting to job transfers within an organization. When individuals transfer from one job to another within an organization, they typically are not seen as "new" employees and thus are not provided formal socialization experiences. Yet, these individuals must still cope with new job requirements, new social relationships, and sometimes a new location. Kramer's work has highlighted the ways in which transferring from one job to another constitutes part of the continuing socialization experience and how communication with the supervisor and coworkers in the new job can serve to ease the transition experience.

Content of Socialization

In addition to considering the socialization process over time (the *when* of socialization), researchers have also looked at the content of socialization—what must be learned in order to adapt to the organizational context. For example, Louis distinguished two classes of information that must be grasped during the socialization process: **role-related information** and **cultural information**. Role-related information encompasses the information, skills, procedures, and rules that an individual must grasp to perform on the job. For example, a new secretary might need to learn about the organization's word-processing programs, filing system, and bookkeeping procedures to adapt to his role in the organization.

A new organizational member must also learn about the organizational culture. Learning about the organizational culture can be much more complex than comprehending role-related information, as formal documentation regarding cultural norms rarely exists and current organizational members might have a difficult time articulating these values for the newcomer. Indeed, Stohl (1986) found that much of socialization occurs through the communication of "memorable messages"—narratives and cultural truisms that stick with employees as they continue on in their employment with the organization (see also Dallimore, 2003).

Myers and Oetzel (2003) proposed a model that provides greater detail about the processes involved in socialization. Although these processes involve more than just the content of socialization, they are useful for considering the various issues that newcomers must cope with when entering an organization. Specifically, these processes include: developing a familiarity with others, acculturating or learning the culture of the organization, feeling recognized by others, becoming involved in the organization, developing job competency, and role negotiation. Not surprisingly, organizational context will make a difference in terms of which particular processes take precedence in the socialization process. For example, Myers (2005) found that role negotiation was not important among firefighters, but that the specific relational task of establishing trustworthiness was critical.

Summary of Socialization Models

In summary, a variety of models have been proposed to help us better understand the organizational socialization process. Phase models of socialization help us understand the *when* of socialization—how individuals move from anticipating occupational and organizational life to becoming integrated organizational members. Content models of socialization help us understand the *what* of socialization by differentiating between role-related and cultural information. Embedded within these notions of *when* and *what* are a variety of processes through which assimilation occurs: formal training programs, mentoring, interviewing, outside research, and relationships with managers, coworkers, and subordinates.

In the next section, we look more carefully at the role of communication in the socialization process. We first examine three aspects of socialization in which communication plays a crucial role. The first of these—communication during the employment interview—is closely tied to anticipatory socialization. We then consider the second aspect: ways newcomers seek information during the encounter phase of socialization. Next, we discuss the third aspect, which is the ongoing communication in the role development process that characterizes the metamorphosis stage of socialization and the sense of identification that individuals develop with their organizations and careers. Following our discussion of these phases, we will examine the role of communication technologies across a variety of socialization processes. Then, in the final section of this chapter, we will consider communication processes during organizational exit—a sometimes forgotten phase of organizational transition.

COMMUNICATION PROCESSES DURING SOCIALIZATION

Recruiting and Interviewing

Processes involved in getting a job can be very different depending on issues such as the industry involved, the age and experience of the potential employee, and the specific needs of the organization. A new college graduate will typically take advantage of the campus career center and perhaps contacts with friends and family or the college alumni network. For individuals in service or manufacturing sectors, the process is likely to involve Internet searches, consideration of classified advertisements, personal contacts, and sometimes pounding the pavement by visiting possible employers. For some experienced professionals and the companies that hire them, this process might involve a head-hunting firm that tries to match the talents and experiences of the job searcher with the needs of the organization.

The initial phases of this process of matchmaking used to be relatively straightforward. An individual would indicate interest in a job by submitting a job application or a résumé and cover letter. The hiring officer at the company would review the materials and decide if the organization wanted to pursue things further with an interview and the process would move on from there. However, technology

Case in Point: The 140 Character Résumé

You may have heard of the "elevator speech" idea regarding job and career. This idea suggests that you should be able to explain what you want to do in a job or career in a straightforward way to a stranger during an elevator ride. These days, though, a tweet may be "the new elevator pitch" (Silverman & Weber, 2013) so you may need to work on getting all of the key ideas for your value to a company down to 140 characters. Though the use of Twitter hasn't yet revolutionized the job search process, some employees can see the definite advantage to the social networking site as a recruiting tool.

Experts see Twitter being used in a number of ways in the recruiting process (Silverman & Weber, 2013). In addition to evaluating the self-presentation skills demonstrated in a tweeted résumé, employers can watch a candidate's Twitter feed to get a sense of a potential employer. Silverman and Weber (2013) quote a talent acquisition manger named Jocelyn Lai who says, "I watch people interact, learn what their positions are, who their best friends on Twitter are, whether they have a sense of humor. From that you can get a pretty good picture." At this point, the use of Twitter as a recruiting and screening tool hasn't been seen a lot beyond "corners of the job market, such as media and technology" (Silverman & Weber, 2013). It wouldn't be a surprise, though, if the 140 character résumé is "trending" very soon.

now allows for the screening of résumés before they ever hit human eyes through the use of "data extractors" (Ramer, 2003), so job searchers are encouraged to create résumés with the content, key words and phrases, and formatting that will appeal to these technological screening processes (Connolly, 2012). Further, once a prospective employee gets a foot in the door, hiring officers can now access social networking sites to learn more about the potential hire (Bohnert & Ross, 2010; Brown & Vaughn, 2011). Looking at a Facebook timeline can provide positive information about a potential employee's education and experience, but a search could also reveal embarrassing events and photos (Finder, 2006), so job seekers are often advised to clean their pages of troublesome "red Solo Cup®" moments.

Once past these initial steps of search and recruitment, the most widely used tool in the hiring process is the employment interview (Powell & Goulet, 1996). In an employment interview, an organizational representative (or, perhaps, a group of representatives) and a potential employee come together for questions, answers, and conversation. The setting for the interview might be a college placement center, an employment office, the organization itself, Skype, or phone. The outcome of the interview might be an offer of employment, a chance at a second interview, or a polite "thanks but no thanks." The employment interview serves three basic functions. First, as an organizational representative, the interviewer is using the interview to recruit potential employees and make decisions about the quality of those recruits. Second, the applicant is using the interview as a way to find out more about the organization. Third, as a point of first contact between the organization and the applicant, the interview serves as a socialization tool—that is, as a way to facilitate the adaptation of the applicant should he or she be hired.

The Interview as a Recruiting and Screening Tool   From the organization's perspective, the main function of the employment interview is the recruiting and screening of potential employees. The hiring organization has typically already screened résumés and letters of application to cull down the number of candidates considered for a position. Then, in an interview, the organizational representative has precious little time to make assessments about additional factors that aren't obvious on paper—such as the interviewee's motivation, communication skills, and personality. Although there are differences in style from interviewer to interviewer, research points to some definite patterns in how the interview is used to recruit and screen applicants.

First, most interviewers gather information in relatively structured ways. Indeed, reviews of the research literature (e.g., Campion, Palmer & Campion, 1997) indicate that highly structured interviews are better predictors of future job performance than unstructured ones. Some structured interviews are highly formulaic (e.g., the "situational interview," the "behavior description interview," or even the "stress interview"), whereas others involve a variety of questions and answers arranged in a structured form. Second, research suggests that interviewers often cue applicants about appropriate responses through the use of directed or leading questions (Jablin & Miller, 1990). For example, an interviewer might say, "We are a national company with the need for high-mobility employees. Would you be willing to relocate as part of your job?" The preferred answer is clear from the nature of this question. Third, a great deal of variability marks the content of interview questions among different employers and industries (Jablin & Miller, 1990). One interviewer might concentrate on college courses and activities, whereas another might ask about behavior in hypothetical organizational situations. A third might take an even more abstract approach. For example, Poundstone (2003) described an interview in which an applicant for an engineering position is asked to describe November. The expectation in this interview was not for a poetic response about beautiful leaves but a precise answer befitting a future engineer. Interestingly, a top executive at Google recently noted the use of brainteasers in interviews has been found to be of no benefit. "How many golf balls can you fit into an airplane? How many gas stations in Manhattan? A complete waste of time. They don't predict anything. They serve primarily to make the interviewer feel smart" (Bryant, 2013).

The Interview as an Information-Gathering Tool   From the interviewee's perspective, the interview provides a glimpse of a possible future employer. Indeed, Ralston (1993) has found that applicant satisfaction with the interview is a good predictor of the acceptance of second interviews. The ability of the interview to serve this purpose is limited, however, because most interviewees assume that they should play a relatively passive role in the interview process. Indeed, few interviewees ask any questions during the interview until such questions are requested by the interviewer (Babbitt & Jablin, 1985). According to Jablin and Miller (1990), "The average applicant asks about ten questions in an interview, most of which are succinct and closed-ended in form, asked after their interviewers formally seek applicants' questions, and focus on single versus multiple topics" (p. 75).

In spite of limited questioning activity, however, recruits do form impressions during the interview process. For example, McComb and Jablin (1984) have found that if interviewers used probing questions, the recruit perceived the interviewer to be an empathic listener. Applicants were also more satisfied when open-ended questions predominated and when they were given an opportunity to express themselves (Jablin & Miller, 1990). Interviewees receiving second interview offers were likely to be those who confined their questions during the interview to job-related issues (Babbitt & Jablin, 1985). Finally, it is quite possible that interviewees form an opinion about the company based on the questions that are asked and the behavior of the recruiter. For example, interviewees form more positive impressions from interviews that concentrate on job and organization-related information (DeBell, Montgomery, McCarthy & Lanthier, 1998) and from recruiters who have a warm, open, and interested demeanor (Gohtz & Giannantonio, 1995).

The Interview as a Tool for Socialization   Finally, the employment interview can serve to ease a newcomer's adaptation to the organization should she or he be offered a job. Wanous (1992; Wanous & Colella, 1989) develops this position in his support of **realistic job previews** (RJPs). The idea behind RJPs is that if new recruits are provided a realistic picture of their future job, they will be less likely to be disappointed if inflated expectations are not met. Thus, RJPs should serve to reduce voluntary turnover. For example, if a potential receptionist is warned about monotony, overload, and abusive clients through an employment interview, that employee is less likely to quit after a few weeks on the job. Further, practices like this should help to enhance the fit between the person and the organization. For example, recent research found that particular personality types were better fits for different types of organizations (e.g., more conscientious individuals were best fit for hierarchical cultures) though the specifics of the recruiting method used were not found to be as critical as the match itself (Gardner, Reithel, Cogliser, Walumbwa & Foley, 2012).

The effectiveness of realistic job previews may depend on what information is communicated during the interview and how the interaction occurs. As Ralston and Kirkwood (1995) note, "Whatever transpires between the participants can mold expectations about communication within the organization" (p. 85). Popovich and Wanous (1982) suggest that RJPs should be viewed as persuasive communication. This view highlights choices made about message source (e.g., job incumbent versus recruiters), message content, and communication medium (e.g., electronic versus written materials vs. oral presentation). But this view of realistic recruiting also carries risks. Rynes (1990) has argued that some recruits may view negative job characteristics as a challenge and hence not self-select out of inappropriate jobs.

Newcomer Information-Seeking Tactics

A second communication process critical to the adaptation of newcomers occurs primarily during the encounter phase of socialization and emphasizes the proactive role of organizational newcomers (Miller & Jablin, 1991; Morrison, 2003; Reichers, 1987). In this view, newcomers are seen as more than passive recipients of training programs and organizational handbooks. Instead, newcomers actively seek information that will help them adapt to their new roles and the norms and values of the organizational culture.

Table 7.2 | Newcomer Information-Seeking Tactics

Tactic	Definition
Overt questions	Newcomer solicits information by asking direct questions of information targets.
Indirect questions	Newcomer solicits information by asking non-interrogative questions or by hinting.
Third parties	Newcomer solicits information by asking a secondary source (e.g., coworker) rather than a primary source (e.g., supervisor).
Testing limits	Newcomer solicits information by breaking or deviating from organizational rules and observing reactions.
Disguising conversations	Newcomer solicits information by disguising the information-seeking attempt as a natural part of the conversation.
Observing	Newcomer solicits information by watching behavior in salient situations.
Surveillance	Newcomer solicits information by making sense of past observed behavior.

Adapted from Miller, V. D. & Jablin, F. M. (1991). Information seeking during organizational entry: Influences, tactics, and a model of the process. *Academy of Management Review, 16*, 92–120.

Miller and Jablin (1991) have developed the most complete typology of newcomer information-seeking. These scholars posit seven modes through which newcomers seek information. These information-seeking strategies are presented and defined in Table 7.2. As this table indicates, newcomers can seek information in obvious ways (e.g., asking overt questions or questioning third parties) or in a more covert manner (e.g., through observation, surveillance, or disguised conversations). For example, a newcomer trying to learn about norms for weekend work might use an overt question by asking, "Are we expected to work on weekends?" Alternatively, the newcomer might drive by the company on a Saturday to check on cars in the parking lot (observation tactic) or engage in conversations about upcoming weekend activities with coworkers (disguised conversation).

According to Miller and Jablin (1991), use of these information-seeking tactics will vary depending on the extent to which uncertainty needs to be reduced and the social costs of seeking information. The social costs for seeking information might include embarrassment about not knowing something or fear of irritating coworkers with repeated requests for information. For example, a new employee might be interested in knowing how the login and password system works on the company's internal computer network. Uncertainty about this issue might be high, and it is unlikely that the newcomer would perceive a high level of social costs associated with inquiries about the local area network. Thus, the new employee would probably use a relatively straightforward information-seeking tactic, such as an overt question. In contrast, if a newcomer were trying to learn about the appropriate level of formality in addressing supervisors, a more covert tactic (e.g., observation, testing limits, or asking third parties) might be used. Several studies have investigated the use of information-seeking tactics by organizational newcomers

(Comer, 1991; Morrison, 1993; Teboul, 1995) and have been relatively supportive of the ideas about the influence of uncertainty and social cost. For example, Teboul (1995) found that information-seeking by new employees was influenced by the perception of social costs and that those perceptions were created through socialization and social support processes. Use of information-seeking tactics will also depend on the personality (e.g., extroversion) of the newcomer (Gruman & Saks, 2011) and can be enhanced through the relationship-building opportunities of social networking sites (Flanagin & Waldeck, 2004).

Role Development Processes

The final communication process we will discuss in this chapter is an ongoing one that begins at organizational entry and continues through the metamorphosis stage of socialization. This process is concerned with how individuals interact to define and develop their organizational roles. The model was developed by George Graen and his colleagues almost forty years ago, but it is still a model that generates considerable research (see Dulebohn, Bommer, Liden, Brouer & Ferris, 2012 for review). Graen (1976) began with the assumption that "organizational members accomplish their work through roles" (p. 1201) and then theorized that individuals develop those roles through interaction with others in the organization. Graen and his colleagues believe that the supervisor-subordinate dyad is critical in the process of role development. They argue that a role is developed by an organizational member through a social exchange process with his or her leader. Hence, this theory has been labeled **Leader-Member Exchange Theory** (LMX). Graen and colleagues (see, e.g., Dienesch & Liden, 1986; Graen & Scandura, 1987) argue that the role development process begins when a newcomer enters an organization (or a new organizational role) and continues through ongoing interactions with the supervisor and other organizational members. The LMX model divides role development into three interrelated phases: role taking, role making, and role routinization.

Role-Taking Phase   The role-taking period is "the sampling phase wherein the superior attempts to discover the relevant talents and motivations of the member through iterative testing sequences" (Graen & Scandura, 1987, p. 180). During this phase, the leader will request a variety of activities of the member. By observing how the member responds to these requests, the leader will begin to evaluate the talents, skills, and motivation of the subordinate. For example, imagine that Josh is a new sales representative for a pharmaceutical company. Josh's supervisor, Laura, may initially ask Josh to update the client list to include new urgent care facilities in the area. By watching how Josh accomplishes this task, Laura can reach conclusions about Josh's organizational and communication skills and the extent to which he can perform tasks independently. Laura can continue this process by assigning Josh a wide variety of organizational tasks.

Role-Making Phase   The second phase of the role development process marks an evolution from the one-way activity—in which the supervisor "gives" the role and the subordinate "takes" it—to a process in which the member seeks to modify the nature of the role and the manner in which it is enacted. For example, Laura might want Josh to take on more responsibility for tailoring the pharmaceutical company's presence on social media sites. When she asks him to do this, Josh might respond that he needs a break from other organizational responsibilities or that he needs additional staff help to accomplish the task. Through interaction, Josh and Laura will negotiate this and other aspects of Josh's role.

The role-making process involves a social exchange in which "each party must see the other party as valuable and each party must see the exchange as reasonably equitable or fair" (Graen & Scandura, 1987, p. 182). The member can offer time, skills, and effort to the role-making process. The leader can offer formal rewards as well as informal resources, such as information, support, and attention. By exchanging these resources, leader and member work together to develop the member's organizational role.

Role-Routinization Phase   The third phase of the role development process represents the point at which the role of the subordinate and expected behaviors of the supervisor are well-understood by both parties. The sampling of the role-taking phase and the negotiation of the role-making phase have led to an established relationship between supervisor and subordinate. It is important to note, however, that each development process is unique. Thus, a single leader can develop very different types of relationships with different subordinates. Indeed, some scholars suggest that supervisor-subordinate relationships can be arrayed along a continuum from "in-group" relationships—which are characterized by high levels of trust, mutual influence, support, and formal/informal rewards (Fairhurst & Chandler, 1989)—to "out-group" relationships—which are characterized by low levels of trust, support, and rewards and the use of formal authority rather than mutual influence (see Figure 7.1).

Some of these differences in role development might be attributable to the role negotiation process. Role negotiation is the interactive process through which individuals create and alter expectations about how a job is to be done (Miller, Jablin, Casey, Lamphear-Van Horn & Ethington, 1996), and this process is likely to be key in predicting "the newcomer's chances of successfully individualizing his or her role in the organization" (Jablin, 2001, p. 781). In other words, Josh's success in creating and maintaining a meaningful role in the organization might depend both on his job-related skills and efforts and on his ability to communicate effectively in interactions with Laura in the workplace.

Beyond the Leadership Dyad   It is also critical to note that while the leader-member exchange model—and the role negotiation process—is considered in terms of interaction between a supervisor and subordinate, these dyadic exchanges are always embedded within the larger organizational context (see Sias & Jablin, 1995). For example, Teboul and Cole (2005) developed an evolutionary model of workplace integration that highlights social relationships with peers. Scholarship has also pointed to the importance of the workgroup in the socialization process. Myers and McPhee (2006) found that workgroup communication was particularly important to assimilation in organizations where trust among coworkers is critical

Figure 7.1 | The Leader-Member Exchange Role Development Process

(e.g., fire or police departments). Apker, Propp, and Ford (2005) also found that the team was critical in the socialization of nurses, particularly in today's complex health care environment. In other words, when jobs are complex and stressful—as the jobs of firefighters and nurses clearly are—the process of role development is one that cannot involve just the supervisor and subordinate.

ORGANIZATIONAL EXIT

Our discussion of socialization thus far has focused on processes involved in *entering* organizations. From pre-entry anticipation, through the surprises of organizational encounter, to the development of ongoing relationships and roles within an organization, we found that organizational socialization was a communicative process through which sense was made of work life and varying levels of identification were forged. However, the comings and goings of organizational life involve more than socialization. It is also critical to consider the "goings" of organizational exit and disengagement.

A consideration of organizational disengagement is particularly important during the twenty-first century. This is true for demographic, economic, and social reasons. Demographically, the baby boom generation is aging, and more and more individuals are reaching retirement age (and often retiring at earlier ages than previous generations). Thus, organizational disengagement through retirement will become increasingly important (e.g., Shultz, Morton & Weckerle, 1998). Economically, the global and postmodern marketplace is one often characterized by mergers, acquisitions, bankruptcies, and downsizing. For example, the fall of Enron in 2001 involved the layoff of thousands of workers (Schwartz, 2001). Finally, we live in an increasingly mobile society in which people move frequently from job to job and from organization to organization. Thus, exits precipitated by job transfers within and between organizations (Jablin & Kramer, 1998) are common. Indeed, for many individuals today, the notion of a connection to a particular organization is not nearly so important as a connection with a career or occupation (Russo, 1998), and workers today are more likely than in past eras to make radical job switches because of disenchantment with an initial job or career.

Case in Point: The Economics of Exit and Entry

This chapter points to some of the complexities of the socialization process, including the challenges of interviewing for a job, learning about a new organizational culture, and negotiating changing roles with supervisors and coworkers. However, this material might make the likelihood that socialization will happen seem relatively unproblematic. However, experiences during the U.S. 2007–2009 economic recession make it clear that entry into the world of work isn't always a given. The unemployment rate in the United States rose steadily during the recession, reaching a peak of 10.1% in October 2009. During the recession, the unemployment rate was particularly high for certain demographic groups, such as African Americans, men, and—yes—recent college graduates (Lee, 2009).

Most of the readers of this textbook are likely to be in this latter group quite soon. Although the statistics have improved somewhat the years since the official end of the recession, unemployment is still stubbornly above ideal levels, and the economics of exit and entry are likely to be in play for the foreseeable future. What does this mean as you anticipate your own period of organizational socialization? First, the simple fact that older workers' retirement coffers are depleted means that they are likely to stay on the job longer, meaning fewer jobs for current college grads. Furthermore, when employers compare the credentials of experienced applicants looking for work with individuals who have just earned their degrees, the new grad might have to consider a job that isn't a perfect match. These economic factors, then, can complicate the processes of job search and accentuate the importance of organizational socialization in whatever job you eventually land.

In spite of this increase in organizational exits, the research on communication during the disengagement process is still relatively thin. Thus, at this point, it makes the most sense to simply offer a few generalizations about communication during the exit process:

- Like organizational entry, organizational exit is a process, not an event. Individuals often anticipate their exit from an organization, perhaps for many years (in the case of retirement) or for shorter time spans (in the case of job transfers). Even layoffs that are seen from the outside as sudden are often anticipated well in advance by organizational insiders.

- Organizational exit is a process that influences both those who leave and those who are left behind. We often concentrate our attention on the person who has crossed the organizational boundary (the leaver), but those who remain in the organization (the stayers) may experience such diverse emotions as happiness or relief (if the leaver was a disliked coworker), resentment (if the stayer must take on additional work), or even survivor's guilt (if the stayer was spared in a layoff or downsizing).

- Furthermore, organizational exit can have profound effects on the families of those who leave the organization. For example, Buzzanell and Turner (2003) interviewed men who had recently lost their jobs, and they also questioned their families. The interviews suggested that the men and their families had to work to control (or express) feelings of anger and often struggled to maintain a sense of normalcy and to construct a continuing masculine role within the family structure.

- Communication plays a critical role in the disengagement process. At times, communication might spur disengagement, as when messages from coworkers or an unpleasant communication environment motivate an employee to leave (Cox, 1999). Research also suggests that individuals on the periphery of communication networks are more likely to exit an organization (Feeley, 2000). When an organizational exit becomes imminent, communication about the leave-taking becomes more explicit, and Klatzke (2008) has found that leave-takers craft different messages for different audiences in order to facilitate particular impressions. Following the announcement of exit, communication patterns might change as the leave-taker's role shifts from insider to outsider. For example, Roth (1991) found that the period between an announced departure and the actual exit provided the communicative space to discuss numerous taboo topics in the organization, and Gordon (2011) proposed a model for understanding the ways in which the exit interview serves as a venue for self-revelation for the departing employee.

- The final exit from the workplace—retirement—is one that holds particular meaning for individuals throughout employees' lives. Smith and Dougherty (2012) found that American workers held a "master narrative" that situated retirement as the ultimate marker of freedom from routine and the financial need to work. However, that narrative was often "fractured" as individuals contemplated worries about money or the double-edged sword of not having work activities as an ongoing life structure.

SUMMARY

In this chapter, we have looked in detail at the processes through which individuals assimilate to organizational life. We began by considering models of socialization phases and content. We then looked at communication processes that occur during socialization. We looked at the recruiting and interview processes during the anticipatory socialization phase. We then considered information-seeking during the encounter phase and the process of role development. Finally, we explored communication during organizational exit and disengagement. In closing, it is instructive to look back at the various approaches to the study of organizational communication considered in the first half of this book and consider how these approaches would investigate

organizational socialization processes. A number of ideas are presented in Table 7.3.

Most of the research on socialization discussed in this chapter has taken a classical, human resources, or cultural approach. For example, the research on realistic job previews takes a mainly classical view in its emphasis on reducing employee turnover. Work on socialization content and tactics often takes a human resources approaches with the goal of understanding the ways in which socialization programs can be developed to maximize the ability of employees to contribute to the organization. In contrast, work on information-seeking strategies is based to a large extent on cultural approaches because an emphasis is placed on

Table 7.3	Approaches to the Socialization Process
Approach	**How Socialization Would Be Considered**
Classical	Socialization seen as a way to ensure that employees are properly trained for maximum effectiveness and efficiency. Research might evaluate training programs or consider socialization strategies as a means of reducing employee turnover.
Human Relations	Socialization seen as a way to maximize the possibility that employees will be highly satisfied organizational members. Research might evaluate the extent to which socialization practices help employees satisfy higher order needs.
Human Resources	Socialization seen as a way to maximize the contributions employees can make to the organization. Research might consider the extent to which selection processes will attract recruits who can contribute to organizational goals.
Systems	Socialization seen as a boundary transition between the "outside" and the "inside" of the system. Research might consider the role of communication networks on the adaptation of newcomers.
Cultural	Socialization seen as a process through which newcomers come to understand the values and norms of the new organizational culture. Research might consider sensemaking strategies of new employees.
Constitutive	Socialization seen in terms of the membership negotiation flow that constitutes the organization rather than as a transition across the boundaries of a container. Research might look at ongoing discourse processes that contribute to member identification with the organization.
Critical	Socialization seen as a process through which organizational owners and managers develop and maintain hegemonic relationships with employees. Research might consider how socialization tactics serve as instruments of unobtrusive control.
Feminist	Socialization seen as a process that is potentially gendered as new employees are introduced to rational and patriarchal organizational systems. Research might encourage alternative modes of recruitment and assimilation that would encourage alternative and feminine values.

how the newcomer can seek information proactively to make sense of the new culture.

The use of other approaches might deepen your understanding of the organizational socialization process, perhaps through a more explicit consideration of the "membership negotiation flow" pointed to by Four Flows CCO theorists. For example, a feminist approach is advocated by Allen (1996), who argues that a black woman's experience of socialization in the academic environment is very different from the experience of whites or men. Other insights might be made in the study of socialization by looking in more detail at systems concepts, such as boundary permeability, subsystems and super-systems, and communication networks. In short, although our knowledge of communication during the socialization process is already well-established, the use of alternative perspectives might broaden and enhance our knowledge of this important organizational communication process.

DISCUSSION QUESTIONS

1. Anticipatory socialization is a process that begins early in childhood as kids learn about work, careers, and organizations. When you were a child, what did you want to be when you grew up? How realistic were your aspirations? How have they changed based on anticipatory socialization processes?

2. Think about organizations you have worked for or groups you have been a part of. To what extent do your experiences reflect the stages of socialization discussed in this chapter?

3. If you worked for the career center on campus, what advice would you give to individuals signing up for job interviews? What advice would you give to organizations interviewing candidates on your campus? How could the interview process be improved so it would be more productive—and less stressful—for all involved?

KEY CONCEPTS

assimilation
socialization
individualization
anticipatory socialization
encounter stage
metamorphosis stage

role-related information
cultural information
employment interview
realistic job previews
newcomer information-seeking
   tactics

Leader-Member Exchange Theory
role-taking phase
role-making phase
role-routinization phase
organizational exit

CASE STUDY | **The Church Search**

SCENE ONE: OCTOBER—A SUNDAY SCHOOL ROOM IN MICHIGAN

Lisa sighed in frustration. "Why did Joe have to leave? He was a great pastor—he was why I came to this church and stayed here. And now we have to look for someone new. I'll do it. I'll be a part of this search committee. But that doesn't mean I have to like it."

"Well, you could always turn to that old saying of God opening a window when he closes a door," countered Jason. "I'm not happy that Joe left either, but it was a great opportunity for him—we can't begrudge him wanting new challenges. And maybe this provides new opportunities for our congregation—perhaps we've become a bit complacent with Joe's ministry, and this is just what we need to think about where we want to go and what we want to do."

Many at the table nodded in agreement. Seven were gathered around the table, all members of a midsized congregation of a Protestant church. Their longtime pastor had recently accepted a calling to a new church, and these seven had been selected as the search committee for the new pastor. They had a lot of work ahead of them and chose Nancy to head the committee. She got straight to the point.

"OK," said Nancy. "Let's get to work. We need to start by developing a profile of our church and congregation. Who we are, what we do, and where we think we're going? And then we need to think carefully about what kind of pastor we want for our future. What are the critical characteristics for our new minister? Is preaching the most important? Evangelism? Spiritual development? Community service and social justice? And then we need to think about the questions we'll ask when we get to the interview process. Who will be involved? What kinds of activities should we include? And then we need to think about how we'll welcome the new pastor once we make a decision about who it will be. And then ..."

Everyone at the table began to laugh as Nancy's list of "and thens" grew longer and longer. "Uh, Nance," interrupted Rick, "we only scheduled a two-hour meeting. Sounds like you'd like to have us here through the night."

"Nope," Nancy responded, looking at the circle of already tired faces. "We'll just have to have a lot more meetings. But let's get to work for now. And let's have a quick prayer before we get started. I think we'll need it."

SCENE TWO: FEBRUARY—A LIVING ROOM IN MISSOURI

Marsha sat in the middle of the floor, surrounded by piles of spiral-bound documents. "Who knew that so many churches could be looking for a pastor? I mean, it's good news for someone like me, but it makes the whole process so much more confusing."

Marsha's husband Ron—also sprawled on the floor—flipped through some of the papers. "We just have to be systematic in looking through these profiles

and think about what you want in a position and where you can best serve. You have gifts in music ministry and youth ministry that could make a big difference for some congregation." Ron looked up from one profile. "This one, for example, would probably be a bad fit. It's a big church, and they've really divided up the ministerial jobs. I'm not sure you'd ever see the kids in the church much, let alone get to work with them in the way you'd want to."

Marsha looked up. "I know. We should just be careful about looking through everything. It's just such a scary prospect. I've been really comfortable in my role as a youth minister, and moving to a larger role seems like a big step." She started laughing. "I know we've been through all this before, and we'll go where God calls us. But this discernment thing is really tough sometimes!"

Half an hour later, Marsha and Ron were both engrossed in the church profiles. "Hey," Marsha said. "Here's a good possibility. It's not a very big church, but the values and mission really match a lot of my own commitments. And they're clearly big on encouraging music and youth programs. What do you think about moving to Michigan?"

SCENE THREE: APRIL— A RESTAURANT IN MICHIGAN

Nancy looked across the table at Marsha. "I'm so glad to finally have the chance to meet you in person after all our time comparing profiles and talking on the phone. This process is sure a lot more complicated than I ever anticipated!"

Marsha smiled in agreement. "You're telling me— I've almost been tempted to change denominations to one where pastors are appointed by the conference. Sure would make this process simpler."

"True," said Nancy. "But I must admit that I like a system that empowers the congregation and the pastor. I mean, I love our conference minister and have great respect for him, but I've never liked that idea of 'matchmaking' for the church."

Nancy then pulled out a notebook and began sorting through some pages. "As you know, Marsha, we've got a pretty full weekend ahead of us. After we finish dinner, we'll head over to the church, where you'll meet with the entire search committee. And then we have more meetings with the committee in the morning and we'll give you a chance to tour the community and see what life here is like. And then, on Sunday, we've arranged for you to preach at a 'neutral pulpit' so committee members can hear you. And then the committee will be able to make a recommendation to the congregation, and you can think and pray about what you want to do. And then ..."

Marsha laughed. "Rick told me you were the queen of 'and thens.' But, yes, it looks like we have a busy weekend ahead of us and a lot of challenges to consider. Let's start with supper."

CASE ANALYSIS QUESTIONS

1. How have Marsha's experiences so far represented aspects of the anticipatory socialization process? Is it also possible to consider anticipatory socialization from the point of view of the church searching for a new pastor? What does anticipatory socialization look like from the organization's point of view?

2. During the weekend ahead, what questions should Marsha anticipate during the interview process? What questions should she ask? What are the various functions that the interview will serve for both Marsha and the congregation?

3. Assuming that Marsha eventually takes on the role of pastor with this church, what should she anticipate during her first few months in her new role? Are there steps that she can take before and after moving to Michigan to ease her transition? Are there steps the congregation can take to help her make sense of life in the new church?

4. A pastor's role is one in which the supervisor could be seen as the congregation. How could the leader-member exchange model be adapted to account for these kinds of organizational positions?

Decision-Making Processes

CHAPTER **8**

AFTER READING THIS CHAPTER, YOU SHOULD ...

- Appreciate how rational decision making is often hampered by individual and organizational limits and know alternative ways to understand individual and group decision making.
- Be able to describe phase models of group decision making and know alternatives to these models.
- Be familiar with the concept of groupthink and with models of effective decision making that could help organizations deal with groupthink and similar challenges.
- Be able to compare and contrast the affective and cognitive models of participative decision making.
- Be familiar with various ways that participation has been instituted in organizations and be especially aware of the challenges of organizational democracy.
- Appreciate the ways in which collaboration in decision making is critical for global and interorganizational relationships.
- Understand knowledge management systems—both information-based and interaction-based—as ways that contemporary organizations move beyond simplistic visions of decision making.

One of the most critical activities in any organization is decision making. Decisions might involve the strategic direction of the organization (e.g., a decision about a possible merger or acquisition) or might simply deal with the daily activities of employees (e.g., a decision about new procedures for greeting clients on the telephone). Decisions might be made after months of information gathering and deliberation or in an instant with little or no consideration. Decisions might be made by individuals alone, through consultation with relevant organizational members, or in participative groups. And decisions will vary in their levels of effectiveness. Indeed, Nutt (1999) concluded that half of all the decisions made in organizations fail because of the poor use of decision-making tactics by managers as well as problems with communication.

In this chapter, we explore the role of communication in organizational decision making. First, we look at general models of the decision-making process, considering the movement away from rational models toward those based on intuition and other less logical premises. Then, we discuss the small-group context in which many organizational decisions are made. Next, we consider one way in which values about decision making are embedded into organizational work life through processes such as participation in decision making, workplace democracy, collaboration among work groups, and knowledge management systems.

MODELS OF THE DECISION-MAKING PROCESS

Rational Models of Decision Making

In classical theories of organizational behavior, decision making is an entirely rational and logical process. First, organization members notice a problem that requires a decision. After carefully defining the problem, the decision makers then search for all the relevant information that might bear upon it. Next, the decision makers develop a set of decision options and evaluate them according to carefully developed criteria for decision effectiveness. The decision-making process concludes when an optimal decision is identified and decision implementation can begin. This has been labeled the **normative model of decision making** (Nutt, 1984), and it includes five stages: formulation, concept development, detailing, evaluation, and implementation.

Consider, for instance, a team at a consumer products company trying to make a decision about the best way to market a new sports drink. In the *formulation stage* (Stage 1), the team might conduct focus group research with individuals in the target demographic to learn more about their workout habits, their media consumption, and their likes and dislikes. In the *concept development stage* (Stage 2), the marketing team would generate alternative approaches to the campaign, perhaps involving distinct content, activity tie-ins, and media delivery options. During the *detailing process* (Stage 3), additional research might be conducted and evaluated in terms of factors such as reach and impact. During the *evaluation stage* (Stage 4), the information gathered during detailing would be placed under intense scrutiny by the group to determine the cost effectiveness and appeal of each marketing option. Finally, in the *implementation stage* (Stage 5), the chosen marketing campaign (perhaps an ongoing tie-in with marathons and triathlons accompanied by Internet and radio ads) would be rolled out.

Alternatives to Rational Models

This rational and logical process sounds like the ideal way to make an organizational decision. However, scholars long ago recognized that this model was *not* a good representation of how organizational decision makers actually work. The first theorists to suggest an alternative to this model were March and Simon (March & Simon, 1958; Simon, 1960), who characterize the traditional approach to decision making as an *optimizing* model, in which decision makers are attempting to find the single best solution to an organizational problem. They believe that it is more realistic to look at organizational decision making as a *satisficing* process in which the search is not for a single optimal solution but for a solution that will work well enough for dealing with the situation. As Pugh and Hickson (1989) explain, "most decisions are concerned not with searching for the sharpest needle in the haystack, but with searching for a needle sharp enough to sew with. Thus, administrators who 'satisfice' can make decisions without a search for all the possible alternatives and can use relatively simple rules of thumb" (p. 138).

March and Simon (1958) propose that organizational decision makers use satisficing strategies because it is not *possible* to make the ideal rational solution. Rather, organizational decision makers are characterized by **bounded rationality**. That is, decision makers attempt to make logical decisions, but they are limited cognitively (e.g., humans are not always perfectly logical) and by the practical aspects of organizational life (e.g., limits in time and resources). For example, a manager might need to make a decision about what inventory control program to use. If this manager were optimizing, she would undertake a search of all possible programs and evaluate these options against a set of carefully developed criteria. However, there is rarely time or motivation to do this. Instead, our manager might talk to a few colleagues in similar businesses about systems that would be adequate for the organization's needs. Thus, March and Simon propose that decision makers still use logic but do so under personal and organizational constraints.

In support of these ideas, March and Simon proposed ideas about decision making that are far removed from optimizing models than is satisficing. For example, Simon (1987) has proposed that a great deal of organizational decision making can be attributed to the *intuitive processes* of managers. Simon harkens back to early work by Barnard (1938), who suggests a distinction between logical and nonlogical management processes. Barnard argues that decision makers are often forced to

Case in Point: Personal Finance Decisions

Decisions made in the workplace have important implications for organizations and the people who work in and for them. But for the individual, the most important work decisions might be those involving what to do with the money earned on the job. Such decisions will influence the individual's lifestyle, date of retirement, and charitable activities.

You would think, then, that rationality would be front and center in making these decisions that are so important for our lives and our futures. Not so, say experts in "behavioral finance," a field of study investigating the role of motivation and psychology in investment decisions (Bernard, 2004). Instead, most individuals rely on mental shortcuts—"heuristics"— that undercut rational principles of probability in investing. For example, people tend to feel more

secure following the lead of other investors, tend to focus too much on what has happened recently, tend to develop irrational "anchor points" for decisions, are reluctant to realize losses, and tend to treat money differently depending on its source. All these tendencies can lead to flawed investment decisions.

So, what's an investor to do? Well, following the steps for rational decision making laid out in this chapter would make sense. But because we don't have perfect information, unlimited time, or a perfectly rational approach to our own lives and money, this can be difficult. Thus, consulting an expert decision maker might be well advised. As Bernard (2004, p. E5) concludes, "[t]aking the emotion out of the decision increases the chance that it will result in a rational move."

make quick decisions without the opportunity for information search and debate. Managers in these situations often make decisions without conscious knowledge of how these decisions are made. Barnard (1938) notes that:

> [t]he sources of these non-logical processes lie in physiological conditions or factors, or in the physical and social environment, mostly impressed upon us unconsciously or without conscious effort on our part. They also consist of the mass of facts, patterns, concepts, techniques, abstractions, and generally what we call formal knowledge or beliefs, which are impressed upon our minds more or less by conscious effort and study. This second source of non-logical mental processes greatly increases with direct experience, study and education. (p. 302)

Simon (1987) points out that although intuitive decision making is not "logical," neither is it "illogical." Rather, this kind of decision making is based on past experience in similar contexts. One could say that this kind of decision-making is *analogical*. That is, a manager faced with making a decision will consider what has worked in similar situations in the past. By analogy, a similar solution should work again. As Simon (1987) notes, "The experienced manager ... has in his or her memory a large amount of knowledge, gained from training and experience and organized in terms of recognizable chunks and associated information" (p. 61). **Intuitive decision making** depends on the decision-maker accessing the relevant chunk of information and putting it to use.

Case in Point: Big Data

This chapter so far has made the argument that many decisions in organizations are not made rationally through the careful, logical analysis of data. Rather, decisions are often made through intuitive processes or by considering similar situations and past decisions. Furthermore, part of what limits our rationality in decision making is our inability to access and process all the information that would be required for a truly rational decision. Well, it turns out that that might be changing, thanks to high-powered computers and lots of disc space.

In a book entitled *Super Crunchers*, Ian Ayres (2007) argues that we are in the midst of a powerful trend: "the replacement of expertise and intuition by objective, data-based decision making, made possible by a virtually inexhaustible supply of inexpensive information" (Adler, 2007, p. 42). Ayres points out that the vast quantities of information gleaned from electronic sources—together with sophisticated

algorithms for analyzing those data—can assist in decisions made in disparate areas such as marketing, criminal justice, agriculture, and medicine. We are probably all familiar with the use of information to track our online buying preferences, but this trend now infiltrates many phases of organizational life. Manyika and his colleagues (2011) argue that the increasing use of "big data" will become "a key basis for competition, underpinning new waves of productivity growth [and] innovation."

Although these developments may lead to decisions that are better (or at least more thoroughly based on evidence and data), they also take some of the challenge out of people's work. As Adler states, "[J]obs that used to call for independent judgment, especially about other people, are being routinized and dumbed down" (p. 42). In other words, there's less chance of charming that loan officer or convincing her that you're a good risk. Your credit score will say it all.

In summary, in spite of our models of an ideal rational process, decision making rarely follows this pattern. Instead, decision makers typically use truncated decision procedures and rely on intuition or satisficing solutions. In the next section, we consider the small-group context in which a great many organizational decisions are made.

SMALL-GROUP DECISION MAKING

According to an old adage, a camel is a horse designed by committee. This saying points to the pitfalls that can arise in group decision making. However fraught with problems the process might be, the fact remains that a vast majority of organizational decisions are made in the context of a small group, whether that group is a standing committee, a self-managing work team, an ad hoc task force, or a group of colleagues standing around the coffeemaker. In this section, we first explore models that describe the group decision-making process. We then consider factors that contribute to effective or ineffective decisions in small groups.

Descriptive Models of Small-Group Decision Making

Most models of group decision making propose that groups go through a series of phases as they systematically attempt to reach decisions. One representative **phase model of decision making** was proposed by B. A. Fisher (1970). He identifies four phases: orientation, conflict, emergence, and reinforcement. In the *orientation* phase, group members become acquainted with each other and with the problem at hand. During the *conflict* phase, possible solutions to the problem are presented and debated. After this, the group will arrive at some level of consensus during the *emergence* phase, and the decision will be supported during the final group phase: *reinforcement*.

In some ways, these phase models of group decision making mirror the rational model of decision making we considered previously. As Poole and Roth (1989a) note, stage models "explain decision behavior as the result of the group following a systematic logic" (p. 325). Stage models also assume a rigid and unitary sequence of group activities. That is, decision making always begins with orientation to the problem and ends with the emergence and reinforcement of a solution. A number of theorists have objected to this type of model. For example, Cissna (1984) argues that phases do not exist, and Morley and Stephenson (1977) argue that phasic development will vary depending on the type of decision being made by the group. Gersick (1991) has developed a "punctuated equilibrium" model that highlights both the underlying deep structure and the revolutionary shifts that occur in groups.

The most complex response to rational phase models has been mounted by Poole and his colleagues (Poole, 1983; Poole & Roth, 1989a, 1989b). Poole has advanced a **multiple sequence model** that represents the variety of decision paths taken by groups. By coding the continuous interaction of decision-making groups, Poole and Roth (1989a) developed a typology of decision paths typically adopted. The three major types of group decision paths are presented in Table 8.1.

Table 8.1 | Typology of Small-Group Decision Path Types

Decision Path Type	Frequency	Explanation
Unitary sequence path	23%	Group interaction generally followed traditional sequence of orientation, problem analysis, solution, and reinforcement.
Complex cyclic path	47%	Group interaction consisted of multiple problem-solution cycles.
Solution-oriented path	30%	Group interaction involved no activity related to problem definition or analysis.

Based on Poole, M. S. & Roth, J. (1989a). Decision development in small groups IV: A typology of group decision paths. *Human Communication Research*, 15, 323–356.

As Table 8.1 indicates, less than a quarter of the groups studied exhibited the rational sequence prescribed by most stage models. Groups were more likely to engage in complicated sequences of cycles (i.e., breaking the problem down into subproblems and processing these one at a time) or to focus on the solution with little regard to problem definition or discussion. Note the similarity between this and our discussion of alternatives to the rational model of decision making presented earlier. It appears that regardless of the context, decision making is rarely a linear and rational process in which organizational members carefully search for and evaluate decision options.

Effective Small-Group Decision Making

Poole's multiple sequence model is useful in highlighting the varying communicative patterns small groups use when making decisions. However, this model says little about what types of communication lead to *effective* decisions. Is a group better off following the rational model? Should a group concentrate on solutions? How should a group distribute its energy among the wide range of tasks that must be accomplished? What interaction patterns lead to bad decisions? These questions have been the focus of a number of group theorists.

Probably the best-known analysis of dysfunctional decisions has been presented by Janis (1982). Janis studied a number of historically noteworthy decision disasters (e.g., the Kennedy administration's decision to invade Cuba at the Bay of Pigs) and concluded that interaction in these groups was characterized by the property of **groupthink**. Other decisions—such as the space shuttle disasters involving both *Challenger* and *Columbia*, the U.S. government's ongoing decisions to remain involved in the Vietnam War, and the financial collapse of Swissair in 2002—have also been attributed to groupthink. Groupthink refers to "a mode of thinking that people engage in when they are deeply involved in a cohesive in-group, when the members' striving for unanimity overrides their motivation to realistically appraise alternative courses of action" (Janis, 1982, p. 9). Thus, in a group characterized by groupthink, there is more concern with appearing cohesive and maintaining group relations than there is with making a high-quality decision. The major symptoms of groupthink identified by Janis are presented in Table 8.2.

Table 8.2 | Symptoms of Groupthink

Groupthink Symptom	Description
Illusion of invulnerability	The belief that nothing can go wrong within the group
Illusion of morality	The self-righteous belief that the virtues of the group are above reproach
Stereotyping	The categorizing of others outside of the group in ways that see their views as unacceptable
Self-censorship	The overt restraint of group members against offering opinions counter to the prevailing thought in the group
Illusion of unanimity	The statement of group agreement while private doubts and disagreements are suppressed
Direct pressure on dissidents	The coercive force that obliges group members to behave and think in similar ways
Reliance on self-appointed mind guards	The protection of the group from contrary information from outside influences

A profound example of these problems can be found in the organizational decision making that led to the United States' invasion of Iraq in 2003. The bipartisan Senate Intelligence Committee report released in the summer of 2004 suggested that the decision making regarding Iraq might have been driven by a preferred solution rather than by a detailed and rational consideration of the available evidence. As Isikoff (2004) summarizes, "U.S. intelligence officials repeatedly embellished fragmentary and ambiguous pieces of evidence, making the danger posed by Iraq appear far more urgent than it actually was" (p. 37). Even at the highest levels of government, decision makers are influenced by the human desire for things to turn out in a particular way and may therefore see things in a preferred light.

How, then, can a group improve its chances of making an effective decision? Several answers to this question have been proposed by researchers of small groups. Some scholars have suggested that a group's manner of dealing with conflict can influence decision quality. For example, Kuhn and Poole (2000) found that groups that worked through their conflicts in collaborative and integrative ways made more effective decisions. Similarly, Jabs (2005) argued that individuals and groups need to be consciously aware of the communication rules to be followed, as this will keep people from following social norms that might have undesirable effects.

Perhaps the most complete explication of the role communication plays in enhancing decision quality comes from Randy Hirokawa and Dennis Gouran in their **functional theory of group decision making** (see, e.g., Gouran & Hirokawa, 1996). Functional theory argues that effective decision making depends on groups attending to critical functions through group communication. Specifically, these functions are as follows (from Gouran, Hirokawa, Julian & Leatham, 1993, p. 580):

- The group should have a correct understanding of the issues to be resolved.
- The group should determine the minimal characteristics required in order for any alternative to be acceptable.

- The group should identify a relevant and realistic set of alternatives.
- The group should carefully examine the alternatives in relation to each previously agreed-upon required characteristic.
- The group should select the alternative that is most likely to have the desired characteristics.

As this list indicates, functional theory works through the same phases identified as necessary for effective individual decision making (e.g., understanding the problem, identifying alternatives, and determining criteria for evaluating those alternatives) and identifies how group communication can enhance the likelihood of success. A statistical review of research testing the functional group approach to decision making suggested that two factors—problem definition and the negative evaluation of alternatives—were key in leading to high-quality decisions (Orlitzky & Hirokawa, 2001). Interestingly, this review also suggested that generating many possible solutions (i.e., brainstorming) was not strongly linked to high-quality decisions.

Beyond Rational Group Processes

Although research on group decision-making processes and effectiveness has led to a number of important findings, there have also been critiques leveled against these structured and rational approaches to group decision making. For example, group decision-making literature has been criticized as being overly concerned with the *task* functions of groups and for ignoring the socio-emotional and relational aspects of group interaction. One theory that has been proposed to help consider these relational issues is **symbolic convergence theory** (see, e.g., Bormann, 1996): this theory considers the role of communication such as stories and jokes in creating a feeling of group identity. Theories of group decision making have also been critiqued because they often ignore organizational context by studying contrived decision situations by using groups of college students. The **bona fide groups** *perspective* (see, e.g., Putnam & Stohl, 1996) deals with this concern by proposing that group research considers factors such as shifting membership, permeable group boundaries, and interdependence within an organizational context. One study of decision making stemming from a bona fide groups approach considered the importance of "backstage" communication in decision making for an interdisciplinary geriatric health care team (Ellingson, 2003). This research suggested that hallway conversations among team members were just as important in the decision-making process as was interaction in formal group meetings.

PARTICIPATION AND COLLABORATION

Thus far, we have examined the process of making decisions—*how* decisions are made by individuals and small groups. We will now combine these ideas with the question of *who* makes the decision, by looking at the ways in which participation and collaboration are important in organizational decision making. We first discuss some of the founding research on participation in decision making (PDM) and look at two models that attempt to explain the effects of participation. We then consider how participation can be brought to life in organizations through workplace democracy programs, look at the role of collaboration in intergroup and interorganizational decision making, and describe ways in which many organizations have enhanced the complexity of decision making through knowledge management processes.

Participation in Decision-Making

The first major study of participation in decision making was conducted by Coch and French in 1948. These researchers were interested in factors that would enhance employee commitment to organizational decisions and found support for their hypothesis that participation in organizational decisions would make employees less resistant to change. Since this early study, researchers have considered a wide range of attitudinal, cognitive, and behavioral effects of participation (see Seibold & Shea, 2001, for review) including job satisfaction, job involvement, employee understanding of decisions, productivity, and decision effectiveness. One meta-analytic literature review of the most often-studied effects of PDM (Wagner, 1994) concludes that participation has significant and consistent—but relatively small—effects on satisfaction and performance.

Given these effects, it is important to consider the processes through which PDM may produce these outcomes. Miller and Monge (1986) have summarized several models that explicate links between participation, job satisfaction, and productivity. Two of these models—the **affective model** and the **cognitive model**—use notably different frameworks to link PDM to these outcome variables. Both models are described below.

The Affective Model   The affective model of participation is based on the work of human relations theorists (see Chapter 3). This model proposes that PDM is an organizational practice that should satisfy employees' higher-order needs (e.g., esteem needs and self-actualization needs). When these needs are met, job satisfaction should result. Ritchie and Miles (1970) state that proponents of this model "believe simply in involvement for the sake of involvement, arguing that as long as subordinates feel they are participating and are being consulted, their ego needs will be satisfied and they will be more cooperative" (p. 348). Supporters of this model would then argue that satisfied workers are more motivated and hence more productive. The affective model is presented in Figure 8.1.

To illustrate this model, consider Frank, an assembly-line supervisor who needs to make a decision about how to improve product rejection rates at the factory. Frank decides to involve his subordinates in this decision. He reasons that including them in the decision will make them feel needed and important and hence engender

Figure 8.1 | The Affective Model of Participative Decision Making

satisfaction with the job. Believing that happy workers are effective workers, Frank figures that improved productivity is sure to follow.

The Cognitive Model   The cognitive model is based on principles of the human resources approach (see Chapter 3). This model proposes that PDM improves the upward and downward flow of information in the organization. The improvement of upward information flow rests on the notion that individuals close to the work (i.e., at the bottom of the organizational hierarchy) know the most about how to accomplish the work. Thus, when these individuals participate in the decision-making process, a decision is made with higher-quality information. The improvement of downward information flow rests on the idea that individuals who participate in decisions will be better able to implement the decisions down the road. When decisions are made with a better pool of information and are better implemented, productivity should improve. Increased employee satisfaction is then seen "as a by-product of their participation in important organizational decisions" (Ritchie & Miles, 1970, p. 348). The cognitive model is presented in Figure 8.2.

To illustrate this model, let's look at Rosie, another assembly-line supervisor at Frank's factory. Rosie also decides to involve her subordinates in decisions about improving rejection rates, but she does so for reasons different from Frank's. Rosie realizes that her workers spend all their work hours on the line and probably know more about why quality control is slipping than anyone else. She wants their input. She also realizes that changing inspection procedures will be far easier if her workers have had a hand in the change process. Thus, she reasons, productivity will improve through participation. Because her philosophy is "busy hands are happy hands," she assumes her subordinates will also be satisfied.

Evidence for Models of Participation   Some support exists for both of these models of participation. The strongest evidence for the *affective model* comes from the ample research finding a link between general perceptions of participation in decision

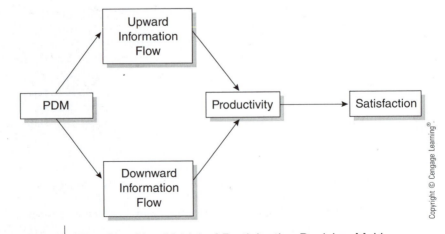

Figure 8.2   The Cognitive Model of Participative Decision Making

making and employee satisfaction (see Miller & Monge, 1986, for a review). This indicates that working in a "participative climate" can meet workers' needs and increase satisfaction. Evidence for the *cognitive model* comes from research linking participation in organizational decisions with productivity increases (Miller & Monge, 1986), as well as research linking participation with organizational knowledge (Marshall & Stohl, 1993). In more recent research, Novak and Sellnow (2009) found that the information flows and mindfulness developed through participation are particularly important when considering ways to reduce risk and avert crises in organizations.

Workplace Democracy

Participation in decision making can be instituted in the workplace in a variety of ways, ranging from casual conversations to formal representative systems and employee ownership. Seibold and Shea (2001) considered the wide array of participation programs used by organizations. These programs varied in terms of type of participation (e.g., consultative or participative), in terms of the content of decision making (including working conditions, company policy, and hiring), and in terms of the locus of participation (e.g., departmental level or organizational level). All of the programs considered, however, had the goal of enhancing organizational effectiveness through employee input and influence.

In recent decades, communication scholars (e.g., Cheney, 1995; Deetz, 1992; Harrison, 1994) have become increasingly interested in *workplace democracy*—the participative ideal for organizations. More than just participation, workplace democracy involves realizing the standards for a democratic society in the workplace and is "grounded in even more fundamental notions of free speech and human dignity" (Budd, Gollan & Wilkinson, 2010). Indeed, Collins (1997) argues that from an economic and political standpoint, participatory management is both inevitable and ethically superior to authoritarian alternatives. Cheney (1995) defines workplace democracy as

> a system of governance which truly values individuals' goals and feelings ... as well as typically organizational objectives ... which actively fosters the connection between those two sets of concerns by encouraging individual contributions to important organizational choices, and which allows for the ongoing modification of the organization's activities and policies by the group, (pp. 170–171)

In other words, participation within a democratic workplace is based on more than mere expediency—it is based on humanistic ideals about how individuals should be treated and involved in society. Participation in such an organization will typically include an actual (rather than just apparent) influence on a large range of organizational processes and issues as well as democracy at all levels of the organization. Not surprisingly, workplace democracy "in action" can involve many challenges and can take a lot of time. For example, in a study of organizational democracy among a community of Benedictine nuns, Hoffman (2002) reported one sister who was frustrated because "sometimes it takes forever to make a decision" (p. 214).

Workplace democracy involves collaboration among "multiple stakeholders" (Deetz, 1995), including workers, investors, consumers, suppliers, host communities, and the world economic community. According to proponents of workplace democracy, shared decision-making among *all* these stakeholders is crucial in today's complicated organizational world. Further, as in politics, it is helpful to differentiate between representative and direct forms of workplace democracy (Knudsen, Busck & Lind, 2011). Some research has suggested that direct workplace democracy has the important advantage of not legitimating additional hierarchical forms of organizing (Kokkinidis, 2011).

Of course, workplace democracy and participation are not easy-to-enact panaceas for the ills of today's organizations. Stohl and Cheney (2001) considered the paradoxes that arise in instituting democratic and participative systems. These paradoxes point out situations in which "the pursuit of an objective involves actions that are themselves antithetical to the desired end" (Stohl & Cheney, 2001, p. 354). Stohl and Cheney highlight fourteen paradoxes of participation that fall into four categories, described in Table 8.3. These paradoxes present a cautionary note about the complexity of instituting participation and democracy within organizations. Ultimately, however, these theorists are hopeful about organizational democracy, and they provide creative, productive ways to handle these paradoxes that could eventually "lead to a much better situation for social actors than had those actors never encountered the paradox in the first place" (Stohl & Cheney, 2001, p. 356).

Collaboration Processes

To this point, we have looked primarily at processes of decision making and participation among members of the same organization. Organizations today, though, are more and more and more likely to be collaborating with each other, crossing the boundaries that have traditionally defined the organizational container. There are several reasons for this. First, as we discussed in Chapter 1, the organizational world is increasingly a global one, and collaborative processes are often necessary as

Table 8.3	Paradoxes of Participative Democracy	
Paradox Type	**Definition**	**What Employees Are Told**
Structure	Paradoxes involving how organizational democracy is planned, designed, and formalized	"Be spontaneous, creative, vocal, and assertive in the way we have planned!"
Agency	Paradoxes concerning an individual's sense of responsibility, autonomy, and cooperation within the participative system	"Do things our way but in a way that is still distinctly your own!"
Identity	Paradoxes concerning issues of inclusion, boundaries, and interests within the participative system	"Be self-managing to reach organizational goals!"
Power	Paradoxes concerning how control and leadership are exercised within the participatory system	"Be independent—just as I have commanded you!"

Adapted from Stohl and Cheney (2001).

multinational companies or nongovernment organizations deal with these global issues. Second, technology allows for enhanced collaboration across organizational boundaries through techniques such as audio, video, and computer conferencing and online collaborative communities. Third, the business, political, and social issues confronting twenty-first century organizations are increasingly complex, and multi-organization solutions are often required to deal with this complexity.

Thus, scholars have become increasingly interested in exploring the ways in which collaboration occurs in intergroup and interorganizational settings. Cooper and Shumate (2012) argue that a bona fide group perspective is appropriate for such scholarship because it emphasizes the dynamic, fuzzy, and multiplex relationships among organizations and organizational actors. Walker and Stohl (2012) used this approach to model the changing networks in interorganizational engineering collaborations. Other scholars have noted that **interorganizational collaboration** can lead to tensions regarding both how contact is structured and how relationships evolve and change (Lewis, Isbell & Koschmann, 2010), although the fluid tension in these relationships can also lead to improvement in the collaborative process (Faraj, Jarvenpaa & Majchrzak, 2011). Finally, several projects have noted that "objects" (such as drawings, photographs, or tables) can be useful in collaborative processes, as these objects can help mediate possible differences in interpretation among multiple groups (Barley, Leonardi & Bailey, 2012; Nicolini, Mengis & Swan, 2012).

Communication and Organizational Knowledge

Finally, it is important to note that, to an ever-increasing extent, organizations no longer see decision making as an isolated process but rather as an ongoing system that is integrated into structures and behaviors throughout and beyond the organization. This is clear from the ideas we have considered about collaboration among organizations and group and organizational democracy—a process that involves a clear conceptual shift by all stakeholders in an organization. This move toward a consideration of knowledge processes has roots in older models of organizing. For example, Canary and McPhee (2010) point to the important role of knowledge in scientific management systems (see Chapter 2) and in human resources approaches to organization (see Chapter 3). However, the complexity of today's organizations and the ability of technology to manage huge amounts of data make the concepts of knowledge even more critical now.

There are a variety of ways to think about organizational knowledge. For example, Tsoukas (2010) draws distinctions among **synoptic knowledge** (abstract representations that might be encoded in instruction manuals or expert systems), **cultural knowledge** that allows organizational actors to act in coordinated ways through understandings of particular sites and systems, and **improvisational knowledge** that people may use when they encounter unusual situations and must move beyond what is encoded in synoptic knowledge. Tsoukas (2010) argues that communication processes allow people in organizations to move among these various types of knowledge. For example, volunteers in a homeless shelter might know the laws regarding shelter operation (synoptic knowledge) and might work together to find the best way to implement those rules in the shelter (cultural knowledge). However, there may be times when the needs of a homeless family don't fit neatly

✳ Spotlight on Scholarship: Who Are the Experts?

One important aspect of knowledge management and decision making in organizations is the idea of expertise. We rely on experts to provide valued information that contributes to workplace decisions. We develop expertise in various areas through ongoing training. We try to be sure that the decision-making groups are populated by organizational members with relevant and up-to-date expertise. And we build critical information into expert knowledge systems that help organizations make decisions in the most effective and efficient ways.

Historically, it has been relatively straightforward to assess expertise as something that individuals "have" or "don't have." For example, one traditional approach to expertise is a cognitive view arguing "that experts have different mental approaches to tasks than other individuals" (Treem, 2012, p. 24) that allow them to identify important patterns in decision-making situations. Another approach to expertise identifies experts as those who have been appropriately trained and legitimated in specific professional areas. For example, a physician is known to have expertise because of graduation from medical school, serving in an appropriate residency, and passing strict tests for state licensure. In both of these situations, expertise is viewed as a property of the individual—a particular organizational actor either has or does not have expertise.

Jeffrey Treem argues, however, that this view of expertise doesn't always work in the "knowledge-intensive" settings that are typical of many of today's organizations. These organizations often include problem-solving situations that are "dynamic, nonrepeatable, and lack objective standards with which to judge performances" (Treem, 2012, p. 25). In these settings, Treem believes it is better to consider expertise as emerging from social relationships rather than as a "there" or "not there" property of individuals.

Treem developed these ideas through a study of two public relations firms, using a research method that included intensive observation of ongoing work behavior, examination of relevant documents, and interviews with workers and with those who could pass judgment on the expertise of the workers. His analyses revealed that workers had consistent ideas about the ways in which expertise is manifest in the work of public relations professionals, and he found that many workers exhibited those behaviors. However, employees who exhibited more of those behaviors were judged as having particular expertise in the field. Thus, in these two firms, expertise could be seen as emerging from the ongoing interactions of employees.

Treem found four themes that characterized expertise in his research. First, he found that experts transcend established procedures through such behaviors as ignoring existing instructions or creating new ways doing a particular task. Second, experts create opportunities to specialize through volunteering for tasks or choosing to work alone. Third, experts handle large quantities of information and demonstrate their ability to find information quickly through the use of tools that others might not utilize. Finally, experts share unsolicited information through highlighting past success and making their experiences visible to those around them.

In some ways, these findings about expertise are encouraging—one doesn't need to necessarily be credentialed to be an expert contributor to a knowledge-intensive organizational system. However, it also paints the somewhat bleak picture of a workplace in which expertise is an ongoing and contested relational battle, a place where "the visible behaviors of workers are judged relative to each other, meaning that to be viewed as an expert one must not merely provide a performance that is reflective of exclusive ability, but do so more frequently, more effectively, or more meaningfully than others" (Treem, 2012, p. 42). In other words, in a workplace without clear markers of quality output, the expert might just be the guy who can "toot his own horn" better than others.

Treem, J.W. (2012). Communicating expertise: Knowledge performance in professional-service firms. *Communication Monographs, 79,* 23–47.

into those rules or applications, and further interaction is needed to find a solution that will keep the family together and off the street for one night or beyond (improvisational knowledge).

Thus, the process of knowledge management involves "identifying and harnessing intellectual assets" to allow organizations to "build on past experiences and create new mechanisms for exchanging and creating knowledge" (Heaton, 2008). Knowledge management involves the use of explicit knowledge that is saved in documents, systems, and programs (typically synoptic knowledge) and tacit knowledge that is held by individuals in an organization (typically cultural knowledge) in ongoing collaboration and, perhaps, improvisation. Nonaka and Takeuchi (1995) argue that a successful system of knowledge management will do two things. First, a successful system will allow individuals in an organization to convert their tacit knowledge into explicit knowledge that can be shared and used in organizational decision making and operations. Second, a successful system will allow organizational members to find ways to make the codified knowledge meaningful once it has been retrieved from organizational systems. For example, knowledge management regarding customer service at a restaurant will involve statistics about restaurant operations *and* the stories of waiters and waitresses about service encounters.

Iverson and McPhee (2002) have argued that the need for these various kinds of knowledge has led to two distinct approaches to knowledge management processes. *Information-based knowledge management* is most concerned with tracking data and developing processes for cataloguing and retrieving those data. In contrast, interaction-based knowledge management is concerned with the tacit knowledge that organizational actors hold and—especially—how interaction patterns in organizational networks can facilitate the sharing of that information. Kuhn and Jackson (2008) argue that the impact of knowledge management systems can be seen most clearly by looking at how organizations deal with difficult situations that might arise during the course of organizational activities. Problematic situations can test the extent to which both tacit knowledge bases and interaction patterns are effective or might lead to unintended consequences. In other words, organizational crises can show the extent to which there is appropriate synoptic knowledge, whether that knowledge has been translated properly to the cultural situation at hand, and whether members of the organizational have the improvisational knowledge to adapt to ongoing contingencies.

SUMMARY

In this chapter, we looked at the activities through which organizational members and groups make decisions, collaborate, and utilize organizational knowledge. We first considered several models of the decision-making process, noting that most scholars have rejected a strictly rational depiction of decision-making in favor of models that include intuition and other nonrational components. We then looked specifically at the small-group context in which a great many organizational decisions are made. Again, we found that most theorists now eschew linear models of decision making in favor of descriptive models that incorporate the complex ebb and flow of communication in small groups. We also looked at group communication processes that result in effective and ineffective decisions, noting that attention to key communication functions in group communication can decrease the risk of groupthink in decision-making collectives. Next, we examined the literature on participative decision making (PDM) by examining two models of the process: the affective model and the cognitive model. Finally, we considered ways in which these ideas regarding decision making have been expanded in recent years to the study of workplace democracy, collaboration among groups and organizations, and systems of knowledge management.

Table 8.4 summarizes the work on decision making in terms of the eight approaches to organizational communication we have discussed in this textbook. It should be clear that the early models of decision making we considered have their roots in the classical approach to organizational communication. The rational models of decision making and the phase models of small-group processing assume that an ideal decision can be made if organizational decision makers are careful in following correct procedures. These models of decision making have been largely rejected, however, in favor of models more in line with human relations, human resources, and systems approaches. The affective and cognitive models of participation, for example, are clearly predicated, respectively, on human relations and human resources principles and the influence of systems approaches can be seen in the work of Poole on decision paths.

Table 8.4	Approaches to the Decision-Making Process
Approach	**How Decision Making Would Be Considered**
Classical	Decision making is seen as a rational and logical process. Emphasis is placed on procedures through which decision makers can reach an optimal solution as efficiently as possible.
Human relations	Participation in the decision-making process is seen as an avenue for the satisfaction of worker needs. Satisfied workers will then be more productive.
Human resources	Participation is seen as an avenue for eliciting valuable information from employees and for ensuring effective implementation of organizational decisions.
Systems	Decision making is seen as a complex process involving multiple and varied stages. Both information and organizational members are seen as part of knowledge management systems.
Cultural	Decision making is seen as a set of practices that reflects organizational values and assumptions. Cultural information is an important facet of embedded knowledge.
Constitutive	Decision making is seen as an interactive site through which organization is constituted. Texts created through conversation can facilitate or impede collaborative processes.
Critical	Decision making is seen as a process through which management can exert control over employees through the definition and acceptance of decision premises and processes.
Feminist	Decision making is seen as one way to enact feminist values such as non-hierarchical structure, collaboration, regard for emotion, and supportive interaction.

More contemporary work in this area has drawn increasingly on other perspectives. Scholars considering organizational knowledge highlight the importance of culture as a site and mediator for synoptic and tacit knowledge. From a critical stance, Tompkins and Cheney (1985) argue that when employees make decisions based on decision-making premises endorsed by management, they are essentially succumbing to unobtrusive control:

> We believe that much of the communication in this entire process is tacit; that is, there are many kinds of suppressed premises, and this is what makes the ... process so elusive, subtle, pervasive, and, from the organization's standpoint, effective. Organizational members often "fill in" premises while nearly always accepting the "master premise" of putting the organization first. (p. 196)

In line with these ideas is the concept of "concertive control" we discussed in Chapter 6. Barker's (1993) study of an organization moving from a hierarchical to a team-based system concluded that, through the influence of participation processes, a team-based organization can exert even stronger control over workers than a hierarchical one. One response to this could be a shift to more "feminist" forms of collaboration and decision-making that value emotion and ongoing collaboration and empowerment or to hybrid forms that account for the linked goals of rationality and support (Ashcraft, 2001). Finally, the research we noted on the influence of objects in collaboration draw on ideas regarding textual agency that we considered in Chapter 5 when exploring the Montreal School's constitutive approach.

DISCUSSION QUESTIONS

1. Think about a decision you've recently made. Did you make that decision in a rational and logical way? If yes, how did you structure your decision-making process? If no, in what ways was your decision-making process not rational?
2. In what ways does group decision making parallel individual decision making? How does group interaction change and influence the decision-making process? If the group is part of an organization, how do organizational factors influence decision making?
3. How do the dynamics of the communication process shift when we move from decision-making among individuals in an organization to collaboration among multiple organizations or groups? How can technology facilitate—or perhaps impeded—the collaboration process?
4. Is organizational democracy merely a utopian goal or is it something that can be achieved in the workplace? What steps would you take to make an organization that you're a part of more democratic?
5. How are people and data linked in systems of knowledge management? Can you think of a job you have had in which your tacit knowledge regarding the culture or improvisational options was different from the explicit knowledge available to organizational decision-makers? How can these two kinds of knowledge be linked through organizational communication processes?

KEY CONCEPTS

normative model of decision
  making
optimizing vs. satisficing
bounded rationality

intuitive decision making
phase models of decision making
multiple sequence model
groupthink

functional theory of group
  decision making
symbolic convergence theory
bona fide groups

affective model
cognitive model
workplace democracy

interorganizational collaboration
synoptic knowledge
cultural knowledge

improvisational knowledge
knowledge management

CASE STUDY | ## Too Many Majors

Chelsea McGuire is the chairperson of a communication department at a university in the southeastern United States. She has been chair for more than five years and has built a successful department. But Chelsea has worried for some time that the department is too successful. Over the last few years, the number of communication majors in the university has steadily increased. When Chelsea took over as chair, there were 500 communication majors. There are now more than 800 such majors, with no indication that this trend will change. Unfortunately, university support for the department has not increased at the same pace, and with only fifteen department professors, Chelsea knows that some kind of action will soon need to be taken.

A month ago, she appointed two separate groups to study the problem and formulate enrollment management plans. First, she formed an ad hoc enrollment management committee to investigate the problem. Second, she asked the standing undergraduate curriculum committee to consider avenues for handling the preponderance of communication majors. Chelsea now has e-mails from each of these committees on her desktop and has scheduled a meeting of the full faculty to discuss options and come to a decision about enrollment management. Let's first take a look at the notes from the two committees:

To: Dr. Chelsea McGuire
From: Dr. Walter Staniszewski
Subject: Enrollment Management Plan

The Ad Hoc Committee on Enrollment Management has met on three occasions in the last month and conducted extensive research into enrollment management systems around the campus. Our goal was to determine the optimal system for stemming the flow of majors into the communication department. In order to reach our goal, we conducted a systematic survey of all other campus departments to determine if they too had experienced problems with over enrollment in the past ten years. If they had experienced this problem, we inquired about plans that had been instituted to deal with the problem and established how well these plans were working. We also carefully compared the characteristics of other campus departments with relevant attributes of the communication department in considering options for dealing with our own enrollment management problems.

After committee evaluation of possible solutions, we have determined that three options are worthy of further departmental consideration:

- Many departments have instituted additional course requirements for majors. These have served to make the major less attractive to many students. Specifically, we might want to consider instituting a requirement of two years of a foreign language or a requirement of math and computer science.

- Some departments have instituted strict grade point requirements for entry into the major. Although the university does not encourage this type of plan, the departments believe it to have been highly successful. Specifically, we might want to consider instituting a 2.5 GPA requirement for entry into the major and continuation in the major.

- A few departments have instituted an application process for admitting students to the major. Although this system would require additional paperwork on the part of the department, it would discourage students who were not truly interested in being communication majors from becoming majors.

The Ad Hoc Committee on Enrollment Management is looking forward to a careful evaluation of these options at the upcoming faculty meeting.

CASE STUDY | **Too Many Majors** *continued*

To: Professor Chelsea McGuire
From: Professor Jerry Gluesing
Subject: Enrollment Management Issue

At its biweekly meeting, the Undergraduate Curriculum Committee took up the issue of enrollment management. We had a lively discussion on the issue, and it quickly became clear that a number of perspectives were possible. The committee was particularly persuaded by the position of Dr. Tanaka, who, as you know, has been with the department for more than thirty years. Dr. Tanaka pointed out that we have had these crises of too many majors (or too few majors) many times in the past and have often spent an inordinate amount of time looking for the proper solution to the problem. Dr. Tanaka argued convincingly that enrollment ups and downs are part of the natural life cycle of an academic department and that we would be rash to institute major curricular or policy changes at this point. Indeed, as Dr. Tanaka pointed out, we have made few major changes to the program in the past twenty-five years, and over the long haul, enrollment has remained at a healthy but manageable level. Thus, although we would certainly enjoy discussing alternative ideas, our committee would suggest that no action be taken at this point. If necessary, we can revisit the issue next year at this time.

With these two memos in hand, Chelsea is now getting set to lead a faculty meeting where the sole agenda item is the discussion of an enrollment management system. Her leadership in the past has always been highly participative. She has generally gone along with the will of the faculty in making departmental decisions, and she has been pleased with the effect of this decision-making style on both the quality of decisions made and on faculty morale. However, she is now concerned that this style might not work for the enrollment management decision, and she is going into this meeting with a bit of trepidation.

CASE ANALYSIS QUESTIONS

1. How would you characterize the decision-making styles of the two committees that considered the enrollment management problem? Would you characterize either of these processes as more effective or appropriate to the decision under consideration?

2. What advice would you give to Chelsea McGuire for the upcoming faculty meeting? Should she retain her typically participative decision-making style? What are the advantages and disadvantages of this kind of style in this type of decision-making situation?

3. Are there specific decision-making strategies that would be helpful in making an effective decision regarding enrollment management? What communication behaviors would you watch for in the upcoming meeting to assess whether an effective decision-making process is being used?

4. How does this case illustrate the various kinds of organizational knowledge and the knowledge management process? Given what you know of this department, do you believe it will be able to adapt to more changes in the organizational environment? How do you think this department would react, for instance, to a call for more online courses as a way to serve even more students?

9 | Conflict Management Processes

AFTER READING THIS CHAPTER, YOU SHOULD ...

- Be able to define organizational conflict and explain its stages and the various levels at which it might occur in the organization.
- Be able to recognize various conflict styles, identify their effectiveness, and appreciate ways in which a styles approach might fall short in analyzing organizational conflict.
- Know about the role of third parties in conflict negotiation, especially the processes of mediation and arbitration.
- Understand how personal, relational, organizational, and cultural factors influence the conflict process.
- Appreciate the need for an alternative approach to conflict, such as the approach suggested by feminist theorists and practitioners.

A manager and an employee of a consulting firm disagree about how to best organize a report for a client. Two coworkers at a fast-food restaurant find themselves in a heated discussion about who is going to be stuck working the weekend shift. Representatives of a school district and a teachers union sit down to hammer out the details of a labor agreement. An automobile company's manufacturing division strongly opposes a set of design changes proposed by research and development.

All these scenarios are examples of a pervasive part of organizational life—conflict. Conflict can be both destructive and productive. It can destroy work relationships or create the impetus for needed organizational change. Through communication, organizational members create and work through conflicts in ways that can be either functional or dysfunctional. In this chapter, we explore the role of conflict in organizational life. First, we conceptualize the issue by defining conflict and then discuss levels of conflict and phases in the conflict process. Following this, we look at communicative processes for managing conflict by considering individual conflict styles, the processes of negotiation and bargaining, and the role of third parties in settling organizational disputes. We then look at personal, relational, and organizational influences on the conflict management process. Finally, we consider a feminist view of conflict and negotiation that shifts our attention from exchange models to a focus on dialogue and community.

CONCEPTUALIZING THE CONFLICT PROCESS

Defining Conflict

What exactly is conflict? Although definitions abound in both academia and everyday life, Putnam and Poole (1987) have developed a definition that is useful in highlighting several critical components of conflict in the organizational arena. They define conflict as "the interaction of interdependent people who perceive opposition of goals, aims, and values, and who see the other party as potentially interfering with the realization of these goals" (p. 552). This definition highlights three general characteristics that we might think of as the **three I's of conflict**: incompatible goals, interdependence, and interaction.

The notion of *incompatible goals* is central to most definitions of conflict and can involve a plethora of issues in the organizational setting. For example, many organizational conflicts stem from contradictory ideas about the distribution of organizational resources. Management and labor negotiate about the distribution of payroll and benefits or the top executive team argues about what capital investments to make in the coming fiscal year. Incompatibility can also disrupt organizational procedures. For example, two social workers might disagree on the best way to conduct home visits for prospective foster families. Or conflict might stem from different value orientations. For instance, in mergers and acquisitions, conflict often arises if the culture of the acquiring company is based on values different from those of the acquired company. In short, the basis of organizational conflict lies in the perception of incompatibility regarding a variety of organizational issues.

However, incompatibility is not a sufficient condition for organizational conflict to result. It is only when the behaviors of the organizational members are *interdependent* that conflict arises. Consider a situation in which one manager supports participative decision making, while another believes in an authoritative management style. This incompatibility can exist harmoniously until interdependencies develop between the two managers. For example, if the two managers are asked to work together on a project or if their subordinates begin to compare notes about bosses, a conflict could well ensue. However, until behaviors are interdependently entwined, incompatibility need not result in conflict.

Finally, our definition of conflict highlights the role of *interaction* in organizational conflict. That is, conflict involves the *expression* of incompatibility, not the mere existence of incompatibility. This idea highlights the importance of communication in the study of conflict. As Putnam and Poole (1987) argue:

> Communication constitutes the essence of conflict in that it undergirds the formation of opposing issues, frames perceptions of the **felt conflict**, translates emotions and perceptions into conflict behaviors, and sets the stage for future conflicts. Thus communication is instrumental in every aspect of conflict, including conflict avoidance or suppression, the open expression of opposition, and the evolution of issues, (p. 552)

Thus, it is through communication that conflict is instantiated and through communication that conflict is dealt with in productive and constructive—or sometimes unproductive and destructive—ways.

Levels of Organizational Conflict

In the examples we've already noted, it's clear that organizational conflict can take place at a variety of levels. By far the most research attention has been paid to the *interpersonal level* of conflict, the level at which individual members of the organization perceive goal incompatibility. However, conflict can also be present in the form of intergroup conflict and interorganizational conflict.

Intergroup conflict considers aggregates of people within an organization (e.g., work teams, departments) as parties in the conflict. As an illustration, two divisions fighting over scarce fiscal resources are involved in intergroup conflict. Not surprisingly, intergroup conflict can become complicated when members of a single group hold varying views about the conflict. For example, in labor negotiations, dissension often occurs among members of the union or members of the management team regarding how the conflict should be resolved. Furthermore, in our increasingly globalized world, work groups from a single organization in different nations might have radically different ideas about work values and procedures.

Interorganizational conflict involves disputes between two or more organizations. This kind of conflict can involve **competition** in the marketplace, perhaps between two stores competing for the same market share or two firms trying to get the same consulting contract. The more interesting interorganizational conflicts, however, may be those among organizations that are *working together,* perhaps in joint operating agreements or community consortiums. This level of conflict, then, emphasizes the role of "boundary spanners"—individuals on the edges of organizations who have significant interorganizational contact. For boundary spanners, interorganizational conflict is particularly stressful because they are asked to understand the needs of both organizational insiders and the outsiders with whom the negotiation takes place (Adams, 1980).

Phases of Organizational Conflict

Individuals in organizations do not move suddenly from peaceful coexistence to conflict-ridden relationships. Rather, people move through phases as conflicts develop and subside. Pondy (1967) has suggested five phases that characterize organizational conflict. A summary of these is presented in Table 9.1.

As Table 9.1 indicates, organizational conflict can go through several phases before it becomes manifest in communicative interaction. The first phase, **latent conflict**, involves a situation in which the conditions are ripe for conflict because interdependence and possible incompatibility exist between the parties. The second phase, **perceived conflict**, occurs when one or more of the parties believes that incompatibilities and interdependence exist. It is possible, of course, to have latent conflict without perceived conflict. For example, two coworkers might have different ideas about the best way to organize a report, but this difference of opinion might not be an issue

Table 9.1 | Phases of Organizational Conflict

Phase	Description
Latent conflict	Grounds for conflict exist because parties are interacting in interdependent relationships in which incompatible goals are possible.
Perceived conflict	One or more parties perceive that their situation is characterized by incompatibility and interdependence.
Felt conflict	Parties begin to personalize perceived conflict by focusing on the conflict issue and planning conflict management strategies.
Manifest conflict	Conflict is enacted through communication. Interaction might involve cycles of escalation and de-escalation as various strategies are used.
Conflict aftermath	Conflict episode has both short-term and long-term effects on the individuals, their relationship, and the organization.

Based on Pondy, L. R. (1967). Organizational conflict: Concepts and models. *Administrative Science Quarterly, 12,* 296–320.

for either of them. It is also possible to have perceived conflict without latent conflict. This situation would exist, for instance, if a manager and a subordinate believed they had different standards about working from home but actually had the same values.

During the third phase of conflict—**felt conflict**—the parties begin to formulate strategies about how to deal with the conflict and consider outcomes that would and would not be acceptable. These strategies and goals are enacted in communication during the **manifest conflict** phase. (Much of the rest of this chapter expands on what goes on during this conflict phase.) Finally, the last phase discussed by Pondy—**conflict aftermath**—emphasizes that conflicts can have both short-term and long-term consequences. Even after a conflict is settled, it can change the nature of the individuals, their relationship, and their functioning within the organization.

MANAGING ORGANIZATIONAL CONFLICT

We have now developed a conceptualization of conflict by defining it and noting its characteristic phases and the levels at which it can materialize. In this section, we look at theory and research about how organizational members attempt to manage conflict. We use the term *conflict management* rather than *conflict resolution* because of the point made previously about the ongoing nature of conflict and because of the complexity of most conflict situations. In discussing conflict management, we first turn to research on the various strategies that individuals use when involved in interpersonal conflict. We then discuss the process of negotiation in managing conflict and examine the role that third parties can play in helping individuals cope with organizational conflicts. Finally, we consider ways in which a feminist view of conflict might provide new directions for conflict research and organizational practice.

Conflict Styles

Description   In Chapter 3, we talked about the Managerial/Leadership Grid developed by Blake and Mouton (1964), who proposed that a manager's leadership style can be characterized in terms of the level of concern shown for productivity and the level of concern shown for people. For example, a manager displaying a high concern for people and a low concern for productivity was characterized as having a "country club" style of management.

Theorists studying organizational conflict have used the basic structure of the Managerial/Leadership Grid as a way of exploring the styles and strategies people use when involved in interpersonal conflict. Indeed, the Managerial/Leadership Grid has been described as the "conceptual grandparent" of conflict style research (Nicotera, Rodriguez, Hall & Jackson, 1995). The analysis of conflict styles was most completely developed by Thomas (1976). In adapting the Managerial/Leadership Grid for conflict situations, Thomas reconceptualized the two dimensions as *concern for self* and *concern for others*. He then identified five conflict styles that would fall at various points on this conflict grid. The conflict grid and resulting styles are presented in Figure 9.1.

These conflict styles can be illustrated by considering a specific conflict situation. Imagine that your boss has come to you with "some good news and some bad news." The good news is that the public relations firm you work for has a chance to attract an important new client. The bad news is that either you or your coworker Wilma

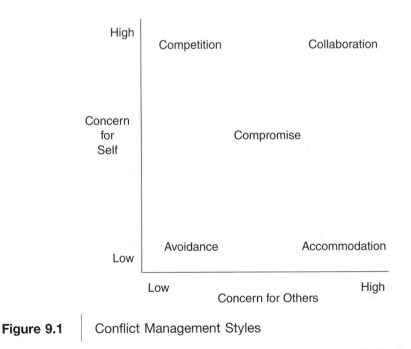

Figure 9.1 | Conflict Management Styles

Adapted from Thomas, W. (1976). Conflict and conflict management. In M. Dunnette (Ed.), *Handbook of Industrial and Organizational Psychology*. Chicago: Rand-McNally. Used by permission of Marvin Dunnette.

will have to spend a healthy portion of the weekend preparing the proposal. Your boss has told you and Wilma to work it out and have a draft of the proposal ready to go on Monday morning. Neither you nor Wilma really wants to work on Saturday, but the work must get done. According to the conflict grid in Figure 9.1, you could approach this conflict in five distinct ways.

First, you could simply decide to not talk with Wilma about the problem because you know that the issue will not be easy to resolve. This strategy—**avoidance**—shows little concern for either your own needs or Wilma's. Not surprisingly, this strategy is rarely effective. Two other strategies emphasize one person's needs at the expense of the other person's needs. For example, by *accommodating,* you could simply volunteer to work on Saturday because you know Wilma wants the day off, and you want to make her happy. This strategy, though, does nothing to satisfy your own needs. Or you could pit your will against Wilma's, insisting that she must work because you cannot. This strategy—competition—might get you what you want, but Wilma's needs will be sacrificed in the process. A fourth strategy—**compromise**—could involve each of you working for four hours on Saturday. Although this strategy seems ideal in some ways, it means that neither you nor Wilma will be able to follow through on your weekend plans because each of you has to work on Saturday, albeit for a shorter period of time. Finally, you might sit down with Wilma and *collaborate* to reach a solution that could benefit both of you. For example, you might find that you both have Thursday and Friday evenings free, and by working together, you can write the proposal without relinquishing weekend plans.

Critique of Conflict Styles Construct   The styles framework suggests that individuals approach organizational conflict in regular and predictable ways. For example, Wood and Bell (2007) found that personality factors, such as agreeableness and extraversion, are predictive of an individual's conflict style preference, and Holmes and Marra (2004) found that effective leaders will choose styles that match the needs of the situation. However, this framework has generated considerable debate about how organizational conflict should be best studied. Knapp, Putnam, and Davis (1988) identified four factors that limit the usefulness of the "grid" approach to organizational conflict. These factors are presented in Table 9.2.

The first criticism presented in Table 9.2 involves the extent to which a grid approach reflects the complex interactive nature of organizational conflict. By arguing that individuals possess particular conflict styles, the grid approach downplays the extent to which individuals change their tactics during interaction with others in conflict situations. For example, an individual might begin by attempting to collaborate but, having little success, might then force a solution on the other party. The second criticism presented in Table 9.2 addresses the two-dimensional nature of the conflict grid. Knapp and associates (1988) argue that issues other than concern for self and concern for others might influence a conflict interaction. For example, individuals might be worried about the political implications of communication or the impact of conflict resolution on the organization as a whole. Third, these scholars believe that research on conflict styles has downplayed the important roles that nonverbal and nonrational communication might play in conflict management. Finally, they contend that by concentrating on individual conflict style, the role of the

Table 9.2	Criticisms of the Conflict Styles Approach
Critique 1	The conflict styles approach treats the individual communicator as the sole benchmark for conceptualizing conflict and for determining how it will develop.
Critique 2	The conflict styles approach relies too narrowly on two- dimensional theoretical models that may not be internally congruent, exhaustive, or representative of conflict-handling modes in organizations.
Critique 3	The conflict styles approach limits communication to verbal behaviors, especially those that are rational and uncomplicated, mutually exclusive across different styles, and static and unchanging.
Critique 4	The conflict styles approach treats the organization as being in the distant background rather than in the center stage of conflict activity.

Based on Knapp, M. L., Putnam, L. L. & Davis, L. J. (1988). Measuring interpersonal conflict in organizations: Where do we go from here? *Management Communication Quarterly, 1,* 414–429.

organizational setting is ignored. An individual might deal very differently with conflict in a highly mechanistic company than in a more democratic and loosely structured one.

New Directions   In recent years, communications scholars have looked beyond general issues of style in considering interpersonal conflict and have begun to pay more attention to details about message style and the perceptions of individuals in the conflict episode. For example, Jameson (2004) explored how individuals in conflict can satisfy a variety of organizational- and individual-level needs through politeness strategies in conflict interaction, and Meiners and Miller (2004) found that the level of formality in conflict interaction influenced the extent to which individuals were direct, detailed in their needs, and willing to make concessions. Gross, Guerrero, and Alberts (2004) considered perceptions of conflict management and found that people viewed controlling strategies as inappropriate when used by others and as highly effective when used by themselves.

A more comprehensive body of research has been developed primarily by Jeffrey Kassing and Johny Garner. This work considers a specific kind of conflict—that which occurs when an employee has a disagreement with the organization or supervisor and chooses to voice that disagreement through **dissent**. Research investigating this specific form of conflict has considered strategies and message types employees use when expressing dissent (Garner, 2009b; Kassing, 2002), the factors that influence the likelihood of speaking up through processes of dissent (Kassing & Armstrong, 2002), the goals that dictate particular expressions of organizational influence (Garner, 2009a), the effectiveness of various dissent messages (Garner, 2012), and the extent to which employees might choose to circumvent their immediate supervisor to express dissent at a higher organizational level (Kassing, 2007). Garner (2013) has summarized much of this work in a practical set of recommendations including the need to express ideas to someone who can make a difference, the importance of package dissent with a solution, and the persuasiveness of direct factual appeals in dissent situations.

Bargaining and Negotiation

A second general strategy for dealing with organizational conflict is bargaining (also referred to as negotiation). According to Putnam and Poole (1987)

> [b]argaining constitutes a unique form of conflict management in that participants negotiate mutually shared rules and then cooperate within these rules to gain a competitive advantage over their opponent ... Bargaining, then, differs from other forms of conflict in its emphasis on proposal exchanges as a basis for reaching a joint settlement in cooperative-competitive situations. (p. 563)

Several characteristics of bargaining are important. First, bargaining is often a *formal* activity in which disputants settle conflicts about scarce resources or policy disagreements. Formal bargaining is marked by a clear understanding of (and adherence to) the rules of the negotiation situation. For example, one rule bargainers often follow is the rule of "mutual concessions." According to this rule, if one party in the conflict gives something up, the other party should concede an issue of like value. Second,

Case in Point: Working with Jerks

For some people, conflict seems to be a way of life. If you have one of these individuals as a coworker—or, even worse, as a boss—your work life can be made miserable. Conflict can shift into bullying and permeate an organizational culture. Robert Sutton, a professor of management science at Stanford University, has heard all the stories about "working with jerks," and wrote The No A****** Rule (2007), see references for uncensored title.

Sutton argues that jerks who elevate the level of conflict and stress in an organization are easy to spot: "[T]he main sign of someone who's a certified jerk is someone who leaves a trail of people feeling demeaned and de-energized. It tends to be more often associated with power dynamics—they kiss up to those above them and kick those beneath them" ("Advice for Tackling Workplace Jerks," 2007). In the language of conflict management styles, these individuals are always confrontational and are unable to collaborate or appreciate the other person's perspective.

What to do if you find yourself working with a jerk? Sutton suggests that organizations can work

to screen these individuals in the hiring process so that jerks don't enter the system. Or you could take the extreme action of quitting if you just can't work with the jerk anymore. But Sutton's best suggestion is to learn to avoid them as much as possible and learn not to care. Sutton recounts one example:

> My favorite story comes from a former CEO who told about her worst board member. When he'd call and scream, she'd lean back in her chair, put her feet on the desk, put him on speakerphone, turn off the volume and do her nails. She would check in from time to time to see if he was still screaming. When he was done, she would reason with him. She put herself in a relaxed position and did something she could control—her nails. ("Advice," 2007)

We may not all be in a position to do our nails in order to cope with a jerk. But the strategy of avoiding and maintaining control is certainly advice we should "file" away.

bargaining often involves individuals who serve as representatives for the parties in the dispute. Third, bargaining is the strategy often used to settle intergroup or inter-organizational conflicts. For example, disputes between labor and management are typically settled through formal negotiation.

An important distinction often made about bargaining is that of *distributive and* **integrative bargaining.** Distributive and integrative bargaining differ in terms of goals, issues, communication processes, and outcomes. These differences are summarized in Table 9.3.

In **distributive bargaining,** the two conflicting parties are working to maximize their own gains and minimize their own losses. The bargaining centers on the limited resources that must be divided in the negotiation (e.g., wages, benefits, hours). Because bargainers are working with a "fixed pot," the only possible outcomes are win-lose solutions or compromises. Finally, because the bargainers are concerned with their own outcomes, communication is marked by withheld information, deception, and attempts to learn as much as possible about the other party's position.

In *integrative bargaining,* the conflicting parties are trying to maximize gains for both parties. Thus, the bargainers discuss issues that could lead to a more creative solution to the problem at hand. Outcomes of integrative bargaining are often solutions that allow both parties to benefit, and communication tends to be marked by open disclosure, careful listening, and multiple communication channels. In its integrative form, bargaining can serve "as a forum for identifying problems, clarifying misconceptions, signaling needs and interests, and negotiating the meaning of organizational events" (Putnam, 1995, p. 196).

Consider, for instance, a labor dispute between a nurses union and the administration of a large hospital. Often, bargainers in this situation take a distributive approach. They concentrate on issues such as salary, working hours, or power to make decisions and try to get as much as possible (or give as little as possible) in the negotiation. The actual bargaining sessions would be marked by distrust and information provided in spurts and starts. However, the parties could choose to take an

---

Table 9.3 | Comparison of Distributive and Integrative Bargaining

	Distributive Bargaining	**Integrative Bargaining**
Goals	Maximize individual gains and minimize losses	Maximize joint gains
Issues	Fixed-sum issues with limited resources	Variable-sum issues shaped by overlapping positions
Outcomes	Compromises, trade-offs, and win-lose results	Creative solutions not attributable to specific concessions
Communication	Information-seeking, withholding data, and deception in disclosures	Open sharing of information; accurate disclosure of needs and objectives

Based on Putnam, L. L. & Poole, M. S. (1987). Conflict and negotiation. In F. Jablin, L. Putnam, K. Roberts & L. Porter (Eds.), *Handbook of Organizational Communication: An Interdisciplinary Perspective* (pp. 549–599). Newbury Park, CA: Sage.

integrative approach to the negotiation. In this case, the bargainers might consider the mutual benefit of a new organizational model in which nurses are part of the fiscal decision-making group and gain more voice in medical collaborations. The development of such a solution would be difficult and would involve intense communication and problem solving but could benefit both parties in the long run.

Third-Party Conflict Resolution

There are times when the individuals (or groups) involved in a conflict are unable to resolve the disagreement on their own either through informal discussion or formal negotiation. At these times, a third party is often relied on to help resolve the conflict. Sometimes, the third party might be a friend or coworker who is brought in to help settle the conflict or to provide support for one of the parties (Volkema, Bergmann & Farquhar, 1997). Especially in conflicts of a relational nature, individuals can often gain important insights from those who are not directly involved in the organizational context (Myers & Larson, 2005).

More often, when conflicts between coworkers stem from differences in working style or personality or when disputes arise over work processes or organizational procedures, a supervisor might be called in to help settle the dispute. A number of scholars have investigated the various roles that managers can play in resolving organizational conflict (see, e.g., Elangovan, 1995). For example, a manager might address a dispute by establishing rules or dictating a specific solution, might reward or punish subordinates in order to facilitate a solution, or might work to change the organization in order to keep similar problems from occurring in the future.

Finally, third parties from outside the organization also sometimes assist in settling disputes (see Lipsky, Seeber & Fincher, 2003, for review). These third parties typically serve as either *mediators* or *arbitrators.* A mediator attempts to help the parties facilitate the dispute but holds no decision power. In contrast, an arbitrator makes decisions (often binding) based on the proposals and arguments of the parties involved in the conflict. For example, professional athletes often go to arbitration to settle contract disputes. The arbitrator hears the proposals and arguments of both the players and team management and decides on one proposal or the other without compromise.

Information sharing and persuasion are important forms of communication in arbitration. However, the role of communication is even more pronounced in **mediation,** as the parties in mediation are working together to develop a viable solution to the conflict at hand. There are a variety of tactics that mediators can use to facilitate effective communication in mediation. These strategies include *directive tactics,* in which the mediator initiates recommendations; *nondirective tactics,* in which the mediator attempts to secure information and clarify misunderstandings; *procedural* tactics, in which the mediator establishes an agenda and protocol for conflict resolution; and *reflexive tactics,* in which the mediator regulates the tone of the interaction by "developing rapport with participants, using humor, and speaking the language of each side" (Putnam & Poole, 1987, p. 572).

The success of mediation and other third party forms of conflict resolution depends to some extent on the outcome, but may depend even more on procedures and communication during the process. For example, Blancero, DelCamp, and

✳ Spotlight on Scholarship: Framing Intractable Conflict

Many of the ideas in this chapter involve individuals or small groups of people working through conflicts and reaching resolutions. However, many organizational conflicts involve larger institutional entities and may continue over many years. Indeed, for some of these conflicts, it seems that no resolution is in sight. It is this kind of conflict—*intractable conflict*—that Linda Putnam and Tarla Peterson consider in their examination of the Edwards Aquifer dispute. An intractable conflict is one that is long-standing and eludes resolution. As Putnam and Wondolleck (2003) explain,

> [i]ntractable conflicts are messy. They are hard to pin down, manage, and analyze, and extremely difficult to resolve. They are intense, frustrating, and complex, with no readily conceivable solutions. (p. 37)

Global warming policy, the Vietnam War, abortion rights and regulations—all of these could be seen as intractable conflicts.

Putnam and Peterson (2003) consider a more regional intractable conflict—that involving the Edwards Aquifer in the south-central region of Texas. The Edwards Aquifer is an underground water formation that provides water not only to a large number of Texans (including the residents of San Antonio) but also to farms in the region and to the native flora and fauna. The aquifer is a renewable resource that is "exceptionally responsive to rainfall and drought" (Putnam & Peterson, 2003, p. 128). That is, when rainfall is plentiful, the aquifer replenishes itself, but in times of drought, the aquifer level drops to a point where the springs cease to flow. This pattern has been exacerbated by the increased use of the aquifer over time.

Not surprisingly, there has been a great deal of conflict over *who* should have control of the Edwards Aquifer and *how* that control should be exercised. Players in the conflict include local, regional, state, and federal agencies, including urban municipalities, organizations of farmers and rural residents, and environmental agencies. The conflict has involved mediation, negotiation, legislation, and litigation. It is, of course, impossible to review all the details of the fifty-plus years of this conflict. However, after considering interviews with seventy stakeholders and the extensive media coverage of the conflict, Putnam and Peterson (2003) conclude that the way the conflict is framed contributes to its ongoing intractability.

Putnam and Peterson (2003) consider three types of **conflict frames**. The first—*identity frames*—refers to how stakeholders describe their own roles in the conflict. Putnam and Peterson note, for instance, that identity frames might involve interests (e.g., private property rights versus the public good), place (e.g., urban versus rural), or institution (e.g., coalitions formed during the conflict). A second type of frame—*characterization frames*—involves how disputants see the other parties in the conflict. In intractable conflicts, these frames often involve polarized and stereotyped categories for understanding others. Finally, disputants use conflict *management frames* to consider ways in which the conflict has been managed in the past or might be managed in the future. For example, if past efforts at mediation and negotiation are framed in negative ways, future frames for conflict negotiation may be more likely to involve resistance strategies than efforts at cooperation. In short, Putnam and Peterson believe these frames often contribute to the seemingly unresolvable nature of intractable conflicts. However, the use of frame analysis also points to the possibility for change and resolution. Indeed, efforts to reframe the conflict in more productive ways have led Putnam and Peterson to a cautiously hopeful prognosis for the Edwards Aquifer case and other seemingly intractable conflicts.

Putnam, L. L. & Peterson, T. (2003). The Edwards Aquifer dispute: Shifting frames in a protracted conflict. In R. J. Lewicki, B. Gray, and M. Elliott (Eds.), *Making Sense of Intractable Environmental Conflicts: Frames and Cases* (pp. 127–158). Washington, DC: Island Press.

Marron (2010) found that factors such as communication style and level of employee input had more influence on perceptions of fairness than actual outcomes. In terms of style of communication, Jameson, Bodtker, and Linker (2010) have recently suggested that one critical factor that is often downplayed—and could enhance mediation outcomes—is the consideration of emotional communication factors during interaction.

FACTORS INFLUENCING THE CONFLICT MANAGEMENT PROCESS

We have now looked at a wide array of conflict management techniques. Individuals involved in interpersonal conflict can and do use a variety of strategies that differ in terms of the attention given to self and other in the conflict. The formal give and take of bargaining and negotiation can be exercised. Or a third party—such as a manager, arbitrator, or mediator—can be brought in to settle conflicts that seem intractable. But when will these various strategies be used? And when will they work to manage the conflict effectively? Although the research on these issues is too vast to summarize here, we will consider three types of factors that influence the conflict management: personal, relational, and cultural factors.

Personal Factors

It might seem that individual characteristics such as personality and gender would strongly influence how conflict is resolved. Indeed, our cultural stereotypes suggest that men are more likely to use competitive strategies, whereas women are prone to accommodate or compromise. It also seems likely that people's conflict management strategies would vary according to their personal characteristics, such as aggressiveness, introversion, or need for control.

However, Putnam and Poole's (1987) review of studies indicates that, on the contrary, personality plays a small role in conflict resolution strategies (although, see Wood & Bell, 2008) and that the findings on gender differences are mixed. Indeed, some of the research findings on gender differences contradict our stereotypical expectations. For example, Turner and Henzl (1987) found that women were very assertive when managing conflict. And Burrell, Buzzanell, and McMillan (1992) found that female managers described conflicts using the typically "male" metaphors of war and aggression. Thus, personality and gender have limited impact on conflict management tactics.

It does appear, however, that the way an individual *frames* a conflict will influence the manner in which the conflict is managed. Framing has been studied as both cognitive representations of the conflict and the way the conflict is enacted during interaction (Dewulf et al., 2009) and involves perceptions of self, of others, or of the conflict itself (Lewicki, Gray & Elliott, 2003). For example, conflict participants might choose to frame others in the conflict as "enemies" in thought or through interaction, and this frame will undoubtedly influence the process and results of the conflict episode. Similarly, individuals in conflict can frame the situation in terms of what they have to lose or in terms of what they have to gain. Neale and Bazerman (1985) found that individuals who frame conflict in terms of losses will be much more likely to take risks than those who frame conflict in terms of gains. Individuals using a frame in terms of loss are also more likely to reach an impasse and seek arbitration.

Relational Factors

In contrast to personal factors, the *relationship* between the conflict parties appears to have a strong impact on conflict resolution. One important characteristic of the relationship between the conflict parties is *power*, or the hierarchical position of the individuals. Putnam and Poole (1987) have reviewed the literature on hierarchical level and conflict styles. Several findings stand out. First, it appears that organizational members generally prefer competitive styles when dealing with subordinates. However, these individuals are likely to use **accommodation** or **collaboration** when dealing with superiors and accommodating or avoiding styles when dealing with peers. Thus, conflict management style depends to a large extent on the hierarchical relationship between the conflict parties. Conflicts with supervisors and administrators are also recalled as more emotionally intense than conflicts with individuals at the same hierarchical level (Gayle & Preiss, 1998).

Another aspect of the relationship between conflict parties is how the relationship influences the interaction through which conflict is managed. For example, Jameson (2004) argued that organizations and their members often struggle with opposing needs for autonomy and connection. That is, workers depend on each other—but also want to maintain independence—and this basic relational contradiction can cause conflict. In a study of conflict between anesthesiologists and certified registered nurse anesthetists, Jameson (2004) found that individuals can use politeness strategies to keep these competing needs balanced and forge more collaborative solutions to conflict situations.

Cultural Factors

Finally, aspects of organizational, national, and ethnic culture might influence the ways in which conflict is enacted and managed in organizations. With regard to national culture, for instance, Brett and Okumura (1998) found that *intercultural* negotiations between U.S. and Japanese negotiators were far less successful than *intracultural* negotiations among these two national groups. These researchers found that U.S. and Japanese negotiators worked from different conflict "scripts," and although the Japanese negotiators understood the U.S. priorities, the U.S. negotiators did not understand the Japanese schema. Ethnic and racial culture also may play a role in conflict negotiation. For example, Turner and Shuter (2004) compared African American women and European American women in terms of their approaches to and perceptions of workplace conflict. Both groups viewed conflict negatively, but the perceptions of African American women were particularly negative and passive. In terms of conflict resolution, European American women were seen as being conflict-avoidant, and African American women were seen as using more direct means of conflict resolution. Generational differences have also recently been considered as a "cultural" factor that influences the likelihood of organizational conflict (Standifer, Lester, Schultz & Windsor, 2013).

Finally, several scholars have investigated how organizational culture can influence the conflict resolution process. This work emphasizes the extent to which conflict resolution can be difficult when organizational subcultures based on professional identity or hierarchical position do not see eye to eye. For example, Geist (1995) examined conflict within hospices, school systems, and hospitals to demonstrate how the culture built around power relationships, technology, and the interests of organizational groups can influence perceptions of conflict and how conflict is managed. Similarly, Smith and Eisenberg (1987) examined a labor dispute at Disneyland, arguing that the subcultures of the workers and management were distinct, with managers seeing Disney as "show business" or "drama" and workers seeing Disney as "family." Thus, in the labor conflict, workers looked at the contract proposals set out by management and were appalled because "this is no way to treat members of your family." In turn, management was shocked when workers went on strike because in showbiz "the show must go on."

A Feminist View of Conflict

To a great extent, the ideas we have looked at so far in this chapter are rooted in a traditional view of conflict. Oh, there are definite differences among the approaches described here. An individual using a "collaborative style" will behave differently in a conflict situation than an individual using either an "accommodating" or "competition" style. And there are clear distinctions between distributive bargaining and integrative bargaining in terms of goals, issues, outcomes, and communication processes. But in spite of these differences, all the research considered here is based on a view of conflict rooted in the concept of *exchange*. In viewing conflict and negotiation as exchange, scholars and practitioners concentrate on goals and resources, on offers and counteroffers, on moves and concessions, and even on creating a "bigger pie" that can satisfy all parties. Indeed, Tjosvold (2008) argues that researchers often conflate "conflict" and "competition" and thus make it less likely that cooperative views of the conflict process will be considered.

Putnam and Kolb (2000) have suggested that these models of conflict that emphasize competition and exchange constitute a *gendered practice*. Specifically, they argue that negotiation

> is gendered in that the qualities of effective bargainers (e.g., individuality and independence, competition, objectivity, analytic rationality, instrumentality, reasoning from universal principles, and strategic thinking) are linked to masculinity. Those attributes typically labeled as feminine (e.g., community, subjectivity, intuition, emotionality, expressiveness, reasoning from particulars, and ad hoc thinking) are less valued. (p. 80)

In response to the masculine exchange model of negotiation, Putnam and Kolb propose a feminist view of conflict based instead on the co-construction of the situation and relationship through collaboration, the sharing of experience and emotion, dialogic interaction, and mutual understanding. For example, their model replaces concepts from the exchange model such as "trades," "mutual gain," "settlement," and "information exchange," with alternative feminist concepts of "mutual inquiry,"

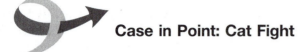

Case in Point: Cat Fight

We've noted in this chapter that some scholars advocate moving from a view of conflict based on masculine ideas such as competition and exchange to one based on feminist ideas such as mutuality and support. Such a move might be difficult, however, as many individuals still hold very stereotypical ideas about women and conflict. A recent study (Sheppard & Aqino, 2012) asked respondents to consider three workplace conflict scenarios that were identical except for the names attached to the conflict: Adam and Steven, Adam and Sarah, or Sarah and Anne. The respondents consistently viewed the conflict between "Sarah and Anne" in a much more negative light than the ones between "Adam and Sarah" or "Adam and Steven."

Why is this the case? It is hard to know for sure, but the researchers suggest that it might be the disjuncture among views about women and conflict. We have cultural language that negatively describes conflicts among women—"catfight" and "Queen Bee syndrome"—with no corresponding terms to refer to other types of conflict. Yet we also have the expectation that women should be "ladylike" and not involved in conflict. As author Sheppard states, "We have this perception that women can be really catty and terrible to each other, but we don't think women *should* be that way. We want to see women supporting one another, because they are a marginalized group" (Silverman, 2013). Sadly, this problem is more than semantic, as "a bias against female-female conflict may affect hiring and promotions for women" (Silverman, 2013). This bias could also hinder both men *and* women from developing more collaborative and effective ways for dealing with workplace conflict.

"mutual understanding," "transformation," and "sharing experiences." This feminist model shifts the emphasis in conflict and negotiation from one that values exchange, problem solving, and rationality to one that considers collaboration, dialogue, and emotion. Putnam and Kolb understand that "at first blush, the alternative approach may seem naive, simple, or unnatural" (p. 81). However, they convincingly argue that their feminist model is an important advance that might be particularly appropriate in situations such as "informal work negotiations, bargaining in long-term relationships, role negotiations, and even intractable disputes" (p. 104). In short, this model provides a new way to think about conflict and perhaps opens new avenues for practice in organizational communication.

SUMMARY

In this chapter, we looked at a ubiquitous facet of organizational life: conflict. We first conceptualized organizational conflict by defining conflict and considering the phases of conflict and the levels at which it can materialize. We then reviewed a number of methods for dealing with organizational conflict. We looked at the literature on conflict style and considered criticisms of the style approach. We then looked at more formal ways of settling organizational dispute: bargaining and negotiation. Then, we considered third-party intervention. In the last section of the chapter, we looked at a number of factors that impinge on the conflict management process, including personal variables, relational variables, and cultural variables. We concluded with a brief look at a feminist view of culture.

The approaches to organizational communication discussed in the first half of this textbook would view conflict as an important and interesting phenomenon, but they would do so in very different ways. As Table 9.4 indicates, classical theorists would see conflict as something that interrupts normal organizational functioning. Thus, the classical manager would try to eliminate conflict in the most efficient way possible. The human relations manager would also want to eliminate conflict but for different reasons. For this manager, conflict is an indication that relationships are not all they could be in the organization. Conflict should thus be dealt with in ways that wouldn't rock the boat—perhaps through accommodating, avoiding, or compromising. In contrast, the human resources manager would consider both the functional and dysfunctional aspects of conflict. This manager would see conflict as a pathway to organizational change and would encourage managing conflict in a collaborative manner.

Systems and cultural researchers have also contributed to our understandings of conflict. A systems approach would look at the cycles of conflict and consider the role of the larger organizational system in encouraging or discouraging conflict behavior, while a cultural approach would consider the extent to which cultural markers such as values and metaphors contribute to and reflect conflictual relationships in the organization. Constitutive theorists might be particularly interested in how culture emerges through individual choices about language in interaction (Holmes & Stubbe, 2003) and the

Table 9.4	Approaches to the Conflict Management Process
Approach	**How Conflict Would Be Considered**
Classical	Conflict is viewed as a breakdown of communication and managed to the extent that the existence of conflict detracts from organizational efficiency.
Human relations	Conflict is viewed as evidence of faulty relationships among organizational members. Parties are encouraged to avoid conflict or compromise in order to return to harmonious work relations.
Human resources	Conflict is viewed as a possible means for growth and development in the organization and conflicting parties are encouraged to collaborate on mutually beneficial solutions.
Systems	Conflict is conceptualized as cycles of activities that can escalate and de-escalate. Conflict is seen as particularly prevalent for highly interdependent parties.
Cultural	Conflict is seen as stemming from the differential value systems of individuals and groups. Factors such as national origin, age, and ethnicity can potentially heighten conflict situations.
Constitutive	Conflict is seen as constituted through the ongoing conversation and discourse of organizational actors. The frames created then shape and constrain subsequent communication in ongoing organizing.
Critical	Superficial organizational conflicts reflect deeper imbalances of power based on issues such as class, culture and economic factors. These imbalances are revealed and sustained through organizational discourse.
Feminist	Conflict is seen as an opportunity to reframe organizational practices away from patriarchal and rational forms and toward patterns that support transformative and collaborative behaviors.

feminist approach we considered above works to reframe conflict through ideals of mutuality. Finally, organizational conflict is central to the work of the critical theorist. The critical scholar, however, would see the enacted conflicts among individuals and work groups as symptomatic of deeper conflicts based on differences of class, power, or economic conditions.

DISCUSSION QUESTIONS

1. Conflict is defined in this chapter as requiring the "three I's": incompatible goals, interdependence, and interaction. Why are these three components necessary? What situations might arise when only one or two of these components are present?

2. Do you believe that you exhibit a typical conflict style? If so, why do you think you use that style? Are there aspects of a situation or of the other parties in a conflict that influence the conflict style you use?

3. What are the differences between integrative and distributive strategies in conflict situations? Why would you use one type of strategy over another? What are the costs of using each of these strategies?

4. What do you think about the feminist reframing of conflict? Is it possible to recast an idea like "conflict" in a way that emphasizes mutuality and collaboration? What are the implications of this reframing for organizational practice?

5. Would you want to have an organization that is free of conflict? Why or why not?

KEY CONCEPTS

three I's of conflict
levels of organizational conflict
latent conflict
perceived conflict
felt conflict
manifest conflict

conflict aftermath
avoidance
accommodation
competition
compromise
collaboration

dissent
distributive bargaining
integrative bargaining
mediation
conflict frames
conflict as gendered practice

CASE STUDY | ## The Problem with Teamwork

Mike Garcia and Jill Hendrickson have been butting heads for months. Mike is a manufacturing manager at Auto Safety Products, a firm in the Midwest that designs and produces automobile seat belts and infant and child safety seats. Jill is a design engineer for the same firm. Recently, top management at Auto Safety Products instituted "concurrent engineering," a team-based system that integrates manufacturing and design processes. Concurrent engineering is intended to eliminate the problems that often occur in industry when designers are unaware of the needs of manufacturing and vice versa. Through concurrent engineering, management hopes to improve attention to all elements of the product life cycle

and manufacture a quality, low-cost product that will meet user needs. The company is also hoping to decrease the amount of time it takes to move from initial conceptual design to actual production.

Mike and Jill are both on the team working on toddler booster seats. This is an important product for Auto Safety Products, as research has indicated that parents do not use safety seats once children reach toddler age, in part because they are difficult to use in cars and uncomfortable for children. As a result, many parents don't use the booster seats correctly, cancelling out any safety benefit. Thus, the team at Auto Safety Products is working to make the seats easier for parents to use by making them more comfortable, more portable, and more compatible with a range of automobiles—from small sports cars to sedans to minivans to SUVs.

Mike is fifty-five years old and has worked in manufacturing for most of his life—twenty-two years with Auto Safety Products. He has always felt some animosity toward the design side of the firm. He finds the engineers uppity and unwilling to listen to the problems faced in manufacturing. He has often complained that the design department generates pie-in-the-sky projects that run into all sorts of practical problems once they hit manufacturing. He approached the new concurrent engineering program at Auto Safety Products with a grain of salt. He thought that it was a good idea in principle ("Those guys in design could use a dose of reality"), but he was not convinced that it would ever work in actuality.

Jill is a twenty-five-year-old mechanical engineer who has been with Auto Safety Products since her college graduation three years ago. She is assertive and strong-minded—she believes she has to be to be effective in the male-dominated world of engineering. She learned about the concurrent engineering concept when she was in school and believes it can greatly improve the effectiveness of design and manufacturing. Unfortunately, it does not seem to be working at Auto Safety Products. The manufacturing side has not really bought into the process, and management did not take the time to introduce the team management system properly and train people to work together. Even though she tries to be open to the ideas of manufacturing, she does not feel this effort is being reciprocated. Her concerns go in one ear and out the other. She is having an especially hard time with Mike Garcia, the lead manufacturing representative on her team. Recently, the two of them have had to work together frequently on a booster seat design problem, trying to adapt the design so it will work in a variety of minivans. Their inability to work together has gotten so bad that their supervisor has set up a meeting to help them deal with the problem.

Adam Shapiro is a project supervisor at Auto Safety Products. He oversees the booster seat project team that Mike and Jill work on. He knows the two of them have not hit it off on the concurrent engineering team and has decided that the conflict has gotten to the point where he must step in and help them settle it. He first asked each of them separately about the problem.

According to Jill, the problem is that Mike will not listen to her ideas and downplays the contributions that design can make to concurrent engineering. In contrast, she sees design as the most important part of the concurrent engineering process. She suspects that Mike has problems with her because she is young and a woman, and this has made her push even harder for her point of view on project disagreements.

According to Mike, the concurrent engineering system—and the booster seat team in particular—is a joke. He says that the design engineers are still trying to push their ideas down manufacturing's throat, and he's tired of the "team" facade. He would like to go back to doing things the old way. However, if he is forced to continue with the concurrent engineering system, he refuses to simply give in to every one of Jill's whims.

As Adam ponders these divergent positions, Jill and Mike enter his office. Neither of them looks particularly happy.

CASE ANALYSIS QUESTIONS

1. What kind of predispositions are Mike and Jill taking into this conflict situation? How might these predispositions influence the way they frame the conflict and the way they approach each other?

2. If Mike and Jill were to attempt to deal with this conflict on their own, what conflict style would you recommend? Given what you know about Jill and Mike, do you think they would use an effective conflict resolution style?

3. If you were Adam, how would you approach this conflict? What strategies should you use to help Mike and Jill deal with their ongoing problems? Would you consider bringing in a mediator to help them work through their issues?

4. How would a feminist approach to conflict see this situation? Is it possible to use an alternative model that would recast this situation in a more productive frame?

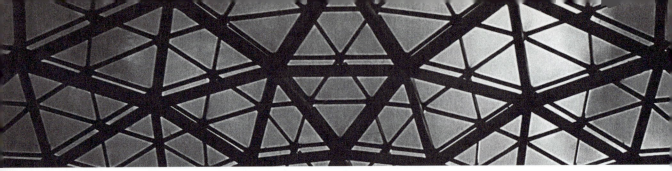

10 | Organizational Change and Leadership Processes

AFTER READING THIS CHAPTER, YOU SHOULD ...

- Appreciate that change is often a natural part of organizational life cycles that can appear in the guise of organizational crisis or be carefully planned and implemented.
- Know the typical problems associated with planned change processes, and be aware of the communication strategies that can address these problems.
- Understand the stages of organizational crisis as forms of unplanned change.
- Be able to trace the development of leadership models from trait and style theories through contingency theories to contemporary theories, such as the transformational leadership model and discursive leadership approaches.
- Appreciate the complex communicative choices that leaders must make, and be able to describe specific tools for delivering leadership messages.
- Understand the distinction between traditional approaches of leadership and models of discursive leadership that highlight the constitutive role of communication.

As the old saying goes, there is nothing so constant as change. Indeed, the constancy of change becomes increasingly apparent as we move further into this new millennium, and the rate of change seems to increase on a daily basis. Zorn, Page, and Cheney (2000) have argued that organizational practitioners today are "Nuts about Change," as the mantra chanted both within the organization and from management gurus is that organizations must "organize for continuous change, to become a flexible organization that can adapt quickly to environmental changes" (pp. 516–517). Zorn et al. believe that we should perhaps question the wisdom of this mantra, but the fact remains that in terms of rhetoric and action, change is likely to remain a central concern in organizational life.

Although change is an enduring feature of organizational life, the degree and impact of that change can vary substantially. Sometimes, the change is huge and life-altering. Imagine, for instance, the changes that could occur if your company merged with another organization, possibly forcing layoffs, job redefinitions, and massive shifts in company mission and processes. Sometimes, the change is large but seems more manageable. For example, a doctor's office might need to revamp a variety of systems as it adjusts to changes in new national health care laws. Most of the time, though, the changes are more mundane and simply a part of the fabric of organizational life. Your boss might ask you to write reports in a different way or the food pantry you volunteer for might adopt new methods for sorting and storing donations.

In this chapter, then, we will consider processes of organizational change and the role of communication in these processes. We will first look at scholarship on planned and unplanned change in organizations. We will consider models of how change occurs in organizations, the roles and reactions of employees, and how communication is woven into change experiences. We will also consider times of major change when organizations face crises. And as we consider the change process, we will find that—as in much of organizational life—the success of such processes often depends on having effective leadership. The second portion of this chapter, then, will consider classic and contemporary models of leadership and look at the role of communication in the leadership process.

ORGANIZATIONAL CHANGE PROCESSES

The Complexity of Organizational Change

No organization that remains static—stuck in particular ways of doing things and particular modes of thinking—will survive long. We can all, for example, think of products such as eight-track audiotapes and beta videotapes that have been lost to history because their makers did not anticipate changes in consumer tastes and habits or changes in the industrial marketplace. Similarly, organizations that get stuck in procedural or managerial ruts are often not long-lived. However, many organizations naturally evolve and adapt to environmental needs.

There are models of **organizational life cycles** (Kimberly & Miles, 1980) and the evolution of organizational populations (Hannan & Freeman, 1989) that consider the "natural" ways in which organizations and groups of organizations change with the ebb and flow of institutional life and industry history. As a highly simplistic example, the natural life cycle of a consulting firm might include a start-up phase in which the company develops a market and creates systems and procedures; a growth phase in which client relationships are developed and the size of the company grows; a steady "harvest" phase in which the company serves existing clients; and a decay stage in which the consulting firm's services become less relevant to the marketplace and the firm eventually folds or is bought by another company.

Other considerations of organizational change look at situations in which there is a *planned* change. Oftentimes, organizations are confronted with problems in the environment or with internal contingencies that suggest that current "ways of doing things" are not effective. Perhaps a competitor starts cutting into the market share of a consumer products company. Or perhaps the new company president decides that it is critical to develop a new culture that emphasizes enhanced customer service. In these cases, many organizations will begin a purposeful process of change over time. This change over time may involve a process in which the organization explores the need for change and possible solutions, plans for how that change is to be instituted, implements the change and disseminates information about the change, and then integrates those changes into the day-to-day operations of the organization.

Of course, the implementation of planned change is not a simple and straightforward process. For example, Jian (2007) argued that there are many unintended consequences of planned change, especially because the senior managers who initiate the change might have very different ideas about the change than the employees who implement the change. Given the complicated nature of communication within each of these groups and the sometimes limited interaction between top management and employees, even a meticulously planned change can have unanticipated outcomes.

Consider, for example, a school system that is instituting a new method for teaching reading. This change might be brought into play because of national standards—such as the institution of Common Core Curriculum requirements—because of changes in the school population, or because of new and exciting developments in elementary school pedagogy. Regardless of the impetus for the change, factors such as individual school culture, existing textbooks and lesson plans, and community involvement and pressure will make this change process an extremely complicated undertaking.

Reactions to Organizational Change

Given these complexities, it is little surprise that change does not often proceed in a particularly smooth fashion. Perhaps change would be easy if members of organizations were like the cogs described in classical and mechanistic views of organizational behavior (see Chapter 2). In such an organization, the "thinking" management could devise ideal processes for changing organizational activity and simply tell the workers what changes should be made. However, as we know from alternative models of organizing, such a simple process is both unlikely and undesirable. Instead, we now appreciate that organizations are cultural and political systems inhabited by thinking and feeling human beings. Thus, it is critical to look at how employees might react to and influence the organizational change process. For example, Kuhn and Corman (2003) argue that organizational members have **schemata**—or knowledge structures—that define individual and collective beliefs about how organizations work and how change happens. In organizational change processes, these schemata may be either confirmed or disrupted, leading to tensions in the change process that must be effectively managed by change agents, often through developing a sense of connection between organizational members and the change process (Barge, Lee, Maddux, Nabnng & Townsend, 2008).

Much of the work in this area has considered typical problems associated with organizational change. For example, Covin and Kilmann (1990) asked managers and consultants involved in change efforts to identify factors that often have a negative impact on change. Their responses, presented in Table 10.1, indicate that change can be thwarted by a variety of obstacles at numerous levels of the organization. This suggests that responding to change at each stage of the change process (i.e., during change development, program planning, and change implementation) is critical to organizational and individual outcomes. Three themes run through much of the literature on key responses to the change process.

Table 10.1	Typical Problems Identified in Organizational Change Process

Problems Identified in Change Process
Lack of management support
Top managers forcing change
Inconsistent action by key managers
Unrealistic expectations
Lack of meaningful participation
Poor communication
Purpose of program was not clear
Responsibility for change not properly identified

Based on Covin, T. J. & Kilmann, R. H. (1990). Participant perceptions of positive and negative influences on large scale change. *Group and Organizational Studies, 15*, 233–248.

First, as indicated by the first three "problems" identified in Table 10.1, **management support** for the change process is critical. As Fairhurst (1993) argues, "[Conventional wisdom suggests that it is senior management who has the most impact on change" (p. 334). When senior management is not seen as backing the change effort or when senior management's vision is not effectively shared with others in the organization, it is unlikely that a change effort will be successful. This may be particularly true when there is an external change agent involved in the change process. For example, if change is initiated by external consultants or by government or community mandate, the perceived support for the change by organizational management can be critical.

Medved et al. (2001) call this the **ownership tension** inherent in the change process, in which the successful implementation of change efforts is contingent on ownership of the problem and ownership of the change process by those in critical positions in the organization. Consider, for instance, our school district changing to a new system of teaching reading. The new system may be mandated by a state or local board of education. If this is the case, successful change may well depend on the extent to which local administrators and school principals feel ownership of both the problem (ineffective methods for teaching reading) and the solution (the new method being proposed).

A second area of concern in the change process has been typically labeled as *resistance* to the change process. Resistance could be seen as the management "ownership" issue transplanted to lower-level employees; Markus (1983, p. 433), for example, defines resistance as "behaviors intended to prevent the implementation or use of a system or to prevent system designers from achieving their objectives." Lewis (2000) points out that resistance might also include problems such as ignorance of a change initiative, inadequate training, or fear. **Resistance to change** is often related to political behavior in organizations because there are often many who have a great deal to win or lose in a change initiative. Regarding our school district moving to a new teaching method for reading, many teachers might have a great deal invested in the tried-and-true system—lesson plans, teaching materials, ways of interacting with the class. Because of this investment and belief in existing methods, teachers might be highly resistant to change efforts.

A final important reaction to organizational change efforts is uncertainty on the part of organizational members. It has long been known that uncertainty about organizational processes can result in stress on the part of employees, and this is particularly true during times of change (Miller, Joseph & Apker, 2000). Although complete information about organizational change might be counterproductive, it is clear that uncertainty about what is happening in the change process causes heightened anxiety on the part of workers. As Harter and Krone (2001) point out, "[A]ny attempt to work with change needs to take into consideration those individual and organizational defense mechanisms against anxiety that structure and form managerial and organizational responses to change." One of the most straightforward ways to deal with this uncertainty and the anxiety it provokes is through communication and the provision of information. Indeed, Miller and Monge (1985) found that employees preferred having *negative* information about an upcoming organizational change to having *no* information about organizational change. For our school district, a great deal of stress about change might be related to a lack of information about the change itself (e.g., "What is entailed in this new teaching method?") and about how the change will be instituted (e.g., "How soon will I have to begin using this new method? Can I adapt it to my own classroom style?"). Any information about these issues can be helpful in reducing uncertainty about the upcoming change.

Communication in the Change Process

The reactions to organizational change highlighted previously—ownership, resistance, and uncertainty—all point to the importance of communication in the organizational change process. For those involved in **planned organizational change**, there are a great many choices that must be made about communication during the change process. For example, Timmerman (2003) points out that a variety of communication media can be used when communicating with employees and people outside the organization during planned organizational change. How much communication should take place in face-to-face meetings? How much can be accomplished through written directives or the Internet? These are choices that must be made. Similarly, change agents must make decisions about whom to communicate with during the change process. Lewis, Richardson, and Hamel (2003) found that change agents communicate first and most frequently with individuals inside or close to the organization.

In considering ways of communicating with employees, some research has considered specific strategies that management can use during the implementation process. Clampitt, DeKoch, and Cashman (2000) have categorized these top-down communication strategies, which are summarized in Table 10.2. Clampitt et al. (2000) believe that the *Underscore and Explore* strategy is most effective and that the *Spray and Pray* and *Withhold and Uphold* strategies are least effective. The two remaining strategies were seen as moderately effective. In essence, these authors argue for a strategy of involving employees in the change process in appropriate areas by providing relevant information. Recent interviews with change implementers at a variety of organizations found, however, that most change agents favored a strategy in which participation was "restricted" or just used in an "advisory" capacity (Lewis & Russ,

Table 10.2 | Managerial Strategies for Communicating about Change

Strategy	Definition
Spray and Pray	Management showers employees with all kinds of information in the hope that employees will be able to sort out significant and insignificant information.
Tell and Sell	Management selects a limited set of messages regarding core organizational issues. Management "tells" employees about these issues and then "sells" employees on the wisdom of the chosen approach.
Underscore and Explore	Management focuses on fundamental issues related to change success and allows employees the creative freedom to explore various possibilities.
Identify and Reply	Management listens to and identifies key concerns of employees and then responds to those issues as they are brought up.
Withhold and Uphold	Management withholds information as much as possible. When management is confronted with questions or rumors, they uphold the party line.

Adapted from Clampitt, P. G., DeKoch, R. J. & Cashman, T. (2000). A strategy for communicating about uncertainty. *Academy of Management Executive*, 14(4), 41–57.

2012). Other research has considered the issue of uncertainty highlighted above in exploring possible communication strategies. Though early research (Miller & Monge, 1985) suggested that, for uncertain employees, even *negative* information about a change is seen as preferable to no information, more recent scholarship has found that previewing the potential pain and stress associated with change might do little to influence beliefs about the favorability of the change or perceptions of the credibility of change implementers (Lewis, Laster & Kulkarni, 2013).

In the last several decades, the most comprehensive research program on organizational communication and change has been undertaken by Laurie Lewis and her colleagues (see Lewis, 2011 for a comprehensive summary). Space doesn't permit full coverage of this scholarship, but several highlights are helpful to summarize the current literature regarding communication and organizational change. First, Lewis emphasizes that though change is often valuable and called for in the workplace, there are also times when change is driven by current fashion or fads. Second, Lewis reminds us that we can't judge the success of change simply in terms of the implementers' initial desires—that is, change is an ongoing process and it is critical to evaluate the ebbs and flows of that process rather than seeing change as a simple input-output process. Third, Lewis complicates our understanding of participation in the change process by highlighting that soliciting input from others can either be *symbolic participation* (i.e., creating the impression of support and buy-in during the change process) or *participation as resource* (when information gained through participation is actually used in the change initiative).

Finally, Lewis conceptualizes the entire change process as one in which a wide variety of *stakeholders* must be considered. These stakeholders are those who have any kind of stake in the organization. Employees are the obvious and most-often considered stakeholders in the change process. But there are other stakeholders as well—customers, financial investors, community members, regulators, and the list could continue. Lewis believes that it is critical to understand the perceptions and concerns of these stakeholders, to take those perceptions and concerns into account in designing communication strategies for various groups, and to understand that these stakeholder groups do not live in bubbles—rather, they interact with each other and will influence the ongoing trajectory of the change process. Lewis's stakeholder model of communication in the organizational change process is presented in Figure 10.1. This figure highlights the complexity of the change process and the importance of understanding the communicative choices and reactions of both implementers and a wide range of stakeholders.

"Unplanned" Change: Organizational Crisis

Up to this point in the chapter, we have considered organizational change as largely a planned and manageable process. However, there are many times when change is thrust upon an organization in the wake of a variety of events. Ulmer, Sellnow, and

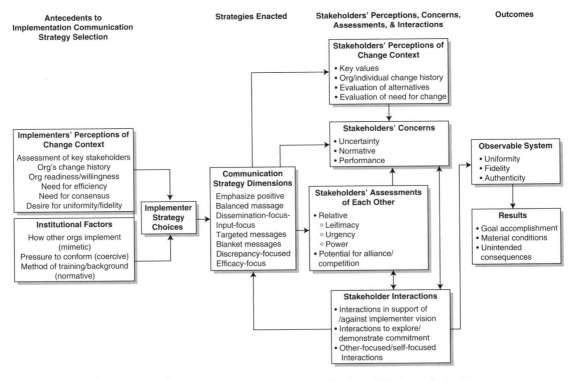

Figure 10.1 | A Model of Implementation Communication Strategy Selection, Stakeholder Concerns, Assessments, Interactions, and Outcomes

From Lewis, L. K. (2007). An organizational stakeholder model of change implementation communication. *Communication Theory, 17,* 176–204.

Seeger (2010) highlight the wide range of organizational crises by dividing them into categories such as natural disasters (e.g., Hurricane Katrina, the Haiti earthquake, or the Moore, Oklahoma tornado), financial crises (e.g., the Enron crisis, the collapse of Lehman Brothers, the auto industry bailout), terrorism (e.g., 9/11, the Boston Marathon bombing), industrial accidents (e.g., the BP oil disaster, the collapse of a garment factory in Bangladesh), and outbreaks of food-borne illness (e.g., recent concerns about tainted spinach and apple juice). In the Mandarin language, the symbol for *crisis* is two characters that are typically interpreted as "dangerous opportunity" and this is the essence of **organizational crisis** and communication—the crisis is dangerous and threatening in many ways, but it also provides opportunity to both address the crisis at hand and reshape perceptions through communication.

Communication scholars who are experts in crisis communication (see, e.g., Coombs, 2012; Ulmer et al., 2010) provide a great deal of insight in terms of how we should think about crises and the communication surrounding them. For example, crises are moments in an organization's history that are characterized by surprise, threat, and the need to respond quickly. They are unpredictable, but not typically unexpected. Crises can be threatening to an organization—on-going projects and goals can be disrupted, performance can be hampered, and reputations damaged in serious ways. Yet crises also create opportunities to communicate in effective ways with stakeholders and to better prepare the organization for similar events moving into the future.

Most scholars describe organizational crisis as evolving in three stages: precrisis, crisis, and postcrisis. Coombs (2012) divides the *precrisis* stage into three subprocesses: signal detection, prevention, and crisis preparation. These sub-processes will take precedence in different ways for different crises. For example, residents of "tornado alley" in the midsection of the United States know that there is little to do to prevent a tornado. However, it is possible to improve the tracking of tornadoes (signal detection) and to let the public know exactly what should be done if a tornado is imminent (crisis preparation). In contrast, the sub-process of prevention can be seen as central to the precrisis stage in the case of terrorism. During the *crisis* stage, there is a trigger (e.g., product failure, natural disaster) that threatens an organization's survival or reputation (Ulmer et al., 2010). During this period, there is a great deal uncertainty, and people inside and outside the organization try to make sense of what is happening (Weick, 1988). After this initial process of recognition, communication during the crisis stage shifts to processes of crisis containment (Coombs, 2012) such as mitigating damage and dealing with immediate issues of information dissemination. In the *postcrisis* stage, communication focuses on determining responsibility, communicating with a wide range of stakeholders, perhaps apologizing (Benoit, 1995), and establishing systems for coping with similar crises in the future. For example, the disastrous grounding of the Costa Concordia cruise ship in 2012 led to important recommendations about safety for both the cruise lines and for passengers (Hetter, 2013). In all three stages, communication processes play a key role in coping with a wide range of these unplanned change processes.

Communication in organizational crises must deal with both external stakeholders—such as the customers, regulators, and the general public—and internal stakeholders—such as employees and these various stakeholders will process and interpret events differently depending on factors such as severity, perceived

✳ Spotlight on Scholarship: Equivocal Reponses to Crisis

It has become a staple of news broadcasting: A corporate spokesperson stands at a podium facing reporters in the beginning phases of an organizational crisis. Perhaps it is a toy manufacturer announcing a recall because of safety concerns. Perhaps it is a financial institution explaining irregularities that are being investigated by the Securities Exchange Commission. Perhaps it is a government agency explaining a slow response to a weather disaster. Whatever the specifics, we find ourselves wondering about how the spokesperson will respond and may criticize the response as not properly addressing the needs of the public. Susan Kline, Bethany Simunich, and Heath Weber were interested in these situations when they conducted research on the use of equivocal messages in responding to corporate crises.

Kline and her colleagues begin with the simple observation that although audiences typically prefer communication that is open and honest, there are situations in which candor might not be appropriate. Scholars advocating the use of "strategic ambiguity" in organizational communication (e.g., Eisenberg, 1984) argue that equivocal messages might be enacted when organizations have multiple goals or when there are distinct audiences that must be addressed. Kline et al. suggest that these situations are likely to be present during initial stages of an organizational crisis and outline four situational features that might warrant the use of equivocal messages: (1) when there is a limited amount of meaningful information, (2) when there is the potential for litigation, (3) when employee privacy or proprietary information is at issue, and (4) when the organization has competing and conflicting objectives. When a crisis situation has any or all of these features, Kline et al. argue that a variety of message forms might be employed. For example, a spokesperson could talk about the company's disclosure policies, could promise to provide additional information when available, or could redirect attention to other aspects of the organization.

In their research, Kline and her colleagues surveyed over one hundred public relations professionals, providing them with scenarios of organizational crises and possible corporate responses to those crises. Not surprisingly, they found that communication professionals believed that equivocal messages were most appropriate when the company was faced with an "avoidance-avoidance" situation in which "the spokesperson had to respond to the reporter's question, but s/he could not be completely direct for a variety of reasons, such as risking the disclosure of proprietary information or violating legal or corporate policies" (Kline et al., 2009, p. 46). In contrast, unequivocal messages were preferred for straightforward situations. Interestingly, the findings in this research from communication professionals were not as strong as in a previous study using a sample of college students, suggesting that "professionals' assessments of equivocal messages in situations with different goal types appear to be constituted by factors other than just multiple goal enactment" (Kline et al., 2009, p. 46). In other words, there are a lot of factors at play in organizational crisis situations. Kline and her colleagues conclude that in a real-life crisis situation, it is critical that organizational representatives have a clear understanding of multiple goals facing that company and that they consider educating their audiences about those goals. Furthermore, they advocate messages that take account of multiple goals by shifting "the focus to a message that portray[s] the company as a public ally, thereby reducing social and power distance and increasing communal support" (Kline et al., 2009, pp. 54–55).

Kline, S. L. Simunich, B. & Weber, H. (2009). The use of equivocal messages in responding to corporate challenges. *Journal of Applied Communication Research, 37*, 40–58.

responsibility for the event, and moral outrage (Fediuk, Coombs & Botero, 2010). Miller and Horsley (2009) considered many external stakeholders in their examination of crisis management in the coal industry and found that though companies place substantial emphasis on technical responses to crises, they are often ill-prepared to counter existing negative perceptions of the industry during the crisis period. In contrast, Downing's (2007) case study of American Airlines in the wake of the terrorist attacks of September 11 emphasized the importance of rebuilding employee confidence and morale after a crisis of this nature rocks an organization. Recent events also highlight the ways in which the Internet and social media can contribute both to the creation of a crisis and methods of coping with the crisis. For example, when a Domino's employee posted a YouTube video in 2009 of pizzas being prepared with mucus (a clip soon revealed as a prank) it went viral. Domino's eventual response was one that took full advantage of its website, Twitter, and blogging and was effective in countering the hoax and restoring consumer confidence (see Gregory, 2009; Veil, Sellnow & Petrun, 2012).

ORGANIZATIONAL LEADERSHIP

As our discussion thus far reveals, organizational change involves a complex process of communication among a many stakeholders in and around the organization. For example, we found that it is critical that a wide array of organizational participants be informed about the change and feel that they are a part of the decision-making process. It is also important, however, that management in an organization is seen as clearly understanding the organization's problems, supporting appropriate change efforts, and being prepared for dealing with organizational crises. Thus, effective leadership is critical in the organizational change process.

Of course, the importance of leadership is not limited to times of change and upheaval. Indeed, we have seen many examples in recent years of how ineffective leadership during normal organizational operations has led to disastrous results for a company. For example, in the trial regarding the collapse of WorldCom in 2002, a major defense of Bernard Ebbers, the ex-CEO of the company, was that he really wasn't aware of issues of technology or finances within the organization. As Ackman (2005) reports, "Ebbers' basis for defense in the criminal case against him … is that he never looked at the numbers. He had people for that, and the people, his lawyers will say, let him down as much as anyone." However, many stockholders—and many scholars too—see this not as a failure of "his people" but as a failure of his leadership. Similar arguments have been made in recent years about leadership at Enron, BP, cruise lines, and a host of banks, mortgage lenders, and Wall Street firms during the housing and economic collapse. Similarly, bottlenecks in decision making in the U.S. Congress are often blamed on a failure of leadership. Thus, it is important to consider the ways in which we have come to understand leadership in organizational contexts. In this section, we will first consider some models of leadership and then look at the role that communication plays within current understandings of the leadership process.

Models of Leadership

Scholars and commentators on political and organizational processes have been interested in leadership for many years. Early thinking that leaders are born, not made was reflected in **trait theories** of leadership. These theories propose that there are particular qualities that will tend to be associated with leaders and that will result in

Case in Point: Leaderless Music

At the beginning of a symphony orchestra concert, the formally dressed conductor comes on stage, bows to the audience, and raises a baton—and moments later, music fills the auditorium. Well, at the beginning of most symphony orchestra concerts. The exception is a performance of the Orpheus, a New York orchestra that has been operating for more than thirty years without a conductor (Lieber, 2007). Orpheus was founded on the principles that guide smaller chamber music groups—that the best art comes from intimacy and connectedness among musicians. As Julian Fifer, the orchestra's founder, recounted, "I wanted to bring that camaraderie and spirit into a larger setting. And in order for everyone to be able to communicate more effectively, it seemed necessary to do without a conductor" (Lieber, 2007).

In the early years of Orpheus, the group made every decision about phrasing, dynamics, tempo, and so on, through a process of participation and unanimous agreement. That approach proved cumbersome and time consuming, and the group now operates through systems of rotating leadership in which smaller groups consult about initial interpretation and then bring ideas to the larger group during rehearsals. Leadership in the orchestra is not just dispersed, however, it is also organic. "Alert audience members will notice a musician use a nod of a head or a gesture of a bow, in a way inviting a fellow musician to join the 'conversation' by offering that person a chance to pick up a musical thought" (Lieber, 2007). In this group, then, everyone is a leader and everyone is a follower—and the result is beautiful music.

success in leadership activities. For example, Northouse (1997) reviews a number of studies of leadership traits and characteristics and concludes that the most common traits associated with leadership are intelligence (verbal ability, perceptual ability, and reasoning), self-confidence (belief that one can make a difference), determination (the persistent desire to get the job done), integrity (honesty and trustworthiness), and sociability (being friendly and outgoing). Organizations advocating a trait approach to leadership might use personality tests to select people with the right combination of characteristics or might use these traits to help organization members in self-assessment. Related to trait approaches to leadership are models that suggest that leaders have particular behavioral styles that make them more or less effective leaders. We saw one of these **style theories** in Chapter 3 when we considered Blake and Mouton's Leadership Grid. Recall that this grid suggested evaluating leaders in terms of their "concern for production" and "concern for people" and argued that the most effective leadership style was a team management style that maximized both of these goals. Thus, this style approach is essentially a way of translating preferred traits into preferred behaviors.

There is certainly much to say for trait and style approaches to leadership—we like to think of leaders as special kinds of people who can do extraordinary things and we can probably think of some people who appear to be born leaders. However, in recent years, trait and style approaches have fallen into disfavor, as many scholars and practitioners are uncomfortable with the notion of a set list of specific characteristics that defines all leaders. Furthermore, these approaches suggest that a particular leader will be effective across all situations and all followers, and this does not fit well with either research or experience. For example, we learned about the Leader-Member Exchange model in Chapter 7. The LMX model proposes that leaders develop different (and perhaps more or less effective) leadership relationships with different subordinates. Thus, the idea of having one ideal type of leader is contrary to much of our experience in which leaders work in different ways with different people.

The more widespread critique of trait and style approaches, though, has come with regard to the idea of leadership behaviors across situations. This critique argues that different individuals might be differently suited for various leadership situations. For example, following our discussion of organizational life cycles earlier in this chapter, the kind of leader who is good at managing a young start-up company might be different from the kind of leader who is appropriate for managing a mature organization. Or, more specifically, some leaders might be good at running structured meetings and others might be more comfortable in freewheeling brainstorming sessions or presenting large-scale public speeches. Not surprisingly, then, when many scholars rejected a trait approach to leadership, they turned to ideas that emphasized the "match" of the style of the leader to the characteristics of the situation. The best known of these theories is **contingency theory** (Fiedler & Garcia, 1987). Contingency theory would predict, for example, that a leader who likes to focus on tasks would be more effective in structured situations than a leader who likes to focus on relationships. More contemporary scholars argue that there are many situations in which a single person is not adequate for the needs of the situation and leadership functions must be shared by several individuals in a group or organization (e.g., Kramer, 2006).

Even a contingency approach to leadership, however, still emphasizes the characteristics and the style of the leader and the needs of particular situations. What is still left out of this and other classic models is the role of those *being led* in the organization. Also missing from these models is the role of communication, especially in establishing relationships between leaders and those in the organization. Thus, in recent years, models that look more closely at leadership as a process of communication and as a process of establishing relationships have been proposed. An example of this relational approach is the concept of transformational leadership that highlights the ways that leaders secure "extraordinary levels of follower trust and inspire followers to emulate their behavior" (Gardner, 2003, p. 503).

The **transformational leadership model** (Bass, 1985) makes a distinction between transactional leaders and transformational leaders. Transactional leadership refers to a relationship in which there is an exchange of some sort between leaders and followers. For example, a political transactional leader exchanges a promise of social security reform for the promise of a vote. A managerial transactional leader exchanges a pay raise, a promotion, or verbal praise for hard work on a project. In contrast, transformational leaders—through communication processes—create a relationship between leaders and followers that helps followers reach their full potential and has the potential for transforming both the leader and the follower. As Northouse (1997, p. 131) explains with regard to Mahatma Gandhi, "Gandhi raised the hopes and demands of millions of his people and in the process was changed himself." Gardner (2003) argues that central to transformational leadership is the concept of **exemplification**. That is, leaders who want to instill the ideals of hard work and ethical behavior would do so by exemplifying those ideals in their own behaviors. Both

Case in Point: Horse Whispering for Leaders

We usually think about a "horse whisperer" as someone who has a special way with animals and can calm even the wildest stallion with words, touch, and eye contact. But what if we turned that equation around and thought about what the horses could be teaching us? Lisa Arie, a former advertising executive, has done this with a ranch that serves as a learning center for leaders from all walks of life—a center "where seven spirited horses are the teachers" (Reed, 2012).

Leaders come to this ranch one at a time for three to four custom designed days of interspecies interaction. The leaders come with varying levels of comfort or concern, but "nearly everyone who participates admits to some kind of epiphany. By working with the horses, most say they become better communicators … break personal logjam … [or] suddenly realize what's behind their management style" (Reed, 2012). Research on participants indicates measurable increases in social and emotional receptivity, social optimism, and being able to see the big picture.

How does this work? Perhaps by getting leaders out of their comfort zones and interact with others (the horses) in ways they've never tried before. One attendee reported that in working with the horses, he was often struck with uncertainty about how to behave and that it was only by getting out of old patterns and just acting that he was able to move ahead with the horse. He recounts: "I stepped forward and let go. I just got out of my head. The horse just looked at me and did everything I wanted it to do" (Reed, 2012). So perhaps that is one of the secrets with people, as well as horses. To ignore the assumptions that constrain our behavior and hold us back. In other words, to loosen the reins.

words and deeds are critical to the transformational leader—it is a model of "do as I say *and* as I do."

In summary, then, models of leadership have moved from relatively simplistic ideas about the traits and styles of effective leaders, through models that suggest that different styles and skills are appropriate in different situations, to models that see leadership as a process of building relationships through interaction with followers and modeling desired values. Clearly, communication processes are central to these new theories of leadership. Thus, in the next section, we will briefly consider several communication factors that have been associated with effective leadership.

COMMUNICATION AND LEADERSHIP

The role of communication in the leadership process can be looked at in several different ways. It is important, for example, to look at what is said—the content of communication. Of course, the appropriate content of communication will vary from situation to situation, but research does give us some ideas about what effective leaders say. For example, several studies have demonstrated that leaders who use "visionary" content in their communication are more effective than those who use more pragmatic content (Awamleh & Gardner, 1999; Holladay & Coombs, 1993). Clearly, Martin Luther King's "I Have a Dream" speech would not have been as effective in motivating citizens if the content had merely listed "ten steps toward racial equality." Saying the right thing can be particularly important for leaders facing crisis situations. For example, in a study of two organizations facing the crisis of fire, Seeger and Ulmer (2002) found that effective leadership discourse was characterized by a strong commitment to stakeholders, an immediate commitment to rebuild, and the opportunity for renewal through the crisis.

Perhaps more important than what is said, though, is *how* it is said. For example, in Seeger and Ulmer's study of crisis communication, timing was critical—the leaders started talking while the fires were still burning. How a message is communicated includes its delivery. Experimental studies have indicated that strong delivery styles (e.g., eye contact, appropriate use of facial expressions and gestures, increased vocal variety) led to higher ratings of leadership effectiveness (Awamleh & Gardner, 1999; Gardner, 2003; Holladay & Coombs, 1993). These findings suggest that individuals could be trained to be more effective (or at least to be seen as more effective) through careful attention to nonverbal behaviors.

A particularly important consideration of communication and leadership stems from the work of Gail Fairhurst and Robert Sarr (1996) regarding the ways in which leaders "frame" their language in interaction with a variety of constituencies. Fairhurst and Sarr see leadership as a "language game," and they argue that the most essential skill for this game is the ability to frame. **Framing** is a way of managing meaning in which one or more aspects of the subject at hand are selected or highlighted over other aspects. For example, in the case study examined by Seeger and Ulmer (1992) that we discussed above, the leader at one of the organizations, Malden Mills, had to find a way to frame a fire that destroyed a textile plant, resulted in serious injury, and placed many jobs in jeopardy. It would be easy to frame this as a disaster, an act of God, or an accident. But in this case, the leader framed the event as a chance to demonstrate his commitment to his workers and to rebuild and renew the company. This emphasizes the notion that leadership is not about events or situations but is instead a process of managing meaning (Turner, 2003). Indeed, framing might be especially important for leaders in "failure" situations (Liu, 2010).

Fairhurst and Sarr (1996) argue that effective leaders begin the framing process by having a clear understanding of their own view of reality and their own goals for the organization and for communication. That is, effective leaders know where they are and know where they want to go. Effective leaders are also those who pay attention to the context, recognizing times and situations in which there are opportunities for shaping meaning or when there are constraints that will hamper the framing process. Finally, effective leaders use language in ways that manage meaning in powerful and appropriate ways. As Fairhurst and Sarr (1996, p. 100) state, "[J]ust as an artist works from a palette of colors to paint a picture, the leader who manages meaning works from a vocabulary of words and symbols to help construct a frame in the mind of the listener." The use of language in framing can involve a variety of communicative strategies that can help others see the world in the way you want them to see it. These linguistic framing devices for managing meaning are presented in Table 10.3. Of course, these strategies can be overused or used in inappropriate contexts. For example, we are all well aware of the overuse of spin following presidential debates and other political events. However, these framing strategies point to a variety of ways that effective leaders can shape their messages to form valued relationships with others and help them see the world in a particular way.

Table 10.3 | Tools for Framing in Leadership

	Metaphors	Jargon/Catchphrases	Contrast	Spin	Stories
Function	They show a subject's likeness with something else.	They frame a subject in familiar terms.	It describes a subject in terms of its opposite.	It puts a subject in a positive or negative light.	They frame a subject by example.
Use It Because	You want a subject to take on new meaning.	Familiar references can enhance meaning. Jargon and catchphrases help communicate a vision's "god" and "devil" terms.	It is sometimes easier to define what your subject is not than state what it is.	It can reveal your subject's strengths or weaknesses.	Stories attract attention and can build rapport.
Avoid It When	They mask important alternative meanings.	A word or phrase is in danger of overuse.	Meaning can be skewed by a poor contrast.	The ratio of spin to reality is excessive.	They mask important alternative meanings.
Example	"I feel our relationship is formal, like punching a ticket."	"We've got to break the squares today."	"It's a choice between raising my hand for the teacher to ask if it's OK or just telling it like it is."	"Which Ray will show up? The one who's cooperative and generous or the egotist who constantly reminds others of his successes?"	"In my first three or four years here, I was a lot like you. I thought …"

From Fairhurst, G. T. & Sarr, R. A. (1996). *The Art of Framing: Managing the Language of Leadership*. San Francisco: Jossey-Bass, p. 101.

All these considerations of communication and leadership view communication as a tool that can be used to enhance the effectiveness of leaders in a variety of ways, including the use of nonverbal behavior, word choice, timing, or framing devices. However, in recent years, communication scholars have shifted their view of communication and leadership by moving to a model in which communication is not a tool in service of effective leadership but is actually the medium through which leadership relationships are constructed. This move is in line with the constitutive approach to organizational communication discussed in Chapter 5, and it has been led by Gail Fairhurst and her consideration of **discursive leadership** (Fairhurst, 2007, 2008). The idea of discursive leadership moves from the views of leadership outlined earlier in this chapter to one that considers the ways in which leadership is socially constructed through interactions among organizational actors (see Fairhurst & Grant, 2010). In this view, Fairhurst sees leadership as "exercised when ideas expressed in talk and action are recognized by others as capable of progressing tasks or problems which are important to them" (Robinson, 2001, p. 93). That is, leadership is accomplished through interaction with others, is a process of meaning management, and is grounded in the accomplishment of tasks. This view of leadership, then, replaces simplified concepts of leaders using the tool of communication to influence followers with a consideration of the ways in which leading is constructed through the discourse of a dispersed group of actors in an organizational context.

SUMMARY

Although it often seems that our work lives are mundane, there are change processes that permeate many aspects of organizational life. Organizations change in the natural course of adapting to their environments, and they change when managers or employees perceive a need to adjust things at either the individual or organizational level. Furthermore, although many players are critically involved in these change processes, the roles of leaders become particularly pronounced. In this chapter, we have examined these related processes of organizational change and leadership. We first considered several models of how change occurs, looked at problems that often arise during planned change efforts, considered the special case of organizational crisis, and considered the role of communication in a variety of change situations. We then turned our attention to leadership, examining traditional models of leadership that emphasize traits, styles, and situations and more contemporary models that see leadership in terms of communication and the building of relationships with followers. We then considered the role of communication in leadership, looking at the role of communication content and delivery, the importance of framing in the management of meaning, and the move of contemporary scholars to a consideration of discursive leadership that highlights the role of communication in constituting leadership.

Clearly, much of the theory and research we have considered in this chapter is rooted in classical, human resources, and systems approaches to organizational communication (see Table 10.4). Indeed, classical approaches to organizations (especially Taylor's Theory of Scientific Manage-ment) are built around the need to control the behaviors of workers in organizations and plan all changes that they encounter. The influence of systems theory can be seen in the importance of goals and communication in the organizational change process, and the human resources approach can be seen in the emphasis on maximizing the effectiveness of leaders through behavioral and communicative choices and in the belief that organizational change can be enhanced by involving employees at all organizational levels in the change process.

However, as Table 10.4 indicates, other approaches to the study of organizational communication could further enhance our understanding of organizational change and leadership. For example, in our discussion of leadership, we considered how effective leaders understand the context in which meaning is being created. In other words, leadership depends to a large extent on understanding organizational culture. Further work on the ways in which leaders use discursive resources to constitute relationships with other would also advance our knowledge. Critical theorists also have much to say about organizational change. Of course, at a basic level, critical theorists hope for emancipatory change in organizations brought on as employees realize the imbalance of power in most organizational settings. However, this emancipatory change is not the kind of change envisioned by the research discussed throughout most of this chapter. Indeed, critical theorists would be very concerned about the processes of "planned change" and "leadership" discussed here because such processes could well perpetuate the hegemonic relationship

Table 10.4 | Approaches to Change and Leadership Processes

Approach	How Change and Leadership Would Be Considered
Classical	Change is viewed negatively, unless that change is carefully controlled by management. Leadership is based on defined traits and abilities that only managers have.
Human relations	Change is seen as a human process that should factor in employee concerns. Leaders are encouraged to satisfy needs of workers to foster job satisfaction.
Human resources	Employees are encouraged to participate in the change process in substantive ways, and the skills of leaders are adapted to specific situations.
Systems	Change is viewed as a complex process involving interaction among multiple stakeholders. Leaders are encouraged to harness the power of communication network connections.
Cultural	Chance practices are seen as reflections of organizational practices and assumptions and effective leadership will depend on an understanding of prevailing values and beliefs.
Constitutive	Change is an inevitable aspect of the processes through which organizations are constituted and reconstituted. Leadership is a discursive process of meaning creation.
Critical	Planned change and many leadership processes can be viewed as mechanisms through which management established power and authority. Truly democratic change can enhance employee voice in the organization.
Feminist	Alternative approaches to change and leadership are encouraged which emphasize the nonrational aspects of organizational functioning and encourage attention to mutual goals.

between management and employees in organizational settings. For example, it could be argued that when employees participate in planning organizational change, they are legitimizing organizational goals at the expense of individual employee goals. In short, by adopting new approaches to the study of change processes, we gain important insights into some of the less obvious functions that these processes play in organizational life.

DISCUSSION QUESTIONS

1. Organizational change can be an anxiety-producing process. What are ways that change can be managed to reduce the level of anxiety experienced by organizational participants? Are there times when uncertainty and anxiety about change might be a good thing?

2. What is the role of leadership in organizational change? Which of the models of leadership discussed in this chapter are most appropriate for times of change? Would the different models advocate different kinds of leadership communication during planned change?

3. In what ways is leadership a "language game" and a process of "managing meaning"? How does communication content and style influence this language game? How do leaders manage meaning through framing techniques?

KEY CONCEPTS

organizational life cycle	uncertainty about change	style theories
schemata	organizational crisis	contingency theory
management support of change	precrisis phase	transformational leadership model
ownership tension in change	crisis phase	exemplification
resistance to change	postcrisis phase	framing
planned organizational change	trait theories	discursive leadership

---

CASE STUDY | ## Leading Nurses through Hospital Change

Few industries are confronted with more change and more turbulence than the health care industry. As the perusal of any newspaper or news website will indicate, there is constant pressure on health care organizations to provide quality care in a cost-controlled environment that is characterized by ever-increasing regulation. This pressure can be seen most clearly in the advent of managed care during the 1980s and beyond. Managed care involves integrated and comprehensive systems of health care providers, insurance companies, and government programs, coordinated around specific care plans and guidelines designed to simultaneously enhance the quality of care provided, control the cost of that care, and maintain access to care for as many people as possible. As you might guess, it's pretty much impossible to succeed in all three of these important goals of cost, quality, and access, but hospitals and other health care organizations keep on trying.

I've run into many such organizations in my research on communication in health care organizations. One of these organizations—we'll call it University Hospital—is discussed in several of my publications (Miller, 1998; Miller et al., 2000). University Hospital is a large teaching hospital that employs nearly 5,000 individuals and is responsible for half a million patient visits a year. University Hospital is acknowledged as a very high-quality medical center—for example, it typically scores extremely well on accreditation surveys. However, like all health care organizations, University Hospital needed to improve in a number of financial areas, including average length of stay and cost per discharge.

My involvement with University Hospital began when I learned of changes that were occurring in the nursing department and was asked to be a part of understanding and instituting those changes. As part of a hospital-wide effort to improve financial and care performances, the nurses were beginning a program of "differentiated nursing practice" (Hoffart & Woods, 1996) in which nursing roles were defined on a variety of specific levels of responsibility. These roles would require new training, new responsibilities, and a new orientation toward the systematized provision of care. The centerpiece of this program was the "care coordinator" role.

Care coordinators were defined as registered nurses charged with coordinating care for patients "from admissions to discharge." This coordination involved communication with relevant physicians, social workers, allied health personnel, insurance representatives, and families. The nurses selected for these roles were the best and the brightest that University Hospital had to offer.

Sounds like a good change, right? Coordinated care from admissions to discharge is certainly an admirable goal. However, remember that the nurses selected for these positions were trained in traditional, clinical nursing. They were then thrown into a role that required them to work with individuals from a variety

CASE STUDY | Leading Nurses through Hospital Change *continued*

of hospital disciplines (with different turf issues and different levels of power) within an incredibly complex organizational structure. And they were doing this with little or no training and with a job description that was purposefully ambiguous; nurses were asked to design the job in the best way possible. Indeed, the final line of the job description for care coordinators read "Role in development/work in progress"!

So, imagine you are me, asked to help the leaders of the nursing department take their nurses—and especially the new care coordinators—down this path of organizational change. The department is directed by two nurses—we'll call them Hannah and Jen—who have an incredible amount of energy. Both are well-liked by the nurses they supervise. Hannah has been with the hospital for many years and knows all the ins and outs of the system. She is the steady hand guiding the nursing department, and she feels a bit overwhelmed by all the change she is being asked to institute. Jen has been with University Hospital for only a few years but has made quite an impact as a charismatic leader who wants University Hospital—and especially the nursing department—to be on the cutting edge of managed care initiatives. Jen is a proponent of all sorts of New Age things, and she is particularly smitten with "chaos theory" as a way to manage organizational change. She figures that they have selected the best people they can for the care coordinator roles, and she trusts that they will use their own imagination and ingenuity to craft roles that will work for the new system. Indeed, when a care coordinator complained about the stress of the changes they were going through, Jen quoted her favorite chaos theorist, saying, "Chaos is the rich soil from which creativity is born" (Merry, 1995, p. 13). Oddly enough, the nurse did not feel comforted.

CASE ANALYSIS QUESTIONS

1. How does the nursing department at University Hospital exemplify ways that organizations often react to planned organizational change? Are there ways in which the nature of the change—or the way it is being instituted at University Hospital—differs from traditional patterns?

2. If you were taking on a "care coordinator" role at University Hospital, what kind of information would you want to have? Do you like the idea of an unstructured role that you can develop on your own? What are the advantages and disadvantages of this kind of organizational ambiguity?

3. How would you choose to lead this department through the change they are experiencing? Would you rather have Jen or Hannah as your leader in this process?

4. What are some ways that Jen and Hannah could work together to make the change process successful?

Processes of Emotion in the Workplace

CHAPTER **11**

AFTER READING THIS CHAPTER, YOU SHOULD ...

- Appreciate the ways in which traditional organizing has been portrayed as rational and logical and be able to provide arguments for why emotion should be considered an integral part of organizational life.
- Understand the concept of emotional labor as communication that is in some way inauthentic and performed for the benefit of the organization.
- Be able to contrast emotional labor with emotional work—authentic emotions that are also a part of many workers' jobs.
- See the ways in which emotion permeates our relationships with coworkers in both satisfying and destructive ways.
- Understand the role of communication both in causing stress and burnout and in helping organizations and individuals cope with stress and burnout.

There is a tradition of rationality in our consideration of organizational life. Think, for example, about some of the models of organization we looked at in the first half of this book—maximizing efficiency in a machine-like factory, enhancing the effectiveness of organizational systems, making the most of human resources, even managing corporate culture—all these models suggest that organizations run through reasoning. The same is true of the processes we've considered so far in the second half of this book, including decision making, conflict management, and leadership and organizational change. Even when we look at current trends in the popular management literature—everything from knowledge management and learning organizations to "money ball" strategies in baseball and business—the presumption has been that successful organizations are places where cool heads and logical thinking prevail.

Since the early 1990s, however, there has been a growing interest in the emotional side of organizational life and a growing appreciation for the tension between emotion and rationality in the workplace. Many decades ago, human relations scholars advocated looking more closely at human feelings in the organization, but the only feeling considered in those years was "satisfaction." However, researchers are now beginning to see just how complex emotional life in organizations is. In this chapter, we explore these issues by first considering how scholars have been moved to look at emotion in organizational life. We will examine emotion as part of the job and look at the ways in which emotion permeates organizational relationships. We will then consider one area of emotion in the workplace that has received a great deal of research attention: the study of stress, **burnout**, and social support in organizations.

EMOTION IN THE WORKPLACE

Most models of organizational life see the workplace as a setting governed by logic and rationality. According to these models, jobs consist of tasks and the cognitive functions required for those tasks. We train people in the logic and mechanics of how to do their jobs. We manage conflict and change by thinking logically about what is best for the company and the employees. And when we make decisions, we carefully weigh the pros and cons of each decision and make a logical choice that will maximize gains and minimize losses.

Of course, anyone who has spent any time in an organization recognizes how inaccurate the above description really is. Our interactions are often governed by hot emotion rather than cool logic. We typically make choices about job and career based on gut feeling rather than a spreadsheet of pros and cons. Unfortunately, it has taken organizational theorists awhile to catch up with these commonsense ideas about organizational life. But scholars are now on board in appreciating the emotional nuances that are so prevalent in the workplace.

This shift in focus can be illustrated with a look back to our discussion of decision making in Chapter 8. We noted in that chapter that scholars rarely see decision making as a purely logical and data-driven process. People (in the workplace or otherwise) don't often follow the prescribed steps of defining the problem, establishing criteria, searching for information, evaluating alternatives, and reaching a decision. But even when theorists moved away from this purely logical model, they moved to models that considered the concept of *bounded rationality* in the workplace (e.g., March & Simon, 1958; Simon, 1987). Decision making couldn't be perfectly rational because of cognitive and situational limits on rationality. But rationality was still the norm; it was merely limited. However, communication scholars Dennis Mumby and Linda Putnam (1992) turned this notion on its head by suggesting that instead of looking at bounded rationality, we should consider **bounded emotionality**. That is, these scholars asked us to begin looking at emotional life as a central focus of organizational research and to consider the ways in which paying attention to emotion might lead to new ways of understanding the workplace.

We turn now to several areas of research in which scholars have heeded this call by looking at emotion in organizational life (see Miller, 2013, for a full review of this literature). We look first at scholarship that has considered emotion as part of the job. We will then look at the organizational emotion that arises through relationships with coworkers and others and consider more general ideas about emotion rules and emotional intelligence.

Emotion as Part of the Job

A wide range of occupations exist in which interaction with clients is a central aspect of the job. In many of these, communication between employees and clients involves some degree of emotional or affective content (see Waldron, 1994). Some examples are obvious. Nurses and physicians interact with dying patients in a hospice, deal with stressed-out families in an intensive care unit, and share the elation of birth in a maternity ward. Ministers counsel troubled parishioners, comfort grieving families, and rejoice with newlyweds. Emotional communication is also a requirement in less obvious occupations. The flight attendant must appear happy and attentive throughout a long cross-country flight (at least in first class!). A bill collector must remain stern and avoid any trace of sympathy in interactions. A cock tail waitress's tips depend to a large extent on maintaining a friendly and cheerful demeanor.

Arlie Hochschild was the first scholar to deal systematically with this phenomenon in her book *The Managed Heart* (1983). She uses the term **emotional labor** to refer to jobs in which workers are expected to display certain feelings in order to satisfy organizational role expectations. Hochschild argues that when performing emotional labor, workers can engage in either **surface acting** or **deep acting**. For example, Hochschild's original study of emotional labor involved airline flight attendants. Flight attendants involved in surface acting might just paste on a smile to satisfy the airline's requirement of a friendly face in the cabin. However, flight attendants might also try to evoke more realistic emotional displays by using deep acting techniques,

Case in Point: "The Cruise from Hell"

On February 7, 2013, the *Carnival Triumph* set sail from the port of Galveston, Texas. Then, in the early morning darkness of February 10, a fire broke out in the engine room and all of the passengers made their way to muster stations. For the next few days, the cruise ship was adrift in the Gulf of Mexico and the experience came to be known as the "Cruise from Hell": "the tilting boat with sewage seeping down the walls, urine-soaked floors, and passengers sleeping in the cold and rain to avoid the noxious fumes inside their cabins" (Conant, 2013). There was limited food, unbearable heat, and with toilets broken, passengers were given red biohazard bags for disposing feces. And through it all, who was charged with picking up those bags and doing everything possible to raise the spirits of miserable passengers? Members of the crew, of course.

It wasn't an easy task. One strategy was "Free beer and wine for everybody" (Drash, 2013) but alcohol could only do so much to appease people in a nasty situation who were expecting a relaxed vacation. So crew members went into high "emotional labor" mode. They "worked around the clock to make the situation somewhat bearable. They constantly checked on passengers, often with smiles on their faces" (Drash, 2013). Many passengers reported being amazed and noted that they did the dirty work that no one would want to do. Crew members agreed that the situation was stressful, but they kept trying to push through it without showing signs of strain. And in the true spirit of the emotional labor concept, one crew member explained why: "It's very simple … It's a part of the job."

such as imagining the airplane cabin as a friendly living room or sympathizing with the stress that irate passengers might be feeling.

Since Hochschild's book, the notion of emotional labor has been further developed by scholars in a variety of disciplines, including sociology, management, and communication. Some of the research has involved case studies of workers in jobs involving emotional labor, including waitresses (Leidner, 1993), flight attendants (Murphy, 1998), workers in emergency call centers (Shuler & Sypher, 2000; Tracy & Tracy, 1998), cruise ship employees (Tracy, 2000), financial advisors (Miller & Koesten, 2008), correctional officers (Tracy, 2005), firefighters (Scott & Myers, 2005), and judges (Scarduzio, 2011). Other work has attempted to develop models of the emotional labor process (e.g., Kruml & Geddes, 2000; Morris & Feldman, 1996) that consider factors such as the antecedents of emotional labor (e.g., gender, task requirements, closeness of monitoring), dimensions of emotional labor (e.g., frequency of emotional display, variety of expressed emotion, degree of emotional dissonance), and consequences of emotional labor (e.g., burnout and job dissatisfaction).

Several generalizations can be forwarded about the body of work on emotional labor:

- Most research considers frontline service workers in organizations that sanction (and pay for) emotion in the service of customers. Thus, emotional labor is seen as a way to increase the success—and profits—of the organization.
- Most research considers emotion that is explicitly controlled through training and employee manuals. For example, Steinberg and Figart (1999, p. 9) quote an employee handbook at a gourmet deli as directing: "Under no circumstance should a customer ever wonder if you are having a bad day. Your troubles should be masked with a smile."
- Most research considers emotional displays that are created through deep acting or surface acting—in other words, emotional displays that are in some way not authentic expressions of current or enduring emotion.
- When workers enact emotional labor, they are very aware that they are acting for the purpose of managerial and (sometimes) personal profit (Miller, Considme & Garner, 2007).
- Emotional labor carries with the potential for negative job outcomes such as stress and anxiety, particularly when workers feel dissonance from the belief that they are "faking it" on the job.

Not all job-related emotion has these characteristics, however. Ashforth and Humphrey (1993) point this out when they state: "The problem with this conception of emotional labor is that it does not allow for the instances whereby one spontaneously and genuinely experiences and expresses the expected emotion" (p. 94). Clearly, there are times when workers feel emotions on the job and express those emotions in interactions. For example, a teacher might feel joy—and express that joy—when a student finally understands long division. A nurse might feel sorrow—and express that sorrow—on the death of a patient. This kind of genuine emotion on the job— what Miller et al. (2007) call **emotional work**—involves people who are not in frontline service jobs but instead hold professional positions in industries such as health care, education, or human services. Workers in these roles rarely have instructions on emotion management that are explicitly spelled out in employee handbooks or during training sessions. However, such individuals clearly do deal with a lot of emotion on the job—both of a genuine and managed variety. For example, a nurse must cope with genuine emotion (e.g., the sorrow of having a patient die) and express emotions that he may not actually feel (e.g., dealing with difficult patients in a cheerful or professional way).

A number of scholars have further investigated the importance of emotion in work in a consideration of *compassion* in the workplace. For example, Miller (2007) looked at a number of jobs that involve emotional work in her consideration of workers who are engaged in **compassionate communication**. In her interviews with workers in a wide range of human service occupations, she found that workers communicate emotionally in ways that involve processes of noticing, connecting, and responding (see also Kanov et al., 2004). Workers engaged in emotional work must *notice* the need for compassion and the details of clients' lives that will lead to appropriate communication. They must then *connect* to clients by taking the others' perspective and establishing an empathic bond. Finally, they must *respond* with verbal and nonverbal behaviors that can make a difference for troubled clients. Way and Tracy (2012) further developed this model in a study of hospice workers. These researchers highlighted both the rewards that workers gain through compassionate work—even, perhaps especially, in a setting such as hospice—and the importance of communication in compassion.

Emotion as Part of Workplace Relationships

Emotion is not just important when it is a prescribed part of a person's job. Indeed, individuals in *all* organizational roles feel emotion in the workplace. Several scholars have argued that we should be looking less at emotions required by the job and more at emotions that emerge from relationships in the workplace (Waldron, 2012). Miller et al. (2007) have called this type of emotion in the workplace **emotion at work**, and Sandelands and Boudens (2000) make a forceful case for looking not at the nature of the job but at relationships with others in the workplace as the major source of organizational emotion. After reviewing many narratives of work life, these scholars conclude:

> When people talk about their work and their feelings they rarely speak about what they do on the job or the meaning of the job. They talk almost exclusively about their involvement in the life of the group.... Feelings are not identified with evaluations of the job, even less with personal growth and development. Instead, feelings are strongly identified with a person's place and activities in the life of the group and the place of their work in the larger scheme of things. (Sandelands & Boudens, 2000, p. 52)

A number of aspects of work relationships are largely emotional. We often have coworkers (or bosses or employees) that we like or dislike, that evoke joy or irritation, that are exhilarating or maddening. Our work with these coworkers might create and sustain emotions, including anger, frustration, elation, excitement, or boredom. On the positive side of this emotional spectrum is the emotion of compassion highlighted in the last section. In addition to considering compassion as part of the job, scholars have also worked at ways in which organizational members

✳ Spotlight on Scholarship: Lining Up for Emotion

You get to the airport early because you know the lines might be long—and they are. You shuffle with other passengers through the snaking queue, using the time to stare at your smartphone—checking e-mail, scrolling through your newsfeed on Facebook, catching up on your Words with Friends games—anything to tamp down the stress you always feel in airports and to avoid talking with others in line. As you progress, you hear commanding voices of TSA agents reminding you to pull out your laptop, remove your shoes, have your liquids in 3-ounce containers stored in a quart size plastic bag. You see a seasoned traveler sigh with exasperation as she is held up by a family negotiating the security line with two small children. You hold your arms up in the scanner and wait until the TSA officer gives you the "all clear" sign – at least you won't have to be patted down. You then move on to your gate to begin the next phase of your anxiety-filled day of travel.

This all-too familiar scenario was the focus of Shawna Malvini Redden's recent article investigating the emotional experiences of passengers in airports. Nearly two million people fly on commercial airliners in the United States every year, and Malvini Redden notes that "passengers bring emotional baggage to the airport along with their carry-on luggage" (Malvini Redden, 2013, p. 123). As this chapter documents, most of the research on emotion in organizations has concentrated on the experiences of organizational members and, often, employees who are providing service to customers and clients. Malvini Redden wanted to look at emotion from the vantage point of customers by examining the repercussions of interactions between airport personnel and passengers. Her research centered on thirty-six one-way flights over a six-month period that involved a variety of airports (primarily Sky Harbor in Phoenix and Sacramento International Airport). She observed

behavior in security lines and elsewhere, talked with many passengers, and conducted formal interviews with nineteen men and women.

Malvini Redden found that a variety of emotions characterized the experiences of passengers: occasionally positive emotions such as excitement and anticipation, but more often negative emotions such as anxiety and frustration or neutral emotions of disengagement. For TSA employees, neutral emotions may stem from boredom but "passengers feel they must contain, inhibit, or mask their feelings to avoid censure, additional scrutiny, or punishment" (Malvini Redden, 2013, p. 136). This is not surprising, as the organizational setting of the airport in our post–September 11 culture turns the table from a situation in which the customer is always right to one in which the customer is an ongoing target of suspicion and surveillance. This shift is obviously stressful, and the need to stand in lines only serves to escalate anxiety. Malvini Redden argues that there is "considerable effort for travelers as they try to 'act right' in line" (p. 140). Further, because standing in line is compulsory at airports, the need to control emotion can be seen as an emotional tax that must be paid in order to successfully move to the next phase of the trip. "For most air passengers, the emotional tax is likely small, similar to a mandatory bridge toll … For others though, emotional taxes may be more significant, like bribes extracted to cross third-world borders" (p. 141).

There is an old saying that the only sure things in life are death and taxes. In today's world of travel, we could also add airport security lines to that list, and Malvini Redden's work suggests that there is an emotional cost to be paid for the experience.

Malvini Redden, S. (2013). How lines organize compulsory interaction, emotion management, and "emotional taxes": The implications of passenger emotion and expression in airport security lines. *Management Communication Quarterly, 27,* 121–149.

communicate compassion in workplace relationships (see Spotlight on Scholarship in Chapter 4). These scholars see compassion as a form of "everyday talk" in the organization (Frost et al., 2006) and believe that a culture of compassion can be nurtured through effective leadership: "there is always grief somewhere in the room ... You can't eliminate such suffering, nor can you ask people to check their emotions at the door. But you can use your leadership to begin the healing process" (Dutton, Frost, Worline, Lilius & Kanov, 2002, p. 61).

At the other negative end of the spectrum, the emotional content of workplace relationships can include psychological abuse of others through **workplace bullying**. As Lutgen-Sandvik (2006) describes, bullying is "persistent, verbal, and nonverbal aggression at work that includes personal attacks, social ostracism, and a multitude of other painful messages and hostile interactions" (p. 406). Bullying is reportedly experienced by 90% of adults at some point in their work life and can cause great pain to its victims (Tracy, Lutgen-Sandvik & Alberts, 2006). For example, Lutgen-Sandvik (2008) reports on the trauma and stigmatization of bullying as workers try to make sense of the abuse in light of their ideas about themselves and others. These bullying victims find themselves "dealing with the perceived loss of professional reputation, organizational identity and self-confidence, and the long-term loss of core beliefs in justice or fairness" (Lutgen-Sandvik, 2008, p. 110). Like the creation of cultures of compassion, however, it is possible that organizational leaders and members can play a role in transforming a negative bullying environment (Cowan, 2012; Lutgen-Sandvik & Tracy, 2012).

In addition to these examples of compassion and bullying, feelings and emotional display—both positive and negative—are rampant in all types of organizational relationships. Waldron (2000) has argued that there are several aspects of work relationships that create potential for intense emotion in organizations. These include:

- *The* tension *between the public and the private in work relationships:* Consider, for example, a case where friends outside the workplace are supervisor and subordinate within the workplace. Or consider a situation in which a private disclosure is revealed in a public meeting. In short, emotion is prevalent in the workplace because the private and the public are often in conflict in organizational life.

- *Relational networks and emotional "buzzing":* Waldron (2000) also points out that emotions can spread like wildfire in the workplace. One negative comment in a meeting can lead to a general uprising. A rumor about a possible downsizing leads to widespread panic. Or, on an everyday basis, ongoing complaints about the workplace can "spread like a contagion from worker to worker" (Korkki, 2013).

- *Conflicting allegiances:* Because organizations are complex systems, workers often feel many loyalties. These conflicts might involve a distinction between what's best for the individual and what's best for the company. Or an individual might feel conflicting loyalties to various departments or individuals in an organization. Or allegiances might develop to subcultural groups that have formed in the workplace. In any of these cases, intense emotions (betrayal, dedication, jealousy) might be found.

- *Emotional rights and obligations at work:* Finally, Waldron (2000) argues that most workplaces include a strong sense of relational morality—what is fair, right, and just in workplace relationships. When these norms are disrupted, strong emotions can be seen. For instance, Waldron (2000) quotes a woman who has been accused of "sleeping her way to a promotion" by a coworker: "I took my fist and cold-cocked that little sucker, and said [to him] 'file a grievance.' I have never had another comment, to my face, about what I have done" (Waldron, 2000, p. 72).

Emotion Rules and Emotional Intelligence

Emotion, then, is a central part of organizational life both in terms of interaction with customers or clients and in terms of interaction with other members of the organization. Some scholars have recently looked across these areas by trying to understand the **emotion rules** for emotional display in the workplace and by understanding the role that **emotional intelligence** might play in a wide variety of workplace interactions. For example, Kramer and Hess (2002) surveyed a wide range of workers to learn about the perceived rules that govern emotional life in an organization. These rules are summarized in Table 11.1. The fact that workers perceived these rules to exist clearly suggests that there are standards for emotional expression both with coworkers and with customers and clients. For example, the most often cited rule involved the need to be "professional." This rule suggests standards for emotional control while interacting with clients and coworkers. For example,

Table 11.1 | Emotional Display Rules

Rule	Explanation
"Express emotions in a professional way."	An individual should have control over emotions and maintain a businesslike atmosphere in the workplace.
"Express emotions to improve situations."	Emotional display should be managed in order to prevent or correct problems and create a positive work climate.
"Express emotions to the right people."	Positive and negative emotions should be directed to the appropriate person in the appropriate setting.
"Express emotions to help individuals."	Emotional display should be managed to provide support and assist others.
"Do not manage emotions for personal benefit to the detriment of others."	Emotional display should not be managed in a manner that is purely for self-promotion.
"The expression of certain emotions is always inappropriate."	Workers should maintain role-appropriate control of positive emotions and should not abuse others.

Table developed from Kramer, M. W. & Hess, J. A. (2002). Communication rules for the display of emotions in organizational settings. *Management Communication Quarterly, 16,* 66–80.

expressing anger through yelling and cussing would probably be seen as a violation of this rule, as would an expression of frustration or sadness through crying. It should be noted, however, that these emotional display rules are not hard-and-fast laws but will vary from workplace to workplace and will change over time. For example, Scott and Myers (2005) describe the ways in which rookie firefighters must be socialized into strategies for managing the emotions of their highly stressful jobs, and Morgan and Krone (2001) studied the extent to which "improvisations" in emotional behavior can lead to a bending of the rules of professional display in the workplace.

Finally, it is important to consider the concept of emotional intelligence that has recently become widely known in the popular management press (Goleman, 1995). This concept suggests that there are some people who are naturally better at understanding and managing the emotional content of workplace relationships and that emotional intelligence is also a skill that can be developed through training. Emotional intelligence involves both a clear understanding of the emotional needs of the situation and the self-awareness and self-control necessary for using the right emotional display to cope with the situation. In essence, those who have a high "emotional intelligence quotient" (EQ) have a clear understanding of the rules of emotional display and an ability to follow and adapt those rules as necessary. Although the concept of emotional intelligence has been embraced by many practicing managers, it has also been criticized by some scholars (see Dougherty & Krone, 2002; Fineman, 2000) who argue that the concept of emotional intelligence is one more example of how organizations are attempting to transform emotion into a marketable product that will enhance organizational profits—perhaps to the detriment of the authentic feelings of organizational members. Further, some scholarship has questioned popular recommendations regarding emotional intelligence as "misleading in that they seem to present scientific studies supporting their claims, while in fact failing to do so" (Zeidner, Matthews & Roberts, 2004, p. 393).

STRESS, BURNOUT, AND SOCIAL SUPPORT IN THE WORKPLACE

In this chapter so far, we have considered the centrality of emotion in the workplace. In the remainder of this chapter, we will look at one area of emotion that has received a great deal of attention from organizational scholars: the consideration of stress and burnout and the role of communication in causing and coping with these critical workplace emotions.

The investigation of stress in the workplace has led to a proliferation of terms used to describe various aspects of the phenomenon. In some cases, the use of these terms can be confusing. Consider, for example, the central concept of *stress*. Some scholars use the term to refer to aspects of the workplace that are difficult to deal with, whereas others use it to refer to the negative outcomes that accrue from these work conditions. For the purposes of this chapter, we will talk about stress as a general area of investigation and use more specific terms to refer to detailed aspects of the stress process.

The stress process can be best conceptualized as one in which some aspects of the environment—called **stressors**—create a strain on the individual—called **burnout**—which can lead to negative psychological, physiological, and organizational outcomes.

Stressors	Burnout	Outcomes
Environmental factors that are difficult for an individual to deal with:	Strain that results from ongoing stressors:	Physiological, attitudinal, and organizational results of burnout:
workload, role conflict, role ambiguity, life events, home/work conflict	emotional exhaustion, depersonalization, decreased personal accomplishment	coronary heart disease, high blood pressure, lower job satisfaction, less commitment, turnover

Figure 11.1 | Basic Model of Stress in the Workplace

This basic model is illustrated in Figure 11.1. The following few sections flesh out this model by considering burnout, stressors, and outcomes. We start in the middle of the model by exploring the concept of burnout.

Burnout

The term *burnout,* which was first coined by Freudenberger (1974), refers to a "wearing out" from the pressures of work. Burnout is a chronic condition that results as daily work stressors take their toll on employees. The most widely adopted conceptualization of burnout has been developed by Maslach and her colleagues in their studies of human service workers (Maslach, 1982; see also Cordes & Dougherty, 1993). Maslach sees burnout as consisting of three interrelated dimensions. The first dimension—**emotional exhaustion**—is really the core of the burnout phenomenon. Workers suffer from emotional exhaustion when they feel fatigued, frustrated, used up, or unable to face another day on the job. The second dimension of burnout is a **lack of personal accomplishment**. This aspect of the burnout phenomenon refers to workers who see themselves as failures, incapable of effectively accomplishing job requirements. The third dimension of burnout is **depersonalization**. This dimension is relevant only to workers who must communicate interpersonally with others (e.g., clients, patients, students) as part of the job. When burned out, such workers tend to "view other people through rust-colored glasses—developing a poor opinion of them, expecting the worst from them, and even actively disliking them" (Maslach, 1982, p. 4).

Consider, for example, Rhoda, a social worker who has been working with inner-city families for more than fifteen years. Rhoda entered her occupation as a highly motivated and idealistic worker. However, over the years, she has become burned out from the daily grind of her job. Rhoda exhibits all three dimensions of burnout outlined above. Over time, she has quit seeing her clients as individuals with special problems and now refers to them by case number. She has even been heard to call some particularly difficult clients "lowlifes." Not surprisingly, Rhoda has trouble motivating herself to get to work every day and is physically exhausted and mentally drained by the time she gets home. When she thinks back on what she originally wanted to accomplish as a social worker, Rhoda gets very depressed, feeling that she has made little difference to anyone she serves.

Leading to this burnout syndrome are a wide array of organizational stressors, although not all stressors will lead to burnout for all individuals. Three of the most frequently identified workplace stressors are workload, role conflict, and role ambiguity (Miller, Ellis, Zook & Lyles, 1990). Workload has been linked to burnout both quantitatively—having "too much" work to do—and qualitatively—having work that is "too difficult." Workload stress can stem from a variety of organizational sources. For example, a teacher might feel overloaded because of the number of students he teaches and the need to serve on school committees and process reams of paperwork. Role conflict and role ambiguity are also important stressors in the workplace. *Role conflict* involves having two or more role requirements that clash with each other, and *role ambiguity* exists when there is uncertainty about role requirements. Burnout can also result from stressors outside the workplace including major life events such as divorce, retirement, pregnancy, or moving that have a spillover impact on burnout experienced at work. Perhaps more important than these major life events, however, are the day-to-day hassles and the emotional strain of balancing work and home life (see, e.g., Golden, Kirby & Jorgenson, 2006). As any working parent knows, it is virtually impossible to maintain home and office as separate spheres, and stressors in one domain invariably influence the other. We consider the issue of the intersection of work and home more completely in Chapter 12.

On the other end of the model, Figure 11.1 indicates that burnout can have a variety of physiological, attitudinal, and organizational effects. Physiologically, burnout has been associated with such outcomes including coronary heart disease and high blood pressure. More research has investigated attitudinal outcomes of burnout. For example, scholarship considering a wide range of occupations and workers has linked burnout with lowered levels of job satisfaction (Miller et al., 1990). Similarly, burned-out workers often have lower levels of commitment as they become disenchanted with a stressful organization or occupation. As Maslach (1982) notes with respect to human service workers: "A psychiatric nurse becomes a carpenter, or a counselor turns to farming. They swear they will never return to their original occupation with its crush of people and emotional demands" (p. 81). Finally, the most prevalent behavioral outcome linked with burnout in the organization is turnover (e.g., Ellis & Miller, 1993).

Communication as a Cause of Burnout

There are numerous ways in which communication contributes to the experience of burnout in organizations. Several workplace characteristics have already been identified—workload, role conflict, and role ambiguity—that can serve as stressors and cause burnout. One way that communication in the workplace can influence burnout is through these variables. Communicative interactions, for example, obviously contribute substantially to an individual's workload. Communication can also influence the experience of role conflict and role ambiguity. For example, Graen's model of role development (Graen & Scandura, 1987) that we discussed in Chapter 7 describes the ways in which supervisor-subordinate interaction helps to define expectations as an individual learns about the job and the organization. If communication in this crucial stage of socialization is inadequate, role conflict and role ambiguity are likely to result.

Thus, communication can play a role in causing burnout through its influence on workplace stressors such as load, role conflict, and role ambiguity. These are not the only ways that communication plays a role in the burnout process, however. Indeed, communication also plays a role in creating stress through processes of emotional communication discussed earlier in this chapter. We will now consider two ways in which the emotional aspects of work contribute to stress and burnout.

Emotional Labor as a Contributor to Burnout   As discussed earlier in this chapter, emotional labor is the term used to describe jobs in which specific emotions are required as a part of the job. Workers in service jobs requiring emotional labor must act in ways prescribed by the organization—the cheerful checkout clerk, the stern prison guard, the sympathetic counselor. So, what does emotional labor have to do with burnout? Many researchers argue that they are closely linked. For example, Hochschild's original development of the emotional labor concept suggests that workers involved in emotional labor are at serious psychological risk. It is argued that a major danger of emotional labor is the display of emotions that are not truly felt. Morris and Feldman (1996) have called this "emotional dissonance" and contend that it is the major factor leading to negative consequences such as burnout, job dissatisfaction, and turnover. Although research on the link between emotional labor and burnout is somewhat mixed, there is clearly the possibility that the display of false emotions can—in some situations—have detrimental effects on workers.

Empathy, Communication, and Burnout   A second area of emotion and burnout research has considered not the "prescribed" and "managed" emotions of emotional labor but instead the natural emotions that often emerge in human service work. Specifically, Miller, Stiff, and Ellis (1988) have explored the role of emotional communication and burnout by developing and testing a model of communication, empathy, and burnout for human service workers. They first noted that individuals often choose these occupations (e.g., health care, social work, teaching) because they are "people oriented" and feel a high degree of empathy for others. Miller and colleagues (1988) then draw a distinction between two kinds of empathy—**emotional contagion** and **empathic concern** (Stiff, Dillard, Somera, Kim & Sleight, 1988). Emotional contagion is an affective response in which an observer experiences emotions parallel to those of another person. For example, a funeral director who always feels sad when talking to grieving clients is experiencing emotional contagion. In short, emotional contagion involves "feeling with" another. In contrast, empathic concern is an affective response in which an observer has a nonparallel emotional response. For example, a counselor dealing with a hysterical client might feel concerned but not share the client's hysteria. Thus, empathic concern involves "feeling for" another.

How do these two dimensions of empathy influence the communication of human service workers? Miller and her colleagues (1988) speculate that empathic concern should help an employee communicate effectively, whereas emotional contagion should hinder effective interaction. Their reasoning is similar to the argument offered by Maslach (1982):

> Understanding someone's problems and seeing things from his or her point of view should enhance your ability to provide good service or care. However, the vicarious experience of that person's emotional turmoil will increase your susceptibility to emotional exhaustion. Emotional [contagion] is really a sort of weakness or vulnerability rather than a strength. The person whose feelings are easily aroused (but not necessarily easily controlled) is going to have far more difficulty in dealing with emotionally stressful situations than the person who is less excitable and more psychologically detached. (p. 70)

Miller and colleagues (1988) further hypothesize that workers who are communicatively responsive would experience less burnout and more commitment to their occupations. The model the researchers developed is presented in Figure 11.2. In a study of hospital workers, they found support for their model, ascertaining that empathic concern enhanced communicative responsiveness, whereas emotional contagion decreased responsiveness. Furthermore, they found that communicatively responsive caregivers were less likely to experience burnout. Their model has been further supported and extended by research on workers providing services for homeless clients (Miller, Birkholt, Scott & Stage, 1995), nurses (Omdahl & O'Donnell, 1999), financial planners (Miller & Koesten, 2008), and human service workers (Snyder, 2012). Emotional contagion has also been linked to burnout among teachers (Bakker & Schaufeli, 2000) and oncology care workers (LeBlanc et al., 2001).

This research provides evidence that emotional communication in the workplace can be detrimental but only under certain conditions. Specifically, when an individual in a caregiving situation feels with the client and communicates

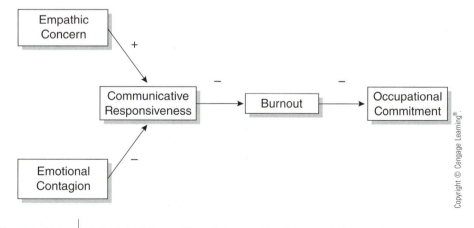

Figure 11.2 | Model of Empathy, Communication, and Burnout

accordingly, burnout is the likely result. In contrast, a caregiver who feels for the client and communicates accordingly is unlikely to suffer the effects of burnout. This pattern led to early recommendations that physicians and other human service workers attempt to adopt a stance of **detached concern,** in which concern for clients can be maintained independent of strong emotional involvement (Lief & Fox, 1963). More recently, scholars have become concerned about the danger of health care workers becoming overly detached—to the detriment of clients and families (Fox, 2006; Halpern, 2001). Thus, some experts have turned to recommending that physicians can combat burnout by engaging in the more genuine empathy embodied in the processes of deep acting we considered earlier in this chapter (Larson & Yao, 2005).

Coping with Burnout

Thus far, we have looked at the genesis of burnout in the workplace, painting a somewhat bleak picture of organizational life. However, there are ways of coping with burnout. In this section, we first look briefly at individual and organizational strategies for handling burnout and then we expand on the role of participation in decision making and social support as communicative strategies to reduce burnout.

Individual and Organizational Coping Strategies   There are many ways an individual might react to burnout. Some of these reactions—such as excessive drinking, drug use, and absenteeism—are clearly dysfunctional. However, an individual might also cope in ways that could serve to ameliorate the experience of burnout and its negative outcomes. For example, some scholars have pointed to different types of coping for dealing with life stress and organizational stress (Folkman, Lazarus, Gruen & DeLongis, 1986). Three types of coping have been identified. **Problem-centered coping** involves dealing directly with the causes of burnout. **Appraisal-centered coping** involves changing the way one thinks about the stressful situation. **Emotion-centered coping** involves dealing with the negative affective outcomes of burnout.

Consider Peter, an engineer who feels overwhelmed by the amount of work he must accomplish. His job leaves him no time for his family, and he is under constant pressure from his supervisor to do more and more on the job. There are several ways Peter could cope with this situation. He might employ emotion-centered coping by using relaxation techniques designed to release job-related tension. Or he might use appraisal-centered coping by convincing himself that he needs to work hard in order to advance in the company and that short-term family sacrifices are necessary for long-term security. Or he might use problem-centered coping by delegating some of his responsibilities, talking to his supervisor about work reduction, or using time-management techniques. These strategies would probably vary in their effectiveness in reducing Peter's stress. However, it is likely that problem-centered coping will generate the most enduring and satisfying reduction in job-related burnout.

The organization can also play a role in reducing burnout (see Pines, Aronson & Kafry, 1981). Socialization programs can be designed to enhance the clarity of employee role definitions. Workload can be carefully monitored and controlled. Workers involved in high-stress or emotional occupations can be provided "timeouts" during the workday or occasional sabbaticals to recharge. The conflict between home and work can be acknowledged through the provision of flextime and onsite day care. All these organizational strategies can serve to eliminate the causes of burnout or lessen its negative effects. Perhaps the most important ways of coping with burnout, however, arise through communicative interactions. Let's look at two important communicative ways of dealing with burnout: participation in decision making and social support.

Communicative Coping: Participation in Decision Making   A first communicative strategy for coping with workplace burnout is participation in decision making (PDM). We have already looked extensively at the participation process in Chapter 8. Specifically, we noted that PDM can improve both worker satisfaction and productivity through enhanced information flow (cognitive model) and the satisfaction of workers' higher-order needs (attitudinal model). Research has also indicated that PDM can decrease burnout in the workplace. Miller and colleagues (1990) found that perceived participation reduced burnout in a sample of hospital employees. Ray and Miller (1991) reached similar conclusions in their study of elementary school teachers. In an experimental study, Jackson (1983) found that employees who had an opportunity to participate in decisions experienced lower levels of strain and fewer intentions to leave their jobs.

Why should PDM work to reduce job-related burnout? Several explanations are feasible. First, it is possible that PDM serves to reduce two of the workplace stressors we talked about earlier in this chapter—role conflict and role ambiguity. As Jackson (1983) notes, PDM should lead to "more accurate knowledge of (a) the formal and informal expectations held by others for the worker, and (b) the formal and informal policies and procedures of the organization, as well as the discrepancies between the two" (p. 6). In addition to this effect on role definition, it is also possible that employees who participate feel more valued by the organization and feel a greater sense of influence and control in the workplace.

Communicative Coping: Social Support   A second communicative avenue for coping with workplace stress and burnout is social support. Voluminous research exists on social support as a means of protecting individuals from the major and minor stresses of life (see Albrecht, Burleson & Goldsmith, 1995, for a review). In this section, we focus on the role of social support as a means of coping with job-related stress and burnout by considering the functions social support can play, the sources of social support for reducing strain in the workplace, and the mechanisms through which social support reduces burnout. It should be noted, however, that social support is not a panacea and that not everyone in the workplace has the communicative competence to provide effective support (Wright, Banas, Bessarabova & Bernard, 2010).

A wide variety of typologies have been proposed to categorize social support (see, e.g., House, 1981). Most typologies involve three major functions of social support:

- *Emotional support* involves letting another person know that they are loved and cared for. Emotional support might involve a message that boosts another's self-esteem ("I know you're bright enough to do well on the test") or a message that indicates unconditional regard ("You know I'll be proud of you

Case in Point: Stretched Thin in the Emergency Room

As the scholarship discussed in this chapter makes clear, workers in human service careers, such as health care, face emotionally burdensome jobs. These workers interact with the sick and their families, dealing with stressed-out people during the most troubling times of their lives. Obviously, this is never an easy task, and it can be the source of both great rewards and intense burnout. However, the struggles of this kind of work become increasingly difficult when the load of health care workers increases.

Paul Duke (2004) makes this argument with regard to workers in his career: emergency room nursing. Duke points out that the load of emergency room (ER) nurses has increased substantially in recent years. This increase can be traced to a variety of sources: fewer qualified nurses, an aging population, more underinsured people using the ER as their first-line source of health care. For all these reasons, ER nurses now must deal with many more patients than in the past, and those patients often have increasingly serious needs. Duke reports that he, like many nurses, is pulled apart emotionally by the stress. He says, "After all this you must wonder why I don't quit. The truth is, I love nursing. It's what I am good at. I love the challenge of not knowing what will come crashing through the doors. Emergency-room nurses rise to the occasion. But we are being steam-rolled, stretched thin and beaten down, and the best of us are frustrated" (p. 12).

In this emotional struggle between the love of nursing and the frustration of increasing patient loads, we can only hope that the love of nursing continues to win out or that we find a way to cope with the pressures of an increasingly congested health care system.

no matter what you do"). Or emotional support might involve the provision of a shoulder to cry on or a friend to gripe to ("You can always come to me when you have problems").

- *Informational support* involves the provision of facts and advice to help an individual cope. Several types of informational support could be helpful in the workplace. First, information might serve to decrease job-related stressors such as role conflict and workload (e.g., clarifying a job description or providing strategies for time management). Second, informational support might provide suggestions for dealing with the strain of burnout (e.g., suggesting a good health club for exercise).

- *Instrumental support* involves physical or material assistance that helps an individual cope with stress and strain. For example, a coworker might pitch in to help someone finish a project when that person is fighting a tight deadline. A supervisor might send an employee to a management seminar for extra job-related training. One's spouse might cook dinner. In short, instrumental support involves providing the resources and labor employees need to cope with workplace burnout.

A variety of people can provide individuals the support they need to cope with burnout. The three most common sources are supervisors, coworkers, and friends and family:

- *Support from supervisors* is most likely to come in the form of instrumental and informational support. A supervisor has the knowledge to provide informational support and the access to resources to provide instrumental support. For example, a supervisor can reduce role ambiguity by sitting down with an employee and clarifying job expectations (informational support). A supervisor could also reduce workload by informing management of the need for additional workers (instrumental support).

- *Support from coworkers* is most likely to come in the form of informational and emotional support. Coworkers (especially long-term employees) can often provide valuable information about how to deal with organizational stressors. Coworkers are also crucial as sources of emotional support because they have a clear understanding of the workplace context. Ray (1987) quotes a day care center worker on this topic: "When I try to tell my husband or friends what it's like at work, to deal with 15 screaming, fighting, attention-demanding kids for 8 hours straight, they don't really understand. The only people who really feel like I do are the people I work with" (p. 174). Recent research points to the possible dangers of type of support, however, as interaction with others in the workplace can sometimes draw attention to just how stressful the workplace can be (Beehr, Bowling & Bennett, 2010).

- *Support from friends and family* will typically come in the form of emotional and instrumental support. Friends and family know an individual well enough to provide esteem support and a shoulder to lean on. Friends and family can also provide instrumental support by freeing an individual from home responsibilities. For example, a woman might take charge of the children for an evening to allow her husband to put in some extra time catching up with an office project.

SUMMARY

In this chapter, we have looked at an important emerging area of scholarship in organizational communication: the consideration of emotion in the workplace. We first looked at several areas of scholarship that emphasize the role of emotion in organizations. These include the consideration of emotional labor, the consideration of emotion in human service occupations, and the investigation of emotion in ongoing organizational relationships. We then turned to a consideration of a specific area of workplace emotion and communication: research on stress, burnout, and social support. We first looked at the burnout syndrome and then at workplace antecedents and outcomes of burnout and the role of communication in both causing and helping individuals cope with burnout.

As in previous chapters, it is instructive to look at our topic in the light of the various approaches to organizational communication (see Table 11.2). The classical approach to organizational communication largely ignores emotion in general and burnout in particular. Indeed, a burned-out employee is simply a cog in the machine that must be replaced. Emotion has similarly been ignored by many scholars in the human relations, human resources, and systems approaches. Although human relations theorists consider feelings such as job satisfaction and all these theorists would see burnout as a problem to be solved, emotion takes a backseat in the work of all these approaches.

Much of the emerging work on emotion in organizations has developed from cultural and

Table 11.2 | Approaches to the Emotion Process

Approach	How Emotion Would Be Considered
Classical	Emotions are not seen as an issue except to the extent that they lower worker productivity. If working conditions cause burnout, employees can be replaced quickly.
Human relations	The only emotion considered is job satisfaction. Stress and burnout are dealt with through emotional support or other means of boosting employee self-esteem.
Human resources	Emotions rarely considered in rationally designed organizations. Stress and burnout are likely to be dealt with through participation or structural changes designed to enhance employee control.
Systems	Emotions are seen as *sensemaking* opportunities. Stress and burnout could be reduced through communication in networks of information sharing and social support.
Cultural	Different organizational cultures provide different value systems regarding emotional expression, compassion, and negative emotional displays such as bullying.
Constitutive	Emotional organizational systems and conditions that breed stress and burnout are socially created through the interaction of organizational participants.
Critical	Emotions are seen as an indicator of inequality in the workplace. Critical scholars would want to educate workers to resist the acceptance of conditions that lead to stress and burnout.
Feminist	The shift to a consideration of emotions is seen as an important move away from patriarchal understandings of organizing. Feminist values would encourage compassion as a workplace value.

feminist approaches to organizational scholarship. For example, Meyerson (1994, 1998) has contrasted the cultures of two health care settings with regard to stress and burnout. Her analysis points to differences in organizational culture (e.g., one culture saw burnout as a "disease," whereas the other saw it as a natural outcome of social work) that highlighted emotional aspects of organizational culture and the power of more feminine modes of organizing. Relatedly, some researchers have argued that the performance of emotional labor is a "gendered" process (e.g., Hall, 1993). Finally, in the area of social support, Kirby (2006) has argued that many organizational programs and policies now take on the support tasks that were once the purview of family and friends. This development is in line with critical scholarship in pointing to the increasing ways in which organizations maintain control over ever-increasing areas of our lives.

DISCUSSION QUESTIONS

1. How does a consideration of emotion change the way we view basic processes of organizational life, such as conflict, decision making, socialization, and organizational change? Is it possible to balance concerns for rationality and emotion? How can this be accomplished?

2. How is the experience and expression of emotion different in different types of jobs?

Compare, for example, emotion in the work of a minister, a store clerk, and a data processor. Are the emotional demands of some jobs more challenging than others?

3. As a student, you sometimes experience stress and burnout. How do your experiences compare with the discussion of stress and burnout in this chapter? How do you cope with stress and burnout as a student?

KEY CONCEPTS

bounded emotionality
emotional labor
surface acting
deep acting
emotional work
compassionate communication
emotion at work
workplace bullying

emotion rules
emotional intelligence
stressors
burnout
emotional exhaustion
lack of personal accomplishment
depersonalization
emotional contagion

empathic concern
detached concern
problem-centered coping
appraisal-centered coping
emotion-centered coping
emotional support
informational support
instrumental support

CASE STUDY | # Inexplicable Events

- On November 18, 1999, on the campus of Texas A&M University, the Aggie bonfire collapsed, killing twelve students and injuring many more. The collapse of the bonfire was a hugely emotional event for students at Texas A&M, for faculty and staff, and for members of the surrounding community. Investigations regarding the decades-old tradition followed, and no on-campus bonfire has been burned since.

- On September 11, 2001, planes piloted by terrorists were flown into the twin towers of the World Trade Center in New York and the Pentagon in Washington, D.C. Another plane crashed in a rural Pennsylvania field. Thousands were killed, and 9/11 will forever be a dividing day in history, marking the beginning of an era in which terms such as *war on terror* and *homeland security* became common parlance. The emotional toll of September 11 on our individual, national, and global psyches will last for untold years to come.

- On August 29, 2005, Hurricane Katrina made landfall along the gulf coast of the United States. Hours later, many levees were breached in New Orleans, leading to the flooding of over 80% of the city. For days, New Orleans residents sought refuge in shelters, in the ill-prepared Superdome, and in neighboring and distant states. More than 1,800 people died, and many more lost homes or were displaced for many months. Criticisms of local and national authorities for their handling of the storm were widespread.

- On April 16, 2007, the deadliest school shooting in U.S. history occurred on the campus of Virginia Tech University in Blacksburg, Virginia. In shootings two hours apart, Seung-Hui Cho, a mentally ill English major at the school, shot thirty-two people before committing suicide. The campus community mourned the loss of both students and faculty, and the incident led to national discussions regarding issues ranging from gun control to campus security to the treatment of the mentally ill.

These events—spread over less than a decade—took place in various locations of the U.S. geography. These events can be attributed to very different causes: terrorism, a natural disaster, a deranged student, a tragic accident. These events varied in terms of their long-term influence on our national and global consciousness—from a ripple in the aftermath of the bonfire collapse to the huge changes in both institutional systems and individual mind-sets brought on by the 9/11 terrorist attacks. But these events—and others like them in the intervening years such as the elementary school shooting in Newtown, Connecticut—also share important characteristics. Although in retrospect they can be "explained" to a greater or lesser extent, at the time they occurred, the events were seen as somehow inexplicable. They were a breach to our beliefs about how things happened in a rational and predictable world. They shifted our organized ways of coping—sometimes for a few days or a few weeks and sometimes forever. Thus, individuals working with and around these events can shed important light on the role of emotion in organizational communication. Consider just a few of the possibilities.

EMOTION IN THE MIDST OF THE INEXPLICABLE

In each of these events, "first responders" worked with the immediate onset of the disasters. Firefighters rushed to the World Trade Center and the Pentagon. Rescue teams hovered in helicopters, plucking New Orleans residents off of rooftops. Campus police worked to secure the safety of students on the Virginia Tech campus. Emergency medical personnel worked in the early morning hours to pull injured students out of "the stack" in College Station, Texas. These first responders were, in one sense, just doing their jobs. These were highly trained men and women who understood the needs of individuals in disasters and understood the ways that the work needed to be accomplished. First responders understand the emotional aspects of their jobs and have special education to deal with stress. However, that does not mean they are immune to the emotional effects of working in the midst of a disaster. Indeed, recent research suggests that social workers who work with disaster victims have a heightened

chance of experiencing post-traumatic stress disorder (Adams, 2007).

EMOTION IN THE AFTERMATH OF THE INEXPLICABLE

In the days and weeks following these events, a variety of workers had to cope with a huge number of organizational problems. In my experience as a professor at Texas A&M University following the bonfire collapse, I found that instructors and staff members were asked to deal with an incredible range of student emotions, and we weren't trained for it. As I wrote afterward, "As professional academics, we were prepared to impart knowledge, to conduct research, to serve on committees, to provide career counseling, and so on…. We weren't prepared to deal with the emotional turmoil that ensued when 12 young people were wrenched from a community in the prime of their lives" (Miller, 2002, p. 589). And there are a myriad of other job tasks that must be accomplished in the aftermath of a disaster. In New Orleans, thousands of people needed to be housed and fed, paperwork needed to be processed to provide money for immediate needs and long-term relief, funds needed to be solicited from donors around the country, and planning needed to be started to consider ways in which the next hurricane could be coped with in a better way. Many of these tasks are bureaucratic and, on the surface, highly rational. However, in the aftermath of the inexplicable, even these rational tasks can be overridden by emotion.

EMOTION IN THE NEW NORMAL

And finally, we move past the disaster and beyond the inexplicable. Or do we? Can our personal and organizational lives ever return to the rationality of the times before the inexplicable? Do we just recreate new sets of logic to encompass that which we do not want to accept? Or was any of it ever all that logical to begin with? In the years since the 9/11 terrorist attacks, we have—in many ways—returned to a new normal. But this is a new normal in which media reports regarding war and terrorism are commonplace. It is a new normal when we know that we need to take off our shoes in airport security lines. It is a new normal when a

| **Inexplicable Events** *continued*

widespread power outage causes rampant speculation about what group might be attacking us. It is a new normal when the possibility of surveillance from our government—and the organizations we work for—is much more conceivable than it was a decade ago. In all these ways in which the inexplicable has somehow been made explicable, we find the tight weaving of emotion and rationality in our lives and in our work.

CASE ANALYSIS QUESTIONS

1. In what ways do the special cases of organizational life discussed in this case bring processes of rationality and emotion into sharp relief? Is emotion more "present" in these cases? Are different kinds of emotion brought to the forefront?

How does the everyday nature of most of our work lives blind us to processes of emotion?

2. How are the specific processes of emotion discussed in this chapter—emotional labor, emotional work, and compassion, stress, and burnout—illustrated in these examples of the inexplicable? Are particular processes of emotion in the workplace especially apparent in the midst of the inexplicable, in the aftermath of the inexplicable, or in living in the new normal?

3. How could organizations and employees in those organizations be better prepared to cope with the emotion of these inexplicable events? And could those lessons be translated into practices that lead to more healthy and happy organizational life during the more mundane days, as well?

12 | Organizational Diversity Processes

AFTER READING THIS CHAPTER, YOU SHOULD ...

- Be able to describe how the workplace is changing in terms of the representation and participation of women and minorities.
- Appreciate how the experiences of women and minorities in the workplace might differ from the experiences of white males.
- Understand the ways in which diversity in the workplace extends beyond the experiences of women and racial and ethnic minorities to other co-cultural groups such as disabled and LGBT employees.
- Be able to explain various approaches to the multicultural workplace and consider the ways in which diversity can make organizations more effective and better places to work.
- Know about the challenges of the diverse and multicultural organization, including dealing with resistance to diversity management program and balancing work and home.

As we move further into the twenty-first century, the workforce continues to reflect the dramatic demographic changes that began many years ago. Women continue to join the workforce in increasing numbers and are now entering careers that were once the exclusive bastions of men. As of a 2012 report, the percentage of women in the U.S. workforce was 47%, and it is anticipated that women will outnumber men in the workforce by 2020 (Burns, Barton & Kerby, 2012). Various factors have contributed to these changes over the last several decades, including increased career aspirations, changes in educational systems, and the development and growth of workplace support schemes, such as child care and flextime. It is notable, however, that the U.S. lags behind other countries in terms of women's participation in the work force—in 1990 the United States ranked sixth among twenty-two developed nations in terms of percentage of women working, but by 2013 the ranking fell to seventeenth (Covert, 2013). As of 2012, 36% of the U.S. workforce identified as a member of a minority group (e.g., Hispanic, African American, Asian American) and as the nation moves toward becoming a "majority minority" nation, these groups' participation in the labor force will continue to grow.

What is it like to be a woman or a person of color in today's workplace? What factors contribute to their organizational experiences? What are the benefits and challenges of a culturally diverse workplace? And what strategies can be instituted to enhance the effectiveness of culturally diverse organizations? In this chapter, we discuss these issues and consider the implications of the changing workplace. First, we examine the experiences of people of color and women in the workplace, attempt to answer questions about how those experiences are changing, and consider diversity beyond the issues of gender, race, and ethnicity. Then, we discuss the notion of a "multicultural organization" and consider the advantages and challenges of such a workplace. Finally, we look at some strategies for developing, managing, and celebrating a culturally diverse organization.

Before we delve into these topics, however, it is worthwhile to briefly consider the terminology that will be used in this chapter. Writing about organizational diversity can be a challenge, as terms used to describe people can be viewed as having a variety of meanings depending on who is involved in the conversation and the norms of particular contexts of time and place. In this chapter, I will use the term *white* rather than the term *Euro-American,* which was used in a previous edition of this textbook. I use this terminology not only because this is the term typically used in conversations about race but also because "whiteness" has become a concept of theoretical interest to scholars in recent years (see, e.g., Alley-Young, 2008). I will use the terms *people of color* and *minorities* in this discussion, as well, although it is certainly true that white is also a color and that the term *minority* might at times be misleading when we consider sheer numbers. What is more important than the terminology, of course, is an understanding of the communication and experiences of a wide range of individuals and groups within increasingly diverse organizational settings.

WOMEN AND MINORITIES IN TODAY'S ORGANIZATIONS

As noted above, women and people of color are entering the workforce in increasing numbers. But what are their experiences in the workplace? Are these experiences similar to those of white males? The consistent answer to this question is that the workplace experiences of women and people of color are vastly different from that of white men (Allen, 2000; Gates, 2003).

Consider first the case of women. For decades, commentators have talked about the phenomenon that has come to be known as the **glass ceiling**. As Morrison and Von Glinow (1990) explain, "The glass ceiling is a concept popularized in the 1980s to describe a barrier so subtle that it is transparent, yet so strong that it prevents women and minorities from moving up in the management hierarchy" (p. 200). Heilman (1994) laid out the relevant statistics from more than twenty years ago: "While women occupy 36% of the management positions in the United States … less than 3% of the top executives in *Fortune* 500 companies are women" (p. 126). Have things improved since then? Hardly. By 2012, the percentage of women who were CEOs of Fortune 500 companies had only risen to 3.6% (Burns et al., 2012).

Beyond the executive suite, the picture has improved slightly but remains disheartening. President Kennedy signed the Equal Pay Act in 1963. In the half century since, women's pay has moved from 59 cents for every dollar a man earns to 77 cents. In 2009, the first bill President Obama signed during his presidency was the Lilly Ledbetter fair pay act, making it easier for women to sue for pay inequity. Thus, there has been progress, but it has been limited. Pay fairness also remains difficult for young women just starting out in their careers. Recent analysis notes that "a year out of school, despite having earned higher college GPAs in every subject, young women will take home, on average across all professions, just 80 percent of what their male colleagues do" (Bennett, Ellison & Ball, 2010, p. 43).

The situation is even grimmer for people of color. The Equal Employment Opportunity Commission reports that "color discrimination in employment seems to be on the rise" ("Why Do We Need E-Race?" 2007). For example, studies have found that black job applicants with lighter skin were more likely to be hired than those with darker skin, even when identical qualifications were presented (Cazares, 2007). There are also differences in various sectors of the labor market. For example, although black men are now less likely to be discriminated against in jobs requiring technical skills, discrimination still exists in jobs that require more social skills (Kim & Tamborini, 2006), and black men experienced greater levels of unemployment in the recent recession than any other demographic group (Cawthorne, 2009). Continuing issues with black unemployment may be driven in part by differential access to relevant social networks (DeTomoso, 2012). And, although representation of minorities throughout the U.S. labor force is 36%, minority representation is significantly lower in important sectors, such as nonprofit organizations and government (Burns et al., 2012). In sum, then, three aspects defining the experience of women and minorities in today's organizations are a relatively greater difficulty in getting

Case in Point: Judging Women

On August 7, 2010, Elena Kagan was sworn in as associate justice of the Supreme Court. This appointment can be seen as a movement toward increased diversity, as now three out of nine Supreme Court justices are women. However, Kagan's nomination process also points to ways in which women's choices play a critical role in organizational experience even in this most exclusive of workplaces.

Lisa Belkin makes this point by comparing the two most recent female justices (Kagan and Sonia Sotomayor) with the first two women appointed to the Supreme Court (Sandra Day O'Connor and Ruth Bader Ginsburg). Belkin (2010) notes that while O'Connor and Ginsburg are both married and mothers, Kagan and Sotomayor are both single and childless. This could be coincidence, or it could point to ways in which women's lives have changed over the years. Belkin argues that O'Connor and

Ginsburg came of age at a time in which "not much was given to or expected of women ... which created a paradoxical freedom." In contrast, Kagan and Sotomayor are of a time in which a great deal more is expected of women. "Expectation brings obligation, and Sotomayor and Kagan were of the generation facing new tradeoffs. Pursue the career and sacrifice the family. Have the family and ratchet back the career ... There would be no taking five years off to stay home with your children if you hoped for a seat on the Supreme Court" (Belkin, 2010). Although this sample of four Supreme Court justices is obviously not representative of all working women, this comparison does point to continuing struggles for women in the workplace. As Belkin concludes, " [F]or men, having a family is an asset when pursuing a demanding career. For women, it is still a complication."

jobs, widespread pay inequity, and challenges with representation in particular sectors and at upper levels of the organizational hierarchy.

There are also other obstacles. We talked earlier about the glass ceiling that hampers advancement for women. Additional buzzwords describe further problems in the workplace. Several decades ago, Schwartz (1989) differentiated between women on a career track and women on a **mommy track**, who were assumed to want flexible work arrangements and family support in exchange for fewer opportunities for advancement. More recent catchphrases in this area suggest enhanced flexibility for women as they choose to *opt-in* and *opt-out* of work (Conant, 2007) or as they take the *off-ramp* from the workplace to have children and then take the *on-ramp* back into a career several years later (McGinn, 2006). However, these transitions aren't always easy. For example, Hewlett (2007) reports that when women wanted to on-ramp back to work, only about three-quarters found a job and only 40% returned to full-time work. Thus, women are now being advised to **lean in** to career and leadership opportunities (Sandberg, 2013). Finally, both women and people of color are often hampered by restricted access to power and by being assigned suboptimal tasks in the workplace (see, e.g., Ohlott, Ruderman & McCauley, 1994); many women and people of color find themselves marginalized, taking on the role of the *outsider within* established organizational systems (Allen, 2000).

Thus, women and people of color do indeed have different organizational experiences than white men. In the next few sections, we'll explore those differences further by considering the concepts of discrimination and relational barriers in the organization and by looking at some of the unexpected experiences brought on by gender diversity in the workplace.

Stereotyping and Discrimination

One of the most basic ways that the experiences of women and people of color differ from those of white men is in the perceptions and attitudes that many people have about the two former groups—and in the behavior that sometimes results from these perceptions and attitudes. In essence, others often view women and people of color in biased ways, and these biases may result in significantly different treatment within the organization. Such bias in the organization has two components: "**Prejudice** refers to negative attitudes toward an organization member based on his/her culture group identity, and **discrimination** refers to observable behavior for the same reason" (Cox, 1991, p. 36). For example, a manager may believe, based on cultural **stereotypes**, that Japanese American workers are unassertive or that Mexican American workers are lazy. A patient might believe that only men have the mental capacity to be physicians or that only women have the nurturing qualities to be nurses. A customer might think that an elderly salesperson must be senile. This process of stereotyping is widespread in society and often serves to reinforce status differences for particular cultural groups (DiTomaso, Post & Parks-Yancy, 2007). For example, stereotypes about women in leadership positions could make it particularly difficult to advance in the organization. As Anna Quindlen argues, "[M]en are judged by a male standard of control and strength; female leaders are judged by that standard and also by a separate stereotypically female standard that assesses everything from bringing people together to projecting approachability" (Quindlen, 2008, p. 86).

The stereotyping of women and minorities in the workplace is not always overt and simplistic, however. Osland and Bird (2000), for instance, note that people in organizations often move beyond irrational stereotypes, such as "The (fill in the blank) are lazy, dirty thieves, and their women are promiscuous" (p. 66) but still engage in stereotyping that might be seen as more sophisticated (e.g., "gays and lesbians tend to be politically progressive") or as helpful (e.g., "individuals who are in wheelchairs prefer to be treated no differently than others"). However, even this sophisticated stereotyping can be dangerous because it is typically incomplete and misleading (and often just plain wrong) when applied to individual members of a cultural group.

Relational Barriers in Organizational Systems

The experiences of stereotyping, prejudice, and discrimination are typically seen as individual-level phenomena. That is, these are problems based on the mental models of individuals, although these mental models are often shared by large segments of the organizational population. However, there are also aspects of organizational relationships and systems that lead to differential experiences for women and minorities in organizations. Three of these issues will be discussed in this section.

First, there is compelling evidence that women and ethnic minorities experience limited access to or exclusion from informal communication networks (see Ibarra, 1993, for a review). This is critical because of the widespread importance of informal communication networks in such processes as socialization, decision making, and conflict management. Thus, as Ibarra (1993) notes, "Limited network access, therefore, produces multiple disadvantages, including restricted knowledge of what is going on in their organizations and difficulty in forming alliances, which, in turn are associated with limited mobility and 'glass ceiling' effects" (p. 56). Although in recent years there has been increasing attention given to the support provided by **minority employee networks** (also known as *affinity groups*) in which members of a particular gender or ethnic background meet (e.g., Friedman & Craig, 2004), Ibarra (1995) found that minority employees experience the most success when they develop a differentiated network consisting of both majority and minority members and of individuals on a wide range of hierarchical levels.

It is not always easy to fit into these networks, however. Ragins, Townsend, and Mattis (1998) report that successful executive women often had to develop an interpersonal communication style that men were comfortable with in order to be successful. One vice president reported that she had to learn "how to act with men who had never dealt with women before, and how to be heard, and how to get past what you looked like, and what sex you were, and into what kind of brain you had" (Ragins et al., 1998, p. 30). These difficulties can be particularly challenging in fields that are typically dominated by males such as engineering and the sciences (Kantrowitz & Scelfo, 2006) and for women entrepreneurs (Gill & Ganesh, 2007).

A second relational experience that is both important and challenging women and people of color is establishing mentor-protégé relationships. Kram (1985) was one of the first researchers to discuss the importance of **mentoring relationships**, defining a mentor as "an experienced, productive manager who relates well to a less-experienced employee and facilitates his or her personal development for the benefit of the individual as well as that of the organization" (Noe, 1988, p. 65). Indeed, research indicates that that mentorship is a critical way of providing support in an organization encouraging a diverse workforce (Ragins, 1997; Clutterbuck & Ragins, 2002).

Especially in careers that are stereotypically male, research has found that a male mentor who works with a female protégé *signals* to others that she is someone to be reckoned with in the organization (Ramaswami, Dreher, Bretz & Wiethoff, 2010). However, these relationships can be extremely difficult to establish and maintain for the woman (Noe, 1988). For example, if Deidre were looking for a mentoring relationship, she might be hampered because she knows few people in the management ranks, because her upbringing makes her reluctant to initiate relationships with men, and because she is worried about how others might construe a mentoring relationship between herself and a man.

Mentoring can also be extremely beneficial for minority employees trying to move into the executive suite. For example, a study of African American managers at Fortune 500 companies found that career development was positive affected by these kinds of relationships (Bristol & Tisdell, 2010). However, establishing these relationships can be challenging. Thomas (1993), in a study of cross-ethnic mentorship, found that successful mentorship could be achieved in relationships in which ethnicity was either openly discussed or suppressed, as long as the mentor and protégé agreed on the appropriateness of the chosen interaction style. However, establishing such a relationship can be difficult.

A third systemic aspect of organizational life that confronts women and minorities is **tokenism**. In many organizations, white males represent the vast majority of employees, especially among the ranks of management. Thus, women and people of color in managerial positions are often tokens or highly visible representatives of their gender or ethnic minority (Ilgen & Youst, 1986). According to Morrison and Von Glinow (1990), "Tokens' performances are hindered because of the pressure to which their visibility subjects them and because members of the dominant group exaggerate differences according to stereotypes" (p. 203). That is, the only African American in a workgroup might be pressured to always represent the "black viewpoint," or men in a workgroup might joke about having to curb their language because there is a "lady" in the room. For example, Janna Levin—an astronomer who studies the origin of the universe—was asked for years about what it was like to be a woman scientist. She's now rejected that role as a spokesperson: "It took me 10 years to get back the confidence I had at 19 and to realize that I didn't want to deal with gender issues. And I didn't have to. Why should curing sexism be yet another terrible burden on every female scientist?" (Levin, 2006, p. 72).

Beyond Women and Minorities

Much of our discussion to this point has centered on issues concerning women and ethnic and racial minorities, as these groups have garnered the most attention both in terms of academic research, legislative action, and practical concern. However, diversity in the workplace also accounts for others who in some way are different from the norm. For example, in a review of the diversity literature, Shore et al. (2009) consider ethnic diversity, gender diversity, age diversity, disability diversity, cultural diversity, and sexual orientation diversity. Orbe (1998) calls these groups *co-cultural groups* in moving beyond issues of race and gender to consider groups who are in some way different from the norm in the organizational setting. We'll talk about age diversity in Chapter 14, but in the following paragraphs we'll briefly consider two other important co-cultural groups: employees with disabilities and lesbian, gay, bisexual, and transgender (LGBT) employees.

The **Americans with Disabilities Act** (ADA) was enacted in 1990, and major amendments to the act were added in 2008. This legislation prohibits discrimination based on disability and requires that organizations make "reasonable accommodations" for disabled workers. The ADA has had historical effects on access in public and workplace, but scholars and activists note that there is still work to be done, as "these solutions have yet to alter fundamentally the social motifs of public life" (Harter, Scott, Novak, Leeman & Morris, 2006, p. 4). This need for additional progress is clearly indicated by the fact that although 11% of the U.S. population is disabled, only 21% of these individuals are members of the labor force (Burns et al., 2012). Disabled individuals in the workplace can face discrimination (Nelson & Probst, 2004) or may be treated differently because of a "kindness norm" (Miller & Werner, 2005). Activist Joel Solkoff believes that these patterns of differential treatment often occur because "institutions often strive to follow the legal letter of the ADA but not its inclusive spirit" (Phillips, 2010).

For LGBT organizational members, however, the situation is somewhat different. There has been rapid progress in many areas of gay rights. As I write this chapter, the Defense of Marriage Act has just been declared unconstitutional and marriage equality is the law in thirteen states and the District of Columbia. However, with regard to the workplace, there has not been wide-ranging legislative action similar to the ADA, and NPR labeled being "gay in the office" as the "last frontier of workplace equality" ("Being Gay," NPR, 2010). There has been some movement, however. Individual states began instituting antidiscrimination laws regarding sexual orientation in 1982, and more than twenty states now prohibit discrimination based on sexual orientation or gender identity. At the national level, the **Employment Non-Discrimination Act** (ENDA) that was first introduced as in Congress in 1994 and has been discussed and reintroduced—but never passed—a number of times. Even without legislative mandate, though, many businesses have included sexual orientation in their nondiscrimination policies. Reasons for taking this lead include both fairness and business concerns. For example, a Hewlett-Packard vice president stated that "in terms of the types of benefits we provide, we know it really is smart business and gives us a competitive advantage to have the LGBT community included in our non-discrimination policies" (Joyce, 2005). Over 6% of the U.S. workforce reported being gay or transgender as of 2012 (Burns et al., 2012) and their experiences and comfort with issues of identity depend a great deal on issues such as "organizational policy and procedures, transparency of decision making, and the presence of other 'out' individuals" (Clair, Beatty & MacLean, 2005).

In summary, then, the organizational experiences of members of various co-cultural groups—women, people of color, people with disabilities, and LGBT workers—are likely to differ substantially from the experiences of white men. To varying degrees, these employees are confronted with stereotyping and prejudice, with relational and systemic barriers, and with lack of legal protection. Thus, today's

Case in Point: Sensitivity Training

Increased attention to a variety of diversity issues has been a learning opportunity for many organizations. For example, in 2005, a Chicago Transit Authority (CTA) employee sued the agency for failing to intervene after he was harassed for being gay. As part of the ruling in favor of this employee, the CTA began to train all of its employees about sensitivity to LGBT issues in the workplace ("CTA Rolling Out," 2013). The training program has had a few bumps—for instance, in developing the understanding that sexual *orientation* harassment is a very different thing from sexual harassment—but officials and employees are now making a difference. One manager noted that "the best part of the training is seeing someone who is resistant to the information settling in and becoming more receptive" ("CTA Rolling Out," 2013).

The training involves both issues of understanding and communication with LGBT employees and customers, and starts at very basic levels of understanding—e.g., "a person who is transgender is not necessarily gay, bisexual or lesbian. And someone who identifies as queer is not necessarily any of those things" ("CTA Rolling Out," 2013). The training then moves on to the presentation of scenarios regarding harassment based on sexual orientation or gender identity. The program has borrowed from related programs in public schools, where there is the understanding that "it's that low level language that really starts to wear on people on a day to day basis" and that at the CTA "they really have situations where people don't really feel like a team member and it really makes it hard for people to go to work" ("CTA Rolling Out," 2013). Thus, there is clearly a continuing need for training about a variety of issues regarding diversity in the workplace—the learning curve might be steep, but it's worth it.

organizations can sometimes be an unfriendly place for many individuals who are different from the white male norm of the past. But what will tomorrow's organizations look like? Can these difficulties be overcome? In the next few sections, we will explore the notion of a **multicultural organization** by considering what such an organization looks like, the opportunities and challenges of a multicultural organization, and steps for developing one.

THE MULTICULTURAL ORGANIZATION

Moving beyond the stereotyping and discrimination found in many of today's organizations is a difficult task. To illustrate this, Morrison and Von Glinow (1990) have described three phases of workplace development in the area of cultural and gender diversity. In the first stage—*first-generation affirmative action*—the organization is concerned with meeting legally mandated requirements for gender and ethnic diversity. Unfortunately, "simply responding to legislative mandates does not seem to automatically result in greater minority inclusion" (Gilbert & Ivancevich, 2000, p. 93). Indeed, the focus on numbers and quotas in these firms can lead to intergroup conflict, distrust, and hostility. In the second stage of development, organizations reach *second-generation affirmative action*. At this stage, the firm has met affirmative action goals in terms of numbers, and the emphasis shifts to supporting female and minority employees. Finally, a *multicultural organization* moves beyond the concept of support for minority members to the institution of policies that deliberately capitalize on cultural and gender diversity. As Gilbert and Ivancevich (2000) contend, "[R]ather than simply making a commitment to valuing diversity, creating an atmosphere of inclusion requires change on many fronts, including fairness, empowerment, and openness" (p. 93).

More than twenty years ago, Cox (1991) provided a detailed description of a multicultural organization that is still helpful today. He identified six critical dimensions: acculturation, structural integration, informal integration, cultural bias, organizational identification, and intergroup conflict. These dimensions are defined in Table 12.1.

According to Cox (1991), a multicultural organization is marked by the full structural integration of women and people of color. Women and minorities—and other co-cultural groups—are proportionally represented at all levels of an organization and in all workgroups. A multicultural organization is also marked by full informal integration. That is, co-cultural group members are not excluded from social activities or from mentoring and other developmental processes. A multicultural organization is also marked by an absence of discrimination, low levels of intergroup conflict, and high levels of organizational identification for all organizational members, regardless of gender, ethnicity, culture, age, sexual orientation, or disability status.

It should be noted, however, that developing this kind of diversity does not necessarily mean that members of the diverse organization will always agree with each other. Hafen (2003), for example, talks about how the dominant metaphor of pluralistic diversity involves having a wide range of voices singing together in a single organizational chorus. However, Hafen believes that this chorus might not always be harmonious, and she argues for "letting all voices on and (arguably) off key, into the choir, without flinching at discordant notes, without wishing that they would

Table 12.1 | Dimensions for Describing a Multicultural Organization

Dimension	Definition
1. Acculturation	Modes by which two groups adapt to each other and resolve cultural differences
2. Structural integration	Cultural profiles of organization members, including hiring, job placement, and job status profiles
3. Informal integration	Inclusion of minority-culture members in informal networks and activities outside of normal working hours
4. Cultural bias	Prejudice and discrimination
5. Organizational identification	Feelings of belonging, loyalty, and commitment to the organization
6. Intergroup conflict	Friction, tension, and power struggles between cultural groups

From Cox, T. H. (1991). The multicultural organization. *Academy of Management Executive*, 5(2), 34–47. Reproduced with permission of the Academy of Management (New York).

just be silent" (Hafen, 2003). In other words, a diverse organization provides both opportunities and challenges, some of which will be considered in the following sections.

The Diverse Organization: Opportunities

Probably few organizations today would meet Cox's (1991) description of a multicultural organization. The achievement of full structural and informal integration is the first difficult step. Attitudinal and behavioral changes following integration pose even greater difficulty. However, a number of organizations are moving toward this goal (see Gilbert & Ivancevich, 2000, for examples). Diversity, of course, should be valued in and of itself, not simply as a means to an end (Ashcraft & Allen, 2003). However, it is also useful to consider the outcomes that can arise from diversity in the workplace. We have already talked about some of the advantages that might accrue to the individual in a multicultural organization (e.g., opportunities for advancement, equitable job opportunities). Organizations can also realize a number of opportunities as they move toward the multicultural model.

Cox and Blake (1991) argue for six important competitive advantages that can be gained through the insightful management of cultural diversity (detailed in Table 12.2). Advantages such as these have come to be known as the **business case for diversity** or the *value-in-diversity perspective* (Herring, 2009), suggesting that an argument for diversity can be made based on the extent to which a diverse organization will provide bottom-line benefits for the company.

There is research to support much of this business case for diversity, but it is not always straightforward. For example, Robinson and Dechant's (1997) survey of human resources managers at Fortune 100 companies points to many bottom-line advantages of a diverse workforce and these advantages can be especially pronounced when the diverse organization is representative of the larger community (Hur, 2012; King et al., 2011). However, there is also evidence that "the potentially positive effects of diversity on group performance may only obtain up to a certain level of diversity, beyond which the lack of a common frame of reference may get in the way of fully appreciating all group members' contributions" (Knippenberg & Schippers, 2007, p. 532).

Arguments for increased creativity and enhanced problem solving through diversity both rest on the contention that a diversity of employees will translate into a diversity of viewpoints. There is evidence that supports this contention (Knippenberg & Schippers, 2007), especially in a global marketplace in which a variety of backgrounds and viewpoints are needed to cope with problems stemming from many national and cultural locations (see, e.g., Carroll, 2007). However, there are also caveats regarding this portion of the business case. For example, Pitts and Jarry (2007) found there were times that diversity hurt performance because of process-oriented problems and concluded that benefits drawn from a diversity of viewpoints could be "overshadowed by communication and collaboration problems" (Pitts & Jarry, 2007, p. 233). The best way to combat these problems is with a very purposive strategy of including members of co-cultural groups in strategy and decision-making processes (Richard, Kirby & Chadwick, 2013).

Table 12.2 | Opportunities Realized through Diversity

1. Cost argument	As organizations become more diverse, the cost of a poor job in integrating workers will increase. Companies who handle diversity well will create cost advantages over those that do not.
2. Resource-acquisition argument	Companies develop reputations as prospective employers for women and ethnic minorities. Those with the best reputations for managing diversity will win the competition for the best personnel. As the labor pool shrinks and changes composition, this edge will become increasingly important.
3. Marketing argument	For multinational organizations, the insight and cultural sensitivity that members with roots in other countries bring to the marketing effort should improve that effort in important ways. The same rationale applies to marketing in subpopulations within domestic operations.
4. Creativity argument	Diversity of perspectives and less emphasis on conformity to norms of the past (which characterize the modern approach to management of diversity) should improve the level of creativity.
5. Problem-solving argument	Heterogeneity in decision making and problem solving groups potentially produces better choices through a wider range of perspectives and more critical analysis of issues.
6. Systems flexibility argument	An implication of the multicultural model for managing diversity is that the system will become less determinant, less standardized, and therefore more fluid. The increased fluidity should create greater flexibility to react to environmental changes (i.e., reactions should be faster and at less cost).

From Cox, T. H. (1991). The multicultural organization. *Academy of Management Executive, 5*(2), 34–47. Reproduced with permission of the Academy of Management (New York).

It is clear, then, that managing culturally diverse groups poses communicative challenges. For example, Watson, Kumar, and Michaelsen (1993) found that realizing the advantages of diversity takes time and effort. Specifically, these researchers found that when first formed, diverse groups were inferior to homogeneous groups in both performance and in managing the process of group interaction. However, over time, the diverse groups developed communicative strategies for encouraging participation and eventually generated a wider range of alternatives and perspectives on a problem than homogeneous groups. As noted earlier, however, a critical facet of this process is allowing for many voices to be heard (Hafen, 2003). Indeed, Kirby and Harter (2001) suggest that the concept of "managing" diversity—with the implication of management on the bottom line—can be problematic if it leads to valuing the profit-driving impact of diversity more than the people involved.

✳ Spotlight on Scholarship: Questioning the Business Case

The business case for diversity rests on the argument that organizations can improve their effectiveness and efficiency through the advantages created through a diverse workforce. Those who advocate for the business case believe that this argument about bottom-line advantages is a critical reason for encouraging diversity of both demography and ideas. Linda Perriton, however, argues that reliance on the business case is troubling because it has "crowded out a range of other ways of thinking about and responding to problems" (Perriton, 2009, p. 240). Her conclusions stem from a critical analysis of discourse—from both experts and practitioners—about the role of women in the contemporary workplace.

Perriton (2009) begins her article by laying out key aspects of the business case for diversity. These include the ideas that diversity will expand recruiting possibilities, will increase the range and depth of skills, will enhance customer and client service, will improve staff retention, and will boost an organization's reputation in the community. Perriton further notes that the business case is well-accepted and points to her own experiences as a consultant to argue that the business case is pervasive and that "failure to communicate using the dominant (or 'preferred') discourse is interpreted as incompetence" (Perriton, 2009, p. 221). She then investigates these ideas by carefully analyzing transcripts from a "Women and Leadership" corporate workshop conference attended by over 200 delegates (almost all women).

Perriton's analysis of the discourse from this conference involved both qualitative interpretation and a quantitative assessment of how various words and themes co-occurred as conference participants talked about issues including developing diversity programs, how to enhance inclusion in the workplace, and concerns with balancing work and home life. Through her analysis, Perriton identified a number of discursive "rules" that stemmed from the emphasis on the business case for diversity. These included rules such as:

- Avoid complaint.
- Sell diversity as a product.
- Emphasize rationality.
- Talk about "men and women" or "people."
- Work–life balance is a personal responsibility.

Perriton argues that these discursive rules are evidence that the business case for diversity can have the effect of limiting women's linguistic and action choices (she cites one conference participant who noted that "we don't want complaining women") and does not really benefit women in organizations. As a result, Perriton rejects the argument that "the business case discourse is a neutral medium through which to transmit the idea of gender and racial equity" (Perriton, 2009, p. 241) and believes that this case "is problematic because it constrains, rather than opens up, the discussion of social justice issues in the workplace" (Perriton, 2009, p. 240). Perriton concludes by calling for a wider range of voices commenting on workplace diversity and an openness to all kinds of discourse. In short, she believes that "what we need, contrary to what the organizers of events like the 'Women and Leadership' conference would have us believe, are more complaining women" (Perriton, 2009, p. 241).

Perriton, L. (2009). "We don't want complaining women!": A critical analysis of the business case for diversity. *Management Communication Quarterly, 23*, 218–243.

The Diverse Organization: Challenges

The challenges of managing and working in culturally diverse organizations are just beginning to be understood. For example, we have already talked about the glass ceiling phenomenon, the off-ramps and on-ramps of careers, and the difficulty of managing cultural diversity in a way that values—rather than minimizes or ignores—differences. In this section, we consider two additional challenges that face organizations as the workplace becomes increasingly diverse. The first of these is instituting diversity management programs in ways that avoid the negative consequences associated with these programs. The second challenge is most notably associated with gender diversity: achieving a balance between work and home.

Avoiding Negative Effects of Diversity Management Programs   The Civil Rights Act of 1964 marked the beginning of programs designed to ensure equal opportunity in the workplace. The **affirmative action** programs that stemmed from this act aim "to remedy discrimination and increase the representation of designated disadvantaged groups, namely, women and ethnic minorities" (Heilman, 1994, p. 126). As discussed earlier in this chapter, subsequent legislation—such as the ADA (passed in 1990) and the ENDA (still being debated in Congress)—looks to provide similar protections to disabled and LGBT workers. However, debates continue about the efficacy of these programs, their impact on workers and organizations, and indeed their future as policy in the United States. Indeed, Harris (2009) believes that "affirmative action has represented one of the most divisive issues and public policies of our time" (p. 367), and the Supreme Court has made a number of rulings in recent years that have an impact on affirmative action practices in both business and educational settings.

It is clear that affirmative action programs have resulted in many desired employment gains: "As a result of affirmative action, the standing and presence of women and minorities have increased throughout all organizational levels" (Harris, 2009, p. 367). These results have not always been as powerful as hoped; the glass ceiling still exists, and there are still major pay inequities and stereotypes about gendered roles in the workplace. However, there have been important gains that influence both individual workers and organizations.

There are also problems, however. Heilman and her associates (Heilman, 1994; Heilman, Block & Stathatos, 1997) have discovered a number of negative consequences for those the programs are trying to help, for those who feel "victimized" by the programs, and for others in the organization. Although the research on this issue is complicated, several generalizations are possible. First, affirmative action programs can affect how an individual benefitting from the program views his or her competence, and this *self-view of competence* can in turn impact work behavior and communication. Second, affirmative action leads others in the workplace to *stigmatize* as incompetent those individuals assumed to have benefitted from these programs. Third, "affirmative action initiatives are often seen as unfair, unjust, or unethical" by others in the organization (Fubara, McMillan-Capehart & Richard, 2008).

To deal with these possible negative consequences, Heilman (1994) recommends that organizations emphasize the use of merit criteria in addition to some preferential criteria in making hiring and promotion decisions. Heilman et al. (1997) also argue that it is critical for organizations to provide "unambiguous, objective, and public information regarding the job qualifications and performance of individuals associated with affirmative action" (Nye, 1998, p. 89). Such information can serve to minimize or eliminate problems associated with victimization and stigmatization. Finally, Kalev, Dobbin, and Kelly (2006) argue that some of the negative effects of affirmative action can be mitigated through the use of mentoring and networks and through establishing organizational commitment and responsibility for diversity programs.

Balancing Work and Home   Finally, individuals and organizations are increasingly faced with the daunting challenge of balancing the needs of work and home. More and more women are entering in the workforce—some for their entire lives and others for shorter time periods throughout the life span. The needs of older women in the workplace might be quite different from those of younger women or of midlife men. For example, younger women have serious concerns about the logistics of child care and the creation of flexible work plans. For older women, the concerns often shift to balancing the needs of child care, elder care, and self-care and to planning for future retirement. Furthermore, both women and men may now find themselves trying to make sense of the work of staying at home with children. For example, Medved and Kirby (2005) argue that women who have taken an off-ramp from work construct "corporate mothering discourses" that see a stay-at-home mother as a "professional, well-educated, highly skilled, irreplaceable worker who is able to choose this supposed career path" (Medved & Kirby, 2005, p. 465).

For both organizations and individuals, the challenges of achieving balance between work and home are myriad. For the organization, the first challenge rests in the institution of **family-friendly programs**, such as flextime, onsite day care, job sharing, family leave policies, and telecommuting (see Friedman, 1987) and in making these policies usable by employees (Kirby & Krone, 2002). The second challenge for the organization involves the creation of a culture that values various aspects of employees' lives. The development and maintenance of such a culture can be extremely difficult in a diverse workplace. For example, employees who do *not* have children may resent the special benefits provided for employees with children and may feel bitter about needing to work late or on holidays so others can be with children (Flynn, 1996). Furthermore, organizations that have many institutionalized programs for assisting in the balance of work and home life may be seen as taking over in even the private sectors of employees' lives (Kirby, 2006).

For the individual, the challenges of balancing work and home are both personal and interpersonal. At the personal level, there are challenges of identity and defining self in both work and home roles. For example, Gregory (2001) found that individuals in the "new economy" often shape identities with values such as "family first" and "don't sweat the small stuff" as defining principles. Buzzanell and Liu (2005) found that negotiating identity was particularly difficult for women during the process of negotiating and experiencing maternity leave (see also Meisenbach, Remke, Buzzanell & Liu, 2008). For example, one woman noted the contrast between a "working" self and a "mothering" self: "You don't feel like the same ... You're used to working every day ... You're cleaning, cooking and stuff and that's not you" (Buzzanell & Liu, 2005, p. 12). There are also interpersonal challenges for workers as they attempt to negotiate tasks and identities with others in the workplace and with family members (Golden, 2001, 2009). These negotiations are complicated by culturally defined notions of gender and work that may limit choices. As Kirby et al. (2003) argue,

> If women are (or want to be) the primary caretakers—especially because new mothers nurse babies, women "intuitively" know how to do household chores, and women who fail to enact caregiving are derided as selfish—then women should downscale their careers, be "stay-at-home" mothers, or expect to participate in a second shift that may include eldercare. (p. 19)

Expectations such as these can make the negotiation of both job and home roles fraught with difficulty.

Managing (and Celebrating) Cultural Diversity

We have now talked about a number of advantages and challenges that can accrue from an organization with cultural and gender diversity. Demographic trends indicate that most organizations will have no choice but to become more diverse in the future, and many organizations are already working on ways to increase and capitalize on the benefits that come from a diverse workforce. However, this is not an easy task. In this section, we briefly consider some strategies organizations can use to gain effectiveness as a multicultural organization. Most of the scholarly and popular writing on this issue uses the term *managing* diversity to talk about these issues. However, as we noted earlier, if management becomes equated solely with bottom-line concerns with profit, the people who make the organization diverse can get lost in the shuffle (Kirby & Harter, 2001). Thus, some scholars have suggested that we think not about the business case for diversity but about the celebration of diversity in organizational and cultural life (Said, 2001).

In considering both the management and celebration of diversity, it is critical to consider many different areas of organizational functioning. For example, Cox and Blake (1991) identify a number of "spheres of activity" that must be dealt with when living life in a culturally diverse organization: education programs, the human resources system, organizational culture, mind-sets about diversity, and programs that support work–family health and combat problems such as sexism and discrimination. These spheres of activity highlight several points. First, life in a diverse organization involves both attitude and action. Managers and employees must view diversity as a challenge and as an opportunity rather than as a problem that must be dealt with, and they must become knowledgeable about the needs and contributions of diverse organizational members. But knowledge and attitude change are not enough; specific action must also be taken to ensure an educated workforce, the elimination of discrimination, a bias-free human resources system, and work options that ease the conflict between job and family.

How can an organization work to change its culture to embrace diversity as a core value? Page (2007) makes the argument for the value of diversity in the workplace and then presents "lessons learned" from organizations that have been successful in enhancing the value of a diverse workplace. These lessons emphasize the value of various kinds of diversity, argue for the importance of interaction, caution against stereotyping in the diversity process, and argue for a continued focus on ability to accompany diversity efforts. Page believes that heeding these lessons will enhance the chance that organizational diversity efforts will lead to new ideas that will benefit both organizations and society. As he notes, "[T]he sources of innovation remain mysterious; life experiences can serendipitously provide insights. By building diverse teams of employees, organizations increase their chances of making a breakthrough" (Page, 2007, p. 19).

SUMMARY

In this chapter, we have looked at the changing face of organizations by considering the explosion of diversity in today's workplace. We began this chapter by considering several aspects of the experiences of women and minorities in organizations today. We found that women and people of color often deal with stereotyping and discrimination as well as systemic and relational barriers in the workplace. We then considered the concept of a multicultural organization and discussed the opportunities and challenges posed by diversity.

We concluded by outlining steps organizations can take in moving toward multiculturalism.

As seen in Table 12.3, the notion of diversity would be viewed very differently by different types of organizational communication scholars and practitioners. Managers taking a classical approach would probably go to great lengths to avoid diversity. After all, the classical approach is based on the concept of standardization, and there is nothing standardized about a diverse work population. Human relations proponents would strive to

Table 12.3 | Approaches to Organizational Diversity

Approach	How Diversity Would Be Considered
Classical	Because diversity would limit the homogeneity of the workforce and hence be distracting or detrimental to morale, diversity would be discouraged.
Human relations	Diversity would be neither encouraged nor discouraged. Emphasis would be placed on meeting the needs of women, minorities, and other co-cultural groups.
Human resources	Diversity would be encouraged by increased creativity and new ideas would increase the competitive advantage for the organization. Emphasis would be placed on maximizing the contributions of all employees.
Systems	Diversity would be seen as one avenue for the organization to adapt effectively to a turbulent global environment. Integration of women and minorities into formal and informal networks would be emphasized.
Cultural	Diverse organizations would be seen as important sites where organizational culture intersects with national and ethnic culture and with the values of various co-cultural groups.
Constitutive	Emphasis would be placed on the processes through which the intersections of various value systems are negotiated through ongoing interaction.
Critical	Diverse organizations would be seen as an arena in which subjugated groups must deal with the dominant class. Emphasis would be placed on the perpetuation of—or emancipation from—hegemonic relationships.
Feminist	Scholarly and activist attention would be given to the ongoing challenges faced by women and other co-cultural groups in diverse organizations such as harassment and home–work balance.

meet the needs of a diverse workforce but would probably do little to either encourage or discourage diversity. In contrast, individuals from the human resources school would embrace diversity if they were convinced that a diverse workforce could provide a competitive advantage. The arguments we discussed regarding increased creativity and improved decision making would probably convince human resources managers to work toward the goal of an effective multicultural organization.

A systems researcher would be particularly interested in the structural challenges facing diverse employees. As mentioned earlier, women and people of color are often excluded from formal and informal communication networks, and a systems approach would be a viable avenue for explaining and rectifying this problem. Scholars taking a cultural approach to the study of organizational communication would also be vitally interested in diversity as an organization with employees representing a variety of co-cultural groups can be viewed as an intersection of cultural values. For the constitutive scholar, interest would turn to the discursive processes through which this cultural system is created and re-created. Finally, critical scholars have already taken an interest in some of the power discrepancies that can arise in a diverse organization, and feminist scholars are, of course, concerned with the challenges faced by women in a patriarchal organizational context.

DISCUSSION QUESTIONS

1. What have your experiences told you about the differences in organizational life for white men and for women and people of color? If you are a white male, do you believe these differences are real and viable? If you are a woman or a person of color (or both), do you think your workplace experiences are influenced by your gender, culture, or ethnicity? How do factors such as disability and sexual orientation make a difference in organizational life?

2. What is the difference between *managing* diversity and *celebrating* diversity? Is this a valuable distinction to make or merely a matter of semantics?

3. What do you think about affirmative action programs—both at the university level and in the workplace? Are these programs important to increasing diversity? Is affirmative action an equitable way of dealing with this issue?

4. Has the challenge of balancing home and work life been an issue in your family? If you are a traditional college-aged student, how did this issue play out as you were growing up? Will the way your parents dealt with this issue influence your career and work choices?

KEY CONCEPTS

glass ceiling
mommy track
opt-in
opt-out
lean in
prejudice

discrimination
stereotypes
minority employee networks
mentoring relationships
tokenism
Americans with Disabilities Act

Employment Non-Discrimination
   Act
multicultural organization
business case for diversity
affirmative action
family-friendly programs

CASE STUDY | The Complex Challenges of Encouraging Diversity

The San Lucas Unified School District has a very aggressive affirmative action program. San Lucas, a midsize city in the Southwest, has a population that is approximately 50% white, 10% African American, and 40% Hispanic (mostly Mexican American). School district officials are strongly committed to recruiting and retaining teachers who represent this diverse population. They believe that students should have positive role models from their own ethnic groups and also think that a diverse teaching staff is best able to deal with student differences stemming from unique cultural backgrounds. The school district's goal is to achieve a teaching staff that has the same proportion of minority groups as in the local population. District officials realized early on that achieving this goal would be no easy task, so they instituted a set of hiring procedures they hoped would attract minority applicants. Then, they worked to make especially attractive offers to these candidates and instituted special programs (mostly seminars and workshops) designed to aid in these recruits' adjustment and to decrease turnover.

The officials hoped that Maria Sanchez would be one of their early success stories. Maria was hired straight out of the state university into a position at San Lucas High School. She specializes in the science curriculum, teaching mostly courses in biology and general science. Hired at the highest salary possible for a new graduate, Maria also negotiated several conditions that were not part of the traditional employment contract. She felt she needed an extra dedicated laptop to prepare exercises and graphics for her classes, and the school board provided one. She wanted her classes to have additional access to the school's iPads. She also asked for an extra free period each day for class preparation. She felt this was necessary because much of her afterschool time would be taken up by extracurricular activities and counseling the Hispanic students at the high school. The school board also complied with this request, agreeing that Maria's role in providing social support for the students was an important one.

Some rough times marked the first two years of Maria's contract with San Lucas High School. Her teaching evaluations were uneven because she had trouble maintaining control in the classroom and had difficulty explaining basic concepts to her first-year classes. She was much more effective in her advanced biology classes, where she could use extended simulations to illustrate complex processes. In general, the students liked her, but some complained that she played favorites. She also ran into problems with her coworkers. Most of the teachers were friendly with her on an interpersonal level, but they were concerned that she was rarely willing to serve on curriculum, planning, or special-events committees.

After two years, Maria's probationary period was over, and it was time to make a decision about a long-term contract. Three representatives of the school district were meeting to discuss this issue: Jan Dobos, director of minority recruitment for the district; Raul Rivera, the principal at San Lucas High School; and Zoe Grainger, head of the teachers' union.

Jan opened up the discussion. "It looks like Ms. Sanchez is doing a reasonably good job at the high school, and I definitely think she should be given a long-term contract. She's doing great work providing advice for many of the Latina girls who have no one else to talk to. And her teaching is beginning to shape up. I think with a bit more support from the district, she can develop into a really valuable contributor."

"We've got a problem here if you're talking about giving Maria even more support," Zoe interrupted. "There's already some discontent among the high school teachers about the special perks Maria got when she signed on here. She has more computing support than they do, and they resent the fact that she only has four classes a day while they're teaching five. It's not that they don't support the diversity program here, but they see it coming out of their own hides. We've been told that we're now living in a 'post-racial society' but it doesn't feel that way here."

"And aren't we forgetting something here?" added Raul. "What about what's best for Maria?"

Zoe laughed. "Most of the teachers don't think Maria's needs are being forgotten! Quite the contrary, it seems that Maria's needs are being considered over everyone else's—other teachers' and the students'!"

"That's just what I'm getting at," said Raul. "I've talked to Maria a lot about this, and I don't think you've taken her perspective at all. She's in a tough situation here. She feels like she's expected to be the perfect cultural role model for students and the school board alike. And she doesn't have anyone to serve as a role model for her; she's just feeling her way through the system. Maria's under a microscope—expected to advise minority students as well as serve in outreach programs. You may not think she pulls her weight with school committees, but you don't know the half of what she does with community programs."

"So, what do we do?" asked Jan. "We need to make an immediate recommendation to the school board. Does she get a long-term contract, and if so, what should it look like?"

CASE ANALYSIS QUESTIONS

1. What do you think of the cultural diversity program in the San Lucas school district? Are the goals of this program reasonable? Are good systems in place for reaching these goals? What alternative ideas could you suggest to the school district for improving its program?

2. What should this committee recommend to the school board with respect to retaining Maria Sanchez? What other recommendations should they make to the board given what they have learned from their experiences so far?

3. How can you explain the very different experiences of Maria and other teachers at the high school? Is there an avenue that could be taken to cope with these differences? How could this situation be managed to improve the situation for Maria, for other teachers, for the students, and for the community?

Technological Processes

CHAPTER 13

AFTER READING THIS CHAPTER, YOU SHOULD ...

- Be familiar with information and communication technology in the workplace and appreciate how these technologies might differ from more traditional modes of communication.
- Be able to explain the process of technology adoption and use in an organizational setting, differentiating between a focus on the attributes of the media and a focus on communication and social relationships.
- Understand that technology can have a variety of effects on organizational processes including decision making and power.
- Appreciate the role of social media in processes ranging from the communication of corporate identity to organizing for social justice.
- Understand how technology can radically change organizational structures, especially in the form of telework and virtual teams.

Consider the changes that have taken place in workplace communication over the past hundred years. To create a simple document, we have moved from handwriting to typing to word processing. To produce multiple copies of that document, we have moved from copying the document by hand to carbon paper to high-speed copying machines. To store those documents, we have moved from boxes to file cabinets to floppy disks to hard drives, servers, CDs, and flash drives and now to cloud storage. To send those documents over long distances, we have moved from stagecoaches to airmail to express mail to facsimile to PDF files. To exchange messages over long distances, we have moved from messengers to telegraph to telephone to voice mail and electronic mail. To get together as a group, we have moved from formal meeting rooms to conference calls to video conferencing to computer conferencing and online chat rooms. To keep in touch with a wide array of contacts, we have moved from newsletters to blogs, Facebook, and Twitter. To prepare presentations, we have moved from paper flipcharts to overheads to PowerPoint. In short, the workplace in the early twenty-first century bears little resemblance to the workplace of a hundred years ago, and many of the workplace changes we observe are the result of technological innovations.

When I was finishing up graduate school, my fiancé and I were excited to buy our first computer. We went top-of-the-line, spending almost $7,000 (in 1985 dollars!). But we felt we were getting our money's worth because the computer had a dot matrix printer that worked at three different speeds, an internal dial-up modem (it was $500 just for that feature), and ten megabytes' worth of storage capacity. We couldn't imagine ever using up that much space on the hard drive. My, how times have changed. For less than one-tenth of the cost, you can now get a computer that is thousands of times better. And, of course, the basic PC is only the beginning. Not so long ago, I couldn't have imagined my everyday world today, with e-mail, texting, Web shopping on my smartphone, Pandora music, Facebook, fantasy football drafts via online chat rooms … and I'm not technologically advanced. Of course, for most of you reading this book, many of these technologies have been a part of your lives for as long as you can remember—you are "digital natives"—so it's difficult to imagine what changes you may experience decades from now.

In this chapter, we examine some technological changes that have influenced organizational communication in recent years. We first look at some of these communication technologies and differentiate them from more traditional communication media. We then consider models that attempt to explain the process through which organizational members come to use these communication technologies. Finally, we examine the effects of communication technology on a variety of organizational communication processes, with specific attention to the impact of social media and telework. Before we begin our discussion, however, several caveats are in order. First, any discussion of "new" communication technologies is sure to be quickly outdated as innovations replace what is currently in vogue. Indeed, each new edition of this book requires the consideration of additional "new" technologies as well as new ways of using more dated technologies. Second, the introduction of new technologies does not always lead to the demise of older technologies. Although the copy machine largely eliminated carbon paper and the computer did away with—for most practical purposes—the typewriter, there are also counterexamples. The existence of computer conferencing has not made the old-fashioned in-person meeting obsolete nor has e-mail put the postal service out of business (at least, not yet). Businesses and individuals in high-tech Japan continue heavy use of fax machines in the Internet age (Fackler, 2013). And although experts were predicting the advent of the "paperless office" with the increased use of computer technology, most businesses go through more paper now than ever before. With these caveats in mind, let us move on to a discussion of technologies that have made an important impact on organizational communication processes.

TYPES OF ORGANIZATIONAL COMMUNICATION TECHNOLOGY

The range of technologies introduced to the workplace in recent years is mindboggling. Voice mail, conference calls, e-mail, texting, management information systems, fax machines, smartphones, social media—all of these advances in information and communication technology (ICT) have radically shifted the ways in which organizations ranging from the smallest mom and pop store to nonprofit service providers to huge multinational corporations accomplish their goals on an ongoing basis. In this

Case in Point: Don't Forget the Thank-You Note

This chapter makes the point that new technologies don't always replace old ways of doing things. However, this idea can be called into doubt when considering the fate of personal handwritten notes. Personal letters only arrive at American homes once every seven weeks, and "some might claim that in a wired world—where e-mails, tweets, and text messages are more accessible than handwritten notes—this is the natural evolution of communication" (Coleman, 2013).

Coleman (2013) believes that it is premature to write off the value of the personal and handwritten note. He argues that this form of communication still has great value in the Internet age for several reasons. First, "handwritten notes mean more because they cost more" (Coleman, 2013). E-mails, tweets, and Facebook messages cost little or nothing in terms of time and money. In contrast, a handwritten note requires stationery, stamps, time for writing, and a trip to the mailbox. Second, the meaning— even just a simple message of "thank-you"—is amplified in a handwritten note. "In a world where so much communication is merely utilitarian, these simple acts of investment, remembrance, gratitude, and appreciation can show the people who matter to your life and business that they are important to you" (Coleman, 2013). Third, these handwritten notes can be saved in drawers, closets, or shoe boxes. We know that e-mails are permanent in one sense, but "they aren't tangible and enduring in the same way" as a thank-you note you can save or see every day under a refrigerator magnet.

So listen to the nagging you probably received from your mom or dad after a birthday party. Write that thank-you note. It could mean as much to a business contact as it did to your grandparents.

section, we will briefly consider some facets of two of the most relevant developments in ICT: electronic mail and the World Wide Web. Electronic mail has clearly changed both personal and organizational life in the last twenty years. Indeed, it is likely that most people reading this page have checked their e-mail at least once already today (and also logged onto Facebook multiple times). Consider the quick march of history. In 1996 there were 400 million e-mail messages sent daily, 16 billion messages in 2001, 60 billion messages in 2006, 145 billion messages in 2012, an estimated 192 billion messages by 2016. A very large portion of these messages are business e-mails and consumer e-mails ("Email statistics report," 2012; Jones, 2002). This growth is a global phenomenon—nearly half of worldwide e-mail users are located in the Asia Pacific Region, 22% of e-mail users in Europe, and 14% in North America ("Email statistics report," 2012). In short, e-mail is a ubiquitous form of organizational communication that can be used to send instant messages to targeted individuals, to broadcast information to a large organizational group, to chat with collaborators across the country or world, and to exchange and revise long, complex documents.

The World Wide Web is another aspect of Internet technology that has radically changed the way organizations operate. For the individual worker, the Web can be used to gather relevant technical or policy information, to check on the activities of partners and competitors, to access timely news on a minute-by-minute basis, or to shop for just about anything. For the organization, the Web serves as a forum to promote a desired image, to communicate with customers, and to conduct business of all kinds. Social media outlets such as Facebook and Twitter have been particularly influential in all of these processes, as has the growth in mobile technology that allows employees and consumers to carry the Internet in their back pockets. But, of course, the Web can also serve to drain organizational productivity. People routinely check personal e-mail and social networking sites from the workplace. And the Monday after Thanksgiving is now popularly referred to as "cyber Monday," as individuals return to work and surf the Web for holiday shopping bargains. Cyber Monday is one of the busiest online shopping days of the year, and if that much shopping is occurring, there is also some work that is not occurring.

What features make these and other ICT channels different from more traditional organizational communication options? A number of characteristics do set these technologies apart, although these characteristics vary from technology to technology. First, many ICT options allow *faster message transmission* than that of traditional organizational communication media. Electronic and voice messages are delivered in seconds, and facsimile machines and PDF files have provided a high-speed alternative to overnight mail delivery. Second, ICT allows communication among *geographically dispersed* participants. For example, a simple conference call or an online conferencing system allows participants at many locations to take part in meetings that formerly would have required hours or days of travel. Similarly, with electronic mail and other online tools, individuals can be productive at home and avoid long commutes to and from the office. Third, new technologies allow **asynchronous communication**—that is, communication between individuals at different points in time. For example, communication by means of e-mail can be accomplished effectively even if the two people communicating are never logged on to the computer or checking their cell phones at the same time.

These basic features of ICT—fast asynchronous message transmission over vast geographical distance—lead to some emergent aspects of technology in organizational communication today. First, technology can greatly enhance the possibility for *collaboration* across time and space. For example, wiki technology now allows dispersed groups to collaboratively create and change content in organizational documents (Wagner & Schroeder, 2010). Second, for good or bad, these factors can lead to communication going viral either within an organizational system or around the world. Jones (2011) notes that viral marketing has the potential to both promote and destroy a brand, and provides advice for companies such as "embrace the weirdness" and "let the community have control."

Some other features of new organizational communication media are less obvious. For example, new media often change ways of addressing messages. With most communication channels, the sender must specifically address a particular receiver (or group of receivers). However, in online chat rooms, on Reddit, or in the blogosphere, users can communicate with an unknown group of people who are interested in a particular topic. This *anonymity* can provide comfort for those uncomfortable sharing information. However, anonymity can also lead to negative communication patterns such as **flaming** and cyberbullying or can serve as a shield for those engaged in criminal or unethical activities. New communication technologies also differ from traditional organizational communication forms in terms of **memory, storage, and retrieval features**. Many conferencing systems allow decision-making groups to create a full written transcript of meeting proceedings and Internet search engines allow for the instant retrieval of even the most arcane bit of information. These features can also clearly be seen as double-edged swords as we learn more about the implications of the fact that "the Internet is forever" and that both businesses and governments have access to aspects of our communicative lives that we may prefer to keep private.

Finally, many new technologies differ in terms of the cues that are available in the communication process (Short, Williams & Christie, 1976). Compare, for example, a traditional meeting with a meeting conducted via conference call or an online computer conference. In a phone conference call, participants are unable to assess nonverbal communication cues that are available in face-to-face settings. In a computer conference, even more communication cues are *filtered out* as participants look only at typed messages and are unable to gain information from vocal or visual channels. Sometimes, the elimination of cues is intentional, as users work to use the technology as efficiently as possible. For example, many older parents still have a difficult time deciphering the text messages of their teenage children, as such messages are often written with a very specific code. And, of course, users of technologies can often enhance the content of their messages through codes such as emoticons, such as ☺, developed specifically for the technology.

In summary, ICT offers organizational participants a wide array of interaction and decision-making options that can differ substantially from traditional ways of working. In considering the impact of these technologies on the workplace, two important questions must be answered (Yates & Orlikowski, 1992). First, what are the factors that will lead organizational members to choose particular types of technologies for their communication needs? Second, once these technologies are used, do they have a discernible impact on organizational communication processes? The remainder of this chapter will address these two fundamental questions. After examining models that predict the adoption and use of communication media, we will discuss the effects of these media on organizational functioning.

UNDERSTANDING TECHNOLOGY ADOPTION AND USE

Once a new ICT hits the scene, most users do not quickly and automatically embrace it. Although their ranks are becoming increasingly thin, there are still people who are reticent to use a computer and many more who cringe at the thought of creating a personal website. There are others, of course, who adopt each new technology with great enthusiasm. Consider, for example, the explosion in recent years of blogs and bloggers on the Web. What factors predict the extent to which various communication media will be used in accomplishing organizational tasks or perhaps distracting workers from those tasks? Several theoretical positions have been offered on this question. For example, Markus (1990) suggests that new communication technologies will not be widely embraced until there is a **critical mass** of individuals who use the technology. The idea of critical mass is particularly important for communication technologies that require connectivity. For example, instant messaging did not take off in the late 1990s until a critical mass of individuals were online with the technology for IM'ing available. However, the adoption of technologies involves more than just numbers. This section presents several important ways of understanding organizational communication media use. We will first consider the idea that the features of the technology—in conjunction with issues such as the nature of the task—are critical for understanding patterns of ICT usage. We will then consider work that emphasizes the importance of the social network in explanations of ICT adoption and implementation.

The Importance of Technology Attributes

One of the first models proposed to understand the choices organizational members make about communication technology use was the **media richness model** proposed by Richard Daft and Robert Lengel (1984, 1986). These scholars were interested in how managers choose one communication medium over another for an array of organizational tasks. For example, if a manager were faced with the task of reminding employees about an upcoming meeting, what communication medium would be used to send the message: face-to-face communication, phone, memo, or e-mail? Or what would be the preferred communication medium for firing an employee or for resolving a conflict between two subordinates?

To explain such communication choices, these theorists first suggested that organizational communication tasks vary in their level of ambiguity. *Ambiguity* refers to the existence of conflicting and multiple interpretations of an issue. Consider, for example, the situations described previously. The manager informing employees about an upcoming meeting is faced with a relatively unambiguous task because multiple interpretations about a simple reminder are unlikely. In contrast, the manager who must resolve a conflict between two subordinates is faced with a communicative situation that has great potential for misunderstanding and emergent meaning. Thus, this communicative interaction would be characterized as much more ambiguous.

Daft, Lengel, and Trevino (1987) then argue that communication channels available to the organizational manager differ markedly in their capability to convey information based on factors such the use of multiple cues, the availability of feedback, and the personal focus of the medium. Given these factors, various communication media can be placed on a continuum ranging from *rich* (e.g., face-to-face communication) to *lean* (e.g., a flyer placed in a mailbox). Between the endpoints of rich and lean would fall media such as the telephone, e-mail, voice mail, written memos, Web postings and others.

Media richness theorists then combine the notion of **task ambiguity** with the notion of **media richness** and argue that managers will choose media that *match* the ambiguity of the message. That is, when dealing with highly ambiguous tasks, managers will choose to use a rich communication medium (e.g., face-to-face interaction), but when dealing with a communication message low in ambiguity, managers will opt for a lean communication medium (e.g., a memo). These theorists further argue that managers will be more effective if they choose a communication medium that is a proper match for the ambiguity of the task at hand. These ideas regarding communicative effectiveness are illustrated in Figure 13.1. In general, there has been support for the basic tenets of the media richness model. Research has found that managers tend to choose rich media to deal with ambiguous tasks and lean media to deal with unambiguous tasks (see, e.g., Russ, Daft & Lengel, 1990); furthermore, there is some evidence that managers and work teams who follow this trend are more effective (see, e.g., Maznevski & Chudoba, 2000).

	Unambiguous Task	Ambiguous Task
Rich Media	**Communication failure.** Data glut. Rich media used for routine tasks. Excess cues cause confusion and surplus meaning.	**Effective communication.** Communication success because rich media match ambiguous tasks.
Lean Media	**Effective communication.** Communication success because media low in richness match routine messages.	**Communication failure.** Data starvation. Lean media used for ambiguous messages. Too few cues to capture message complexity.

Figure 13.1 | Effective Media Predictions

Adapted with permission of the publisher, from Lengel, R. H., & Daft, R. L. (1988). The selection of communication media as an executive skill. *Academy of Management Executive*, 2, 225–232. Reproduced with permission of Academy of Management (NY) via Copyright Clearance Center.

However, scholars still debate whether the media richness model provides a thorough explanation for the process of technology use in organizations (e.g., Sheer & Chen, 2004). Thus, several other theorists have proposed models to better understand the characterization of various communication media as "rich" or "lean." For example, in their **channel expansion theory**, Carlson and Zmud (1999) consider the ways in which richness perceptions will depend on an individual's personal experience with a specific medium. For example, an individual may not understand all the richness of a particular smartphone until after having several weeks of experience using the phone. In support of this idea, D'Urso and Rains (2008) found that richness perceptions varied depending on interpersonal factors and media experience. The **dual capacity model** also complicates the idea of media richness by proposing that every organizational medium has both "data-carrying capacity" that is analogous to media richness, and "symbol-carrying capacity" that involves additional meaning an individual might have for a particular medium (Sitkin, Sutcliffe & Barrios-Choplin, 1992). According to the dual capacity model, the choice of communication channel will depend on both of these factors. So even if a task such as a meeting reminder could be accomplished with a quick e-mail, the personal touch of a phone call might be called for in some organizational cultures.

Other theorists have provided additional concepts to understand choices about technology in organizations. For example, in their **media synchronicity theory**, Dennis, Fuller, and Valacich (2008) argue that the choice of communication media should depend on the extent to which a medium supports a shared pattern of coordinated behavior among coworkers. Ideas about media synchronicity are important because they clearly acknowledge the fact that communication technology choice often involves more than one individual working on a task and might well involve multiple media. This point is also emphasized by Watson-Manheim and Belanger (2007), who contend that it is important to think about **communication media repertoires** that individuals choose among as they consider how to accomplish individual and joint tasks in organizations.

The Importance of Social Factors

The ideas we considered in the last section emphasize the importance of understanding the nature of various ICT options and the ways those options might match the needs dictated by tasks or organizational or individual values. In contrast to these models highlighting the nature of the technology, Janet Fulk and her colleagues have proposed that the adoption of organizational technologies (and the use of all organizational communication media) can be more fully explained by looking at the social environment of the organization (Fulk, Schmitz & Steinfield, 1990; Fulk, Steinfield, Schmitz & Power, 1987). The **social information processing model** proposed by these theorists argues that communication between coworkers, supervisors, customers, and others affects media usage.

Consider, for example, an academic department that wants to increase the use of online courses. A media richness approach would suggest that this communication channel would be adopted whenever it provides a proper match for the ambiguity of the communicative task. However, a social information processing approach suggests that an individual's use of Web-enhanced instruction will also be influenced by interaction with others in the department. Let's look at Rebecca, an instructor in our example department. Rebecca may have heard a great deal through the grapevine about how difficult it is to prepare the lectures and slides during the initial start up and how challenging it can be to encourage appropriate student interaction in online discussion groups. This social information influences her perception of the medium's characteristics. Similarly, she might talk a great deal with students who have hated online instruction in other courses. Because of these and other social influences, Rebecca might not choose to teach an online course, even if it provides an appropriate match to the ambiguity of the task at hand.

The social information processing model is depicted in Figure 13.2. As this figure illustrates, this approach sees the use of a communication technology as a complex function of (1) the objective characteristics of the task and media, (2) past experience and knowledge, (3) individual differences, and (4) social information. Because the model shows the objective characteristics of task and media (i.e., task ambiguity and media richness) as influencing media use, it can be seen as an extension of the media richness theory. In support of the social information processing model, evidence suggests that communication patterns do have an influence on technology adoption (Fulk, 1993; Rice & Aydin, 1991; Schmitz & Fulk, 1991). For example, a study by Contractor, Seibold, and Heller (1996) found that perceptions of a group decision-making system were more strongly influenced by the attitudes of others than by demographic characteristics or system attributes.

Recent research has expanded these ideas by considering more details about what kinds of social information are most critical with regard to ICT usage and how the process of social influence works. For example, Zorn, Flanagin, and

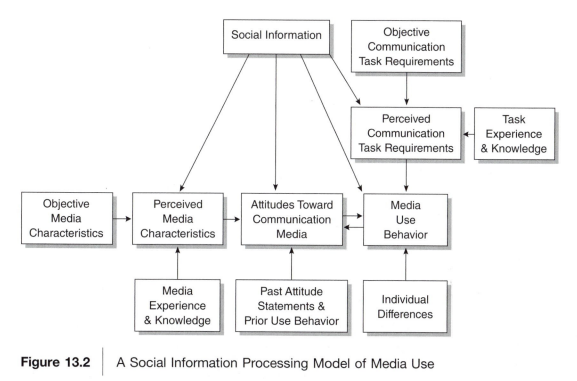

Figure 13.2 | A Social Information Processing Model of Media Use

From Fulk, J., Steinfield, C. W., Schmitz, J., & Power, J. G. (1987). A social information processing model of media use in organizations. *Communication Research*, 14, 529–552. Reproduced with permission of Sage Publications Inc. Journals via Copyright Clearance Center.

Shoham (2011) found that leaders of nonprofit organizations often look especially to leaders outside of their organization and emulate those who are seen as having technological expertise. The nature of relationship can also matter, as Scott, Dam, Paez, and Wilton (2012) found that decisions to telework were most strongly influenced by closely connected friends, neighbors, and colleagues.

In summary, then, these ideas point to the likelihood that organizational media choices are determined by a complex combination of all these factors: the richness of the medium, the ambiguity of the task, the symbolic value of the medium, the extent to which coordination with others is required, and the social information received in the organizational setting and from institutional leaders, friends, and families. It is also worth noting that individuals in organizations often have little choice about the adoption of new technologies, especially given the technological sophistication of many organizations. However, these models are useful in helping us understand the attitudes of people using technologies in the workplace and in understanding various patterns of media use.

EFFECTS OF INFORMATION AND COMMUNICATION TECHNOLOGY

The second general question to be answered with regard to ICT concerns the impact that those technologies can have on communication in organizations. We now examine this question by considering a number of outcomes that have come through the use of ICT in organizing. It is important to remember, however, that technologies do not *determine* particular outcomes and that the effects of any communication technology will depend on the manner in which it is employed or appropriated by the users (Poole & DeSanctis, 1992). For example, the user of a smartphone has an incredible range of functions and applications available—surfing the Internet, playing games, accessing music and videos, getting directions to and reviews of a restaurant, organizing appointments. Yet, it is also still possible to use the phone just to make and receive phone calls. Thus, the effects of a particular technology will depend both on its features and on how those features are used by the individual, group, or organization. With this caveat in mind, it is possible to point to a large range of ways in which the use of ICT has influenced workplace life.

Some of the effects of technology are obvious. One of these stems from our earlier observation that new technologies augment existing technologies rather than replace them. Because of this, organizations that adopt new communication technologies are marked by an overall increase in the amount of communication. For example, when videoconferencing and computer conferencing are available, they will typically be used in addition to face-to-face meetings (not instead of them), increasing the overall level of organizational communication.

One disturbing result of this information increase is that we often feel that we are drowning in data and are constantly besieged with information from e-mail, texts, phone calls, social media, and assorted other mass-media sources. Jones (2002) reports that even CEOs of major corporations often spend hours a day writing and responding to e-mail. Furthermore, the proliferation of junk e-mail (spam) has implications for individual irritation, for organizational productivity, and for the ability of computer systems to process the proliferation of data on the information highway (Padilla, 2010). Though it is possible to "use technology to impose order on chaos" ("Drowning in data?" 2013), the sheer mass of information we deal with on a daily basis can be overwhelming.

Other effects of communication technology have been found regarding communication patterns and power in the workplace. For example, electronic connections such as e-mail and texting can enhance the development of workplace friendship (Sias, Pedersen, Gallagher & Kopaneva, 2012) and there is some evidence that computer technology will lead to greater equality of participation in group interactions (Fulk & Collms-Jarvis, 2001). Not surprisingly, one of the most widespread effects of communication technology is the increased prominence of individuals knowledgeable about the technology (Ducheneaut, 2002). For example, Soukup (2003) reports the growing importance of consultants who secretly teach CEOs the basics of computer technology and Day, Paquet, Scott, and Hambley (2012) report on the importance of ICT support for enhancing employee well-being. The effects of information technology can be particularly pronounced during times of organizational crisis, when technology can be used to inform the public in emergencies (Stephens, Barrett & Mahometa, 2013), and for coordination among organizations in the aftermath of disaster (Chewning, Lai & Doerfel, 2012).

Perhaps the two most prevalent ways in which we can consider the effects of ICT, however, are in looking at the recent impact of social media on organizing and in the development of virtual work. We now turn to these specific issues.

Spotlight on Scholarship: Doodling in the Age of Technology

You can probably recall many a meeting or class period during which you looked around the room and saw that most attendees were not fully engaged with the speaker or the PowerPoint slides being displayed on the screen at the front of the room. Instead, people might be looking at open laptops on the conference table or surreptitiously tapping on a smartphone. What were these people doing? Perhaps checking their e-mail or calendars. Perhaps gathering information for additional insight into a point just made during a presentation. Perhaps ordering a take-out meal to be picked up on the way home from the office. Perhaps playing Angry Birds. Regardless of the relevance of the activity to the meeting, these individuals were multitasking—engaging in different activities at the same time. Although doodling during meetings is a time-honored tradition, multitasking has become ubiquitous in the age of communication technologies such as notebook computers and cellular phones. This trend caught the eyes of communication scholars Keri K. Stephens and Jennifer Davis, who conducted research to investigate the factors that influence individuals to engage in electronic multitasking during meetings (Stephens & Davis, 2009).

Stephens and Davis drew on the social influence model described in this chapter as a way of understanding electronic multitasking with information and communication technologies (ICTs) because this theory "accounts for the interdependence of social and technical considerations when making ICT use decisions" (Stephens & Davis, 2009, p. 66). Following this theory, Stephens and Davis hypothesized that electronic multitasking would depend on (1) an individual's experience with the technology, (2) an individual's level of communication load, (3) the observation of others engaged in electronic multitasking, and (4) beliefs about organizational norms regarding electronic multitasking. They investigated their hypotheses in an Internet survey study of 119 workers from approximately twenty organizations in diverse industries, such as engineering, finance, software, energy, and advertising.

The results of this research were quite clear-cut. An individual's level of "communication overload" did not influence multitasking, and experience with ICTs had only a small effect on multitasking. The strongest predictors of multitasking were clearly the observation of others engaging in electronic multitasking and beliefs about what others in the workplace would think about them for multitasking. These two factors explained almost 50% of the variance in the extent to which an individual multitasked during meetings, suggesting that "social influences are playing a major role in how people engage ICTs during [face-to-face] meetings" (Stephens & Davis, 2009, p. 75).

These results have implications for both theory and practice. In terms of theory, this study provides strong support for the social information processing model of media use; as individuals saw others using ICTs to multitask, they were more likely to engage in this behavior. The pragmatic implications of this are a bit more complicated though. Given these results, should organizations follow the trend of several companies that have gone "laptop-less" and banned electronic devices during meetings? Perhaps, as this study clearly indicates that the use of ICTs may be contagious, and "some people claim their meetings are now shorter and more productive without the distraction of technology" (Stephens & Davis, 2009, p. 77). However, this policy direction is not necessarily a good one because "it is highly likely that these ICTs are also being used to enhance meeting processes" through accessing information that is not available in the room (Stephens & Davis, 2009, p. 77). Doubtless, there are a variety of motivations for multitasking during meetings. This study clearly suggests, however, that—for good or ill—once the behavior starts in an organization, it might be hard to stop.

Stephens, K. K., & Davis, J. (2009). The social influences on electronic multitasking in organizational meetings. *Management Communication Quarterly, 23,* 63–83.

Social Media: From Public Relations to Politics and Justice

It could be argued that the online technology with the most potential to change organizational communication patterns is the increasing prevalence of social media sites, such as Facebook, Twitter, and YouTube (and related business sites such as LinkedIn). For the individual, we already considered ways in which social media can contribute (both positively and negatively) to processes such as the job search (see Chapter 7). Social media can also have an effect on larger workgroups, as these sites "provide simple, inexpensive ways to organize members, arrange meetings, spread information, and gauge opinion" (Ellison, Lampe & Steinfield, 2009, p. 8). These tasks can be facilitated through dedicated software that "can help workers find the right colleague to help them complete a task, can help organize and locate internal data more easily and can boost productivity and reduce redundancy by better sharing what everyone is doing" (Swift, 2010).

Beyond connecting employees within an organization, however, social media have developed a huge role in representing an organization to its public. We will talk a bit more about this issue of organizational identity in Chapter 14, but the importance of Facebook, Twitter, and other social media outlets in this process cannot be under-emphasized in this day and age. For example, in a study of Whole Foods, Gilpin (2010) found that the company used various social media outlets to various aspects of its corporate image. Though communication converged on key aspects of what Whole Foods meant, different outlets could be used to address divergent issues and audiences. Similarly, Schultz, Utz, and Goritz (2011) found that the ability of an organization to use a variety of media outlets was critical for organizational crisis response. The importance of social media for representation to key stakeholders also extends to nonprofit organizations (Lovejoy & Saxton, 2012).

Finally, in moving beyond the idea of "organization" to the constitutive concept of "organizing," it is important to note the role of ICT channels—and especially social media—on the processes of organizing in political and social justice movements. In the United States, the importance of social media can be seen in movements on both ends of the political spectrum—from the Tea Party to Occupy Wall Street—as organizers use the power of Facebook, Twitter, and blogging to attract supporters, publicize beliefs, and organize events on a moment's notice. Jonathan Alter (2013) attributes much of Barack Obama's success in the 2012 election to the ability of his campaign to harness the power of social media and data gathering techniques in a way that enhanced the shoe leather approach of grassroots campaigning. And the importance of social media in movements for social justice and democracy can clearly be seen around the globe (Loader & Mercea, 2011). Recent scholarship has pointed to the central role of ICTs in organizing the global social justice movement in New Zealand (Ganesh & Stohl, 2010), oppositional political movements in Egypt (Lim, 2012), protests against the global economic crisis (Bennett & Segerberg, 2011), and the Guatemalan justice movement (Harlow, 2011).

Virtual Organizing and Telework

Finally, it is becoming increasingly clear that technology can change the very way we structure work and design organizations. Because ICTs allow communication at great distances and at asynchronous times, it is often not necessary for people working together to be in the same place. Grantham (1995) introduced the complications of these issues in his discussion of **distributed work**. By examining both the time and place at which work is accomplished, four variations of work distribution become apparent. When work is accomplished by people in the same time and the same place, we have a classic example of a *central office*. When work is accomplished at the same time in a different place, we have **telework**, whereas work done at the same place and different time exemplifies **flextime**. The most radical new form of organizations created through technology is the **virtual organization** that has no brick-and-mortar presence at all (Shekhar, 2006). Rather, virtual work is accomplished at different times and different places through the use of multiple information and computer technologies. Shockley-Zalabak (2002) calls these virtual organizations "protean places" after Proteus, a being in Greek mythology who could transform his shape to meet the changing requirements of a situation.

There are several ways to think about virtual work. First, for many, virtual work involves working from home, and this kind of arrangement is on the rise, especially given increasing concerns about the environment and work/family balance. For example, recent research indicates that in 2011, more than 3 million Americans worked from home multiple days per week and 2.5% of the workforce consider home their primary place of work ("Latest Telecommuting Statistics," 2012). These and similar numbers have been increasing steadily over recent years and can be seen across for profit, nonprofit, and government sectors. There are strong economic reasons for telework, as analysts estimate that a typical business would save $11,000 per person per year, the telecommuters save between $2,000 and $7,000 per year, and the environment benefits from a reduction in greenhouse gases ("Latest Telecommuting Statistics," 2012). Further, given the increasing portability and connectivity of through mobile phones and tablets, it is clear that work *can* take place anywhere, although organizations have sometimes questioned the wisdom of some of these locations. One commentator considering the practice of "working while driving" notes that "a growing body of research shows that splitting attention between activities like working and driving often leads to distracted conversations and bad decisions" ("At 60 M.P.H.," 2010).

A second way to think about the virtual organization is to consider virtual teams (sometimes called "geographically dispersed teams") that work across borders of time, space, and, often, organizational boundaries. Virtual teams might be groups of individuals working on a particular project, parallel teams working in different locations, or service teams providing around-the-clock technical help. With the help of advanced technology, virtual teams work across time zones and across cultures, and this makes virtual teamwork particularly challenging. Meyer (2010) suggests that the key to success for virtual teams involves changing sometimes entrenched ideas about leadership, decision making, building trust, and communication. Some of these keys involve an understanding of different global business cultures, while others involve challenges related to the virtual nature of the team. For example, Meyer (2010) argues that "trust takes on a whole new meaning in virtual teams. When you meet your workmates by the water cooler or photocopier every day, you know instinctively who you can and cannot trust. In a geographically distributed team, trust is measured almost exclusively in terms of reliability."

Case in Point: Caring at a Distance

We often think about the ways in which communication technology can influence business organizations, service companies, or even educational endeavors. However, in the field of medicine, the technology advances we think of more often are advances in surgical procedures, pharmaceuticals, or biotechnology. But communication technologies can also make a huge difference in the provision of quality care. For example, for many years, individuals in rural communities have been able to discuss diagnoses, have tests analyzed, and have x-rays read by physicians who are many miles away. In recent years, though, even the highly involved care provided by an intensive care unit has been assisted by communication technology.

Stern (2007) examines such a system of "eICU" that has been adopted at several hospitals in the United States. In this system, critical care nurses and doctors can monitor patients from afar, relying on multiple monitors and webcams. These remote caregivers supplement the on-floor staff, relying on tracking software that allows for early detection of possible problems. These systems are expensive to license and install, but Setara Healthcare in Virginia reports that they are worthwhile both for the bottom line and for patient care. Stern (2007, p. E18) notes that in this hospital system, there was a "27 percent reduction in the ICU's mortality rate, a 17 percent reduction in length of stay and savings of $2,150 per patient—or $3 million systemwide." These systems have not met with total enthusiasm, however, as some hospitals have not found them to be a cost-effective way to provide care. And even though there has been little criticism of these systems from the medical community, it's clear that long-distance medicine still requires lots of direct contact between physicians and patients. As Stern (2007, p. E18) concludes, "[E]ven in the digital age, the need for good bedside manners remains."

Recent research helps us understand some of the complications of various kinds of virtual work. For the organization, the challenge is finding ways to harness the advantages of telework with its possible pitfalls. Though work from home provides cost savings, there are also worries about productivity loss as there is less control over workers from a distance. For example, one survey of teleworkers found that 43% report that they've watched television or a movie while on the "company clock" (Hu, 2013). Further, employees who work for telecommuting managers report lower-quality work experiences than others (Golden & Fromen, 2011) and employees who telecommute tend to identify less strongly with the organizations they work for (Fay & Kline, 2011; Fonner & Roloff, 2012).

There are also concerns for employees. For example, teleworkers may feel isolated and cut off from the culture of the organization. A report from NPR pointed to the increasing trend of telecommuters gathering at private homes to work on their own projects but to share space and social interaction ("Work Groups," 2007). Further, for the individual worker, the challenges of balancing work and home that we discussed in Chapter 12 can become particularly difficult as the time and space boundaries dividing work from home break down (Golden, 2013). As a result, for both teleworkers and those who spend most of their time in a traditional office, "work bleeds into just about every vacant space of time—from checking Blackberrys and iPhones at school drop-offs, on the way from happy hour and just after the alarm clock rings" (Kang, 2012).

Given these concerns, it is not surprising that there has been some push back. For example, one organization recently told employees to stay away from e-mail and other work-related communication on the weekend as "part of a growing effort by some employers to rebuild the boundaries between work and home that have crumbled amid the do-more-with-less ethos of the economic downturn" (Kang, 2012). In a highly publicized move, Marissa Mayer, CEO of Yahoo, decided in 2013 to no longer allow employees to work from home. She argued that this was a move made to enhance the quality of decision making and work life at the Internet giant: "To become the absolute best place to work, communication and collaboration will be important, so we need to be working side-by-side" (Hu, 2013).

In summing up advantages and challenges of telework and virtual organizing, Pearlson and Saunders (2001) discuss three important paradoxes that illustrate the difficulties facing both organizations and individuals:

- *Paradox 1: Increased Flexibility and Increased Structure.* One of the attractions of telework is the increased flexibility afforded to the employee. However, telework also requires the manager to keep better track of schedules and meetings because "chance encounters and informal discussions do not occur" (Pearlson & Saunders, 2001, p. 118).
- *Paradox 2: Greater Individuality and More Teamwork.* Teleworkers are isolated on an individual basis, but they are also required to coordinate work to a high degree. For example, Hylmo and Buzzanell (2002) report that the telecommuters they studied often saw basic procedures as "mysterious" because they were expected to be independent and yet still adapt to the rules and regulations of the central organization.
- *Paradox 3: More Responsibility and Less Control.* The nature of telework requires tasks that can be accomplished independently. However, managers often fear losing control of workers who are out of sight (Fritz, Narashim & Rhee, 1998). Similarly, teleworkers fear that if they are out of sight, they will be less likely to be considered for promotions (Hylmo & Buzzanell, 2002).

As these paradoxes illustrate, virtual work opens up new avenues and new concerns for both individuals and organizations. Indeed, this uncertainty characterizes many of our predictions about the impact of communication technology in the workplace. Some forecasters (**Utopians**) are quite hopeful about the positive impacts of technology on organizations, whereas others (**Luddites**) are more pessimistic. Turnage's (1990) observation from twenty-five years ago still ring true today:

> The optimists view technology as increasing both productivity and employee quality of work life. They see the computer as freeing employees to work on more challenging tasks by taking over the routine aspects of jobs, thus increasing productivity and competition and creating more employment in the long run. The pessimists ... associate automation with loss of employment, de-skilling (i.e., lowering the skill requirements for job incumbents), physical and mental problems, and a tightly controlled work environment. (pp. 171–172)

SUMMARY

In this chapter, we have examined the role of information and communication technologies (ICTs) in organizational life. We began by considering a wide array of ICTs and differentiated these technologies from traditional organizational communication media. We then considered several approaches of organizational communication media adoption use. The first of these approaches views media choice as a process of matching various aspects of the medium (richness, symbolic value) to the aspects of the task, work group, and organization. The second approach emphasizes the role of communication and social relationships in creating and sustaining attitudes and behaviors relating to communication technol-

ogy. After considering these ideas about media adoption and use, we reviewed research on the effects of ICT options in the workplace. We discussed a number of ways in which technology can influence communication patterns and relationships, and we paid particular attention to the influence of social media on processes ranging from identity promotion to social justice and the ways technology has influenced organizational structure through telework and virtual workplaces.

As we have done with other topics, it is useful to consider how different theoretical approaches would consider the issue of organizational communication technology (see Table 13.1). Early classical theorists such as Taylor and Fayol would

Table 13.1	Approaches to Communication Technology Processes
Approach	**How Communication Technology Would Be Considered**
Classical	Communication technology is seen as a tool that can be used to enhance the efficiency of organizations by supplementing or replacing efforts of human workers.
Human relations	Communication technology is seen as an avenue for freeing workers from mundane tasks and allowing them to engage in activities that satisfy higher-order needs.
Human resources	Communication technology is seen as an opportunity for enhancing organizational effectiveness when used in combination with human workers. Decision-making technologies are particularly relevant.
Systems	Communication technology is seen as a way to link individuals and organizational subsystems. Special attention is paid to the impact of technologies on communication networks.
Cultural	Communication technology is seen as a symbolic manifestation of organizational culture and as a medium through which cultural values are communicated.
Constitutive	Communication technology is seen as an aspect of the socially constructed organization rather than as an entity that determines particular processes and outcomes.
Critical	Communication technology is seen as a means for repressing workers through de-skilling jobs and information control. Alternatively, technology could enhance democratization through social media tools.
Feminist	Communication technology viewed as a tool that can both enhance the patriarchal control of organizational systems or contribute to activist feminist movements in positive ways.

probably be amazed at the technological advancements in today's workplace. These classical theorists would see these technologies as tools through which the efficiency and productivity of workers could be maximized. In contrast, human relations theorists might be excited about the extent to which technologies could free employees from the drudgery of mundane work and offer them more intrinsically rewarding work. Human resources theorists would be most interested in how communication technologies could enhance information flow and how decision-making technologies could maximize workers' effectiveness.

A great deal of the research conducted to date on organizational communication technology has taken a systems point of view. The ability of these technologies to link disparate parts of the organization and to transform organizational processes makes a systems perspective especially appropriate. We have also already noted the impact of cultural theorists on the study of communication technology. When we considered the dual capacity model of media adoption, we indicated the important role of technologies as symbols and as carriers of organizational values.

Constitutive scholars are particularly interested in the ways in which technologies and their use are socially constructed and the extent to which technology wields a patterned (though not deterministic) influence on communication (Leonardi & Barley, 2010). Finally, critical theorists make valuable contributions to our understanding of communication technologies by considering the impact of these technologies on the distribution of power within the organization. As Huber (1990) has pointed out, there are mixed ideas about the impact of technologies on power distribution within the organization. Some scholars argue that technologies allow top managers to exercise greater power, whereas others believe that technologies serve to decentralize decision making and power, as lower-level employees have greater access to information. There is little doubt, though, that technological innovations will lead to shifts in information access and resulting shifts in organizational power. Thus, a central role for critical theorists is the study of technologies in their capacity as tools for both oppression and emancipation.

DISCUSSION QUESTIONS

1. Reflect on changes in communication technology during your lifetime. Are there communication technologies you use now that were not available when you were a child? What about changes experienced by your parents or grandparents? Do you think the pace of technological change is increasing or decreasing?

2. Which ideas about communication media use seems most appropriate for describing the process through which you choose what technology to use? Are you rational in your choices? Are you swayed by what others say about a technology or the symbolic value of the technology?

3. Consider all the effects of communication technology discussed in this chapter. What do you see as the most positive effects? What effects are indicative of a dark side to communication technology? Given your beliefs about technology, would you consider yourself to be a "utopian" or a "Luddite"?

KEY CONCEPTS

asynchronous communication
memory, storage, and retrieval
   features
filtering of social cues

critical mass
media richness model
social information processing
   model

task ambiguity
media richness
channel expansion theory
dual capacity model

media synchronicity theory
communication media repertoires
flaming

distributed work
telework
flextime

virtual organization
Utopians
Luddites

| ## High-Tech Gardening

Hank Pembrook is the owner of The Greenery, a chain of a dozen plant nurseries in a large western metropolitan area. The Greenery has been very successful and has the largest market share of any nursery in the area. Not surprisingly, Hank is pleased with his nurseries. They stock a wide selection of trees, plants, and gardening supplies, and The Greenery customers come back because the staff is highly knowledgeable and extremely helpful. Hank has never been one to rest on his laurels (even box laurels!), though, so he has been looking at ways to improve customer service and enhance the overall profitability of his nurseries.

Hank has a good friend, Felipe, who is a bit of a computer nerd. For years, Felipe has bombarded Hank with ideas about how he could improve Hank's business through the wonders of technology. Hank has finally agreed and has instituted two systems designed to improve business at The Greenery.

The first is a wireless information system designed to improve communication and inventory control among the various branches of The Greenery. All associates at The Greenery now have personal digital assistants that allow them to schedule appointments and send and receive e-mail. In addition, the system allows for immediate updating of inventory and pricing, which can be shared at all branches of The Greenery. Adopting this system required outfitting each person with his or her own PDA, as well as purchasing the complex business software for inventory control. It cost Hank about $25,000 for the necessary hardware and software.

The second system is one designed to enhance customer service. This system includes a touch-screen computer for each store equipped with software that helps customers select plants appropriate for their particular landscaping needs. For example, if a customer is looking for a small flowering bush that requires little water and would thrive in full sunlight, the computer would provide a list of plants that might fit the bill. Furthermore, a full-color picture of each plant would appear on the screen so customers could actually see the variety of plants that might work for their needs. With the touch-screen computer, the menu-driven program is easy to use, and pilot tests with consumers have indicated that most gardeners find it helpful, educational, and fun to use. It cost Hank more than $5,000 per store to install these computer assistance centers.

Although Hank has spent a lot of money on the wireless data system and computer assistance centers, he is confident that the investments will pay off. The wireless data system has the potential to make the entire chain work more effectively because information can be easily disseminated to all stores, individual branches can transfer data and messages with minimum hassle, and individuals can keep track of appointments and contacts and easily share that information with others. Furthermore, the computer assistance centers promise to give The Greenery an important edge over the competition. No other nurseries in the area can provide such detailed information and advice for clients at the touch of a fingertip.

There are only two problems. First, managers and employees are not using the wireless data system. Instead, they continue to keep in contact by phone, track inventory via paper forms, and keep relevant contact and scheduling information stored in day planners or in their heads. Second, customers are not using the new assistance centers. Some customers try the computers out of curiosity, but few go beyond the stage of checking them out. Clearly, neither system is

CASE STUDY | **High-Tech Gardening** *continued*

being used to its full potential. Because Hank has sunk nearly $90,000 into the new systems, he is understandably concerned.

Well, perhaps "concerned" is an understatement: Hank is panicked. The next time he sees Felipe, he flies off the handle: "Felipe, what am I going to do? My staff doesn't use their PDAs, and my customers don't use the assistance centers! What should I do? More documentation? More training? More advertising? Bonuses for use? New software? New hardware? New employees? New customers? Should I just dump the whole idea?"

Felipe leans back in his chair. "Gee, Hank. I'm more of a systems guy. You've got good technology, but you're gonna have to talk to a people person to figure out how to get folks to use it."

CASE ANALYSIS QUESTIONS

1. As a "people person," how would you advise Hank? What can he do to increase the use of his wireless data system and his customer assistance centers?

2. What different kinds of suggestions for increased adoption of these systems might be made by supporters of the media richness model, the social information processing model, and the dual capacity model? Is there a way to combine these approaches to help Hank out of his bind?

3. Was Hank realistic in his assessment of the possible advantages of these systems? What would research tell us about the likely outcomes of wireless data systems and the customer assistance centers?

14 | The Changing Landscape of Organizations

AFTER READING THIS CHAPTER, YOU SHOULD ...

- Be able to distinguish between *modern* organizations stemming from the Industrial Revolution and *postmodern* organizations stemming from the Information Revolution.
- Understand the nature of a global organizational environment and appreciate the practical and cultural challenges of working within such an environment.
- Be familiar with the role of organizational and personal identity in postmodern organizations, especially during times of change and crisis.
- Recognize the contemporary shift from a manufacturing to a service economy and be familiar with the communication challenges of providing service.
- Recognize the forces that contributed to an increase in the contingent workforce and see how temporary workers (and the organizations they work for) are challenged by this shift.

We began, in Chapter 1, with a consideration of the ways in which our organizational world of today is complicated. This complexity was illustrated with such issues as globalization, terrorism, climate change, and shifting demographics. I suggested that equally complex views of organizational communication are needed to effectively address these issues. In the following twelve chapters, our journey introduced you to ways of approaching organizational communication as well as to specific processes—such as conflict, socialization, and emotion—that are vital to considering organizational communication.

This journey began, in Chapter 2's discussion of classical approaches to organizational communication, with a consideration of the organizational world brought on by the Industrial Revolution. This was the **modern era**, ushered in by the logic and rationality of science and technology and nurtured by the managerial search for effectiveness and efficiency. This modern era or *industrial age* spawned many of the corporations and organizations with which we are most familiar and was the basis for many of the ideas about organizational communication that you have encountered in this book. These ideas about approaches ranging from human relations to systems to culture and about processes including decision making, conflict, change, emotion, diversity, and technology are highly relevant in today's organizations. But the world of organizations is changing, and in this chapter, we conclude our journey with a look at some of the major alterations to the organizational landscape.

If the Industrial Revolution ushered in the modern era of efficient organization and society, many would say that the **Information Revolution** has ushered in the **postmodern era**, where everything moves fast and life is more fragmented and less consistent. More than two decades ago, in an earlier phase of this revolution, Kenneth Gergen described these societal changes in his book *The Saturated Self* (1991):

> An urgent fax from Spain lay on the desk, asking about a paper I was months late in contributing to a conference in Barcelona. Before I could think about answering, the office hours I had postponed began. One of my favorite students arrived and began to quiz me about the ethnic biases in my course syllabus. My secretary came in holding a sheaf of phone messages, and some accumulated mail.... My conversations with my students were later interrupted by phone calls from a London publisher, a colleague in Connecticut on her way to Oslo for the weekend, and an old California friend wondering if we might meet during the summer travels to Holland. By the morning's end I was drained. (p. 1)

Although Gergen felt drained by these multiple contacts around the world, his experience seems positively quaint by today's standards. Where are the e-mails, the cell phone, and the iPad? Why is Gergen merely concerned about work and not checking on stock prices, on turmoil in the Middle East, on his parents' move to an assisted living facility, and on his child's rescheduled soccer game? What is he doing in an office with a secretary outside rather than working from home, from the local coffee shop, or from halfway around the world? Clearly, we now live in a frenetic, multitasking, quickly changing, immense, and fragmented world. For the individual, this postmodern world has led to what Dalton Conley calls "Elsewhere U.S.A." (2009a), a condition in which "we feel like we are in the right place at the right time only when in transit" and in which "we are haunted by the feeling that we are frauds, expendable in the workplace because so much of our service work is intangible" (Conley, 2009b, p. 59). These problems have been exacerbated by the ongoing effects of the Great Recession of 2008–2010, whose effects will "likely change the life course and character of a generation of young adults" (Peck, 2010, p. 42).

In short, as we demonstrated in Chapter 1, this postmodern world is complicated. In this concluding chapter, then, we will again look squarely at our present and future lives and consider those issues that directly influence our work experiences. To do this, we will revisit one of the issues examined in Chapter 1: how work itself is directly affected by our global economy and related societal shifts. We will also focus on three aspects of our postmodern world that are key to a consideration of organizational communication: the increasing importance of image and identity, the shift to a predominantly service economy, and the prevalence of new employment relationships, such as the "disposable worker."

COMMUNICATION IN THE GLOBAL WORKPLACE

Most likely, many of us have recently called a help line for information about a product or help with computer software or perhaps government benefits. If we managed to get past the automated system and talk to a human, it is likely that our helper was someone located in a call center in another corner of the world. In recent years, for example, when citizens in New Jersey and a number of other states have called for help with their welfare benefits, they found themselves talking to someone in Ireland. Service technicians for one Mexican tourism hotline are located in Oregon. Those looking to choose an offshore call center site must balance the advantages of locations, including India, the Philippines, and South Africa (Asangi & Sathe, 2007). The proliferation of companies choosing to locate call centers in such far-reaching locations is just one example of globalization or "the rapidly developing processes of complex interconnections between societies, cultures, institutions, and individuals worldwide" (Tomlinson, 1997, p. 170).

Other examples abound. As we discussed in Chapter 1, as political changes have broken down many boundaries that once divided countries, business practices have changed too. Many countries that were once considered unable to compete in the global marketplace have developed modernization programs that are helping them meet new challenges. The most obvious example is China, which in 2010 passed Japan to become the world's second-largest economy (with the United States being first). Corporations in developed nations now have branches and manufacturing plants worldwide, as they look for ways to compete in the economic marketplace. Of course, these global production facilities raise important questions about issues ranging from the 2013 industrial accident at a textile factory in Bangladesh (Greenwald & Hirsch, 2013) to worker treatment and human rights at Apple plants in China (Duhigg & Barboza, 2012).

A number of factors have contributed to the rise of globalization. One underlying intellectual impetus for the global economy is **laissez-faire capitalism**: "the assumption that a free-market economic system has sufficient checks and balances in place to ensure that the legitimate interests of all members of a society will be met" (Conrad & Poole, 2004, p. 39). This economic philosophy—which minimizes the role of government—advocates the creation of wealth through free trade and has contributed to the globalization of business during the past few decades. With this globalization movement has come the increasing movement toward the democratization of many world governments, though a consideration of ongoing events in Africa, the Middle East, and other regions of the world suggests that democratization is a continuing struggle. Of course, the economic and political impetus toward globalization has been helped along by many technological factors. Foremost among these are the ease of travel and the advent of advanced communication technologies. Through low-cost air travel, it is possible for companies to employ many "road warriors" to span the globe. And through technologies such as cellphones, the Internet, and Skype, it is possible to conduct business across great distances. (See Chapter 13 for a review of technological advances and their impacts on virtual teams and virtual organizing.)

As a result of these changes, we have moved from a landscape in which companies are largely associated with one country to a landscape where there is a mix of domestic organizations, multicultural organizations, multinational organizations, international organizations, and global organizations (see Table 14.1). As Table 14.1 indicates, the global marketplace contains an array of organizational types. These organizations differ not only in their geographical identity (do they operate in one country? several countries? around the globe?) but also in how they manage the interests and concerns of their employees, customers, and clients.

Table 14.1 | Organization Types in the Global Marketplace

Organization Type	Description
Domestic	An organization that identifies with a single country and predominant culture.
Multicultural	An organization that identifies predominantly with one country but recognizes the needs of a culturally diverse workforce and diverse contacts outside the company.
Multinational	An organization that identifies with one nationality while doing business across several or many nations. Management recognizes the needs of a multinational workforce, customer base, and institutional environment.
International	An organization that identifies with two or more countries with distinct cultural qualities. Distinct national interests are assumed to exist within the company's management, clients, customers, and institutional environment.
Global	An organization that identifies with the global system rather than any particular nation. In a global workplace, organizational membership takes precedence over national allegiances.

Adapted from Stohl, C. (2001). Globalizing organizational communication. In F. M. Jablin & L. L. Putnam (Eds.), *The New Handbook of Organizational Communication: Advances in Theory, Research, and Methods* (pp. 323–375). Thousand Oaks, CA: Sage.

Effects of Globalization

Clearly, economic globalization has substantially changed how we live and how organizations do business. As we noted in Chapter 1, there is considerable debate as to whether these are changes we should applaud or dread. And as Zahra (1999) points out, there are utopian and dystopian views on this subject. In the utopian view:

> Globalization will continue to escalate, transferring technologies, bringing cultures and societies closer, and creating a community of peace loving, intelligent citizens. In this vision of the future, globalization will foster cooperation among nations and create good will. Globalization will be an instrument of peace, growth, progress and prosperity. Competitiveness is viewed as a marathon to achieve and sustain excellence. (Zahra, 1999, p. 36)

For example, Taylor and Doerfel (2003) have described how an interorganizational network of nongovernmental organizations (NGOs) came together in Croatia during that country's transformation from a totalitarian state into the initial phases of a civil society. Positive outcomes of this kind are encouraged when organizations involved in global processes are encouraged in the practice of *corporate social responsibility*—a stance in which businesses attempt to have a positive impact on a variety of stakeholders including the environment, consumers, government, and the communities in which the company is embedded (Roper & Barker, 2011).

In contrast, a variety of dystopian views see globalization in dramatically different terms. For example, Parameswaran (2008) considers the development of call centers in Bangalore, India. She first points to the historical conditions that have led to

India being a source of inexpensive labor for this kind of work and then discusses the ways in which the life of an individual worker—although enriched through better pay than might be available elsewhere in the country—is difficult in many ways. She notes that "the assertion that call centers have provided relatively lucrative employment to hundreds of young women and men is indeed accurate, but to pitch the call center job ... without any consideration of the stress that night shifts, highly repetitive work ... and assumed 'American identities' have caused paints a unidimensional picture of globalization's effects in South Asia" (Parameswaran, 2008, p. 120). Although there are sometimes opportunities for resistance at the level of the individual worker (Pal & Buzzanell, 2013), the oppressive outcomes of a global economy are widespread. For example, Liu and Vlaskamp (2010) have considered similar issues in China, as new college graduates in the global economy are now often unemployed or underemployed and forced to live in slum conditions.

It is likely that both these positive and negative views are playing out on the global stage. As this happens, it is helpful to consider some general effects of globalization and to examine how some organizations adapt to the global workplace. For example, Monge (1998) proposes several ways that globalization influences organizational communication. First, globalization results in **time and space compression**, changing communication patterns and perceptions. In the global workplace, everything moves quickly: You can be in Tokyo one day and Cleveland the next, and it's always the beginning of the workday somewhere around the globe. Space and time are no longer directly connected. Second, globalization enhances our sense of **global consciousness**. When we work in an organization that is global, multinational, or multicultural, we must be aware of the cultures of others and of our own attitudes, beliefs, and behaviors. Kim (2008) has referred to this as a process of developing "intercultural personhood" that includes both patterns of individuation and universalization. Third, globalization leads to *disembedded* organizations and people. In a global society, behavior and interaction are often lifted from their local context and restructured across time and space. While working in a cybercafe, for example, it might be difficult to know if one is in Seattle, Moscow, or Kuwait.

In addition to these specific effects, there are general patterns to consider in how people view the process and outcomes of globalization. Stohl (2001) has noted two such patterns for viewing the challenges and outcomes of globalization within organizational communication research and practices. The first of these—**convergence**—is an approach that emphasizes the need of organizations to adapt their practices to a global marketplace. A convergence approach considers how an organization might adapt its practices to "a global system that requires flexibility, responsiveness, speed, knowledge production, and knowledge dissemination" (Stohl, 2001, p. 325). In this approach, communication is seen as "a conduit for the acquisition of resources, capital, information, and expertise" (Stohl, 2001, p. 325). For example, Roberts, Kossek, and Ozeki (1998) have discussed management challenges in the global workplace and advocated specific strategies for coping with such management challenges. Their ideas about instituting structures such as aspatial careers, awareness-building assignments, corporate SWAT teams, and virtual solutions (see Table 14.2) illustrate a convergence approach to globalization in which the goal is to enhance organizational performance in the worldwide marketplace.

Table 14.2	Strategies for Managing in a Global Marketplace		
Strategy	**What?**	**Who?**	**How?**
Aspatial Careers	A corps of experts with borderless careers on long-term overseas assignments	Mobile and globally oriented employees with proven ability and loyalty	Deploy employees in leadership positions across sites and rotate to develop human resources
Awareness-Building Assignments	Three- to twelve-month assignments in various global locations	High-potential employees who are early in their careers	Deploy employees in global positions to enhance global perspective and skills. Screen employees for the ability to function in other cultures
SWAT Teams	Short-term project-length assignments in worldwide locations	Technical specialists	Provide specialized skills and the transfer of technical processes and systems to global locations on an "as-needed" basis
Virtual Solutions	Allow employees in a wide variety of locations to work together on global solutions to problems	Employees assigned throughout the organization in need of overseas connections	Use electronic communication—such as the Web, intranets, and distance learning—to disperse information across locations

Adapted from Roberts, K., Kossek, E. E. & Ozeki, C. (1998). Managing the global workforce: Challenges and strategies *Academy of Management Executive*, *12*(4), 93–106.

In contrast, the **divergence** approach to the globalizing workplace emphasizes the cultural distinctiveness found around the world. The divergence perspective is less interested in exploring strategies for organizational success than in exploring how meaning is constructed in various cultural settings and the impact of organizational norms and functioning on that construction of meaning. Stohl (2001) argues that "[t]he environmental and technological pressure on contemporary organizations to become more and more similar clash with the proprietary pull of cultural identifications, traditional values, and conventional practices of social life" (p. 326). Thus, it is critical to look at the competing forces of convergence and divergence in examining communication within global organizations.

It is also vital to consider the human effects of globalization as more individuals are working in unfamiliar cultures with people who hold different values and goals. For example, Enghsh-Lueck, Darrah, and Saven (2002) found that it was not only crucial but also quite challenging for high-tech workers to establish trusting relationships in global organizations where workers are separated by great distances and are working under severe time constraints. Similarly, Mattson and Stage (2001) describe a variety of ethical dilemmas faced by workers who confront different cultural norms while working for global organizations. For example, Stage (1999) found that American companies in Thailand had an especially difficult time adapting to the national custom of gift-giving at New Year's. Gifts were expected by clients from the Thai culture but were seen as unethical by many U.S. organizations.

In summary, a variety of economic, political, and technological forces are transforming the workplaces of organizations competing in the global marketplace. In the global marketplace, our perceptions of time and space change, as does our understanding of others and ourselves. Communication in these global organizations will depend largely on balancing the forces of convergence (making us more alike in our search for workplace efficiency) with the forces of divergence (making us appreciate our cultural differences).

COMMUNICATION IN AN ERA OF SHIFTING IDENTITY

As our economy becomes more global, the names of some corporations have become known worldwide. Some critics have talked about the "McDonaldization" of the world (Ritzer, 2000), and names such as Samsung, Disney, Ford, Nike, and CNN are brand names that are clearly recognizable around the globe. The worldwide spread of these corporate monikers suggests the increasing importance of **organizational identity**—knowing an organization, what it sells, and where it stands on relevant issues of the day. Indeed, Cheney and Christensen (2001) argue that "[i]n the contemporary activities of public relations, issue management, marketing, advertising, and the like … the ongoing rhetorical struggle for organizations of most kinds is to establish a clearly distinctive identity and at the same time connect with more general concerns so as to be maximally persuasive and effective" (p. 233).

In addition to worldwide recognition, there are many other reasons for the increased importance of organizational identity in today's economy. For example, with widespread mergers and acquisitions, there is the shifting landscape of "who belongs to whom," causing confusion for a great many individuals and organizations. These mergers and acquisitions are often contentious. Recent mergers among airlines provide an interesting illustration of this branding dynamic. In 2005, US Airways merged with America West, keeping the US Airways name. In 2010, Delta and Northwest completed their merger, keeping the Delta name. Some of these name choices may have been based on size (Delta taking a front seat in branding to the smaller Northwest), but some might also say that the issue of reputation may have also made a difference (as American West was sometimes referred to by customers as "America Worst"). US Airways is likely to lose its name, however, in its planned merger with American Airlines. The merger between United and Continental put another interesting twist on this notion of organizational image during a merger, as the planes now combine the name "United" in block letters on the front fuselage with the Continental logo and colors on the tail.

Organizations often try to be proactive in developing and communicating an organizational identity. Heath (1994) has noted that "[c]ompanies try to impose themselves on their environments, rather than merely adapt to them. They attempt to shape their environment by their presence in it, by what they do and say" (p. 228). Organizations seek to create and maintain positive images in order to achieve long-term goals. As Cheney and Frenette (1993) explain, "The presumed

Case in Point: Image Gone Viral

It started in 2006 when Abercrombie & Fitch CEO Mike Jeffries granted an interview to *Salon Magazine*. When asked about the secret of A&F's success, he said: "...we go after the cool kids...a lot of people don't belong [in our clothes], and they can't belong. Are we exclusionary? Absolutely" (Temin, 2013). Probably not the best thing to say in terms of organizational image, but there wasn't a great uproar and it soon became old news.

Of course, in the Internet age, "embarrassing articles do not die—they just go into hibernation until they are resuscitated" (Temin, 2013). The quote was brought up by an author who was promoting her new book about the retail industry. The fire was fanned with quotes such as "Teen retailer Abercrombie & Fitch doesn't stock XXL sizes in women's clothing because they don't want overweight women wearing their brand" (Temin, 2013). And, not surprisingly, the quotes—and the hit to the Abercrombie & Fitch

image—went viral. Bloggers went crazy. An online petition was opened up to force A&F to make plus sizes. A boycott of the retailer was established. And on and on.

Temin (2013) compares this negative image gone viral with another corporate effort from the same time period—Dove's "Real Beauty Sketches" campaign in which women are encouraged to see themselves in the more positive ways that others see them. Though this campaign has also drawn criticism, the contrast with the A&F image is stark: "Mean, bully-boy culture (A&F) vs. a holistic, self-esteem promoting, we-can-make-the-world-a-better-place sensibility (Dove). Narcissism vs. collectivism; cruelty vs. compassion; me, me, me vs. we" (Temin, 2013). Many years ago, Canon promoted its cameras through an Andre Agassi campaign with the tagline "Image is Everything." If Canon was right, Abercrombie & Fitch ran into a lot of trouble when their image went viral.

circle of influence runs thus: corporation to public to policy makers to corporation" (p. 50). For example, a pharmaceutical company may attempt to enhance its image in a number of ways: by providing free AIDS drugs in sub-Saharan Africa, by distributing prescription discount cards for senior citizens who rely on Medicaid, or by promoting concern for the long-term health of Americans. It is then hoped that this positive image will engender public support that could eventually be parlayed into favorable policy decisions at various levels of government.

It is important to note, however, that organizational images are not always created and maintained through purposive campaigns. Members of the organizational environment form perceptions of an organization's image based on a wide array of messages. Furthermore, sometimes the style or means of communication can be more important than the actual message. As Cheney and Christensen (2001) suggest, "[T]he principal management problem in today's marketplace of goods and ideas is not so much to provide commodities and services or to take stands on the salient issues of the day, but to do these things with a certain distinctiveness that allows the organization to create and legitimize itself" (p. 241). For example, a Samsung advertising campaign positions its phones as more cutting edge than major competitor Apple by showing young and hip college students transferring music through a bump of the phone while their parents stand hopelessly by with their iPhones. As Van Camp (2013) notes, these "ads have been damn effective at making the Galaxy phones look a lot cooler than most things on the market."

Examples of organizational image creation and maintenance abound and illustrate the various communication avenues through which this process occurs. In the late 1970s, Mobil Oil enhanced its image through an advertising campaign that advocated positions on a wide range of public issues. In the fall of 2001, the travel industry as a whole attempted to link its image with patriotism in a post-September 11 public relations campaign. Federal and state government agencies (especially the Federal Emergency Management Association [FEMA]) suffered from severe image concerns in the aftermath of hurricanes Katrina and Rita in 2005. Toyota worked to maintain its strong image with customers in the wake of a wide range of safety concerns. And many corporations quickly severed their spokesperson ties with Tiger Woods when issues in his personal life spiraled out of control in late 2009.

As many of these examples illustrate, image becomes particularly critical during times of organizational crisis (see Chapter 10). Classic examples include Exxon after the Valdez oil spill, Johnson & Johnson after the discovery of tainted Tylenol tablets, Union Carbide after the energy plant disaster in Bhopal, India, and NASA after the explosion of the *Challenger* and *Columbia* space shuttles. More recent examples include a wide variety of food safety issues, such as spinach and eggs, concerns with toy safety dealt with by Mattel, concerns with mine safety in the wake of explosions and collapses, and the BP oil rig disaster. The messages sent by organizational representatives in the face of such events could predict both the short-term image and the long-term survival of the organization.

Issues of identity are not limited to the organizational or corporate level, of course. Individuals, too, see their organizational selves in a particular light that is influenced by ongoing changes in the workplace and can have implications for well-being. For example, Kristen Lucas (2011) argues that identity is particularly problematic for working class employees who find it increasingly difficult to achieve the "American Dream" in the contemporary economy. Though these workers hold onto an identity that she labels the "working class promise"—strong work ethic, providing for family, dignity of work, and humility—this identity can be difficult to maintain when upward mobility is more difficult. Similar issues of individual identity were raised for many in 2013 when news stories publicized the statistic that 40% of American households include a mother who is the sole or primary earner in the family (Rampell, 2013). The increased prevalence of women in the breadwinner role pointed to contemporary trends such as changing gender roles in upper income households and the prevalence of single mother households in lower income households.

In summary, then, the changing landscape of organizations points to important identity shifts for both organizations and individuals. These identity challenges can be particularly difficult during times of crisis and social and economic upheaval.

COMMUNICATION IN A SERVICE ECONOMY

A third aspect of the changing landscape for organizational communication involves the type of business we conduct in today's organizational world. In the years following the Industrial Revolution (see Chapter 2), most organizations counted the creation of "things" as a primary goal. The U.S. economy (and other world economies) was based primarily on manufacturing. At the end of World War II, only 10% of nonfarm jobs were in the service sector ("The American Workplace," 2010), but the

U.S. economy then underwent a radical shift, and today, it can largely be characterized as a **service economy**. There are estimates that service companies (including retail, financial services, transportation, health care, and construction, among others) now employ about 90% of the U.S. economy ("Service Sector," 2012). The shift to a service economy has also fueled rapid growth in global economies, such as in India ("Services," 2010). Though there are some good jobs in sectors of the service economy, it is bad news for many. For example, Davis (2010) notes that "jobs in retail are distinguished by low wages, low tenure, and extremely limited job prospects" (p. 303).

It is hard to deny the importance of service in our daily lives as employees, students, customers, and clients in a wide range of organizational settings. Even a trip to the grocery store involves a service encounter that has implications both for the grocer's profits and for your mood for the rest of the day. Moreover, customer service today extends to a wide range of online and mobile interactions, ranging from the ease of a return at Amazon to the quality of a pedicure purchased through a Groupon opportunity. Thus, it is little surprise that popular business publications tout the importance of service. For example, a recent book examining "high-tech, high-touch customer service" pointed to trends in customer service including the customer's desire for instant gratification, a push toward self-service and customer empowerment, and an appreciation for environmental awareness and values-based buying. Failures in customer service are costly to the organization and frustrating to the consumer, and these failures are widespread. For example, only 37% of brands received "excellent" or "good" customer experience score in a 2012 survey—the rest were rated as "OK," "poor," or "very poor" ("20 Important Customer Experience Statistics," 2012).

The airline industry is a case in point. Flying was a luxury afforded only to a few in the middle part of the twentieth century, but by the 1990s, air travel was a part of everyday life for many. Deregulation had lowered prices, thus increasing the prevalence of business and leisure travel, and with the rising number of travelers came declining service standards. Indeed, in April 2001, *Newsweek* ran an in-depth story entitled "Why Flying Is Hell" (Bryant, 2001) and surveys of service quality have not turned around in recent years. Indeed, when a 2012 survey found that airline performance quality was only "slightly worse" than in 2011, it was viewed as a positive sign for the industry (Brown, 2013). These negative attitudes toward the airline experience are fueled by factors such as airport lines, flight delays, boarding denials, horror stories of hours spent on the tarmac, and an increasing trend toward fees for everything—luggage, food, boarding and seating preferences, and so on. Indeed, in 2013, Spirit Airlines eliminated their toll-free customer service phone number.

Why are there problems with service? Part of the answer may lie in organizational moves, such as corporate downsizing and retrenchment. As Pederson (1997) notes, "While manufacturers can often replace workers with machines, that's usually not an option for services. Some companies—FedEx, UPS, Nordstrom—kept customers happy despite the new pressures. Many others just got surlier" (p. 57). Thus, in a turbulent environment, an organization may choose to sacrifice customer service in the belief that such a move will enhance profits and keep the company economically competitive.

Another answer to problems with service may be in the type of service that is provided and the match of that service communication to the needs of the customers. Ford and Etienne (1994) have suggested that service comes in many guises. For example, a supermarket clerk may strive to be courteous, auto dealers have the reputation of providing manipulative service, and retailers like Nordstrom take great pride in providing personalized service. Ford (1995) has found that these forms of service can have a significant impact on customers' satisfaction and behavior. When customers develop expectations about service, violations of those expectations can either be highly gratifying (e.g., when personalized service is not expected but received) or highly dissatisfying (e.g., when manipulation is encountered in a sales presentation).

Third, as noted in Chapter 11, the provision of service often involves emotional labor and accompanying stress for the service provider. Undoubtedly, worker stress can lead to service that is less than optimal. This problem can be accentuated when service providers are stretched thin by understaffing and unrealistic expectations. Research has found that customers are highly intolerant of negative emotional displays, and the norm of "service with a smile" is particularly pronounced in the United States (Grandey, Rafaeli, Ravid, Wirtz & Steinger, 2010). Consider, again, the airline industry. While passengers become increasingly frustrated with service, those providing the service are also getting mad. In August 2010, this dynamic reached a breaking point for one flight attendant who got fed up with an unruly passenger, grabbed the intercom for a final parting message, activated the emergency chute, and slid down with a beer in each hand. Peggy Noonan (2010) sees this as a sad outcome of the service economy: "Everyone is getting on everyone's nerves.... Everyone wants to tell the boss to take this job and shove it. Everyone wants to take a good, hard, last look at the customer and take the chute."

The challenges of communication in a service environment can be particularly pronounced in the information economy, which is increasingly dominated by electronic transactions, or **e-commerce** (Yoon, Choi & Sohn, 2008). In the early years of e-commerce, growth was slow, perhaps because of challenges in the communication environment. With no face-to-face interaction, service provided largely through self-service transactions, and limited opportunities for complex messages and immediate feedback, there were many communication challenges (Scott, 2001). However, many online retailers and service providers have met these challenges and e-commerce is growing at record and is anticipated to grow at 14% per year in the coming years (Enright, 2013). Much of the new growth is fueled by mobile devices, adding new communication challenges for providing customer service. Research has suggested that one of the most important aspects of maintaining good relationships with customers in this environment is establishing a sense of trust (Kim, Ferrin & Rao, 2009).

In sum, then, we now live in a service economy and hence an organizational world that is dominated by service encounters. Communication in service encounters—whether an ongoing service relationship with a valued massage therapist or a point-and-click encounter when ordering flowers online—can influence customer attitudes and satisfaction as well as organizational profits and the satisfaction and health of service providers.

✳ Spotlight on Scholarship: What Can You Do With That Major?

This chapter highlights many ways in which organizational life is continually shifting, in part in response to larger changes in the economy and society. Some of you now reading the end of this book are also looking forward to the end of your college career—if not this semester than in the next year or two. Undoubtedly, the prospect of graduation has you thinking more about the changing landscape of the workplace highlighted in these final pages of this text: What will the next phase of your life look like? What kind of work will you do? How will that work provide meaning to your life? The answers to these questions will obviously be shaped by larger currents in society. As I write these words, the economy is improving after many years of trouble, but it's far from healthy. Thus, those graduating from college continue to face an uncertain and rapidly changing job market—often with the additional worry of student-loan debt. In this environment, it's hardly surprising that many have started questioning the value of higher education, as "students are turning to universities in increasingly vocational terms, dramatically altering social understandings of the meaning and purpose of higher education" (Lair & Wieland, 2012, p. 425).

And in the midst of all this societal turmoil, you still must deal with the ubiquitous question: "What are you going to do with that major?" In many ways, this colloquial and oft-asked question distills our ongoing concerns about education and work, and it served as a focus for a recent investigation undertaken by Daniel Lair and Stacey Wieland. These scholars were interested in knowing more about how students understood the meaning of work and the connection of education to work, and they asked undergraduates to write short essays describing situations in which this question was asked and answered. Their analysis of the narratives revealed interesting patterns about the ways in which today's college students frame the work world they are about to enter.

Lair and Wieland found widespread acknowledgement that this question is ubiquitous and often emotionally charged—typically in a negative way.

They note that "one student reported 'having a mini heart attack' every time she is asked" (Lair & Wieland, 2012, p. 433). The researchers also found that the question serves three broad functions: as small talk in everyday conversation, as an opportunity for exploration and self-reflection, and as an expression of judgment about major and career choice.

On a more abstract level, Lair and Wieland analyzed the narratives to better understand how respondents conceptualized the "connection" between work and education. Most students accepted the dominant interpretation that an acceptable answer to the question was one that demonstrated a sensible plan that promised future success—especially in financial terms. This majority of respondents "understood the meaning of work—and subsequently, education—first and foremost in economic terms" (Lair & Wieland, 2012, p. 440). However, a small portion of respondents (10%) resisted this dominant interpretation, either by refusing to engage the question or by rejecting the premise of the question. These students questioned the tight coupling of academic major and planned career and rejected the notion that they should already have a linear career path in mind. According to Lair and Weiland, "these alternative interpretations of the work-education relationship helped relieve the pressure around major selection by emphasizing students' potential to use education creatively to succeed over their long-term working lives" (2012, p. 443). One student (but only one) even rejected the notion that what you "do" with a major necessarily relates to paid employment—she instead stated that because of her international studies major she would be able to participate in significant conversations through the rest of her life. And although it is important to not discount the importance of work and career, let's hope that one important function of college education continues to be these ongoing dialogues.

Lair, D. J., & Wieland, S. M. B. (2012). "What are you going to do with that major?" Colloquial speech and the meaning of work and education. *Management Communication Quarterly, 26,* 423–452.

COMMUNICATION IN THE AGE OF THE DISPOSABLE WORKER

A final factor to consider in the changing landscape of the workplace involves the roles that individuals play in the new global economy. In the past, many people stayed with one or perhaps two organizations throughout their working lives. As Reich (2000) notes, "[T]wo-thirds of senior executives surveyed in 1952 had been with the same company for more than twenty years" (pp. 93–94). And most people working at a given company were permanent, full-time employees of that organization. These circumstances created strong connections between an individual and the company with which he or she worked—what William Whyte called *The Organization Man* (Whyte, 1956). As Holstein and Gubrium (2000) explain, "[T]he Organization Man (and presumably woman) … puts the organization's interests above individual goals and priorities" (p. 45). And in exchange for that loyalty, the organization was supposed to take care of all the organizational men and women.

But times have changed. By the turn of the twenty-first century, the global economy, increased technology, weakened labor unions, and an extremely competitive organizational environment had contributed to what Robert Reich called "the end of employment as we knew it" (Reich, 2000) and what Conrad and Poole (1997) labeled "the age of the disposable worker." During the first decade of the twenty-first century, the situation intensified, and a *Business Week* cover story in early 2010 noted that the Great Recession's "unusual ferocity… accelerated trends— including offshoring, automation, the decline of labor unions' influence, new management techniques, and regulatory change—that already had been eroding workers' economic standing" (Coy, Conlin & Herbst, 2010). The trend continues, as human resource advisors argue that a contingent workforce "provides employers with flexibility and control when you need to make changes in [the] workforce quickly" ("Employment Trends," 2013). In short, today's workforce is comprised to an ever-increasing degree of **contingent workers**—individuals without a permanent and full-time connection to an organization. The college or university you're now enrolled in is probably a case in point—the ranks of adjunct and part-time professors have exploded by 300 percent since 1975 (Weissmann, 2013).

Some workers are contingent by choice—they are not forced into alternative work arrangements but intentionally opt for an employment situation that bears little resemblance to Whyte's "Organization Man" (or woman). Individuals may choose to work as temps, telecommute, work part-time, or enter and exit the workforce at various stages of their lives. These choices can be motivated by a variety of factors. Some workers want to concentrate on an avocation rather than a vocation. Some workers simply enjoy the liberty of being "temporary." Erickson (2012) summarizes many of the motivations for choosing a contingent work life:

> Some contingent workers say they are seeking better work/life balance; others want to create or design their own careers by choosing the kind of work or projects that create a unique set of skills, making them more desirable prospective employees. Contingent employment can expose individuals to a broad variety of challenges, demanding constant learning and new skills, which make work more interesting for them.

For these kinds of contingent workers, there are great rewards, as a recent survey found that the happiest workers in the United States were independent workers who did not have a connection to a specific organization (Shaughnessy, 2012). From the organization's perspective, the need to attract these high quality "free agents" creates challenges for relationship building and communication. Frauenheim (2012) calls this the "arm's-length embrace" in which "companies respect contingents' independence yet nonetheless show them more love—in the form of invitations to social gatherings, improved communication, greater recognition and the like."

For many workers, however, being contingent is not a choice. For many years, organizations have worked to streamline and downsize their workforce to deal with the uncertainties of the contemporary business landscape. Coy et al. (2010) note, "[T]he trend toward a perma-temp world has been developing for years" and that "26% of the U.S. workforce had jobs in 2005 that were in one way or another 'nonstandard.'" However, this trend accelerated rapidly during the recent recession and has not changed substantially. Employers have increasingly relied on temporary workers in order to lower costs and gain flexibility. Furthermore, this trend has hit workers at all levels of the organization, in a wide range of work sectors, and for longer periods of time. Work is increasingly becoming what Kalleberg (2009) calls "precarious"—"uncertain, unpredictable, and risky from the point of view of the worker" (p. 2).

It is clear, then, that the nature of the workforce is rapidly changing and is not likely to shift back into old patterns. We are now increasingly temporary, part-time, independent, freelancing, e-lancing, and telecommuting workers. What are the implications of these basic changes in work as we know it? A few issues are highlighted below.

There are, of course, financial implications for the disposable worker. Those who are unemployed, underemployed, working in temporary jobs, or in and out of the workforce will most often earn less money over their lifetimes than will a lifetime corporate employee. Individuals who finish college during a recession (and are hence likely to be underemployed or contingent workers) suffer from lower wages for a decade or more after graduation (Marray, 2009). A second financial implication involves employment benefits. For example, Reich (2000) notes that "in 1980, more than 70 percent of workers received some form of health benefit from their employers. By the late 1990s, that percentage had slipped to about 60 percent. And even when employees have some coverage, it has become less generous" (p. 99). A 2010 report portrayed a telling contrast regarding the contingent workforce: While 86% of full-time U.S. workers receive health care benefits, such benefits were available to only 24% of part-time workers ("Employee Benefits," 2010).

There are additional concerns beyond pay and benefits. For example, contingent workers are at higher risk for work-related injury, illness, and death than other workers (Cummings & Kreiss, 2008). There are also social and psychological effects, as a disposable workforce feels less connection to the organization and vice versa. For example, Gossett (2002) found that many contemporary companies could be described as "organizations of free agents," where lack of interaction and purposeful organizational policies limited the extent to which temporary workers felt connected to the organization and might feel stigmatized by others in the organization (Boyce, Ryan, Imus & Morgeson, 2007). Furthermore, a lack of employee identification has implications for personal and organizational decision making (see the discussion in Chapters 6 and 8) and for job satisfaction and turnover. The implications of an employer's lack of commitment to the worker is also clear: "Part-time jobs are … the first to go in an economic downturn" (Greenberg, 2001, p. 55). Furthermore, in

Case in Point: Generation Y in the Workplace

Part of the changing landscape of work stems from younger workers arriving in organizations. The most recent influx of workers has come from Generation Y, often defined as those born in the 1980s and 1990s. These new workers are seen as different from the preceding baby boomers and Gen-Xers. Tim Irvin, a corporate psychologist, explains: "They come in with very high expectations.... Their parents have told them from the moment they were born that they were special. These Gen Y'ers believe it. The thought of having to pay dues for a long time to get into a corner office is kind of jarring to them" (Osburn, p. DI, 2007).

Now, if you are someone born in the 1980s or 1990s—a member of Generation Y—this description might seem a bit insulting. Perhaps you would not agree with the assessment that indulgent parents have produced "workers without a sense of responsibility, accountability, or commitment" (Osburn, 2007, p. D6). However, these generational differences can clearly influence relationships in the work-

place, and the prevailing perception of younger workers can be seen as a disturbing trend for both employers and for workers. However, there's another side of the story. For example, Generation Y workers are also seen as being highly motivated, willing to stay with a company if they are challenged and given opportunities, and very aware of the technology options that are vital to today's workplace. One of these Gen Y'ers, Anthony Oni, describes it this way: "For the 76 million or so Gen Y'ers in the world, we are trying to find our place in the business community. Sometimes it doesn't always happen the first time. Young people are graduating college and exploring and seeking their niche in a community and taking advantage of great opportunities. This may be confused with impatience" (Osburn, 2007, p. D6). Indeed, these words might describe you: exploring, looking for opportunity, impatiently finding your place—difficult and challenging tasks in the changing world of work.

addition to feeling a limited connection to the organization, contingent workers often receive directives from both the staffing agency and the organization that contracts for their work. This situation can lead to role conflict and the need for temporary workers to choose between the desires of these competing organizations (Gossett, 2007).

It is possible, though, to see a silver lining around this dark cloud. That is, a contingent workforce has the potential to continuously breathe new life into organizations. As Conrad and Poole (1997) argue, "Temporary or part-time workers bring new ideas and new ways of doing things.... They may also bring a useful candor; they may be less strategically motivated and less concerned with impression management than employees with their future at stake" (p. 590).

SUMMARY

In this chapter, we have considered a number of factors critical to a continuing understanding of organizational communication. The landscape of the work world has shifted substantially in the last twenty years, and it continues to change.

First, the organizational landscape has become global. Second, this globalization—along with other aspects of the "new economy"—has heightened the importance of understanding the creation and maintenance of organizational image. Third, the economy is increasingly dominated by organizations that provide services rather than products. Finally, workers in today's economy increasingly hold temporary and contingent positions that make them more expendable and that change the basic relationship between workers and organizations.

This changing nature of the organizational world does not diminish the value of other concepts we have considered in this text. People still enter and leave organizations, make decisions, manage conflict, deal with change, balance emotional and rational needs, and organize in the midst of diversity and technological change. And these constitutive processes can still be understood through lenses that include systems, cultural, critical, and feminist perspectives. But knowing about the changes in our organizational landscape helps to highlight areas of increasing importance in the workplace, such as managing diversity in a multicultural organization or understanding the comings and goings of temporary workers. And knowing about the changing nature of organizations provides a new lens for the consideration of organizational communication processes.

KEY CONCEPTS

modern era	global consciousness	service economy
information revolution	disembeddedness	e-commerce
postmodern era	convergence	contingent workers
laissez-faire capitalism	divergence	
time and space compression	organizational identity	

CASE STUDY | ## Charting the Changing Nature of Work

In this final case study, we turn away from looking at fictional (or occasionally factual) organizations for information and inspiration. Instead, as we close our examination of organizational communication, I ask you to look at yourself and others close to you as a way of understanding how the work world—and communication within that world—has changed in recent years and will continue to change in the future.

Throughout this chapter, we have highlighted ways that society has been transformed in recent decades and the implications of those transformations for organizational communication. Our economy is now primarily a service economy. We live in a global village dominated by business conducted in the global marketplace. Many workers are "disposable," moving in and out of organizations, as temporary and contract work become more common. These workers are sometimes (but certainly not always) disposable by choice. At a more macro level, companies merge and acquire with such frequency that the question of "who owns whom" is often difficult to answer, and loyalties toward organizations are not at all straightforward. In short, we live in an organizational world that is far different from the one inhabited by workers one hundred, fifty, or even twenty years ago.

As you conclude this course in organizational communication, then, I would like you to first take a look at those who have worked in organizations for many years. Talk to your parents and grandparents, aunts and uncles, brothers and sisters, or old family friends. Ask these people how the work world has changed in the years they have been employed. Here are some issues you might raise with them:

- Have they worked for one or two organizations throughout their lives or have they changed jobs frequently? What kind of loyalty do they feel to their organizations and occupations?
- Has technology transformed the nature of their work? Do they feel these shifts are for the better or worse?
- Do they feel the impact of globalization in their work? How do other nations and cultures

influence their work lives and the flow of business in their organizations?

- How have economic shifts affected them? Have they ever been laid off or downsized? Have they chosen alternative work arrangements like contract work or temporary work? Have they started their own businesses as a result of economics (or other factors)? And how have all these alternative work arrangements influenced the quality of their work and family lives?

- Are the people you talk to happy with their work lives? Do they enjoy their work? Do they like the amount of time they spend working? If they could go back in time and make different choices about work, what would those choices be?

These questions—and the stories they spur in the people you talk with—will help you understand the changing nature of work in a very personal way. Consider the brief stories of my family as an example. My grandparents labored during the early part of the twentieth century in working-class jobs typical of the time. One grandfather was a printer, and the other was a bookkeeper. They worked to keep food on the table during the Great Depression and the time surrounding it, and they thought little about the intrinsic rewards of work. The question of whether work made them feel happy would seem quite ludicrous to them. My grandmothers both cared at home for their families, although one grandmother was trained as a schoolteacher.

My parents—born in the 1920s—both went to college and worked as journalists. My father worked for a large daily newspaper for more than thirty years and felt a strong connection to the organization and to the union. And the corporation he worked for (with some prodding from the union) reciprocated through steady employment, a pension, and retirement benefits. My mother was a journalist during World War II; in the decade after, she dropped out of the workforce to have her children. She returned to a newspaper job when the youngest was in school and continued to work

for many years. Her career trajectory was typical of working women of her generation.

My parents' children (four girls) have had varied career paths, which are typical of late baby boomer children. One daughter is a college professor; one teaches music in a rural school district; another—originally trained as a computer engineer—returned to school to earn a teaching degree and now teaches fifth grade; and another also returned to school after her children entered elementary school, and after completing her education degree, she is now a third-grade teacher who has gone on for a graduate degree. None of us feel tied to a particular organization as our parents did, although we all enjoy our workplaces and colleagues. All of us define ourselves more in terms of our profession and our family. Indeed, I have recently shifted from a tenured position to one that affords me more flexibility for a variety of academic and nonacademic pursuits. And when I turn the future, I consider the career prospects for my daughter, now a college junior. She'll have a fine education when she has completed her degree, but is still not at all sure of what the future holds for her—perhaps a nonprofit job promoting social justice, perhaps graduate school at some point, undoubtedly a decision to make family a central aspect of her future life. In short, and you can see that the notion of there being a single way to work and communicate in organizations is as outdated as an eight-track tape player.

So, what are the stories of the people you know? And what do you think your own story will be? Will you stay in one career or explore various options throughout your life? Will your job take you to various parts of the globe or will others from worldwide cultures be an important part of your work life at your home base? Will you work in a manufacturing industry, a service industry, an information age industry, or perhaps an industry we have not yet dreamed of? How will you fit family into the mix of your work life? These questions will take many years to explore. Hence, these questions serve as a fitting end to our consideration of organizational communication.

Glossary

Accommodation (Chapter 9) Conflict style that shows low concern for self and high concern for others.

Activism (Chapter 6) The commitment to do more than talk about a problem but rather seek tangible forms of justice that enhance the lives of real people.

Activity Coordination Flow (Chapter 5) The ongoing interaction that is necessary to get work done in an organization.

Affective Model (Chapter 8) Participatory decision-making process that seeks to satisfy employees' higher-order needs in order to increase job satisfaction.

Affirmative Action (Chapter 12) Efforts to remedy discrimination and increase the representation of designated disadvantaged groups, namely, women and ethnic minorities. (Heilman, 1994, p. 126)

Agency (Chapter 5) The possibility that people can act otherwise in a situation.

Americans with Disabilities Act (Chapter 12) Legislation that prohibits discrimination based on disability and requires that organizations make reasonable accommodations for disabled workers.

Anticipatory Socialization (Chapter 7) Socialization process that occurs before an individual actually enters an organization, such as learning about a particular occupation or organization.

Appraisal-Centered Coping (Chapter 11) Changing the way one thinks about a stressful situation.

Assimilation (Chapter 7) The ongoing behavioral and cognitive processes by which individuals join, become integrated into, and exit organizations. (Jablin & Krone, p. 712)

Asynchronous Communication (Chapter 13) Communication between individuals at different points in time.

Avoidance (Chapter 9) Conflict style that shows low concern for self or others.

Bona Fide Groups (Chapter 8) Naturally occurring groups that deal with factors such as shifting membership, permeable group boundaries, and interdependence within an organizational context.

Bounded Emotionality (Chapter 11) Looking at emotional life as a central focus of organizational research and considering the ways in which paying attention to emotion might lead to new ways of understanding the workplace.

Bounded Rationality (Chapter 8) The cognitive (e.g., humans are not always perfectly logical) and practical (e.g., limits in time and resources) limitations that exist when making a decision.

Burnout (Chapter 11) Strain that results from ongoing stressors, such as emotional exhaustion, depersonalization, and decreased personal accomplishment.

Business Case for Diversity (Chapter 12) Recognizing the competitive advantages that can be gained through the insightful management of cultural diversity.

Centralization (Chapter 2) Managerial control over decision making and employee activities.

Channel Expansion Theory (Chapter 13) The ways in which perceptions of technological richness will depend on an individual's personal experience with a specific medium.

Channels of Communication (Chapter 2) Means through which information is communicated, such as face-to-face, writing, telephone, computer, and so on.

Charismatic Authority (Chapter 2) Power based on an individual's personality and ability to attract and interact with followers.

Climate Change (Chapter 1) The upward shift in overall global temperature, rising sea levels, and extreme weather events.

Closed Systems (Chapter 2) To the extent possible, a bureaucracy will shut itself off from influences of the outside environment because environmental interruptions could hamper its smooth functioning.

Cognitive Model (Chapter 8) Participatory decision-making process that seeks to improve the upward and downward flow of information in the organization by including those closest to the work.

Collaboration (Chapter 9) Conflict style that shows high concern for self and others.

Communication Media Repertoires (Chapter 13) Range of technology choices that individuals choose from as they consider how to accomplish individual and joint tasks in organizations.

Communicative Constitution of Organization (CCO) (Chapter 5) The processes through which interactions create, re-create, and change organizations.

Compassionate Communication (Chapter 11) Emotionally communicating in a wide range of human service occupations in ways that involve processes of noticing, connecting, and responding to troubled clients.

Competition (Chapter 9) Conflict style that shows high concern for self and low concern for others.

Compromise (Chapter 9) Conflict style that shows moderate concerns for both self and others.

Concertive Control (Chapter 6) Control in which the locus of power in an organization shifts from management to workers who collaborate to create rules and norms that govern their behavior. (Barker, 1993, p. 413)

Conflict Aftermath (Chapter 9) Conflicts can have both short-term and long-term consequences that can change the nature of the individuals, their relationship, and their functioning within the organization.

Conflict as Gendered Practice (Chapter 9) Recognizing that most traditional conflict models are linked to masculinity (e.g., competition, instrumentality, objectivity) while more feminine models (e.g., community, emotionality, expressiveness) are less valued.

Conflict Frames (Chapter 9) Ways of viewing intractable conflict, including identity, characterization, and management.

Constitutive Model of Communication (Chapter 1) View of communication as a process that produces and reproduces meaning.

Constraint (Chapter 5) The ability of structures to limit our behavior by giving us specific directions about how to act.

Container Metaphor (Chapter 5) Understanding of organizations that highlights the ability of an organizational form to hold and shape the communication within it and influences the nature of processes.

Contingency Theory (Chapter 10) Leadership perspective that emphasizes the match of the leader's style to the characteristics of the situation.

Contingent Workers (Chapter 14) Workers without a permanent and full-time connection to an organization.

Convergence (Chapter 14) The need of organizations to adapt their practices to a global marketplace.

Crisis Phase (Chapter 10) The trigger (e.g., product failure, natural disaster) that threatens an organization's survival or reputation and creates a great deal uncertainty.

Critical Mass (Chapter 13) The amount of adopters communication technologies need before they are widely used.

Cultural Fragmentation (Chapter 4) Multiple manifestations of organizational culture that are difficult to interpret.

Cultural Information (Chapter 7) The norms, behaviors, narratives, truisms, and the like that an individual must understand to function within an organization.

Cultural Knowledge (Chapter 8) Understandings of particular sites and systems that allow organizational actors to act in coordinated ways.

Cultural Performances (Chapter 4) Interactional, contextual, episodic, and improvisational interactions that create and recreate organizational cultures.

Deep Acting (Chapter 11) Evoking realistic emotional displays in the workplace by using techniques such as imagining friendly environments or sympathizing with customers.

Degrees of Separation (Chapter 5) The process through which the original intent of a speaker is embedded in conversation and then distanced from that conversation through its transformation into text.

Demographics (Chapter 1) Statistical descriptions of characteristics of a population, such as age, race, income, educational attainment, and the like.

Depersonalization (Chapter 11) A dimension of burnout in which service workers objectify their clients in order to protect themselves. (Maslach, 1982, p. 4)

Descriptive Approach to Culture (Chapter 4)   A view of organizational culture that identifies culture as the emerging—and sometimes fragmented—values, practices, narratives, and artifacts that make a particular organization what it is.

Detached Concern (Chapter 11)   Attempting to adopt a stance in which concern for clients can be maintained, independent of strong emotional involvement.

Deviation-Amplifying Feedback (Chapter 4)   Information that serves to change system functioning through growth and development.

Deviation-Reducing Feedback (Chapter 4)   Information that serves to keep organizational functioning on a steady course.

Discipline (Chapter 6)   Techniques developed through communicative interaction to reward and punish behavior that conforms with or deviates from the values identified as important by the work group.

discourse and Discourse (Chapter 5)   The distinction between the study of talk and text and social practices (discourse) and general and enduring systems of thought (Discourse).

Discrimination (Chapter 12)   Observable behavior resulting from negative attitudes toward an organization member based on his or her culture group identity. (Cox, 1991, p. 36)

Discursive Leadership (Chapter 10)   Leadership perspective that considers the ways in which leadership is socially constructed through interactions among organizational actors.

Disembeddedness (Chapter 14)   Behavior and interaction are lifted from their local context and restructured across time and space in a globalized world.

Dissent (Chapter 9)   Specific kind of conflict in which an employee has a disagreement with the organization or supervisor and chooses to voice that disagreement.

Distributed Work (Chapter 13)   Work that does not require people who work together to be in the same place.

Distributive Bargaining (Chapter 9)   Strategy in which conflicting parties work to maximize their own gains and minimize their own losses.

Divergence (Chapter 14)   The need of organizations to emphasize the cultural distinctiveness found around the world.

Division of Labor (Chapter 2)   Assigning employees to a limited number of specialized tasks.

Domains of Communication Theory (Chapter 1)   Seven different ways of thinking about how communication works in the world, which include rhetorical, semiotic, phenomenological, cybernetic, sociopsychological, sociocultural, and critical.

Dual Capacity Model (Chapter 13)   Every organizational medium has both data-carrying capacity that is analogous to media richness and symbol-carrying capacity that involves additional meaning an individual might have for a particular medium.

Duality of Structure (Chapter 5)   The process of producing and reproducing the structures that enable and constrain our behavior.

E-commerce (Chapter 14)   Financial transactions via technology.

Elements of Management (Chapter 2)   Five aspects of classical management theory that deal with what managers should do, including planning, organizing, command, coordination, and control.

Emancipation (Chapter 6)   The liberation of people from unnecessarily restrictive traditions, ideologies, assumptions, power relations, identity formations, and so forth that inhibit or distort opportunities for autonomy, clarification of genuine needs and wants, and thus greater and lasting satisfaction. (Alvesson & Willmott, 1992, p. 435)

Emotion at Work (Chapter 11)   Emotions that emerge from relationships in the workplace.

Emotion Rules (Chapter 11)   Guidelines for emotional display in the workplace.

Emotion-Centered Coping (Chapter 11)   Dealing with the negative affective outcomes of burnout.

Emotional Contagion (Chapter 11)   An affective response in which an observer experiences emotions parallel to those of another person.

Emotional Exhaustion (Chapter 11)   Feelings of fatigue, frustration, or being unable to face another day on the job.

Emotional Intelligence (Chapter 11)   Idea that there are some people who are naturally better at understanding and managing the emotional content of workplace relationships and that emotional intelligence is also a skill that can be developed through training.

Emotional Labor (Chapter 11)   Jobs in which workers are expected to display certain feelings in order to satisfy organizational role expectations.

Emotional Support (Chapter 11)   Letting another person know that they are loved and cared for.

Emotional Work (Chapter 11)   When workers feel genuine emotions on the job and express those emotions in interactions.

Empathic Concern (Chapter 11)   An affective response in which an observer empathetically feels concerns for another without having a parallel emotional response.

Employee Involvement (Chapter 3)   Participative processes in the workplace designed to enhance employee commitment and organizational productivity. (Cotton, 1993)

Employment Interview (Chapter 7)   A meeting between an organization's representatives and a potential employee for the purpose asking questions, seeking answers, and engaging in conversation.

Employment Non-Discrimination Act (Chapter 12)   Proposed antidiscrimination laws regarding sexual orientation and gender identity that have been discussed and reintroduced but never passed.

Enactment of Information (Chapter 4)   The process of individuals creating the environment that confronts them through social interaction and sensemaking.

Encounter Stage (Chapter 7)   Socialization process that occurs at the organizational point of entry, when a new employee first encounters life on the job.

Equifinality (Chapter 4)   The idea that a system can reach the same final state from differing initial conditions and by a variety of paths. (Katz & Kahn, 1978, p. 30)

Equivocality (Chapter 4)   The unpredictability inherent in the information environment of an organization.

Exemplification (Chapter 10)   Leadership that instill the ideals of hard work and ethical behavior by exemplifying those ideals in the leader's own behaviors.

Family Metaphor (Chapter 3)   A comparison used to describe a human relations approach that emphasizes that people thrive when needs are fulfilled and opportunities are provided for self-actualization.

Family-Friendly Programs (Chapter 12)   Efforts to achieve balance between work and home, such as flextime, on-site day care, job sharing, family leave policies, and telecommuting.

Felt Conflict (Chapter 9)   When parties in conflict begin to formulate strategies about how to deal with the conflict and consider outcomes that would and would not be acceptable.

Feminism (Chapter 6)   Approach to power that begins with the basic idea that organizations—in their traditional and bureaucratic forms—are inherently patriarchal and seeks to uncover the power relations that reproduce these structures.

Filtering of Social Cues (Chapter 13)   New technologies differ in terms of the cues they make available and filter out in the communication process.

Flaming (Chapter 13)   Hostile communication on the Internet.

Flextime (Chapter 13)   Work that is done at the same place but at different times.

Framing (Chapter 10)   Leadership process of managing meaning in which one or more aspects of the subject at hand are selected or highlighted over other aspects.

Functional Theory of Group Decision Making (Chapter 8)   Model that argues that effective decision making depends on groups attending to critical functions through group communication.

Generational Cohorts (Chapter 1)   Divisions of populations by similarities in birth year and associated similarities in experience.

Glass Ceiling (Chapter 12)   A concept popularized in the 1980s to describe a barrier so subtle that it is transparent, yet so strong that it prevents women and minorities from moving up in the management hierarchy. (Morrison & Von Glinow, 1990)

Global Consciousness (Chapter 14)   Awareness of the cultures of others and of our own attitudes, beliefs, and behaviors.

Globalization (Chapter 1)   The process of our world becoming ever more connected in economic, political, organizational, and personal terms as transportation and telecommunication systems improve.

"Green" Companies (Chapter 1)   Businesses that want to raise their level of environmental responsibility and make decisions with environmental considerations in mind.

Groupthink (Chapter 8)   A mode of thinking that people engage in when they are deeply involved in a cohesive in-group, when the members' striving for unanimity overrides their motivation to realistically appraise alternative courses of action. (Janis, 1982, p. 9)

Hawthorne Effect (Chapter 3) The phenomenon whereby mere attention to individuals causes changes in behavior.

Hawthorne Studies (Chapter 3) Research that attempted to discover aspects of the task environment that would maximize worker output and hence improve organizational efficiency, but which lead to explanations that revolved around the social and emotional needs of workers.

Hegemony (Chapter 6) The process in which a dominant group leads another group to accept subordination as the norm.

Hierarchy of Needs (Chapter 3) Abraham Maslow's idea that proposes that humans are motivated by a number of basic needs, including physiological needs, safety needs, affiliation needs, esteem needs, and self-actualization needs.

Homeland Security (Chapter 1) Communication systems that enhance border security, improve tracking of possible terrorist activities, and develop the ability of first-response organizations to act quickly and appropriately in case of terrorist threats or attacks.

Holism (Chapter 4) System property that suggests that a system is more than the sum of its parts.

Human Relations Approach (Chapter 3) View of organizations that emphasizes the importance of human needs in the workplace.

Human Resources Approach (Chapter 3) View of organizations that acknowledges contributions of classical and, especially, human relations approaches to organizing approach that concentrate on the contributions of all employees in reaching organizational goals.

Ideal Type Theory (Chapter 2) A theory that does not advocate a particular organizational form as best but rather lays out the features of an abstract—or idealized—organization of a given type.

Identification (Chapter 6) The perception of oneness with or belongingness to a collective, where the individual defines him or herself in terms of the collective in which he or she is a member. (Mael & Ashforth, 1992, p. 104)

Ideology (Chapter 6) The taken-for-granted assumptions about reality that influence perceptions of situations and events. (Deetz & Kersten, 1983, p. 162)

Improvisational Knowledge (Chapter 8) Understandings people use when they encounter unusual situations and must move beyond what is encoded in synoptic knowledge.

Individualization (Chapter 7) When an employee changes some aspect of the organization to better suit his or her needs, abilities, or desires.

Information Environment (Chapter 4) The nonphysical environment within an organization that does not exist in an objective manner, but rather is created through everyday organizing processes.

Informational Support (Chapter 11) Providing facts and advice to help an individual cope.

Innovation-Related Communication (Chapter 2) Communication about new ideas in the workplace.

Institutional Positioning Flow (Chapter 5) The processes in which organizations create relationships with other entities in the environment and establish ways that information and other resources can move among relevant organizations.

Instrumental Support (Chapter 11) Providing physical or material assistance that helps an individual cope with stress.

Integrative Bargaining (Chapter 9) Strategy in which conflicting parties try to maximize gains for both parties.

Interdependence (Chapter 4) The need of system components to rely on other components in order to function.

Interorganizational Collaboration (Chapter 8) Collaboration in intergroup settings that emphasizes the dynamic, fuzzy, and multiplex relationships among organizations and organizational actors.

Intuitive Decision Making (Chapter 8) Accessing relevant information and experience in order to make decisions.

Knowledge Management (Chapter 8) Identifying and harnessing intellectual assets to allow organizations to build on past experiences and create new mechanisms for exchanging and creating knowledge. (Heaton, 2008)

Lack of Personal Accomplishment (Chapter 11) When workers see themselves as failures and incapable of effectively accomplishing job requirements.

Laissez-Faire Capitalism (Chapter 14) The assumption that a free-market economic system has sufficient checks and balances in place to ensure that the legitimate interests of all members of a society will be met. (Conrad & Poole, 2004, p. 39)

Latent Conflict (Chapter 9) A situation before manifest conflict in which the conditions are ripe for conflict because interdependence and possible incompatibility exist between the parties.

Leader-Member Exchange Theory (Chapter 7)   The role-development process of role taking, role making, and role routinization that occurs through ongoing interactions with a supervisor or other organizational leaders.

Lean In (Chapter 12)   Advice given to women to do more to develop their career and leadership opportunities.

Learning Organizations (Chapter 3)   Workplaces that emphasize mental flexibility, team learning, a shared vision, complex thinking, and personal mastery.

Levels of Organizational Conflict (Chapter 9)   Areas in which conflict can take place, including interpersonal, intergroup, and interorganizational.

Link Properties (Chapter 4)   Characteristics of network links that include strength, symmetry, and multiplexity.

Luddites (Chapter 13)   Forecasters who are pessimistic about the impacts of technology on organizations.

Machine Metaphor (Chapter 2)   An understanding of organizations that highlights the ways in which organizations are specialized, standardized, and predictable.

Maintenance-Related Communication (Chapter 2)   Communication about social topics that maintains human relationships.

Management Support of Change (Chapter 10)   When senior management is not seen as backing the change effort or when senior management's vision is not effectively shared with others in the organization, it is unlikely that a change effort will be successful.

Managerial/Leadership Grid (Chapter 3)   Robert Blake and Jane Mouton's tool for training managers in leadership styles that would enhance organizational efficiency and effectiveness and stimulate the satisfaction and creativity of individual workers.

Manifest Conflict (Chapter 9)   When parties in conflict enact available strategies and goals in communication during conflict.

Markers of Organizational Culture (Chapter 4)   Rites, ceremonies, values, belief systems, metaphors, stories, and communication rules.

Materiality (Chapter 5)   Physical aspects of the organization including buildings, technology, and bodies.

Media Richness (Chapter 13)   The capability of a technology to convey information based on factors

such the use of multiple cues, the availability of feedback, and the personal focus of the medium.

Media Richness Model (Chapter 13)   Framework for understanding which communication technologies to use for various tasks that requires a determination about the ambiguity of the message and leanness or richness of the medium.

Media Synchronicity Theory (Chapter 13)   The choice of communication media should depend on the extent to which a medium supports a shared pattern of coordinated behavior among coworkers.

Mediation (Chapter 9)   Third-party conflict resolution process in which both parties work together with a mediator to develop a viable solution to the conflict at hand.

Member Negotiation Flow (Chapter 5)   The processes through which people who bring an organization into existence, enter and exit it over time.

Memory, Storage, and Retrieval Features (Chapter 13)   The ability of technology to create records of both important and arcane communication that can be retrieved at any time.

Mentoring Relationships (Chapter 12)   Establishment of mentor-protégé relationships to facilitate personal development for the benefit of the individuals and organizations.

Metamorphosis Stage (Chapter 7)   Socialization process that occurs when the new employee has made the transition from outsider to insider, being accepted by colleagues and learning new behaviors and attitudes or modifying existing ones.

Minority Employee Networks (Chapter 12)   Specific networks in which members of a particular gender or ethnic background meet to create opportunities for advancement and leadership.

Modern Era (Chapter 14)   Consideration of the organizational world brought on by the Industrial Revolution that focused on the logic and rationality of science and technology and the search for effectiveness and efficiency.

Modes and Means of Production (Chapter 6)   Marxist perspective of power that examines the ways in which capitalist owners control the economic conditions that underlie the production process (mode) as well as how products are made and services rendered (means).

Mommy Track (Chapter 12)   Career track for women who want flexible work arrangements and family support in exchange for fewer opportunities for advancement.

Multicultural Organization (Chapter 12)   Moves beyond the concept of support for minority members to the institution of policies that deliberately capitalize on cultural and gender diversity.

Multiple Sequence Model (Chapter 8)   The variety of decision paths taken by groups, including the unitary sequence path, complex cyclic path, and solution-oriented path.

Multiplexity (Chapter 4)   The number of different kinds of content that flow through a particular network link.

Negative Entropy (Chapter 4)   The ability of systems to sustain themselves and grow.

Network Properties (Chapter 4)   Characteristics of a network that include content, mode, and density.

Network Roles (Chapter 4)   The ways in which individuals in a network are connected with each other.

Newcomer Information-Seeking Tactics (Chapter 7)   Actively seeking information that helps new organizational members adapt to their roles and the norms and values of the organizational culture, such as overt questions, indirect questions, third parties, testing limits, disguising conversations, observing, and surveillance.

Normative Model of Decision Making (Chapter 8)   Rational and logical decision-making process in which organization members notice a problem, carefully define it, search for relevant information, develop a set of options, and evaluate them according to carefully developed criteria.

Opt-In (Chapter 12)   Metaphor used to describe when women move back into a career several years after leaving the workplace to have children.

Opt-Out (Chapter 12)   Metaphor used to describe women who leave the workplace to have children.

Optimizing Model (Chapter 8)   Attempting to find the single best solution to an organizational problem.

Organizational Crisis (Chapter 10)   Potentially dangerous or threatening circumstances that also provide opportunity to both address the crisis at hand and reshape perceptions through communication.

Organizational Discourse (Chapter 6)   Communicative interaction that socially constructs organizational realities that can become sites of domination as they create and recreate power structures.

Organizational Exit (Chapter 7)   The process of disengaging from and leaving an organization.

Organizational Identity (Chapter 5)   The image that an organization creates and maintains in order to successfully position itself with other organizations in the larger environment or with the public.

Organizational Identity (Chapter 14)   Knowing an organization, what it sells, and where it stands on relevant issues of the day.

Organizational Life Cycle (Chapter 10)   The natural ways in which organizations and groups of organizations change with the ebb and flow of institutional life and industry history.

Organizational Subcultures (Chapter 4)   Groups within an organization whose inconsistencies among cultural views are expected and often seen as desirable.

Outsourcing (Chapter 1)   The practice of moving manufacturing and service centers to countries where labor is cheap.

Ownership Tension in Change (Chapter 10)   The successful implementation of change efforts is contingent on ownership of the problem and ownership of the change process by those in critical positions in the organization.

Patriarchy (Chapter 6)   Social system in which men serve as primary sources of authority and power.

Perceived Conflict (Chapter 9)   When parties in conflict believe that incompatibilities and interdependence exist.

Permeable Boundaries (Chapter 4)   The ability of system components to allow information and materials to flow in and out.

Phase Models of Decision Making (Chapter 8)   Groups go through a series of phases as they systematically attempt to reach decisions, including orientation, conflict, emergence, and reinforcement.

Pluralist Frame of Reference (Chapter 6)   Political frame used to understand organizations that recognizes many groups with divergent interests and views conflict positively.

Postcrisis Phase (Chapter 10)   Determining responsibility, communicating with a wide range of stakeholders, perhaps apologizing, and establishing systems for coping with similar crises in the future.

Postmodern Era (Chapter 14) Consideration of the organizational world that focuses on how everything moves fast and life is more fragmented and less consistent.

Precrisis Phase (Chapter 10) The processes of signal detection, prevention, and crisis preparation that occur before an actual crisis.

Prejudice (Chapter 12) Negative attitudes toward an organization member based on his or her culture group identity. (Cox, 1991, p. 36)

Prepotency (Chapter 3) Lower-level needs must be satisfied before an individual can move on to higher-level needs.

Prescriptive Approach to Culture (Chapter 4) A view of organizational culture that proposes a single cultural formula for achieving organizational success.

Prescriptive Theory (Chapter 2) A theory that gives specific directions on how an organizational form should best be created and managed.

Principles of Management (Chapter 2) Aspects of classical management theory that deal with power relationships, appropriate rewards, how an organization should be put together, and proper feelings and attitudes of employees.

Problem-Centered Coping (Chapter 11) Dealing directly with the causes of burnout.

Radical-Critical Approach (Chapter 6) Perspective of power that is concerned with the deep structures that produce and reproduce relationships in organizational life and how social and communicative relationships produce and maintain organizational power relationships.

Radical Frame of Reference (Chapter 6) Political frame used to understand organizations that sees the organization as a battleground where competing forces seek to achieve largely incompatible goals.

Rational-Legal Authority (Chapter 2) Power based on the rational application of rules developed through a reliance on information and expertise.

Realistic Job Previews (Chapter 7) A realistic picture of a future job provided by an organization in order to create appropriate expectations and reduce voluntary turnover.

Requisite Variety (Chapters 1 and 4) The need for organizations and groups to be as complicated as the problems that confront them.

Resistance (Chapter 6) The ways in which workers can exert counterpressure on the exercise of power and control.

Resistance to Change (Chapter 10) Behaviors intended to prevent the implementation or use of a system or to prevent system designers from achieving their objectives. (Markus, 1983, p. 433)

Role-Making Phase (Chapter 7) Leader-Member Exchange Theory process that marks an evolution from the supervisor giving the role and the subordinate taking it to the member seeking to modify the nature of the role and the manner in which it is enacted.

Role-Related Information (Chapter 7) The skills, procedures, and rules that an individual must grasp to perform on the job.

Role-Routinization (Chapter 7) Leader-Member Exchange Theory process in which the role of the subordinate and the expected behaviors of the supervisor are well-understood by both parties.

Role-Taking Phase (Chapter 7) Leader-Member Exchange Theory process wherein a superior attempts to discover the relevant talents and motivations of the member through iterative testing sequences. (Graen & Scandura, 1987, p. 180)

Satisficing Model (Chapter 8) Searching for a solution that will work well enough for dealing with a given situation.

Scaling Up Process (Chapter 5) The way in which conversations become textualized and taken up into organizations and institutions, opening up the possibility that texts can have agency apart from the humans who have created them through conversation.

Schemata (Chapter 10) Knowledge structures that define individual and collective beliefs about how organizations work and how change happens.

Self-Structuring Flow (Chapter 5) The processes that serve to design the organization, provide guidance about resource allocation, institute policies and procedures, and create rules about how work is accomplished.

Sensemaking (Chapter 4) The cycles in which organizational members introduce and react to ideas that help to make sense of the equivocal information environment.

Service Economy (Chapter 14) Shift in economic activity to primarily services, including retail, financial, transportation, health care, and construction, among others.

Simple Control (Chapter 6) The direct and authoritarian exertion of control in the workplace.

Social Constructionism (Chapter 5) Theory that suggests reality is not an objective thing but is, instead, an intersubjective construction created through communication.

Social Information Processing Model (Chapter 13) Communication between coworkers, supervisors, customers, and others affects media usage.

Socialization (Chapter 7) The process by which an organization influences the adaptation of individuals as they learn about the requirements of the job, and so on.

Stereotypes (Chapter 12) Viewing a group, such as women and people of color, in biased ways that may result in significantly different treatment within the organization.

Strength (Chapter 4) The ability of network links to endure within a specific exchange or over a long period of time.

Stressors (Chapter 11) Environmental factors that are difficult for individuals to deal with in their workloads, such as role ambiguity and work/life balance.

Structures (Chapter 5) Rules and resources that individuals draw on while they interact in the social world that can also be also be changed during the course of interaction.

Structuration Theory (Chapter 5) Idea that suggests the social world is generated through the agency of active participants.

Style of Communication (Chapter 2) The tone or form of address in a particular communication that can range from highly formal and distant to very informal and familiar.

Style Theories (Chapter 10) Leadership perspective that suggests that leaders have particular behavioral styles that make them more or less effective leaders.

Surface Acting (Chapter 11) Evoking superficial emotional behaviors during workplace interaction to satisfy work requirements.

Symbolic Convergence Theory (Chapter 8) Perspective that considers the role of communication such as stories and jokes in creating a feeling of group identity.

Symmetry (Chapter 4) When two nodes in a network link have the same kind of relationship with each other.

Synoptic Knowledge (Chapter 8) Abstract representations that are encoded in instruction manuals or expert systems.

Systems Metaphor (Chapter 4) Understanding of organizations as complex organisms that must interact with their environment to survive.

Systematic Soldiering (Chapter 2) Social pressure among workers to keep productivity down and wages up.

Task Ambiguity (Chapter 13) The extent to which conflicting and multiple interpretations of an issue exist.

Task-Related Communication (Chapter 2) Communication about specific aspects of a job or work process.

Team Management (Chapter 3) Structuring an organization in ways that maximize the contribution of employees, both individually and collectively.

Technological Control (Chapter 6) Control exerted through technological workplace processes such as assembly lines or computer programs.

Telework (Chapter 13) Work that is accomplished at the same time but with workers in different places.

Terrorism (Chapter 1) A set of strategies (rather than a particular ideology) that involves the use of unpredictable violence against individuals and thus creates ongoing fear and suspicion among large groups of people.

Theory of Bureaucracy (Chapter 2) Max Weber's idea that effective organizations should be operated through a clearly defined hierarchy, characterized by division of labor, and organized under a centralization of decision making and power.

Theory of Classical Management (Chapter 2) Henri Fayol's idea that an effective organization is highly structured and rule-guided, each individual knows where he or she fits, and employees are treated equitably and encouraged to labor strictly for the goals of the organization rather than for their own individual interests.

Theory of Scientific Management (Chapter 2) Frederick Taylor's idea that highlights a clear distinction between managers and employees and focuses on the control of the individual at work.

Theory X (Chapter 3) Assumptions of a manager who is influenced by the most negative aspects of classical management theories.

Theory Y (Chapter 3) Assumptions of a manager who adheres to the precepts of the human relations movement.

Three I's of Conflict (Chapter 9) General characteristics of conflict: incompatible goals, interdependence, and interaction.

Time and Motion Studies (Chapter 2) Research by managers that seeks to find the most time-efficient way for employees to accomplish a specific work task.

Time and Space Compression (Chapter 14)   Space and time are no longer directly connected in a globalized world.

Tokenism (Chapter 12)   Being a highly visible representative of a gender or ethnic minority within an organization who experiences increased pressure because members of the dominant group exaggerate differences according to stereotypes.

Traditional Authority (Chapter 2)   Power based on long-standing beliefs about who should have control that is vested in particular positions within an organizational hierarchy.

Trait Theories (Chapter 10)   Leadership perspective that theorizes that leaders are born with inherent abilities that cannot be learned or developed.

Transformational Leadership Model (Chapter 10)   Leadership perspective that suggests that through communication processes leaders create a relationship with followers that helps followers reach their full potential while transforming both the leader and the follower.

Transmission Model of Communication (Chapter 1)   View of communication as a process of moving information from sources to receivers.

Unitary Frame of Reference (Chapter 6)   Political frame used to understand organizations that emphasizes common organizational goals.

Utopians (Chapter 13)   Forecasters who are hopeful about the positive impacts of technology on organizations.

Ventriloquism (Chapter 5)   The ability of one agent in an organization to speak for other agents through texts.

Vertical Flow of Information (Chapter 2)   Communicating up and (at times) down the organizational hierarchy, particularly in the form of orders, rules, and directives.

Virtual Organization (Chapter 13)   Organization that has no brick-and-mortar presence and whose work is accomplished at different times and different places through the use of multiple information and computer technologies.

War on Terror (Chapter 1)   Military actions and bureaucratic processes that seek to prevent and fight terrorism.

Workplace Alienation and Oppression (Chapter 6)   The estrangement that workers feel when their work becomes repetitive and boring with severe limitations on advancement.

Workplace Bullying (Chapter 11)   Persistent verbal, and nonverbal aggression at work that includes personal attacks, social ostracism, and a multitude of other painful messages and hostile interactions. (SanvikLutgen-Sanvik, 2006)

Workplace Democracy (Chapter 8)   Realizing the standards for a democratic society, free speech, and human dignity in the workplace.

References

20 Important Customer Experience Statistics. (2012, March 26). 20 Important Customer Experience Statistics for 2012. Retrieved on July 3, 2013, from http://fonolo.com/blog/2012/03/customer-experience-statistics-2012/.

A Service Economy. (2007). USA Economy in Brief, International Information Programs. Retrieved on December 8, 2007, from http://usinfo.state.gov/products/pubs/economy-in-brief/page3.html.

Ackman, D. (2005, January 18). Will the Jury Believe Bernie the Believer? Retrieved on December 20, 2007, from http://www.forbes.com.

Adams, J. S. (1980). Interorganizational Processes and Organization Boundary Activities. *Research in Organizational behavior, 2*, 321–355.

Adams, W. L. (2007, February 19). PTSD for Social Workers, the Price of Caring. *Newsweek*, p. 12.

Adler, J. (2007, September 3). Era of the Super Cruncher. *Newsweek*, p. 42.

Advice for Tackling Workplace Jerks. (2007, April 11). *Associated Press*. Retrieved on October 29, 2007, from http://www.msnbc.msn.com/id/17629928.

Albrecht, T. L., Burleson, B. R. & Goldsmith, D. (1995). Supportive Communication. In M. Knapp & G. R. Miller (eds.), *Handbook of Interpersonal Communication* (pp. 419–449). Thousand Oaks, CA: Sage.

Alger, H. (1990; originally published in 1868). *Ragged Dick, Or, Street Life in New York with the Boot-Blacks.* New York: Signet.

Allen, B. J. (1996). Feminist Standpoint Theory: A Black Woman's (Re)View of Organizational Socialization. *Communication Studies, 47*, 257–271.

_____. (2000). "Learning the Ropes": A Black Feminist Critique. In P. Buzzanell (ed.), *Rethinking Organizational and Managerial Communication from Feminist Perspectives* (pp. 177–208). Thousand Oaks, CA: Sage.

Alter, J. (2013). *The Center Holds: Obama and His Enemies.* New York: Simon & Schuster.

Alvesson, M. (1993). *Cultural Perspectives on Organizations.* Cambridge: Cambridge University Press.

Alvesson, M. & Willmott, H. (1992). On the Idea of Emancipation in Management and Organization Studies. *Academy of Management Review, J 7*, 432–464.

Apker, J., Propp, K. M. & Ford, W. S. Z. (2005). Negotiating Status and Identity Tensions in Healthcare Team Interactions: An Exploration of Nurse Role Dialectics. *Journal of Applied Communication Research, 33*, 93–115.

Asangi, S. & Sathe, D. (2007). Choosing an Offshore Call Center. Retrieved on February 19, 2008, from http://www.sourcingmag.com/content/c060619a.asp.

Ashcraft, K. L. (2000). Empowering "Professional" Relationships: Organizational Communication Meets Feminist Practice.

Management Communication Quarterly, 13, 347–392.

_____. (2001). Organized Dissonance: Feminist Bureaucracy As Hybrid Form. *Academy of Management Journal, 44*, 1301–1322.

_____. (2005). Feminist Organizational Communication Studies: Engaging Gender in Public and Private. In S. May & D. K. Mumby (eds.), *Engaging Organizational Communication Theory and Research* (pp. 141–169). Thousand Oaks, CA: Sage.

Ashcraft, K. L. & Allen, B. J. (2003). The Racial Foundation of Organizational Communication. *Communication Theory, 13*, 5–38.

Ashcraft, K. L., Kuhn, T. R. & Cooren, F. (2009). Constitutional Amendments: "Materializing" Organizational Communication. *The Academy of Management Annals, 3*, 1–64.

Ashcraft, K. L. & Mumby, D. K. (2004). *Reworking Gender: A Feminist Communicology of Organization.* Thousand Oaks, CA: Sage.

Ashforth, B. E. & Humphrey, R. H. (1993). Emotional Labor in Service Roles: The Influence of Identity. *Academy of Management Review, 18*, 88–115.

Atouba, Y. & Shumate, M. (2010). Interorganizational Networking Patterns Among Development Organizations. *Journal of Communication, 60*, 293–317.

Awamleh, R. & Gardner, W. L. (1999). Perceptions of Leader Charisma and Effectiveness: The Effects of Vision

Content, Delivery, and Organizational Performance. *Leadership Quarterly, 10*, 343–375.

Ayres, I. (2007). *Super Crunchers: Why Thinking-by-Numbers Is the New Way to Be Smart*. New York: Bantam.

Babbitt, L. V. & Jablin, F. M. (1985). Characteristics of Applicants' Questions and Employment Screening Interview Outcomes. *Human Communication Research, 22*, 507–535.

Baird, S. (2013, March 19). Armstrong Lanced from Livestrong Identity. Retrieved on June 15, 2013, from http://www.duetsblog.com/2013/03/articles/trademarks/armstrong-lanced-from-livestrong-logo/.

Bakker, A. B. & Schaufeli, W. B. (2000). Burnout Contagion Processes Among Teachers. *Journal of Applied Social Psychology, 30*, 2289–2308.

Barge, J. K., Lee, M., Maddux, K., Nabring, R. & Townsend, B. (2008). Managing Dualities in Planned Change Initiatives. *Journal of Applied Communication Research, 36*, 364–390.

Barker, J. R. (1993). Tightening the Iron Cage: Concertive Control in Self-Managing Teams. *Administrative Science Quarterly, 38*, 408–437.

_____. (1999). *The Discipline of Teamwork: Participation and Concertive Control*. Thousand Oaks, CA: Sage.

Barker, J. R. & Cheney, G. (1994). The Concept and the Practices of Discipline in Contemporary Organizational Life. *Communication Monographs, 61*, 19–43.

Barker, J. R., Melville, C. W. & Pacanowsky, M. E. (1993). Self-Directed Teams at XEL: Changes in Communication Practices During a Program of Cultural Transformation. *Journal of Applied Communication Research, 21*, 297–312.

Barley, W. C., Leonardi, P. M. & Bailey, D. E. (2012). Engineering Objects for Collaboration: Strategies of Ambiguity and Clarity at Knowledge Boundaries. *Human Communication Research, 38*, 280–308.

Barling, J., Rogers, K. & Kelloway, E. K. (1995). Some Effects of Teenagers' Part-Time Employment: The Quantity and Quality of Work Make the Difference. *Journal of Organizational Behavior, 16*, 143–154.

Barnard, C. I. (1938). *The Functions of the Executive*. Cambridge, MA: Harvard University Press.

Barron, C. & Barron, A. (2012). *The Creativity Cure*. New York: Scribner.

Bass, B. M. (1985). *Leadership and Performance Beyond Expectations*. New York: Free Press.

Beehr, T. A., Bowling, N. A. & Bennett, M. M. (2010). Occupational Stress and Failures of Social Support: When Helping Hurts. *Journal of Occupational Health Psychology, 15*, 45–59.

Belkin, L. (2010, May 17). Judging Women. *New York Times*. Retrieved on May 19, 2010, from http://www.nytimes.com/2010/05/23/magazine/23FOB-wwln-t.html?r=2.

Bell, E. & Forbes, L. (1994). Office Folklore in the Academic Paperwork Empire: The Interstitial Space of Gendered (Con)Texts. *Text and Performance Quarterly, 38*, 181–196.

Bennett, J., Ellison, J. & Ball, S. (2010, March 29). Are We There Yet? *Newsweek*, pp. 42–46.

Bennett, W. L. & Segerberg, A. (2011). Digital Media and the Personalization of Collective Action: Social Technology and the Organization of Protests Against the Global Economic Crisis. *Information, Communication & Society, 14*, 770–799.

Bennis, W. G. & Nanus, B. (1985). *Leaders: The Strategies for Taking Charge*. New York: Harper & Row.

Benoit, W. L. (1995). *Accounts, Excuses and Apologies*. Albany, NY: SUNY Press.

Berkelaar, B. L., Buzzanell, P. M., Kisselburgh, L. G., Tan W. & Shen, Y. (2012). "First, It's Dirty. Second, It's Dangerous. Third, It's Insulting": Urban Chinese Children Talk about Dirty Work. *Communication Monographs, 79*, 93–114.

Bernard, T. S. (2004, August 29). Examine Your Finances—or Your Head. *The Bryan-College Station Eagle*, p. E5.

Bernstein, R. J. (1976). The Restructuring of Social and Political Theory. Philadelphia: University of Pennsylvania Press.

Beyer, J. & Trice, H. (1987). How an Organization's Rites Reveal Its Culture. *Organizational Dynamics, 15*, 4–35.

Bisel, R. S. (2010). A Communication Ontology of Organization? A Description, History, and Critique of CCO Theories for Organization Science. *Management Communication Quarterly, 24*, 124–131.

Blake, R. & McCanse, A. A. (1991). *Leadership Dilemmas: Grid Solutions*. Houston: Gulf.

Blake, R. & Mouton, J. (1964). *The Managerial Grid*. Houston: Gulf.

Blancero, D. M., DelCampo, R. G. & Marron, G. F. (2010). Just Tell Me! Alternative Dispute Resolution Systems Fair. *Industrial Relations, 49*, 524–543.

Bohnert, D. & Ross, W. H. (2010). The Influence of Social Networking Web Sites of the Evaluation of Job Candidates. *Cyberpsychology, Behavior, and Social Networking, 13*, 341–347.

Boje, D. (1991). The Storytelling Organization: A Study of Story Performance in an Office-Supply Firm. *Administrative Science Quarterly, 36*, 106–126.

Bormann, E. G. (1996). Symbolic Convergence Theory and Communication in Group Decision-Making. In R. Y. Hirokawa & M. S. Poole (eds.), *Communication and Group Decision Making*, 2nd ed. (pp. 81–113). Thousand Oaks, CA: Sage.

Bowes, J. M. & Goodnow, J. J. (1996). Work for Home, School, or Labor Force: The Nature and Sources of Changes in Understanding. *Psychological Bulletin, 119*, 300–321.

Boyce, A. S., Ryan, A. M., Imus, A. L. & Morgeson, F. P. (2007). "Temporary Workers, Permanent Loser?"

A Model of the Stigmatization of Temporary Workers. *Journal of Management, 33,* 5–29.

Braverman, H. (1974). *Labor and Monopoly Capital: The Degradation of Work in the Twentieth Century.* New York: Monthly Review Press.

Bremmer, I. (2012, June 18). The Good, the Bad and the Global Economy. *Reuters.* Retrieved on June 3, 2013, from http://blogs.reuters.com/ian-bremmer/2012/06/18/the-good-the-bad-and-the-global-economy/.

Brett, J. M. & Okumura, T. (1998). Inter- and Intracultural Negotiation: U.S. and Japanese Negotiators. *Academy of Management Journal, 41,* 495–510.

Brief, A. P. (1998). *Attitudes in and Around Organizations.* Thousand Oaks, CA: Sage.

Bristol, T. L. & Tisdell, E. J. (2010). Leveraging Diversity Through Career Development: Social and Cultural Capital Among African-American Managers. *International Journal of Human Resources Development and Management, 10,* 224–238.

Brown, G. S. (2013, April 8). Airline Industry Has "Declined in Overall Performance Quality." *ABC News.* Retrieved on July 3, 2013, from http://abcnews.go.com/Travel/airline-report-names-best-worst-2012/story?id=18904919.

Brown, V. R. & Vaughn, E. D. (2011). The Writing on the (Facebook) Wall: The Use of Social Networking Sites in Hiring Decisions. *Journal of Business Psychology, 26,* 219–225.

Bryant, A. (2001, April 23). Why Flying Is Hell. *Newsweek,* pp. 34–47.

Bryant, A. (2013, June 19). In Head-Hunting, Big Data May Not Be Such a Big Deal. *New York Times.* Retrieved on June 20, 2013, from http://www.nytimes.com/2013/06/20/business/in-head-hunting-big-data-may-not-be-such-a-big-deal.html?pagewanted=all.

Budd, J. W., Gollan, P. J. & Wilkinson, A. (2010). New Approaches to Employee voice and Participation in Organizations. *Human Relations, 63,* 303–310.

Bullis, C. (1993). Organizational Values and Control. In C. Conrad (ed.), *Ethical Nexus* (pp. 75–102). Norwood, NJ: Ablex.

Bullis, C. & Bach, B. W. (1989). Socialization Turning Points: An Examination of Change in Organizational Identification. *Western Journal of Speech Communication, 53,* 273–293.

Burke, K. (1966). *Language as Symbolic Action.* Berkeley: University of California Press.

Burns, C., Barton, K. & Kerby, S. (2012, July 12). The State of Diversity in Today's Workforce. Retrieved on June 28, 2013, from http://www.americanprogress.org/issues/labor/report/2012/07/12/11938/the-state-of-diversity-in-todays-workforce/.

Burrell, G. & Morgan, G. (1979). *Sociological Paradigms and Organizational Analysis.* London: Heinemann.

Burrell, N. A., Buzzanell, P. M. & McMillan, J. J. (1992). Feminine Tensions in Conflict Situations as Revealed by Metaphoric Analyses. *Management Communication Quarterly, 6,* 115–149.

Butts, M. M., Vandenberg, R. J., Dejoy, D. M., Schaffer, B. S. & Wilson, M. G. (2009). Individual Reactions to High Involvement Work Practices: Investigating the Role of Empowerment and Perceived Organizational Support. *Journal of Occupational Health Psychology, 14,* 122–136.

Buzzanell, P. M. (1994). Gaining a Voice: Feminist Organizational Communication Theorizing. *Management Communication Quarterly, 7,* 339–383.

Buzzanell, P. M. & Liu, M. (2005). Struggling with Maternity Leave Policies and Practices: A Poststructuralist and Feminist Analysis of Gendered Organizing. *Journal of Applied Communication Research, 33,* 1–25.

Buzzanell, P. M. & Turner, L. H. (2003). Emotion Work Revealed by Job Loss Discourse: Backgrounding-Foregrounding of Feelings, Construction of Normalcy, and (Re) Instituting of Traditional Masculinities. *Journal of Applied Communication Research, 31,* 27–57.

Campion, M. A., Palmer, D. K. & Campion, J. E. (1997). A Review of Structure in the Selection Interview. *Personnel Psychology, 50,* 655–702.

Canary, H. E. & McPhee, R. D. (2010). Introduction: Toward a Communicative Perspective on Organizational Knowledge. In H. E. Canary & R. D. McPhee (Eds.), *Communication and Organizational Knowledge: Contemporary Issues for Theory and Practice* (pp. 1–14). New York: Routledge.

Carey, A. (1967). The Hawthorne Studies: A Radical Criticism. *American Sociological Review, 32,* 403–416.

Carlson, J. R. & Zmud, R. W. (1999). Channel Expansion Theory and the Experimental Nature of Media Richness Perceptions. *Academy of Management Journal, 42,* 153–170.

Carroll, C. (2007, January 29). Why Different Is Better. *Newsweek,* p. E4.

Casey, C. (1999). "Come Join Our Family": Discipline and Integration in Corporate Organizational Culture. *Human Relations, 52,* 155–178.

Cawthorne, A. (2009, April 15). Weathering the Storm: Black Men in the Recession. Retrieved on August 4, 2010, from http://www.americanprogress.org/issues/2009/04/black_men_recession.html.

Cazares, L. (2007). Study Reveals Skin Color Influences Wages. Retrieved on November 24, 2007, from http://media.www.californiaaggie.com/media/storage/paper981/news/2007/02/02/CityNews/Study.REV-2693981-shtml.

Chaput, M., Brummans, B. H. J. M. & Cooren, F. (2011). The Role of Organizational Identification in the Communicative Constitution of an Organization: A Study of Consubstantialization in a Young

Political Party. *Management Communication Quarterly, 25,* 252–282.

Chatman, J. A., Polzer, J. T., Barsade, S. G. & Neale, M. A. (1998). Being Different Yet Feeling Similar: The Influence of Demographic Composition and Organizational Culture on Work Processes and Outcomes. *Administrative Science Quarterly, 43,* 749–780.

Cheney, G. (1995). Democracy in the Workplace: Theory and Practice from the Perspective of Communication. *Journal of Applied Communication Research, 23,* 167–200.

Cheney, G. & Christensen, L. T. (2001). Organizational Identity: Linkages Between Internal and External Communication. In F. M. Jablin & L. L. Putnam (eds.), *The New Handbook of Organizational Communication: Advances in Theory, Research, and Methods* (pp. 231–269). Thousand Oaks, CA: Sage.

Cheney, G. & Frenette, G. (1993). Persuasion and Organization: Values, Logics, and Accounts in Contemporary Corporate Public Discourse. In C. Conrad (ed.), *The Ethical Nexus* (pp. 49–73). Norwood, NJ: Ablex.

Chewing, L. V., Lai, C.-H. & Doerfel, M. L. (2012). Organizational Resilience and Using Information and Communication Technologies to Rebuild Communication Structures. *Management Communication Quarterly, 27,* 237–263.

Chiles, A. M. & Zorn, T. E. (1995). Empowerment in Organizations: Employees' Perceptions of the Influences on Empowerment. *Journal of Applied Communication Research, 23,* 1–25.

Choi, T. Y. & Behling, O. C. (1997). Top Managers and TQM Success: One More Look After All These Years. *Academy of Management Executive, 11*(1), 37–47.

Cissna, K. (1984). Phases in Group Development: The Negative Evidence. *Small Group Behavior, 14,* 3–32.

Clair, J. A., Beatty, J. E. & MacLean, T. L. (2005). Out of Sight But Not Out of Mind: Managing Invisible Identities in the Workplace. *Academy of Management Review, 30,* 78–95.

Clair, R. P. (1993a). The Bureaucratization, Commodification, and Privatization of Sexual Harassment Through Institutional Discourse: A Study of the "Big Ten" Universities. *Management Communication Quarterly, 7,* 123–157.

_____. (1993b). The Use of Framing Devices to Sequester Organizational Narratives: Hegemony and Harassment. *Communication Monographs, 60,* 113–136.

_____. (1996). The Political Nature of the Colloquialism, "A Real Job": Implications for Organizational Socialization. *Communication Monographs, 63,* 249–267.

Clampitt, P. G., DeKoch, R. J. & Cashman, T. (2000). A Strategy for Communicating About Uncertainty. *Academy of Management Executive, 14*(4), 41–57.

Clegg, S. R. (1990). *Modern Organizations.* Newbury Park, CA: Sage.

Clegg, S. R. & Dunkerley, D. (1980). *Organization, Class and Control.* London: Routledge & Kegan Paul.

"Climate Change." (2007). Environmental Protection Agency. Retrieved on September 17, 2007, from http://epa.gov/climatechange/basicinfo.html.

"Climate Change." (2013). Environmental Protection Agency. Retrieved on June 5, 2013, from http://www.epa.gov/climatechange/basics/.

Cloud, D. S. (2013, June 5). Military Is on the Spot over Sexual Assaults. *Los Angeles Times.* Retrieved on June 6, 2013, from http://articles.latimes.com/2013/jun/05/nation/la-na-rape-military-20130605.

Clutterbuck, D. & Ragins, B. R. (2002). *Mentoring and Diversity: An International Perspective.* Woburn, MA: Butterworth-Heinemann.

Coch, L. & French, J. R. P. (1948). Overcoming Resistance to Change. *Human Relations, 1,* 512–532.

Cohn, D. (2011, April 22). *Census 2010: Household Size Trends.* Retrieved on June 5, 2013, from http://www.pewresearch.org/2011/04/22/census-2010-household-size-trends/.

Coleman, J. (2013, April 5). Handwritten Notes Are a Rare Commodity. They're Also More Important Than Ever. *Harvard Business Review.* Retrieved on June 1, 2013, from http://blogs.hbr.org/cs/2013/04/handwritten_notes_are_a_rare_c.html.

Collins, D. (1997). The Ethical Superiority and Inevitability of Participatory Management as an Organizational System. *Organization Science, 8,* 489–507.

Collins, P. H. (1990). *Black Feminist Thought: Knowledge, Consciousness, and the Politics of Empowerment.* Boston: Unwin Hyman.

Columbia. (2003, August 26). Spouse: Report a Prescription for Change. *CNN.com.* Retrieved on October 11, 2007.

Comer, D. R. (1991). Organizational Newcomers' Acquisition of Information from Peers. *Management Communication Quarterly, 5,* 64–89.

Conant, E. (2007, May 28). Trying to Opt Back In. *Newsweek,* p. 42.

_____. (2013, February 25). *Carnival from Hell.* Retrieved on June 27, 2013, from http://www.thedailybeast.com/newsweek/2013/02/25/triumph-passenger-s-carnival-cruise-from-hell.html.

Concerns Raised That Changes in NASA Won't Last. (2003, August 26). *CNN.com.* Retrieved on October 11, 2007.

Conley, D. (2009a). *Elsewhere U.S.A.* NY: Pantheon Books.

_____. (2009b, January 26). Welcome to Elsewhere. *Newsweek,* pp. 59–60.

Connolly, B. (2012, January 30). How to Get Your Resume Past Computer Screening Tactics. Retrieved on

June 23, 2013, from http://wallstreet jobreport.com/how-to-get-your-resume-past-computer-screening-tactics/.

Conrad, C. (1985). *Strategic Organizational Communication.* New York: Holt, Rinehart & Winston.

Conrad, C. & Poole, M. S. (1997). Introduction: Communication and the Disposable Worker. *Communication Research, 24,* 581–592.

_____. (2005). *Strategic Organizational Communication in a Global Economy,* 6th ed., Belmont, CA: Wadsworth.

Conrad, C. & Ryan, M. (1985). Power, Praxis, and Self in Organizational Communication Theory. In R. D. McPhee & P. K. Tompkins (eds.), *Organizational Communication: Traditional Themes and New Directions* (pp. 235–257). Beverly Hills, CA: Sage.

Contractor, N. S., Seibold, D. R. & Heller, M. A. (1996). Interactional Influence in the Structuring of Media Use in Groups: Influence of Members' Perceptions of Group Decision Support System Use. *Human Communication Research, 22,* 451–481.

Coombs, W. T. (2012). *Ongoing Crisis Communication: Planning, Managing and Responding* (3rd ed.). Thousand Oaks, CA: Sage.

Cooper, K. R. & Shumate, M. (2012). Interorganizational Collaboration Exposed Through the Bona Fide Network Perspective. *Management Communication Quarterly, 26,* 623–654.

Cooper, M. H. (1996). Background: A History of U.S. Intelligence Gathering. *The CQ Researcher, 6*(5), 108–109.

Cordes, C. L. & Dougherty, T. W. (1993). A Review and Integration of Research on Job Burnout. *Academy of Management Review, 18,* 621–656.

Corman, S. R. (Ed.) (2013). *Narrating the Exit from Afghanistan.* Tempe, AZ: Center for Strategic Communication.

Corman, S. R., Trethewey, A. & Goodall, Jr., H. L. (eds.) (2008). *Weapons of Mass Persuasion: Strategic Communication to Combat Violent Extremism.* New York: Peter Lang.

Cote, S. (1999). Affect and Performance in Organizational Settings. *Current Directions in Psychological Science, 8,* 65–68.

Cotton, J. L. (1993). *Employee Involvement: Methods for Improving Performance and Work Attitudes.* Newbury Park, CA: Sage.

Covert, B. (2013, January 16). The U.S. Gets Left Behind When It Comes to Working Women. *Forbes.* Retrieved on June 28, 2013, from http://www.forbes.com/sites/brycecovert/2013/01/16/the-u-s-gets-left-behind-when-it-comes-to-working-women/.

Covin, T. J. & Kilmann, R. H. (1990). Participant Perceptions of Positive and Negative Influences on Large-Scale Change. *Group and Organizational Studies, 15,* 233–248.

Cowan, R. L. (2012). It's Complicated: Defining Workplace Bullying from the Human Resource Professional's Perspective. *Management Communication Quarterly, 26,* 377–403.

Cox, S. A. (1999). Group Communication and Employee Turnover: How Coworkers Encourage Peers to Voluntarily Exit. *Southern Communication Journal, 64,* 181–192.

Cox, T. H. (1991). The Multicultural Organization. *Academy of Management Executive, 5*(2), 34–47.

Cox, T. H. & Blake, S. (1991). Managing Cultural Diversity: Implications for Organizational Effectiveness. *Academy of Management Executive, 5*(3), 45–56.

Coy, P., Conlin, M. & Herbst, M. (2010, January 7). The Disposable Worker. *Bloomsburg BusinessWeek.* Retrieved on August 24, 2010, from http://www.businessweek.com/magazine/content/10_03/b4163032935448.htm.

Craig, R. T. (1999). Communication Theory as a Field. *Communication Theory, 9,* 119–161.

Cross, K. (2000). @ Your Service. *Business 2.0, 5,* 427–428.

CTA Rolling Out LGBT Sensitivity Training. (2013, January 22). *Chicago Phoenix.* Retrieved on June 28, 2013, from http://chicagophoenix.com/2013/01/22/cta-rolling-out-lgbt-sensitivity-training/.

Daft, R. L. & Lengel, R. H. (1984). Information Richness: A New Approach to Managerial Information Processing and Organizational Design. In B. Staw & L. L. Cummings (eds.), *Research in Organizational Behavior, Vol. 6* (pp. 191–233). Greenwich, CT: JAI Press.

_____. (1986). Organizational Information Requirements, Media Richness and Structural Design. *Management Science, 32,* 554–571.

Daft, R. L., Lengel, R. H. & Trevino, L. K. (1987). Message Equivocality and Media Selection: Implications for Information Systems. *MIS Quarterly, 11,* 355–366.

Dallimore, E. J. (2003). Memorable Messages as Discursive Formations: The Gendered Socialization of New University Faculty. *Women's Studies in Communication, 26,* 214–265.

Dandridge, T. (1986). Ceremony as an Integration of Work and Play. *Organization Studies, 7,* 159–170.

Daniels, T. D., Spiker, B. K. & Papa, M. J. (1997). *Perspectives on Organizational Communication,* 4th ed., Dubuque, LA: Brown & Benchmark.

Davidson, A. (2013, May 29). C.E.O.'s Don't Need to Earn Less. They Need to Sweat More. *New York Times.* Retrieved on June 6, 2013, from http://www.nytimes.com/2013/06/02/magazine/ceos-dont-need-to-earn-less-they-need-to-sweat-more.html?pagewanted=all.

Davis, G. F. (2010). Job Design Meets Organizational Sociology. *Journal of Organizational Behavior, 31,* 302–308.

Day, A., Paquet, S., Scott, N. & Hambley, L. (2012). Perceived Information and Communication Technology (ICT) Demands on Employee Outcomes: The Moderating Effect of ICT Support. *Journal of Occupational Health Psychology, 17*, 473–491.

Deal, T. & Kennedy, A. (1982). *Corporate Cultures: The Rites and Rituals of Corporate Life*. Reading, MA: Addison-Wesley.

DeBell, C. S., Montgomery, M. J., McCarthy, P. R. & Lanthier, R. P. (1998). The Critical Contact: A Study of Recruiter Verbal Behavior During Campus Interviews. *Journal of Business Communication, 35*, 202–223.

D'Enbeau, S. & Buzzanell, P. M. (2011). Selling (Out) Feminism: Sustainability of Ideology-Viability Tensions in a Competitive Marketplace. *Communication Monographs, 78*, 27–52.

Deetz, S. (1992). *Democracy in an Age of Corporate Colonization*. Albany: State University of New York Press.

_____. (1995). *Transforming Communication, Transforming Business*. Albany: State University of New York Press.

_____. (2005). Critical Theory. In S. May & D. K. Mumby (eds.), *Engaging Organizational Communication Theory and Research* (pp. 85–111). Thousand Oaks, CA: Sage.

Deetz, S. & Kersten, S. (1983). Critical Models of Interpretive Research. In L. Putnam & M. Pacanowsky (eds.), *Communication and Organizations* (pp. 147–171). Beverly Hills, CA: Sage.

Deetz, S. & Mumby, D. K. (1990). Power, Discourse, and the Workplace: Reclaiming the Critical Tradition. In J. Anderson (ed.), *Communication Yearbook 13* (pp. 18–47). Newbury Park, CA: Sage.

Dennis, A. R., Fuller, R. M. & Valacich, J. S. (2008). Media, Tasks, and Communication Processes: A Theory of Media Synchronicity. *MIS Quarterly, 32*, 575–600.

Dewulf, A., Gray, B., Putnam, L., Lewicki, R., Aarts, N., Bouwen, R. & van Woerkum, C. (2009). Disentangling Approaches to Framing in Conflict and Negotiation Research: A Meta-Paradigmatic Perspective. *Human Relations, 62*, 155–193.

Dienesch, R. M. & Liden, R. C. (1986). Leader-Member Exchange Model of Leadership: A Critique and Further Development. *Academy of Management Review, 11*, 618–634.

DiTomaso, N. (2013, May 5). How Social Networks Drive Black Unemployment. *New York Times*. Retrieved on June 1, 2013, from http://opinionator.blogs.nytimes.com/2013/05/05/how-social-networks-drive-black-unemployment/.

DiTomaso, N., Post, C. & Parks-Yancy, R. (2007). Workforce Diversity and Inequality: Power, Status, and Numbers. *Annual Review of Sociology, 33*, 473–501.

Doerfel, M. L. & Taylor, M. (2004). Network Dynamics of Interorganizational Cooperation: The Creation Civil Society Movement. *Communication Monographs, 71*, 371–394.

Dougherty, D. S. (1999). Dialogue Through Standpoint: Understanding Women's and Men's Standpoints of Sexual Harassment. *Management Communication Quarterly, 12*, 436–468.

_____. (2001). Sexual Harassment as [Dys] Functional Process: A Feminist Standpoint Analysis. *Journal of Applied Communication Research, 29*, 372–402.

Dougherty, D. S. & Krone, K. J. (2002). Emotional Intelligence as Organizational Communication: An Examination of the Construct. In William B. Gudykunst (ed.), *Communication Yearbook 26* (pp. 202–229). Mahwah, NJ: Lawrence Erlbaum Associates.

Downing, J. R. (2007). No Greater Sacrifice: American Airlines Employee Crisis Response to the September 11 Attack. *Journal of Applied Communication Research, 35*, 350–375.

Doyle, K. (1992). Who's Killing Total Quality? *Incentive, 16*, 12–19.

Drash, W. (2013, February 17). On Crippled Cruise Ship, Icky Jobs Fell to "Amazing Crew." *CNN*. Retrieved on June 1, 2013, from http://www.cnn.com/2013/02/15/travel/triumph-cruise-crew.

"Drowning in Data?" (2013, February). Drowning in Data? The Solution is Simple: Use More Technology. *The Guardian*. Retrieved on July 1, 2013, from http://www.guardian.co.uk/technology/blog/2013/feb/02/data-technology-solution-consumer.

Ducheneaut, N. B. (2002). The Social Impacts of Electronic Mail in Organizations: A Case Study of Electronic Power Games Using Communication Genres. *Information Communication & Society, 5*, 153–188.

Duhigg, C. & Barboza, D. (2012, January 25). In China, Human Costs are Built Into an iPad. *New York Times*. Retrieved on July 3, 2013, from http://www.nytimes.com/2012/01/26/business/ieconomy-apples-ipad-and-the-human-costs-for-workers-in-china.html?pagewanted=all.

Duke, P. (2004, February 2). If ER Nurses Crash, Will Patients Follow? *Newsweek*, p. 12.

Dulebohn, J. H., Bommer, W. H., Liden, R. C., Brouer, R. L. & Ferris, G. R. (2012). A Meta-Analysis of Antecedents and Consequences of Leader-Member Exchange: Integrating the Past With an Eye Toward the Future. *Journal of Management, 38*, 1715–1759.

D'Urso, S. C. (2006). Who's Watching Us at Work? Toward a Structural-Perceptual Model of Electronic Monitoring and Surveillance in Organizations. *Communication Theory, 16*, 281–303.

D'Urso, S. C. & Rains, S. A. (2008). Examining the Scope of Channel Expansion: A Test of Channel Expansion Theory with New and Traditional Communication Media.

Management Communication Quarterly, 21, 486–507.

Edersheim, E. H. (2010, June 8). The BP Culture's Role in the Gulf Oil Crisis. *The Conversation – Harvard Business Review*. Retrieved on June 26, 2010, from http://blogs.hbr.org/cs/2010/06/the_bp_cultures_role_in_the_gu.html.

Edley, P. P. (2000). Discursive Essentializing in a Woman-Owned Business: Gender Stereotypes and Strategic Subordination. *Management Communication Quarterly, 14*, 271–306.

Edwards, R. C. (1981). The Social Relations of Production at the Point of Production. In M. Zey-Ferrell & M. Aiken (eds.), *Complex Organizations: Critical Perspectives* (pp. 156–182). Glenview, IL: Scott, Foresman.

Eisenberg, E. M. (1984). Ambiguity as Strategy in Organizational Communication. *Communication Monographs, 51*, 227–242.

Eisenberg, E. M., Farace, R. V., Monge, P. R., Bettinghaus, E. P., Kurchner-Hawkins, R., Miller, K. I. & Rothman, L. (1985). Communication Linkages in Interorganizational Systems: Review and Synthesis. In B. Dervin & M. Voigt (eds.), *Progress in Communication Sciences, Vol. 6* (pp. 231–258). Norwood, NJ: Ablex.

Eisenberg, E. M., Murphy, A. & Andrews, L. (1998). Openness and Decision Making in the Search for a University Provost. *Communication Monographs, 65*, 1–23.

Eisenberg, E. M. & Riley, P. (2001). Organizational Culture. In F. M. Jablin & L. L. Putnam (eds.), *The New Handbook of Organizational Communication: Advances in Theory, Research, and Methods* (pp. 291–322). Thousand Oaks, CA: Sage.

Elangovan, A. R. (1995). Managing Third-Party Dispute Intervention: A Prescriptive Model of Strategy Selection. *Academy of Management Review, 20*, 800–830.

Elison, N. B., Lampe, C. & Steinfield, C. (2009, January/February). Social Network Sites and Society: Current Trends and Future Possibilities. *Interactions*, 6–9.

Ellingson, L. L. (2003). Interdisciplinary Health Care Teamwork in the Clinic Backstage. *Journal of Applied Communication Research, 31*, 93–117.

Ellis, B. H. & Miller, K. I. (1993). The Role of Assertiveness, Personal Control, and Participation in the Prediction of Nurse Burnout. *Journal of Applied Communication Research, 21*, 327–342.

Email Statistics. (2012, April). Email Statistics Report, 2012–2016. *The Radicati Group*. Retrieved on July 4, 2013, from http://www.radicati.com/wp/wp-content/uploads/2012/04/Email-Statistics-Report-2012-2016-Executive-Summary.pdf.

Employee Benefits in the United States. (2010). Retrieved on August 29, 2010, from http://www.bls.gov/news.release/ebs2.nr0.htm.

Employment Trends. (2013). Employment Trends: Contingent Workforce. Retrieved on July 2, 2013, from http://www.bowenworks.ca/blog/2013/04/10/employment-trends-contingent-workforce/.

English-Lueck, J. A., Darrah, C. N. & Saveri, A. (2002). Trusting Strangers: Worker Relationships in Four High-Tech Communities. *Information Communication & Society, 5*, 90–108.

Enright, A. (2013, April 25). U.S. E-Commerce Sales Could Top $434 Billion in 2017. Retrieved on July 3, 2013, from http://www.internetretailer.com/2013/04/25/us-e-commerce-sales-could-top-434-billion-2017.

Erickson, T. (2012, September 7). The Rise of the New Contract Worker. *Harvard Business Review*. Retrieved on June 1, 2013, from http://blogs.hbr.org/erickson/2012/09/the_rise_of_the_new_contract_worker.html.

Everbach, T. (2007). The Culture of a Women-Led Newspaper: An Ethnographic Study of the *Sarasota Herald-Tribune*. *Journalism and Mass Communication Quarterly, 83*, 477–493.

Fackler, M. (2013, February 13). In High-Tech Japan, the Fax Machines Roll On. *New York Times*. Retrieved on June 1, 2013, from http://www.nytimes.com/2013/02/14/world/asia/in-japan-the-fax-machine-is-anything-but-a-relic.html?_r=0.

Fairhurst, G. T. (1993). Echoes of the Vision: When the Rest of the Organization Talks Total Quality. *Management Communication Quarterly, 6*, 331–371.

Fairhurst, G. T. (2007). *Discursive Leadership: In Conversation with Leadership Psychology*. Thousand Oaks, CA: Sage.

_____. (2008). Discursive Leadership: A Communication Alternative to Leadership Psychology. *Management Communication Quarterly, 21*, 510–521.

Fairhurst, G. T. & Chandler, T. A. (1989). Social Structure in Leader-Member Exchange. *Communication Monographs, 56*, 215–239.

Fairhurst, G. T. & Grant, D. (2010). The Social Construction of Leadership: A Sailing Guide. *Management Communication Quarterly, 24*, 171–210.

Fairhurst, G. T. & Putnam, L. (2004). Organizations as Discursive Constructions. *Communication Theory, 14*, 5–26.

Fairhurst, G. T. & Sarr, R. A. (1996). *The Art of Framing: Managing the Language of Leadership*. San Francisco: Jossey-Bass.

Fairhurst, G. T. & Wendt, R. F. (1993). The Gap in Total Quality: A Commentary. *Management Communication Quarterly, 6*, 441–451.

Farace, R. V., Monge, P. R. & Russell, H. M. (1977). *Communicating and Organizing*. Reading, MA: Addison-Wesley.

Faraj, S., Jarvenpaa, S. L. & Majchrzak, A. (2011). Knowledge Collaboration in Online Communities. *Organization Science, 22*, 1224–1239.

Fay, M. J. & Kline, S. L. (2011). Coworker Relationships and Informal Communication in High-Intensity Telecommuting. *Journal of Applied Communication Research, 39*, 144–163.

Fayol, H. (1949). *General and Industrial Management*, C. Storrs, trans. London: Pitman.

Fediuk, T. A., Coombs, W. T. & Botero, I. C. (2010). Exploring Crisis from a Receiver Perspective: Understanding Stakeholder Reactions During Crisis Events. In W. T. Coombs & S. J. Holladay (eds.), *The Handbook of Crisis Communication* (pp. 635–656). Malden, MA: Wiley-Blackwell.

Feeley, T. H. (2000). Testing a Communication Network Model of Employee Turnover Based on Centrality. *Journal of Applied Communication Research, 28*, 262–277.

Fein, M. (1974). Job Enrichment: A Reevaluation. *Sloan Management Review*, 69–88.

Feldman, D. C. & Klaas, B. S. (2002). Internet Job Hunting: A Field Study of Applicant Experiences with On-Line Recruiting. *Human Resource Management, 41*, 175–192.

Ferguson, K. E. (1984). *The Feminist Case Against Bureaucracy*. Philadelphia: Temple University Press.

Fiedler, F. E. & Garcia, J. E. (1987). *New Approaches to Effective Leadership: Cognitive Resources and Organizational Performance*. New York: Wiley.

Finder, A. (2006, June 11). For Some, Online Persona Undermines a Resume. *New York Times*. Retrieved on July 15, 2010, from http://www.nytimes.com/2006/06/11/us/11recruit.html?_r=1&ex=1165467600&en=6eac971bleeb8246&ei=5070.

Fineman, S. (2000). Commodifying the Emotionally Intelligent. In S. Fineman (ed.), *Emotion in Organizations,* 2nd ed., London: Sage.

Fisher, B. A. (1970). Decision Emergence: Phases in Group Decision-Making. *Communication Monographs, 37*, 53–66.

Fisher, K. & Duncan, M. D. (1998). *The Distributed Mind: Achieving High Performance Through the Collective Intelligence of Knowledge Work Teams*. New York: AMACOM.

Flanagin, A. J. (2000). Social Pressures on Organizational Website Adoption. *Human Communication Research, 26*, 618–646.

Flynn, G. (1996). No Spouse, No Kids, No Respect: Backlash. Why Single Employees Are Angry. *Personnel Journal*, 59–69.

Folkman, S., Lazarus, R. S., Gruen, R. J. & DeLongis, A. (1986). Appraisal, Coping, Health Status, and Psychological Symptoms. *Journal of Personality and Social Psychology, 50*, 571–579.

Fonner, K. L. & Roloff, M. E. (2012). Testing the Connectivity Paradox: Linking Teleworkers' Communication Media Use to Social Presence, Stress from Interruptions, and Organizational Identification. *Communication Monographs, 79*, 205–231.

Ford, W. S. Z. (1995). Evaluation of the Indirect Influence of Courteous Service on Customer Discretionary Behavior. *Human Communication Research, 22*, 65–89.

_____. (2003). Communication Practices of Professional Service Providers: Predicting Customer Satisfaction and Loyalty. *Journal of Applied Communication Research, 31*, 189–211.

Ford, W. S. Z. & Etienne, C. N. (1994). Can I Help You? A Framework for the Interdisciplinary Research on Customer Service Encounters. *Management Communication Quarterly, 7*, 413–441.

Foroohar, R. (2006, September 18). Are They Worthy? *Newsweek*. Retrieved on September 25, 2007, from http://www.msnbc.msn.com/id/14752519/site/newsweek.

Forrester, R. (2000). Empowerment: Rejuvenating a Potent Idea. *Academy of Management Executive, 14*(3), 67–80.

Forrester, R. & Drexler, A. B. (1999). A Model for Team-Based Organization Performance. *Academy of Management Executive, 13*(3), 36–49.

Foucault, M. (1976). *Discipline and Punish*, A. Sheridan, trans. New York: Vintage.

Franke, R. H. & Kaul, J. (1978). The Hawthorne Experiments: First Statistical Interpretation. *American Sociological Review, 43*, 623–643.

Frauenheim, E. (2012, August 3). Contingent Workers: Why Companies Must Make Them Feel Values. Retrieved on July 2, 2013, from http://www.workforce.com/article/20120803/NEWS02/120809979/contingent-workers-why-companies-must-make-them-feel-valued.

Freidman, T. J. (2005). *The World Is Flat: A Brief History of the Twenty-First Century*. New York: Farrar, Straus & Giroux.

Freudenberger, H. J. (1974). Staff Burn-Out. *Journal of Social Issues, 30*, 159–165.

Friedman, D. (1987). *Family Supportive Policies: The Corporate Decision Making Process*. New York: The Conference Board.

Friedman, R. A. & Craig, K. M. (2004). Predicting Joining and Participating in Minority Employee Network Groups. *Industrial Relations, 43*, 793–816.

Fritz, M. B. W., Narashim, S. & Rhee, H.-S. (1998). Communication and Coordination in the Virtual Office. *Journal of Management Information Systems, 14*(4), 7–28.

Frost, P. J., Moore, L. F., Louis, M. R., Lundberg, C. C. & Martin, J. (1991). *Reframing Organizational Culture*. Newbury Park, CA: Sage.

Fubara, E. I., Mc-Millan-Capehart, A. & Richard, O. C. (2008). The Role of Organizational Justice and Ethical Frameworks on Attitudes Toward Affirmative Action: The Moderating Role of Organizational Support. *Journal of Diversity Management, 3*(3), 29–40.

Fulk, J. (1993). Social Construction of Communication Technology.

Academy of Management Journal, 36, 921–950.

Fulk, J. & Collins-Jarvis, L. (2001). Wired Meetings: Technological Mediation of Organizational Gatherings. In F. M. Jablin & L. L. Putnam (eds.), *The New Handbook of Organizational Communication: Advances in Theory, Research, and Methods* (pp. 624–663). Thousand Oaks, CA: Sage.

Fulk, J., Schmitz, J. & Steinfield, C. W. (1990). A Social Influence Model of Technology Use. In J. Fulk & C. W. Steinfield (eds.), *Organizations and Communication Technology* (pp. 117–140). Newbury Park, CA: Sage.

Fulk, J., Steinfield, C. W., Schmitz, J. & Power, J. G. (1987). A Social Information Processing Model of Media Use in Organizations. *Communication Research, 14,* 529–552.

Gallagher, E. B. & Sias, P. M. (2009). The New Employee as a Source of Uncertainty: Veteran Employee Information Seeking About New Hires. *Journal of Communication, 73,* 23–46.

Ganesh, S. & Stohl, C. (2010). Qualifying Engagement: A Study of Information and Communication Technology and the Global Social Justice Movement in Aotearoa New Zealand. *Communication Monographs, 77,* 51–74.

Ganesh, S., Zoller, H. & Cheney, G. (2005). Transforming Resistance, Broadening Our Boundaries: Critical Organizational Communication Meets Globalization from Below. *Communication Monographs, 72,* 169–191.

Gardner, W. L. (2003). Perceptions of Leader Charisma, Effectiveness, and Integrity: Effects of Exemplification, Delivery, and Ethical Reputation. *Management Communication Quarterly, 16,* 502–527.

Gardner, W. L., Reithel, B. J., Cogliser, C. C., Walumbwa, F. O. & Foley, R. T. (2012). Matching Personality and Organizational Culture: Effects of Recruitment Strategy and the Five-Factor Model on Subjective Person-Organization Fit. *Management Communication Quarterly, 26,* 585–622.

Garner, J. T. (2009a). Strategic Dissent: Expressions of Dissent Motivated by Influence Goals. *International Journal of Strategic Communication, 3,* 34–51.

_____. (2009b). When Things Go Wrong at Work: An Exploration of Organizational Dissent Messages. *Communication Studies, 60,* 197–218.

_____. (2012). Making Waves at Work: Perceived Effectiveness of Organizational Dissent Messages. *Management Communication Quarterly, 26,* 224–240.

_____. (2013, February 4). How to Communicate Dissent at Work. *Harvard Business Review.* Retrieved on June 1, 2013, from http://blogs. hbr.org/cs/2013/02/how_to_ communicate_dissent_at.html.

Gates, D. (2003). Learning to Play the Game: An Exploratory Study of How African American Women and Men Interact with Others in Organizations. *Electronic Journal of Communication, 13* (2–3).

Gawande, A. (2009). *The Checklist Manifesto.* New York: Metropolitan.

Gay in the Office: The Last Frontier of Workplace Equality. (2010). Retrieved on August 6, 2010, from http://www.npr.org/templates/story/ story.php?storyId=122483892.

Gayle, B. M. & Preiss, R. W. (1998). Assessing Emotionality in Organizational Conflicts. *Management Communication Quarterly, 12,* 280–302.

Geertz, C. (1973). *The Interpretation of Cultures.* New York: Basic Books.

Geist, P. (1995). Negotiating Whose Order? Communicating to Negotiate Identities and Revise Organizational Structures. In A. M. Nicotera (ed.), *Conflict and Organizations: Communicative Processes* (pp. 45–64). Albany: State University of New York Press.

Gergen, K. (1991). *The Saturated Self: Dilemmas of Identity in Contemporary Life.* New York: Basic Books.

Gersick, C. (1991). Revolutionary Change Theories: A Multilevel Exploration of the Punctuated Equilibrium Paradigm. *Academy of Management Review, 16,* 10–36.

Gibson, M. K. & Papa, M. J. (2000). The Mud, the Blood, and the Beer Guys: Organizational Osmosis in Blue-Collar Work Groups. *Journal of Applied Communication Research, 28,* 68–88.

Giddens, A. (1979). *Central Problems in Social Theory: Action, Structure and Contradiction in Social Analysis.* Berkeley: University of California Press.

Gilbert, J. A. & Ivancevich, J. M. (2000). Valuing Diversity: A Tale of Two Organizations. *Academy of Management Executive, 14*(1), 93–105.

Gill, R. & Ganesh, S. (2007). Empowerment, Constraint, and the Entrepreneurial Self: A Study of White Women Entrepreneurs. *Journal of Applied Communication Research, 35,* 268–293.

Gilpin, D. (2010). Organizational Image Construction in a Fragmented Online Media Environment. *Journal of Public Relations Research, 22,* 265–287.

Golden, A. G. (2001). Modernity and the Communicative Management of Multiple Role-Identities: The Case of the Worker-Parent. *The Journal of Family Communication, 1,* 233–264.

_____. (2009). Employee Families and Organizations as Mutually Enacted Environments: A Sensemaking Approach to Work-Life Relationships. *Management Communication Quarterly, 22,* 385–415.

_____. (2013). The Structuration of Information and Communication Technologies and Work-Life Interrelationships: Shared Organizational and Family Rules and Resources and Implications for Work in a High-Technology Organization. *Communication Monographs, 80,* 101–123.

Golden, T. D. & Fromen, A. (2011). Does It Matter Where Your Manager Works? Comparing Managerial Work Mode (Traditional, Telework, Virtual) Across Subordinate Work Experiences and Outcomes. *Human Relations, 64*, 1451–1475.

Goldstein, E. L. & Gilliam, P. (1990). Training System Issues in the Year 2000. *American Psychologist, 45*, 134–143.

Goleman, D. P. (1995). *Emotional Intelligence*. New York: Bantam Books.

Golitz, S. M. & Giannantonio, C. M. (1995). Recruiter Friendliness and Attraction to the Job: The Mediating Role of Inferences About the Organization. *Journal of Vocational Behavior, 46*, 109–118.

Gordon, J. (2007, September 7–13). Parkland Slashes ER Admission Wait Time. *Dallas Business Journal*, p. 13.

Gordon, M. E. (2011). The Dialectics of the Exit Interview: A Fresh Look at Conversations About Organizational Disengagement. *Management Communication Quarterly, 25*, 59–86.

Gore, A. (2006). *An Inconvenient Truth*. New York: Rodale.

Gossett, L. M. (2002). Kept at Arm's Length: Questioning the Desirability of Organizational Identification. *Communication Monographs, 69*, 385–404.

_____. (2007). Falling Between the Cracks: Control and Communication Challenges of a Temporary Workforce. *Management Communication Quarterly, 19*, 376–415.

Gossett, L. M. & Kilker, J. (2006). My Job Sucks: Examining Counterinstitutional Web Site as Locations for Organizational Member Voice, Dissent, and Resistance. *Management Communication Quarterly, 20*, 63–90.

Gouran, D. S. & Hirokawa, R. Y. (1996). Functional Theory and Communication in Decision-Making and Problem-Solving Groups: An Expanded View. In R. Y. Hirokawa & M. S. Poole (eds.), *Communication and Group Decision Making*, 2nd ed. (pp. 55–80). Thousand Oaks, CA: Sage.

Gouran, D. S., Hirokawa, R. Y., Julian, K. M. & Leatham, G. B. (1993). The Evolution and Current Status of the Functional Perspective on Communication in Decision-Making and Problem-Solving Groups: A Critical Analysis. In S. A. Deetz (ed.), *Communication Yearbook 16* (pp. 573–600). Newbury Park, CA: Sage.

Gouran, D. S., Hirokawa, R. Y. & Martz, A. E. (1986). A Critical Analysis of Factors Related to Decisional Processes in the Challenger Disaster. *Central States Speech Journal, 37*, 119–135.

Graen, G. B. (1976). Role-Making Processes Within Complex Organizations. In M. D. Dunnette (ed.), *Handbook of Industrial and Organizational Psychology* (pp. 1201–1245). Chicago: Rand McNally.

Graen, G. B. & Scandura, T. A. (1987). Toward a Psychology of Dyadic Organizing. In B. Staw & L. L. Cummings (eds.), *Research in Organizational Behavior, Vol. 9* (pp. 175–208). Greenwich, CT: JAI Press.

Gramsci, A. (1971). *Selections from the Prison Notebooks*, Q. Hoare & G. Nowell Smith, trans. New York: International Publishers.

Grandey, A., Rafaeli, A., Ravid, S., Wirtz, J. & Steiner, D. (2010). Emotion Display Rules at Work in the Global Service Economy: The Special Case of the Customer. *Journal of Service Management, 21*, 388–412.

Grantham, C. (1995, September/ October). The Virtual Office. At Work: Stories of *Tomorrow's Workplace*, pp. 12–14.

Greenberg, S. H. (2001, January 8). Time to Plan Your Life. *Newsweek*, pp. 54–55.

Greenwald, R. & Hirsch, M. (2013, May 7). Dying for the Shirt on Your Back. *Los Angeles Times*. Retrieved on June 1, 2013, from http://articles.latimes.com/2013/may/07/opinion/la-oe-greenwald-bangladesh-triangle-fire-20130507.

Gregory, K. W. (2001). "Don't Sweat the Small Stuff": Employee Identity Work in the New Economy. Unpublished doctoral dissertation. Department of Communication, University of South Florida.

Gregory, S. (2009, April 18). Domino's YouTube Crisis: 5 Ways to Fight Back. *Time*. Retrieved on June 26, 2013, from http://www.time.com/time/nation/article/0,8599,1892389,00.html.

Gronn, P. (1983). Talk as the Work: The Accomplishment of School Administration. *Administrative Science Quarterly, 28*, 1–21.

Gross, D. (2009). Rules of the Jungle: Wall Street Bonuses Won't Go Quietly. *Newsweek*. Retrieved on May 25, 2010, from http://www.newsweek.com/2009/10/23/rules-of-the-jungle.html.

Gross, M. A., Guerrero, L. K. & Alberts, J. K. (2004). Perceptions of Conflict Strategies and Communication Competence in Task-Onented Dyads. *Journal of Applied Communication Research, 32*, 249–270.

Gruman, J. A. & Saks, A. M. (2011). Socialization Preferences and Intentions: Does One Size Fit All? *Journal of Vocational Behavior, 79*, 419–427.

Gutek, B. A. & Welsh, T. (2000). *The Brave New Service Strategy: Aligning Customer Relationships, Market Strategies, and Business Structures*. New York: American Management Association.

Habermas, J. (1971). *Knowledge and Human Interests*, J. J. Shapiro, trans. Boston: Beacon Press.

Hafen, S. (2003). Cultural Diversity Training: A Critical (Ironic) Cartography of Advocacy and Oppositional Silences. In G. Cheney & G. Barnett (eds.), *Organization Communication: Emerging Perspectives*. Cresskill, NJ: Hampton Press.

Hall, E. J. (1993). Smiling, Deferring, and Flirting: Doing Gender by Giving "Good Service." *Work and Occupations, 20,* 452–471.

Hall, S. (1985). Signification, Representation, Ideology: Althusser and the Post-Structuralist Debates. *Critical Studies in Mass Communication, 2,* 91–114.

Halpern, J. (2001). *From Detached Concern to Empathy: Humanizing Medical Practice.* New York: Oxford University Press.

Halverson, J. R., Goodall, H. L. & Corman, S. R. (2011). *Master Narratives of Islamist Extremism.* New York: Palgrave Macmillan.

Hannan, M. & Freeman, J. (1989). *Organizational Ecology.* Cambridge, MA: Harvard University Press.

Hardy, C. & Clegg, S. R. (1996). Some Dare Call It Power. In S. R. Clegg, C. Hardy & W. R. Nord (eds.), *The Handbook of Organization Studies* (pp. 622–641). Newbury Park, CA: Sage.

Harlow, S. (2011). Social Media and Social Movements: Facebook and an Online Guatemalan Justice Movement that Moved Offline. *New Media & Society, 14,* 225–243.

Harris, G. L. A. (2009). Revisiting Affirmative Action in Leveling the Playing Field: Who Have Been the True Beneficiaries Anyway? *Review of Public Personnel Administration, 29,* 354–372.

Harrison, T. (1994). Communication and Interdependence in Democratic Organizations. In S. Deetz (ed.), *Communication Yearbook 17* (pp. 247–274). Beverly Hills, CA: Sage.

Harter, L. M. & Krone, K. J. (2001). The Boundary-Spanning Role of a Cooperative Support Organization: Managing the Paradox of Stability and Change in Non-Traditional Organizations. *Journal of Applied Communication Research, 29,* 248–277.

Harter, L. M., Scott, J. A., Novak, D. R., Leeman, M. & Morris, J. F. (2006). Freedom Through Flight: Performing a Counter-Narrative of Disability. *Journal of Applied Communication Research, 34,* 3–29.

Health Insurance Coverage. (2007). National Coalition on Health Care. Retrieved on December 8, 2007, from http://www.nchc.org/facts/coverage.html.

Heath, R. L. (1994). *Management of Corporate Communication: From Interpersonal Contacts to External Affairs.* Hillsdale, NJ: Erlbaum.

Heaton, L. H. (2008). *Knowledge Management. International Encyclopedia of Communication.* Boston: Blackledge.

Heaton, L. & Taylor, J. R. (2002). Knowledge Management and Professional Work: A Communication Perspective on the Knowledge-Based Organization. *Management Communication Quarterly, 16,* 210–236.

Heilman, M. E. (1994). Affirmative Action: Some Unintended Consequences for Working Women. In B. M. Staw & L. L. Cummings (eds.), *Research in Organizational Behavior, Vol. 16* (pp. 125–169). Greenwich, CT: JAI Press.

Heilman, M. E., Block, C. J. & Stathatos, P. (1997). The Affirmative Action Stigma of Incompetence: Effects of Performance Information Ambiguity. *Academy of Management Journal, 40,* 603–625.

Heiss, S. N. & Carmack, H. J. (2012). Knock, Knock, Who's There: Making Sense of Organizational Entrance Through Humor. *Management Communication Quarterly, 26,* 106–132.

Herring, C. (2009). Does Diversity Pay? Race, Gender, and the Business Case for Diversity. *American Sociological Review, 74,* 208–224.

Herzberg, F. (1966). *Work and the Nature of Man.* Cleveland, OH: World.

Hetter, K. (2013, January 11). Cruise Safety One Year After Concordia. *CNN.* Retrieved on June 1, 2013, from http://www.cnn.com/2013/01/11/travel/concordia-anniversary.

Hewlett, S. A. (2007). *Off-Ramps and On-Ramps: Keeping Talented Women on the Road to Success.* Cambridge, MA: Harvard Business School Press.

Hirokawa, R. Y. & Salazar, A. J. (1999). Task-Group Communication and Decision-Making Performance. In L. R. Frey, D. S. Gouran & M. S. Poole (eds.), *The Handbook of Group Communication Theory and Research* (pp. 167–191). Thousand Oaks, CA: Sage.

Hirokawa, R. Y. & Scheerhorn, D. R. (1986). Communication in Faulty Group Decision-Making. In R. Y. Hirokawa & M. S. Poole (eds.), *Communication and Group Decision-Making* (pp. 63–80). Beverly Hills, CA: Sage.

Hochschild, A. (1983). *The Managed Heart.* Berkeley: University of California Press.

Hoffart, N. & Woods, C. Q. (1996). Elements of a Professional Practice Model. *Journal of Professional Nursing, 12,* 354–364.

Hoffman, M. F. (2002). "Do All Things with Counsel": Benedictine Women and Organizational Democracy. *Communication Studies, 53,* 203–218.

Hoffner, C. A., Levine, K. J. & Toohey, R. A. (2008). Socialization to Work in Late Adolescence: The Role of Television and Family. *Journal of Broadcasting & Electronic Media, 52,* 282–302.

Holladay, S. J. & Coombs, W. T. (1993). Communicating Visions: An Exploration of the Role of Delivery in the Creation of Leader Charisma. *Management Communication Quarterly, 6,* 405–427.

Holmes, J. & Marra, M. (2004). Leadership and Managing Conflict in Meetings. *Pragmatics, 14,* 439–462.

Holmes, J. & Stubbe, M. (2003). Doing Disagreement at Work: A Sociolinguistic Approach. *Australian Journal of Communication, 30,* 53–77.

Holstein, J. A. & Gubrium, J. F. (2000). *The Self We Live By: Narrative Identity in a Postmodern World.* New York: Oxford University Press.

Horowitz, J. (2013, February 16). Pope Benedict XVI's Leaked Documents Show Fractured Vatican Full of

Rivalries. *Washington Post.* Retrieved on June 3, 2013, from http://articles.washingtonpost.com/2013-02-16/world/37131414_1_benedict-xvi-vatican-insiders-vatican-city.

House, J. S. (1981). *Work Stress and Social Support.* Reading, MA: Addison-Wesley.

Houston, R. & Jackson, M. H. (2003). Technology and Context Within Research on International Development Programs: Positioning an Integrationist Perspective. *Communication Theory, 13,* 57–77.

Hu, E. (2013, February 25). Working From Home: The End of Productivity or the Future of Work? *NPR.* Retrieved on June 1, 2013, from http://www.npr.org/blogs/alltechconsidered/2013/02/23/172792467/working-from-home-the-end-of-productivity-or-the-future-of-work.

Huber, G. P. (1984). Issues in the Design of Group Decision Support Systems. *MIS Quarterly, 8,* 195–204.

_____. (1990). A Theory of the Effects of Advanced Information Technologies on Organizational Design, Intelligence, and Decision Making. *Academy of Management Review, 15,* 47–71.

Hur, Y. (2012). Racial Diversity, Is It a Blessing to an Organization? Examining Its Organizational Consequences in Municipal Police Departments. *International Review of Administrative Sciences, 79,* 149–164.

Huspek, M. (1997). Toward Normative Theories of Communication with Reference to the Frankfurt School: An Introduction. *Communication Theory, 7,* 265–276.

Hylmo, A. & Buzzanell, P. M. (2002). Telecommuting as Viewed Through Cultural Lenses: An Empirical Investigation of the Discourses of Utopia, Identity, and Mystery. *Communication Monographs, 69,* 329–356.

Ibarra, H. (1993). Personal Networks of Women and Minorities in Management: A Conceptual

Framework. *Academy of Management Journal, 18,* 56–87.

_____. (1995). Race, Opportunity, and Diversity of Social Circles in Managerial Networks. *Academy of Management Journal, 38,* 673–703.

Ilgen, D. R. & Youst, M. A. (1986). Factors Affecting the Evaluation and Development of Minorities in Organizations. In K. M. Rowland & G. R. Ferris (eds.), *Research in Personnel and Human Resource Management, Vol. 4* (pp. 307–337). Greenwich, CT: JAI Press.

Isikoff, M. (2004, July 19). The Dots Never Existed. *Newsweek,* pp. 36–38.

Iverson, J. O. & McPhee, R. D. (2002). Knowledge Management in Communities of Practice: Being True to the Communicative Character of Knowledge. *Management Communication Quarterly, 16,* 259–266.

Jablin, F. M. (2001). Organizational Entry, Assimilation, and Disengagement/Exit. In F. M. Jablin & L. L. Putnam (eds.), *The New Handbook of Organizational Communication: Advances in Theory, Research, and Methods* (pp. 732–818). Thousand Oaks, CA: Sage.

Jablin, F. M. & Kramer, M. W. (1998). Communication-Related Sense-Making and Adjustment During Job Transfers. *Management Communication Quarterly, 12,* 155–182.

Jablin, F. M. & Krone, K. J. (1987). Organizational Assimilation. In C. R. Berger & S. H. Chaffee (eds.), *Handbook of Communication Science* (pp. 711–746). Newbury Park, CA: Sage.

Jablin, F. M. & Miller, V. D. (1990). Interviewer and Applicant Questioning Behavior in Employment Interviews. *Management Communication Quarterly, 4,* 51–86.

Jabs, L. B. (2005). Communicative Rules and Organizational Decision Making. *Journal of Business Communication, 42,* 265–288.

Jackson, S. E. (1983). Participation in Decision Making as a Strategy for Reducing Job-Related Strain. *Journal of Applied Psychology, 68,* 3–19.

Jacobson, S. (2010, May 26). Texas Hospital Decreases ER Wait Time as Visits Increase. *Dallas Morning News.* Retrieved on May 27, 2010, from http://emsresponder.com/article/article.jsp?siteSection=1&id=13431.

Jameson, J. K. (2004). Negotiating Autonomy and Connection Through Politeness: A Dialectical Approach to Organizational Conflict Management. *Western Journal of Communication, 68,* 257–277.

Jameson, J. K., Bodtker, A. M. & Linker, T. (2010). Facilitating Conflict Transformation: Mediator Strategies for Eliciting Emotional Communication in a Workplace Conflict. *Negotiation Journal, 26*(1), 25–48.

Janis, I. L. (1982). *Groupthink.* Boston: Houghton Mifflin.

Jassawalla, A. R. & Sashittal, H. C. (1999). Building Collaborative Cross-Functional New Product Teams. *Academy of Management Executive, 13*(3), 50–63.

Jenkins, B. M. (2007). *Basic Principles for Homeland Security.* Santa Monica, CA: RAND Corporation.

Jian, G. (2007). Unpacking the Unintended Consequences in Planned Organizational Change: A Process Model. *Management Communication Quarterly, 21,* 5–28.

Jones, D. (2002, January 4–6). E-Mail Avalanche Even Buries CEOs. *USA Today,* 1–2.

Jones, K. (2011, April 19). How Viral Marketing Has the Potential to Promote or Destroy Your Brand. Retrieved July 1, 2013, from http://searchengineland.com/how-viral-marketing-has-the-potential-to-promote-or-destroy-your-brand-72889.

Joyce, A. (2005, June 6). Workplace Improves for Gay, Transgender Employees, Rights Group Says. *The Washington Post.* Retrieved on

August 5, 2010, from http://www .washingtonpost.com/wp-dyn/ content/article/2005/06/05/ AR2005060501249.html.

Kalev, A., Dobbin, F. & Kelly, E. (2006). Best Practices or Best Guesses? Assessing the Efficacy of Corporate Affirmative Action and Diversity Policies. *American Sociological Review, 71*, 589–617.

Kalleberg, A. L. (2008a). Precarious Work, Insecure Workers: Employment Relations in Transition. *American Sociological Review, 74*, 1–22.

_____. (2008b). The Mismatched Worker: When People Don't Fit Their Jobs. *Academy of Management Perspectives, 22*(1), 24–40.

Kamalanabhan, T. J., Uma, J. & Vasanthi, M. (1999). A Delphi Study of Motivational Profile of Scientists in Research and Development Organisations. *Psychological Reports, 85*, 743–749.

Kanaov, J. M., Maitlis, S., Worline, M. C., Dutton, J. E., Frost, P. J. & Lilius, J. M. (2004). Compassion in Organizational Life. *American Behavioral Scientist, 47*, 808–827.

Kang, C. (2012, September 21). Firms Tell Employees: Avoid After-Hours E-Mail. *Washington Post*. Retrieved September 23, 2012, from http:// articles.washingtonpost.com/2012-09-21/business/35497074_1_e-mail-work-culture-blackberrys.

Kanter, R. M. (1977). *Men and Women of the Corporation*. New York: Basic Books. (1983).

_____. *The Change Masters*. New York: Simon & Schuster.

Kantrowitz, B. & Scelfo, J. (2006, September 25). Science and the Gender Gap. *Newsweek*, pp. 67–72.

Kassing, J.W. (2002). Speaking Up: Identifying Employees' Upward Dissent Strategies. *Management Communication Quarterly, 16*, 187–209.

Kassing, J. W. & Armstrong, T. A. (2002). Someone's Going to Hear About This: Examining the Association Between Dissent-

Triggering Events and Employees' Dissent Expression. *Management Communication Quarterly, 16*, 39–65.

Katz, D. & Kahn, R. L. (1978). *The Social Psychology of Organizations*, 2nd ed., New York: Wiley. (First published in 1966.)

Kerschner, L. (2008, April 28). A Farmer's Labor of Love. *Newsweek*, p. 17.

Kim, C. & Tamborini, C. R. (2006). The Continuing Significance of Race in Occupational Attainment of Whites and Blacks: A Segmented Labor Market Analysis. *Sociological Inquiry, 76*, 23–51.

Kim, D. J., Ferrin, D. L. & Rao, H. R. (2009). Trust and Satisfaction, Two Stepping Stones for Successful E-Commerce Relationships: A Longitudinal Exploration. *Information Systems Research, 20*, 237–257.

Kimberly, J. R. & Miles, T. H. (1980). *The Organizational Life Cycle: Issues in the Creation, Transformation, and Decline of Organizations*. San Francisco: Jossey-Bass.

King, E. B., Dawson, J. F., West, M. A., Gilrane, V. L., Peddie, C. I. & Bastin, L. (2011). Why Organizational and Community Diversity Matter: Representativeness and the Emergence of Incivility and Organizational Performance. *Academy of Management Journal, 54*, 1103–1118.

Kinlaw, D. C. (1991). *Developing Superior Work Teams: Building Quality and the Competitive Edge*. Lexington, MA: Lexington Books.

Kirby, E. L. (2006). "Helping You Make Room in Your Life for Your Needs": When Organizations Appropriate Family Roles. *Communication Monographs, 73*, 474–480.

Kirby, E. L., Golden, A. G., Medved, C. E., Jorgenson, J. & Buzzanell, P. M. (2003). An Organizational Communication Challenge to the Discourse of Work and Family Research: From Problematics to Empowerment. In Pamela J.

Kalbfleisch (ed.), *Communication Yearbook 27* (pp. 1–43). Mahwah, NJ: Lawrence Erlbaum.

Kirby, E. L. & Harter, L. M. (2001). Discourses of Diversity and the Quality of Work Life: The Character and Costs of the Managerial Metaphor. *Management Communication Quarterly, 15*, 121–127.

Kirby, E. L. & Krone, K. J. (2002). "The Policy Exists But You Can't Really Use It": Communication and the Structuration of Work-Family Policies. *Journal of Applied Communication Research, 30*, 50–77.

Klatzke, S. R. (2008). Communication and Sensemaking During the Exit Phase of Socialization. Unpublished doctoral dissertation, University of Missouri.

Kline, S. L., Simumch, B. & Weber, H. (2009). The Use of Equivocal Messages in Responding to Corporate Challenges. *Journal of Applied Communication Research, 37*, 40–58.

Knapp, M. L., Putnam, L. L. & Davis, L. J. (1988). Measuring Interpersonal Conflict in Organizations: Where Do We Go from Here? *Management Communication Quarterly, 1*, 414–429.

Knudsen, H., Busck, O. & Lind, J. (2011). Work Environment Quality: The Role of Workplace Participation and Democracy. *Work, Employment and Society, 25*, 379–396.

Kokkindis, G. (2011). In Search of Workplace Democracy. *International Journal of Sociology and Social Policy, 32*, 233–256.

Kolb, D. M. (1986). Who Are Organizational Third Parties and What Do They Do? In R. J. Lewicki, B. H. Sheppard & M. H. Bazerman (eds.), *Research on Negotiations in Organizations, Vol. 1* (pp. 207–278). Greenwich, CT: JAI Press.

Koontz, H. & O'Donnell, C. (1976). *Management: A Systems and Contingency Analysis of Managerial Functions*. New York: McGraw-Hill.

Korkki, P. (2013, February 23). How Offices Become Complaint Departments. *New York Times*. Retrieved on June 1, 2013, from http://www.nytimes.com/2013/02/24/jobs/how-offices-become-complaint-departments.html.

Koschmann, M. A. (2012). Developing a Communicative Theory of the Nonprofit. *Management Communication Quarterly, 26,* 139–146.

_____. (2013). The Communicative Constitution of Collective Identity in Interorganizational Collaboration. *Management Communication Quarterly, 26,* 106–132.

Kotkin, J. (2010a). 400 Million People Can't Be Wrong: Why America's New Baby Boom Bodes Well for Our Future. *Newsweek*. Retrieved on May 24, 2010, from http://www.newsweek.com/2010/04/15/400-million-people-can-t-be-wrong.html.

_____. (2010b). *The Next Hundred Million: America in 2050*. New York: Penguin Press.

Kramer, M. W. (1993). Communication and Uncertainty Reduction During Job Transfers: Leaving and Joining Processes. *Communication Monographs, 60,* 178–198.

_____. (2006). Shared Leadership in a Community Theater Group: Filling the Leadership Role. *Journal of Applied Communication Research, 34,* 141–162.

Kramer, M. W. & Berman, J. E. (2001). Making Sense of a University's Culture: An Examination of Undergraduate Students' Stories. *Southern Communication Journal, 66,* 297–311.

Kramer, M. W. & Hess, J. A. (2002). Communication Rules for the Display of Emotions in Organizational Settings. *Management Communication Quarterly, 16,* 66–80.

Kruml, S. M. & Geddes, D. (2000). Exploring the Dimensions of Emotional Labor: The Heart of Hochschild's Work. *Management Communication Quarterly, 14,* 8–49.

Kuhn, T. (2008). A Communicative Theory of the Firm: Developing an Alternative Perspective on Intra-Organizational Power and Stakeholder Relationships. *Organization Studies, 29,* 1197–1224.

_____. (2012). Negotiating the Micro-Macro Divide: Thought Leadership From Organizational Communication for Theorizing Organization. *Management Communication Quarterly, 26,* 543–584.

Kuhn, T. & Corman, S. R. (2003). The Emergence of Homogeneity and Heterogeneity in Knowledge Structures During a Planned Organizational Change. *Communication Monographs, 70,* 198–229.

Kuhn, T. & Jackson, M. H. (2008). Accomplishing Knowledge: A Framework for Investigating Knowing in Organizations. *Management Communication Quarterly, 21,* 454–485.

Kuhn, T. & Poole, M. S. (2000). Do Conflict Management Styles Affect Group Decision Making? Evidence from a Longitudinal Field Study. *Human Communication Research, 26,* 558–590.

Lair, D. J. & Wieland, S. M. B. (2012). "What Are You Going to Do With That Major?" Colloquial Speech and the Meaning of Work and Education. *Management Communication Quarterly, 26,* 423–452.

Larson, E. B. (2013). Clinical Empathy as Emotional Labor in the Patient-Physician Relationship. *Journal of the American Medical Association, 293,* 1100–1106.

Latest Telecommuting Statistics. (2012). Retrieved on July 2, 2013, from http://www.globalworkplaceanalytics.com/telecommuting-statistics.

Lawler, E. E. & Finegold, D. (2000). Individualizing the Organization: Past, Present, and Future. *Organizational Dynamics, 29,* 1–15.

LeBlanc, P. M., Bakker, A. B., Peeters, M. C. W., VanHeesch, N. C. A. & Schaufeli, W. B. (2001). Emotional Job Demands and Burnout Among Oncology Care Providers. *Anxiety, Stress, & Coping, 14,* 243–263.

Lee, D. (2009, December 14). Job Market Worsens for Recent College Graduates. *Los Angeles Times*. Retrieved on July 15, 2010, from http://articles.latimes.com/2009/dec/14/business/la-fi-jobs-graduatesl4-2009decl4.

Leidner, R. (1993). *Fast Food, Fast Talk: Service Work and the Routinization of Everyday Life*. Berkeley: University of California Press.

Lengel, R. H. & Daft, R. L. (1988). The Selection of Communication Media as an Executive Skill. *Academy of Management Executive, 2,* 225–232.

Leonardi, P. M. & Barley, S. R. (2010). What's Under Construction Here? Social Action, Materiality, and Power in Constructivist Studies of Technology and Organizing. *The Academy of Management Annals, 4,* 1–51.

Leonsis, T. (2010, April 12). How to Build a Happy Company. *Newsweek*, p. 16.

Levin, J. (2006, September 25). "This Topic Annoys Me." *Newsweek*, p. 72.

Levine, K. J. & Hoffner, C. A. (2006). Adolescents' Conceptions of Work: What Is Learned from Different Sources During Anticipatory Socialization? *Journal of Adolescent Research, 21,* 647–669.

Lewicki, R. J., Gray, G. & Elliott, M. (eds.) (2003). *Making Sense of Intractable Environmental Conflicts: Frames and Cases*. Washington, DC: Island Press.

Lewis, L. K. (2000). "Blindsided by That One" and "I Saw That One Coming": The Relative Anticipation and Occurrence of Communication Problems and Other Problems in Implementers' Hindsight. *Journal of Applied Communication Research, 28,* 44–67.

_____. (2007). An Organizational Stakeholder Model of Change Implementation Communication. *Communication Theory, 17,* 176–204.

_____. (2011). *Organizational Change: Creating Change Through Strategic Communication.* Malden, MA: Wiley-Blackwell.

Lewis, L. K., Isbell, M. G. & Koschmann, M. (2010). Collaborative Tensions: Practitioners' Experiences of Interorganizational Relationships. *Communication Monographs, 77,* 460–479.

Lewis, L. K., Laster, N. & Kulkarni, V. (2013). Telling 'Em How It Will Be: Previewing Pain of Risky Change in Initial Announcements. *Journal of Business Communication, 50,* 278–308.

Lewis, L. K., Richardson, B. K. & Hamel, S. A. (2003). When the "Stakes" Are Communicative: The Lamb's and the Lion's Share During Nonprofit Planned Change. *Human Communication Research, 29,* 400–430.

Lewis, L. K. & Russ, T. L. (2012). Soliciting and Using Input During Organizational Change Initiatives: What Are Practitioners Doing? *Management Communication Quarterly, 26,* 267–294.

Liberto, J. (2012, April 19). CEO Pay is 380 Times Average Worker's – AFL-CIO. *CNNMoney.* Retrieved on June 6, 2013, from http://money.cnn.com/2012/04/19/news/economy/ceo-pay/index.htm.

Lief, H. I. & Fox, R. C. (1963). Training for "Detached Concern" in Medical Students. In H. I. Lief, V. F. Lief & N. R. Lief (eds.), *The Psychological Basis of Medical Practice,* 12–35. New York: Harper & Row.

Likert, R. (1961). *New Patterns of Management.* New York: McGraw-Hill.

_____. (1967). *The Human Organization: Its Management and Value.* New York: McGraw-Hill.

Lilius, J. M., Worline, M. C., Dutton, J. E., Kanov, J. M. & Maitlis, S. (2011). Understanding Compassion Capability. *Human Relations, 64,* 873–899.

Lim, M. (2012). Clicks, Cabs, and Coffee Houses: Social Media and Oppositional Movements in Egypt,

2004–2011. *Journal of Communication, 62,* 231–248.

Lim, V. K. G. (1996). Job Insecurity and Its Outcomes: Moderating Effects of Work-Based and Nonwork-Based Social Support. *Human Relations, 49,* 171–194.

Lipsky, D. B., Seeber, R. L. & Fincher, R. D. (2003). *Emerging Systems for Managing Workplace Conflict: Lessons from American Corporations for Managers and Dispute Resolution Professionals.* San Francisco: Jossey-Bass.

Lithwick, D. (2010, June 14). Our Beauty Bias Is Unfair: But Should It Also Be Illegal? *Newsweek,* p. 20.

Liu, H. (2010). When Leaders Fail: A Typology of Failures and Framing Strategies. *Management Communication Quarterly, 24,* 232–259.

Liu, V. & Vlaskam, M. (2010, June 28 & July 5). Smart, Young, and Broke: White-Collar Workers Are China's Newest Underclass. *Newsweek,* pp. 40–41.

Loader, B. D. & Mercea, D. (2011). Networking Democracy? Social Media Innovations and Participatory Politics. *Information, Communication & Society, 14,* 757–769.

Louis, M. R. (1980). Surprise and Sense-Making: What Newcomers Experience When Entering Unfamiliar Organizational Settings. *Administrative Science Quarterly, 23,* 225–251.

_____. (1985). An Investigator's Guide to Workplace Culture. In P. J. Frost, L. F. Moore, M. R. Louis, C. C. Lundberg & J. Martin (eds.), *Organizational Culture* (pp. 73–93). Beverly Hills, CA: Sage.

Lovejoy, K. & Saxton, G. D. (2012). Information, Community, and Action: How Nonprofit Organizations Use Social Media. *Journal of Computer-Mediated Communication, 17,* 337–353.

Lucas, K. (2011). The Working Class Promise: A Communicative Account of Mobility-Based Ambivalences. *Communication Monographs, 78,* 347–369.

Lutgen-Sandvik, P. (2006). Take This Job and…: Quitting and Other Forms of Resistance to Workplace Bullying. *Communication Monographs, 73,* 406–433.

_____. (2008). Intensive Remedial Identity Work: Responses to Workplace Bullying Trauma and Stigmatization. *Organization, 15,* 97–119.

Lutgen-Sandvik, P. & Tracy, S. J. (2012). Answering Five Key Questions About Workplace Bullying: How Communication Scholarship Provides Thought Leadership for Transforming Abuse at Work. *Management Communication Quarterly, 26,* 3–47.

Lynch, O. & Schaefer, Z. (2012, May). The Good, the Bad, and the Dummie: Now a Non-Profit in Fiscal Crisis Negotiates Authority. Paper presented at the annual meeting of the International Communication Association. Phoenix, AZ.

Mael, F. & Ashforth, B. E. (1992). Alumni and Their Alma Mater: A Partial Test of the Reformulated Model of Organizational Identification. *Journal of Organizational Behavior, 13,* 103–123.

Malvani Redden, S. (2013). How Lines Organize Compulsory Interaction, Emotion Management, and "Emotion Taxes": The Implications of Passenger Emotion and Expression in Airport Security Lines. *Management Communication Quarterly, 27,* 121–149.

Manyika, J., Chui, M., Brown, B., Bughin, J., Dobbs, R., Roxburgh, C. & Byers, A. H. (2011, May). Big Data: The Next Frontier for Innovation, Competition, and Productivity. Retrieved on June 7, 2013, from http://www.mckinsey.com/insights/business_technology/big_data_the_next_frontier_for_innovation.

March, J. G. & Simon, H. A. (1958). *Organizations.* New York: Wiley.

Marcus, A. A. & Fremeth, A. R. (2009). Green Management Matters Regardless. *Academy of*

Management Perspectives, 23(3), 17–26.

Markus, M. L. (1983). Power Politics and MIS Implementation. *Communications of the ACM, 26,* 430–444.

_____. (1990). Toward a "Critical Mass" Theory of Interactive Media. In J. Fulk & C. W. Steinfield (eds.), *Organizations and Communication Technology* (pp. 194–218). Newbury Park, CA: Sage.

Marlon, J. R., Leiserowitz, A. & Feinberg, G. (2013). *Scientific and Public Perspectives on Climate Change.* New Haven, CT: Yale Project on Climate Change Communication.

Marschall, D. (2002). Internet Technologists as an Occupational Community: Ethnographic Evidence. *Information Communication & Society, 5,* 51–69.

Marshall, A. A. & Stohl, C. (1993). Being "In the Know" in a Participative Management System. *Management Communication Quarterly, 6,* 372–404.

Marshall, J. (1993). Viewing Organizational Communication from a Feminist Perspective: A Critique and Some Offerings. In S. Deetz (ed.), *Communication Yearbook 16* (pp. 122–141). Newbury Park, CA: Sage.

Martin, J. (1992). *Cultures in Organizations: Three Perspectives.* New York: Oxford University Press.

_____. (2002). *Organizational Culture: Mapping the Terrain.* Thousand Oaks, CA: Sage.

Martin, J. & Frost, P. (1996). The Organizational Culture War Games: A Struggle for Intellectual Dominance. In S. R. Clegg, C. Hardy & W. R. Nord (eds.), *The Handbook of Organization Studies* (pp. 599–621). Newbury Park, CA: Sage.

Maruyama, M. (1963). The Second Cybernetics: Deviation-Amplifying Mutual Causal Processes. *American Scientist, 51,* 52–64.

Marx, K. (1967). *Writings of the Young Marx on Philosophy and Society.* L. D. Easton & K. H. Guddat, eds. and trans. New York: Anchor Books.

Maslach, C. (1982). *Burnout: The Cost of Caring.* Englewood Cliffs, NJ: Prentice Hall.

Maslow, A. H. (1943). A Theory of Human Motivation. *Psychology Review, 50,* 370–396.

_____. (1954). *Motivation and Personality.* New York: Harper & Row.

Matheson, K. & Zanna, M. (1989). Impact of Computer-Mediated Communication on Self-Awareness. *Computers in Human Behavior, 4,* 221–233.

Mattson, M. & Stage, C. W. (2001). Toward an Understanding of Intercultural Ethical Dilemmas as Opportunities for Engagement in New Millennium Global Organizations. *Management Communication Quarterly, 15,* 103–109.

Maznevski, M. L. & Chudoba, K. M. (2000). Bridging Space Over Time: Global Virtual-Team Dynamics and Effectiveness. *Organization Science, 11,* 473–492.

McComb, K. B. & Jablin, F. M. (1984). Verbal Correlates of Interviewer Empathic Listening and Employment Interview Outcomes. *Communication Monographs, 51,* 353–371.

McCurdy, H. E. (1992). NASA's Organizational Culture. *Public Administration Review, 52,* 189–192.

McDaniel, M. A., Whet zel, D. L., Schmidt, F. L. & Maurer, S. D. (1994). The Validity of Employment Interviews: A Comprehensive Review and Meta-Analysis. *Journal of Applied Psychology, 79,* 599–616.

McGinn, D. (2000, November 13). A Ph.D. Hits the Road. *Newsweek,* pp. 70–72.

_____. (2004, March 1). Help Not Wanted. *Newsweek,* pp. 31–33.

_____. (2004, April 19). Faster Food. *Newsweek,* pp. E20–E22.

_____. (2006, September 25). Getting Back on Track. *Newsweek,* pp. 62–66.

_____. (2007, March 19). You Need to Get to Work! *Newsweek,* pp. E8–E15.

McGinn, D. & Naughton, K. (2001, February 25). How Safe Is Your Job? *Newsweek,* pp. 36–43.

McGregor, D. (1957). The Human Side of Enterprise. *Management Review, 46,* 22–28, 88–92.

_____. (1960). *The Human Side of Enterprise.* New York: McGraw-Hill.

McPhee, R. D. & Iverson, J. (2009). Agents of Constitution in the *Communidad:* Constitutive Processes of Communication in Organizations. In L. L. Putnam & A. Nicotera, (eds.), *Building Theories of Organization: The Constitutive Role of Communication* (pp. 49–87). NY: Routledge.

McPhee, R. D. & Poole, M. S. (2001). Organizational Structure and Configurations. In F. M. Jablin & L. L. Putnam (eds.), *The New Handbook of Organizational Communication: Advances in Theory, Research, and Methods* (pp. 503–543). Thousand Oaks, CA: Sage.

McPhee, R. D. & Zaug, P. (2000). The Communicative Constitution of Organizations: A Framework for Explanation. *The Electronic Journal of Communication, 10* (1, 2).

Medved, C. E. & Kirby, E. L. (2005). Family CEOs: A Feminist Analysis of Corporate Mothering Discourses. *Management Communication Quarterly, 18,* 435–478.

Medved, C. E., Morrison, K., Dearing, J., Larson, R. S., Cline, G. & Brummans, B. H. J. M. (2001). Tensions in Community Health Improvement Initiatives: Communication and Collaboration in a Managed Care Environment. *Journal of Applied Communication Research, 29,* 137–152.

Meiners, E. B. & Miller, V. D. (2004). The Effect of Formality and Relational Tone on Supervisor/Subordinate Negotiation Episodes. *Western Journal of Communication, 68,* 302–321.

Meyer, J. (1995). Tell Me a Story: Eliciting Organizational Values from Narratives. *Communication Quarterly, 43,* 210–224.

Meyer, E. (2010, August 19). The Four Keys to Success with Virtual Teams. *Forbes*. Retrieved on July 2, 2013, from http://www.forbes.com/2010/08/19/virtual-teams-meetings-leadership-managing-cooperation.html.

Meyer, J. W. & Scott, W. R. (1983). *Organizational Environments: Ritual and Rationality*. Beverly Hills, CA: Sage.

Meyerson, D. E. (1994). Interpretations of Stress in Institutions: The Cultural Production of Ambiguity and Burnout. *Administrative Science Quarterly, 39*, 628–653.

_____. (1998). Feeling Stressed and Burned Out: A Feminist Reading and Re-Visioning of Stress-Based Emotions Within Medicine and Organizational Science. *Organizational Science, 8*, 103–118.

Miles, R. (1965). Human Relations or Human Resources. *Harvard Business Review, 43*, 21–29.

Miller, B. K. & Werner, S. (2005). Factors Influencing the Inflation of Task Performance Ratings for Workers with Disabilities and Contextual Performance Ratings for Their Coworkers. *Human Performance, 18*, 309–329.

Miller, B. M. & Horsley, S. (2009). Digging Deeper: Crisis Management in the Coal Industry. *Journal of Applied Communication Research, 37*, 298–316.

Miller, K. (1995). *Organizational Communication: Approaches and Processes*. Belmont, CA: Wadsworth.

_____. (1998). Nurses at the Edge of Chaos: The Application of "New Science" Concepts to Organizational Systems. *Managerial Communication Quarterly, 12*, 112–127.

_____. (2002). The Experience of Emotion in the Workplace: Professing in the Midst of Tragedy. *Management Communication Quarterly, 15*, 571–600.

_____. (2005). *Communication Theories: Perspectives, Processes, and Contexts,* 2nd ed., New York: McGraw-Hill.

_____. (2007). Compassionate Communication in the Workplace: Exploring Processes of Noticing, Connecting, and Responding. *Journal of Applied Communication Research, 35*, 223–245.

Miller, K. (2013). Organizational Emotions and Compassion at Work. In L. L. Putnam & D. K. Mumby (eds.), *The SAGE Handbook of Organizational Communication*, 3rd ed (pp. 569–587). Thousand Oaks, CA: Sage.

Miller, K. I., Birkholt, M., Scott, C. & Stage, C. (1995). Empathy and Burnout in Human Service Work: An Extension of a Communication Model. *Communication Research, 22*, 123–147.

Miller, K. L, Considine, J. & Garner, J. (2007). "Let Me Tell You About My Job": Exploring the Terrain of Emotion in the Workplace. *Management Communication Quarterly, 20*, 231–260.

Miller, K. L, Ellis, B. H., Zook, E. G. & Lyles, J. S. (1990). An Integrated Model of Communication, Stress, and Burnout in the Workplace. *Communication Research, 17*, 300–326.

Miller, K. L, Joseph, L. & Apker, J. (2000). Strategic Ambiguity in the Role Development Process. *Journal of Applied Communication Research, 28*, 193–214.

Miller, K. I. & Koesten, J. (2008). Financial Feeling: An Investigation of Emotion and Communication in the Workplace. *Journal of Applied Communication Research, 36*, 8–32.

Miller, K. I. & Monge, P. R. (1985). Social Information and Employee Anxiety About Organizational Change. *Human Communication Research, 11*, 365–386.

_____. (1986). Participation, Satisfaction, and Productivity: A Meta-Analytic Review. *Academy of Management Journal, 29*, 727–753.

Miller, K. L, Stiff, J. B. & Ellis, B. H. (1988). Communication and Empathy as Precursors to Burnout Among Human Service Workers.

Communication Monographs, 55, 250–265.

Miller, V. D. & Jablin, F. M. (1991). Information Seeking During Organizational Entry: Influences, Tactics, and a Model of the Process. *Academy of Management Review, 16*, 92–120.

Miller, V. D., Jablin, F. M., Casey, M. K., Lamphear-Van Horn, M. & Ethington, C. (1996). The Maternity Leave as a Role Negotiation Process. *Journal of Managerial Issues, 8*, 286–309.

Miller, V. D., Johnson, J. R. & Grau, J. (1994). Antecedents to Willingness to Participate in a Planned Organizational Change. *Journal of Applied Communication Research, 22*, 59–80.

Miner, J. B. (1980). *Theories of Organizational Behavior*. New York: Dryden Press.

_____. (1982). *Theories of Organizational Structure and Process*. New York: Dryden Press.

Mintzberg, H. (1973). *The Nature of Managerial Work*. New York: Harper & Row.

Mohrman, S. A., with Cohen, S. G. & Mohrman, A. M. (1995). *Designing Team-Based Organizations*. San Francisco: Jossey-Bass.

_____. (1998). Communication Structures and Processes in Globalization. *Journal of Communication, 48*(4), 142–153.

Monge, P. R. & Contractor, N. S. (2001). Emergence of Communication Networks. In F. M. Jablin & L. L. Putnam (eds.), *The New Handbook of Organizational Communication: Advances in Theory, Research, and Methods* (pp. 440–502). Thousand Oaks, CA: Sage.

_____. *Theories of Communication Networks*. Oxford: Oxford University Press.

Monge, P. R. & Eisenberg, E. M. (1987). Emergent Communication Networks. In F. M. Jablin, L. L. Putnam, K. H. Roberts & L. W.

Porter (eds.), *Handbook of Organizational Communication: An Interdisciplinary Perspective* (pp. 304–342). Newbury Park, CA: Sage.

Monge, P. R., Heiss, B. M. & Margolin, D. (2008). Communication Network Evolution in Organizational Communities. *Communication Theory, 18*, 449–477.

Monge, P. R. & Miller, K. I. (1988). Participative Processes in Organizations. In G. M. Goldhaber & G. A. Barnett (eds.), *Handbook of Organizational Communication* (pp. 213–229). Norwood, NJ: Ablex.

More, E. (1998). *Managing Change: Exploring State of the Art.* Greenwich, CT: JAI Press.

Morgan, G. (1986). *Images of Organization.* Beverly Hills, CA: Sage.

_____. (1997). *Images of Organization,* 2nd ed., Newbury Park, CA: Sage.

Morgan, J. M. & Krone, K. J. (2001). Bending the Rules of "Professional" Display: Emotional Improvisation in Caregiver Performances. *Journal of Applied Communication Research, 29*, 317–340.

Morley, D. D. & Shockley-Zalabak, P. (1991). Setting the Rules: An Examination of Organizational Founders' Values. *Management Communication Quarterly, 4*, 422–449.

Morley, I. E. & Stephenson, G. M. (1977). The Social Psychology of Bargaining. London: Allen & Unwin.

Morris, J. A. & Feldman, D. C. (1996). The Dimensions, Antecedents, and Consequences of Emotional Labor. *Academy of Management Review, 21*, 986–1010.

Morrison, A. M. & Von Glinow, M. A. (1990). Women and Minorities in Management. *American Psychologist, 45*, 200–208.

Morrison, E. W. (1993). Newcomer Information Seeking: Exploring Types, Modes, Sources, and Outcomes. *Academy of Management Journal, 36*, 557–589.

_____. (2003). Information Seeking Within Organizations. *Human Communication Research, 28*, 229–242.

Morrow, R. A. (1994). *Critical Theory and Methodology.* Thousand Oaks, CA: Sage.

Muchinsky, P. (1977). Organizational Communication: Relationships to Organizational Climate and Job Satisfaction. *Academy of Management Journal, 20*, 592–607.

Mumby, D. K. (1987). The Political Functions of Narrative in Organizations. *Communication Monographs, 54*, 113–127.

_____. (1988). *Communication and Power in Organizations: Discourse, Ideology, and Domination.* Norwood, NJ: Ablex.

_____. (1989). Ideology and the Social Construction of Meaning: A Communication Perspective. *Communication Quarterly, 37*, 291–304.

_____. (1993). *Narrative and Social Control.* Newbury Park, CA: Sage.

_____. (1996). Feminism, Postmodernism, and Organizational Communication Studies: A Critical Reading. *Management Communication Quarterly, 9*, 259–295.

_____. (2000). Common Ground from the Critical Perspective: Overcoming Binary Oppositions. In S. R. Gorman & M. S. Poole (eds.), *Perspectives on Organizational Communication: Finding Common Ground* (pp. 68–86). New York: Guilford.

_____. (2001). Power and Politics. In F. M. Jablin & L. L. Putnam (eds.), *The New Handbook of Organizational Communication: Advances in Theory, Research, and Methods* (pp. 585–623). Thousand Oaks, CA: Sage.

_____. (2005). Theorizing Resistance in Organization Studies: A Dialectical Approach. *Management Communication Quarterly, 19*, 19–44.

Mumby, D. K. & Putnam, L. L. (1992). The Politics of Emotion: A Feminist Reading of Bounded Rationality.

Academy of Management Review, J 7, 465–486.

Murphy, A. G. (1998). Hidden Transcripts of Flight Attendant Resistance. *Management Communication Quarterly, 11*, 499–535.

Murray, S. (2009, May 9). The Curse of the Class of 2009. *The Wall Street Journal.* Retrieved on August 27, 2010, from http://online.wsj.com/article/SB124181970915002009.html.

Myers, K. K. (2005). A Burning Desire: Assimilation into a Fire Department. *Management Communication Quarterly, 18*, 344–384.

Myers, K. K., Jahn, J. L. S., Gailliard, B. M. & Stoltzfus, K. (2011). Vocational Anticipatory Socialization (VAS): A Communicataive Model of Adolescents' Interests in STEM. *Management Communication Quarterly, 25*, 87–120.

Myers, K. K. & McPhee, R. D. (2006). Influences on Member Assimilation in Workgroups in High-Reliability Organizations: A Multilevel Analysis. *Human Communication Research, 32*, 440–468.

Myers, K. K. & Oetzel, J. G. (2003). Exploring the Dimensions of Organizational Assimilation: Creating and Validating a Measure. *Communication Quarterly, 51*, 438–457.

Myers, L. L. & Larson, R. S. (2005). Preparing Students for Early Work Conflict. *Business Communication Quarterly, 68*, 306–317.

Neale, M. A. & Bazerman, M. H. (1985). The Effects of Framing and Negotiator Overconfidence on Bargaining Behaviors and Outcomes. *Academy of Management Journal, 28*, 34–49.

Nelson, N. L. & Probst, T. M. (2004). Multiple Minority Individuals: Multiplying the Risk of Workplace Harassment and Discrimination. In J. L. Chin (ed.), *The Psychology of Prejudice and Discrimination: Ethnicity and Multiracial Identity, Vol. 2* (pp. 193–217). Westport, CT: Praeger.

New Gallup Poll. (2005, December 8). U.S. *Equal Employment Opportunity Commission.* Retrieved on November 24, 2007, from http://www.eeoc.gov/eeoc/newsroom/release/12-8-05.cfm.

Newell, F. (2000). *Loyalty.com.* New York: McGraw-Hill.

New Study Reveals Sweeping Dissatisfaction with Customer Service. (2004, July 19). Retrieved on February 19, 2008, from http://www.instantservice.com/news/20040719_2.html.

Ng, T. W. H., Sorensen, K. L. & Yim, F. H. K. (2009). Does the Job Satisfaction-Job Performance Relationship Vary Across Cultures? *Journal of Cross-Cultural Psychology, 40,* 761–796.

Nicolini, D., Mengis, J. & Swan, J. (2012). Understanding the Role of Objects in Cross-Disciplinary Collaboration. *Organization Science, 23,* 612–629.

Nicotera, A. M., Rodriguez, A. J., Hall, M. & Jackson, R. L. (1995). A History of the Study of Communication and Conflict. In A. M. Nicotera (ed.), *Conflict and Organizations: Communicative Processes* (17–41). Albany: State University of New York Press.

Noe, R. A. (1988). Women and Mentoring: A Review and Research Agenda. *Academy of Management Review, 13,* 65–78.

Nonaka, I. & Takeuchi, H. (1995). *The Knowledge-Creating Company.* Oxford: Oxford University Press.

Noonan, P. (2010, August 13). We Pay Them to Be Rude to Us. *The Wall Street Journal.* Retrieved on August 24, 2010, from http://online.wsj.com/article/SB1000142405274870440 7804575425983109795768.html.

Norander, S. & Harater, L. M. (2012). Reflexivity in practice: Challenges and Potentials of Transnational Organizing. *Management Communication Quarterly, 26,* 74–105.

Northouse, P. G. (1997). *Leadership.* Thousand Oaks, CA: Sage.

Novak, J. M. & Sellnow, T. L. (2009). Reducing Organizational Risk Through Participatory Communication. *Journal of Applied Communication Research, 37,* 349–373.

"Number of Active Users." (2013). Number of Active Users at Facebook Over the Years. *Associated Press.* Retrieved on June 4, 2013, from http://news.yahoo.com/number-active-users-facebook-over-230449748.html.

Nusca, A. (2011, July 28). Rural U.S. Population Lowest in History, Demographers Say. Retrieved on June 5, 2013, from http://www.smartplanet.com/blog/smart-takes/rural-us-population-lowest-in-history-demographers-say/17982.

Nutt, P. C. (1984). Types of Organizational Decision Processes. *Administrative Science Quarterly, 29,* 414–450.

_____. (1999). Surprising But True: Half the Decisions in Organizations Fail. *Academy of Management Executive, 13*(4), 75–90.

Nye, D. (1998). Affirmative Action and the Stigma of Incompetence. *Academy of Management Executive, 12*(1), 88–89.

"Office Romances." (2012, August 26). *Office Romances Often Sparked by Emoticon-Laced Emails: Survey.* Retrieved June 1, 2013, from http://www.huffingtonpost.com/2012/08/26/office-romances-emoticons_n_1828493.html.

Ohlott, P., Ruderman, M. & McCauley, C. (1994). Gender Differences in Managers' Developmental Job Experiences. *Academy of Management Journal, 37,* 46–67.

O'Kane, R. H. T. (2007). *Terrorism: A Short History of a Big Idea.* Harlow, England: Pearson Longman.

Oliver, J. K. (2007). U.S. Foreign Policy After 9/11: Context and Prospect. In M. J. Miller & B. Stefanova (eds.), *The War on Terror in Comparative Perspective: U.S. Security and Foreign Policy After 9/11* (pp. 19–45). New York: Palgrave MacMillan.

Omdahl, B. L. & O'Donnell, C. (1999). Emotional Contagion, Empathic Concern and Communicative Responsiveness as Variables Affecting Nurses' Stress and Occupational Commitment. *Journal of Advanced Nursing, 29,* 1351–1359.

Orbe, M. P. (1998). An Outsider Within Perspective to Organizational Communication: Explicating the Communicative Practices of Co-Cultural Group Members. *Management Communication Quarterly, 12,* 230–279.

Orlitzky, M. & Hirokawa, R. Y. (2001). To Err Is Human, to Correct for It Divine: A Meta-Analysis of Research Testing the Functional Theory of Group Decision-Making Effectiveness. *Small Group Research, 32,* 313–341.

Osburn, L. (2007, September 17). Expecting the World on a Silver Platter. *Houston Chronicle,* pp. D1, D6.

Osland, J. S. & Bird, A. (2000). Beyond Sophisticated Stereotyping: Cultural Sensemaking in Context. *Academy of Management Executive, 14*(1), 65–79.

Ouchi, W. G. (1981). *Theory Z.* New York: Avon Books.

Pacanowsky, M. (1988). Communication in the Empowering Organization. In J. A. Anderson (ed.), *Communication Yearbook 11* (pp. 356–379). Newbury Park, CA: Sage.

Pacanowsky, M. & O'Donnell-Trujillo, N. (1983). Organizational Communication as Cultural Performance. *Communication Monographs, 50,* 126–147.

Padilla, O. (2009, November 5). E-Mail Overload. *Charlotte Florida Weekly.* Retrieved on August 19, 2010, from http://charlotte.floridaweekly.com/news/2009-ll-05/Business_News/Email_Overload.html.

Page, S. E. (2007). Making the Difference: Applying a Logic of Diversity. *Academy of Management Perspectives, 21,* 6–20.

Pal, M. & Buzzanell, P. M. (2013). Breaking the Myth of Indian Call Centers: A Postcolonial Analysis of Resistance. *Communication Monographs, 80,* 199–219.

Parameswaran, R. (2008). The Other Sides of Globalization: Communication, Culture, and Postcolonial Critique. *Communication, Culture & Critique, 1*, 116–125.

Parker, P. S. (2003). Control, Resistance, and Empowerment in Raced, Gendered, and Classed Work Contexts: The Case of African American Women. In Pamela J. Kalbfleisch (ed.), *Communication Yearbook 27,* (pp. 257–291). Mahwah, NJ: Lawrence Erlbaum Associates.

Pearlson, K. E. & Saunders, C. S. (2001). There's No Place like Home: Managing Telecommuting Paradoxes. *Academy of Management Executive, 15*(2), 117–128.

Peck, D. (2010, June). How a New Jobless Era Will Transform America. *The Atlantic,* pp. 42–56.

Pederson, D. (1997, June 23). Dissing Customers: Why the Service Is Missing from America's Service Economy. *Newsweek,* pp. 56–57.

Penelope, J. (1990). *Speaking Freely: Unlearning the Lies of the Fathers' Tongues.* New York: Pergamon Press.

Penn, M. J. (2007). *Microtrends: The Small Forces Behind Tomorrow's Changes.* New York: Hachette Book Group.

Pepper, G. L. & Larson, G. S. (2006). Cultural Identity Tensions in a Post-Acquisition Organization. *Journal of Applied Communication Research, 34*, 49–71.

Peraino, K. (2003, September 8). Good Times in the Skies. *Newsweek,* p. 58.

Perriton, L. (2009). "We Don't Want Complaining Women!" A Critical Analysis of the Business Case for Diversity. *Management Communication Quarterly, 23*, 218–243.

Peters, T. J. & Waterman, R. H. (1982). *In Search of Excellence: Lessons from America's Best-Run Companies.* New York: Harper & Row.

Pfeffer, J. (1998). *The Human Equation: Building Profits by Putting People First.* Boston: Harvard Business School Press.

Pfeffer, J. & Veiga, J. F. (1999). Putting People First for Organizational Success. *Academy of Management Executive, 13*(2), 37–48.

Phillips, A. (2010, July 31). Americans with Disabilities Act Celebrates 20 Years. *VOA News.com.* Retrieved on August 3, 2010, from http://www.voanews.com/english/news/usa/Americans-with-Disabilities-Act-Celebrates-20-Years-99691979.html.

Pierce, T. & Dougherty, D. S. (2002). The Construction, Enactment, and Maintenance of Power-as-Domination Through an Acquisition: The Case of TWA and Ozark Airlines. *Management Communication Quarterly, 16*, 129–164.

Pines, A. M., Aronson, E. & Kafry, D. (1981). *Burnout: From Tedium to Personal Growth.* New York: Free Press.

Pitts, D. & Jarry, E. (2007). Ethnic Diversity and Organizational Performance: Assessing Diversity Effects at the Managerial and Street Levels. *International Public Management Journal, 10*, 233–254.

Pondy, L. R. (1967). Organizational Conflict: Concepts and Models. *Administrative Science Quarterly, 12*, 296–320.

Poole, M. S. (1983). Decision Development in Small Groups II: A Study of Multiple Sequences in Decision-Making. *Communication Monographs, 50*, 206–232.

_____. (1996, February). Another Turn of the Wheel: A Return to Systems Theory in Organizational Communication. Paper presented at the Austin, TX: Conference on Organizational Communication and Change. Austin, TX.

Poole, M. S. & DeSanctis, G. (1992). Microlevel Structuration in Computer-Supported Group Decision Making. *Human Communication Research, 19*, 5–49.

Poole, M. S. & Roth, J. (1989a). Decision Development in Small Groups IV: A Typology of Group Decision Paths. *Human Communication Research, 15*, 323–356.

_____. (1989b). Decision Development in Small Groups V: Test of a Contingency Model. *Human Communication Research, 15*, 549–589.

Popovich, P. & Wanous, J. P. (1982). The Realistic Job Preview as a Persuasive Communication. *Academy of Management Review, 7*, 570–578.

Poundstone, W. (2003). *How Would You Move Mount Fuji? Microsoft's Cult of the Puzzle.* New York: Little, Brown & Company.

Powell, G. N. & Goulet, L. R. (1996). Recruiters' and Applicants' Reactions to Campus Interviews and Employment Decisions. *Academy of Management Journal, 39*, 1619–1640.

Pugh, D. S. & Hickson, D. J. (1989). *Writers on Organizations.* Newbury Park, CA: Sage.

Putnam, L. L. (1983). The Interpretive Perspective: An Alternative to Functionalism. In L. L. Putnam & M. E. Pacanowsky (eds.), *Communication and Organizations: An Interpretive Approach* (pp. 31–54). Beverly Hills, CA: Sage.

_____. (1995). Formal Negotiations: The Productive Side of Organizational Conflict. In A. M. Nicotera (ed.), *Conflict and Organizations: Communication Processes* (pp. 183–200). Albany: State University of New York Press.

Putnam, L. L. & Kolb, D. M. (2000). Rethinking Negotiation: Feminist Views of Communication and Exchange. In P. M. Buzzanell (ed.), *Rethinking Organizational and Managerial Communication from Feminist Perspectives* (pp. 76–104). Thousand Oaks, CA: Sage.

Putnam, L. L. & Nicotera, A. M. (2010). Communicative Constitution of Organization Is a Question: Critical Issues for Addressing It. *Management Communication Quarterly, 24*, 158–165.

Putnam, L. L. & Peterson, T. (2003). The Edwards Aquifer Dispute: Shifting Frames in a Protracted

Conflict. In R. J. Lewicki, B. Gray & M. Elliott (eds.), *Making Sense of Intractable Environmental Conflicts: Frames and Cases* (pp. 127–158). Washington, DC: Island Press.

Putnam, L. L. & Poole, M. S. (1987). Conflict and Negotiation. In F. M. Jablin, L. L. Putnam, K. H. Roberts & L. W. Porter (eds.), *Handbook of Organizational Communication: An Interdisciplinary Perspective* (pp. 549–599). Newbury Park, CA: Sage.

Putnam, L. L. & Stohl, C. (1996). Bona Fide Groups: An Alternative Perspective for Communication and Small Group Decision Making. In R. Y. Hirokawa & M. S. Poole (eds.), *Communication and Group Decision Making*, 2nd ed. (pp. 147–178). Thousand Oaks, CA: Sage.

Putnam, L. L. & Wondolleck, J. M. (2003). Intractability: Definitions, Dimensions, and Distinctions. In R. J. Lewicki, B. Gray & M. Elliott (eds.), *Making Sense of Intractable Environmental Conflicts: Frames and Cases* (pp. 35–59). Washington, DC: Island Press.

Quindlen, A. (2003, October 20). Still Needing the F Word. *Newsweek*, p. 74.

_____. (2008, October 13). The Leadership Lid. *Newsweek*, p. 86.

Quinn, J. B. (2006, December 18). Giving Freely and Wisely. *Newsweek*, p. 51.

Quinn, R. E. & McGrath, M. R. (1985). The Transformation of Organizational Cultures: A Competing Values Perspective. In P. J. Frost, L. F. Moore, M. R. Louis, C. C. Lundberg & J. Martin (eds.), *Organizational Culture* (pp. 315–334). Beverly Hills, CA: Sage.

Ragins, B. R. (1997). Diversified Mentoring Relationships in Organizations: A Power Perspective. *Academy of Management Review*, 22, 482–521.

Ragins, B. R. & Cotton, J. L. (1991). Easier Said Than Done: Gender Differences in Perceived Barriers to Gaining a Mentor. *Academy of Management Journal*, 34, 939–951.

Ragins, B. R., Townsend, B. & Mattis, M. (1998). Gender Gap in the Executive Suite: CEOs and Female Executives Report on Breaking the Glass Ceiling. *Academy of Management Executive*, 12(1), 28–42.

Ralston, S. M. (1993). Applicant Communication Satisfaction, Intent to Accept Second Interview Offers, and Recruiter Communication Style. *Journal of Applied Communication Research*, 21, 53–65.

Ralston, S. M. & Kirkwood, W. G. (1995). Overcoming Managerial Bias in Employment Interviewing. *Journal of Applied Communication Research*, 23, 75–92.

Ramaswami, A., Dreher, G. F., Bretz, R. & Carolyn, C. (2010). Gender, Mentoring, and Career Success: The Importance of Organizational Context. *Personnel Psychology*, 63, 385–405.

Rampell, C. (2013, May 29). U.S. Women on the Rise as Family Breadwinner. *New York Times*. Retrieved on June 29, 2013, from http://www.nytimes.com/2013/05/30/business/economy/women-as-family-breadwinner-on-the-rise-study-says.html.

Ray, E. B. (1987). Supportive Relation ships and Occupational Stress in the Workplace. In T. L. Albrecht & M. B. Adelman (eds.), *Communicating Social Support* (pp. 172–191). Beverly Hills, CA: Sage.

_____. (1993). When the Links Become Chains: Considering Dysfunctions of Supportive Communication in the Workplace. *Communication Monographs*, 60, 106–111.

Ray, E. B. & Miller, K. I. (1991). The Influence of Communication Structure and Social Support on Job Stress and Burnout. *Management Communication Quarterly*, 4, 506–527.

Reed, C. (2012, September 19). How to Horse-Train Leaders. *Fast Company*. Retrieved on June 1, 2013, from http://www.fastcompany.com/3001382/how-horse-train-leaders.

Reed, M. (2010). Is Communication Constitutive of Organization? *Management Communication Quarterly*, 24, 151–157.

Reich, R. B. (2000). *The Future of Success: Working and Living in the New Economy*. New York: Vintage Books.

Reichers, A. E. (1987). An Interactionist Perspective on Newcomer Socialization Rates. *Academy of Management Review*, 12, 278–287.

Reichers, A. E., Wanous, J. P. & Austin, J. T. (1997). Understanding and Managing Cynicism About Organizational Change. *Academy of Management Executive*, 11(1), 48–59.

Rhode, D. (2010). *The Beauty Bias: The Injustice of Appearance in Life and Law*. New York: Oxford University Press.

Rice, R. E. & Aydin, C. (1991). Attitudes Toward New Organizational Technology: Network Proximity as a Mechanism for Social Information Processing. *Administrative Science Quarterly*, 36, 219–244.

Rice, R. E. & Love, G. (1987). Electronic Emotion: Socioemotional Content in a Computer-Mediated Communication Network. *Communication Research*, 14, 85–108.

Richard, O. C., Kirby, S. L. & Chadwick, K. (2013). The Impact of Racial and Gender Diversity in Management on Financial Performance: How Participative Strategy Making Features Can Unleash a Diversity Advantage. *The International Journal of Human Resource Management*, 24, 2571–2582.

Richard, O. C., Murthi, B. P. S. & Ismail, K. (2007). The Impact of Racial Diversity on Intermediate and Long-Term Performance: The Moderating Role of Environmental Context. *Strategic Management Journal*, 28, 1213–1233.

Richel, M. (2009, September 30). At 60 M.P.H., Office Work Is High Risk. *New York Times*. Retrieved on

August 23, 2010, from http://www.nytimes.com/2009/10/01/technology/01distracted.html?_r=l.

Risberg, A. (1999). *Ambiguities Thereafter.* Lund, Sweden: Lund University Press.

Ritchie, J. B. & Miles, R. E. (1970). An Analysis of Quantity and Quality of Participation as Mediating Variables in the Participative Decision Making Process. *Personnel Psychology, 23,* 347–359.

Ritzer, G. (2000). *The McDonaldization of Society.* Thousand Oaks, CA: Pine Forge Press.

Roberts, K., Kossek, E. E. & Ozeki, C. (1998). Managing the Global Workforce: Challenges and Strategies. *Academy of Management Executive, 12*(4), 93–106.

Robinson, G. & Dechant, K. (1997). Building a Case for Diversity. *Academy of Management Executive, 11,* 21–31.

Robinson, V. M. J. (2001). Embedding Leadership in Task Performance. In K. Wong & C. W. Evers (Eds.), *Leadership for Quality Schooling* (pp. 90–102). London: Routledge/Falmer.

Rodrick, D. (2011). *The Globalization Paradox: Democracy and the Future of the World Economy.* New York: Norton.

Roethlisberger, F. J. & Dickson, W. J. (1939). *Management and the Worker.* Cambridge, MA: Harvard University Press.

Roper, J. & Barker, J. R. (2011). Forum Introduction: State-Owned Enterprises, Corporate Social Responsibility, and Organizational Communication. *Management Communication Quarterly, 25,* 690–692.

Roth, N. L. (1991, February). Secrets in Organizations: Addressing Taboo Topics at Work. Paper presented at the annual meeting of the Western Speech Communication Association, Phoenix, AZ.

Russ, G. S., Daft, R. L. & Lengel, R. H. (1990). Media Selection and Managerial Characteristics in Organizational Communications. *Management Communication Quarterly, 4,* 151–175.

Russo, T. C. (1998). Organizational and Professional Identification: A Case of Newspaper Journalists. *Management Communication Quarterly, 12,* 72–111.

Rybicki, M. (2003, March 10). Temporary Worker, Permanent Loser? *Newsweek,* p. 18.

Rynes, S. L. (1990). Recruitment, Job Choice, and Post-Hire Consequences: A Call for New Research Directions. In M. D. Dundee & L. Hugh (eds.), *Handbook of Industrial and Organizational Psychology,* 2nd ed. (pp. 399–444). Palo Alto, CA: Consulting Psychologists Press.

Sager, K. L. (2008). An Exploratory Study of the Relationships Between Theory X/Y Assumptions and Superior Communicator Style. *Management Communication Quarterly, 22,* 288–312.

Said, E. (2001). The Clash of Ignorance. *The Nation, 273*(12), 11–13.

Sandberg, S. (2013). *Lean In: Women, Work, and the Will to Lead.* New York: Alfred E. Knopf.

Sandelands, L. E. & Boudens, C. J. (2000). Feeling at Work. In S. Fineman (ed.), *Emotion in Organizations,* 2nd ed. (pp. 46–63). London: Sage.

Scarduzio, J. A. (2011). Maintaining Order Through Deviance? The Emotional Deviance, Power, and Professional Work of Municipal Court Judges. *Management Communication Quarterly, 25,* 283–310.

Scarduzio, J. A. & Geist-Maratin, P. (2010). Accounting for Victimization: Male Professors' Ideological Positioning in Stories of Sexual Harassment. *Management Communication Quarterly, 24,* 419–445.

Schall, M. (1983). A Communication-Rules Approach to Organizational Culture. *Administrative Science Quarterly, 28,* 557–581.

Schein, E. H. (1985). *Organizational Culture and Leadership.* San Francisco: Jossey-Bass.

_____. (1992). *Organizational Culture and Leadership,* 2nd ed., San Francisco: Jossey-Bass.

_____. (2004). The Culture of Media as Viewed from an Organizational Culture Perspective. *International Journal on Media Management, 5,* 171–172.

Schmitz, J. & Fulk, J. (1991). Organizational Colleagues, Media Richness, and Electronic Mail: A Test of the Social Influence Model of Technology Use. *Communication Research, 18,* 487–523.

Schultz, F., Utz, S. & Göritz, A. (2011). Is the Medium the Message? Perceptions of and Reactions to Crisis Communication via Twitter, Blogs and Traditional Media. *Public Relations Review, 37,* 20–27.

Schuman, H. & Scott, J. (1989). Generations and Collective Memories. *American Psychological Review, 54,* 359–381.

Schwartz, E. I. (2004). *Juice: The Creative Fuel That Drives World-Class Inventors.* Cambridge, MA: Harvard Business School Press.

Schwartz, F. N. (1989). Management Women and the New Facts of Life. *Harvard Business Review,* January/February, 65–76.

Schwartz, N. D. (2001, December 24). Enron Fallout: Wide, But Not Deep. *Fortune,* pp. 71–72.

Scott, C. & Myers, K. K. (2005). The Socialization of Emotion: Learning Emotion Management at the Fire Station. *Journal of Applied Communication Research, 33,* 67–92.

Scott, C. R. (2001). Establishing and Maintaining Customer Loyalty and Employee Identification in the New Economy: A Communicative Response. *Management Communication Quarterly, 14,* 629–636.

Scott, D. M., Dam, I., Páez, A. & Wilton, R. D. (2012). Investigating the Effects of Social Influence on the Choice to Telework. *Environment and Planning A, 2012,* 1016–1031.

Scott, J. (1990). *Domination and the Arts of Resistance: Hidden*

Transcripts. New Haven, CT: Yale University Press.

Seeger, M. W. & Ulmer, R. R. (2003). Explaining Enron: Communication and Responsible Leadership. *Management Communication Quarterly, 17,* 58–84.

Seibold, D. R. & Shea, B. C. (2001). Participation and Decision Making. In F. M. Jablin & L. L. Putnam (eds.), *The New Handbook of Organizational Communication: Advances in Theory, Research, and Methods* (pp. 664–703). Thousand Oaks, CA: Sage.

Senge, P. (1991). *The Fifth Discipline: The Art and Practice of the Learning Organization.* New York: Doubleday/Currency.

Senge, P., Roberts, C., Ross, R., Smith, B. & Kleiner, A. (1994). *The Fifth Discipline Fieldbook.* New York: Doubleday/Currency.

Service Sector. (2012, July 5). Service Sector Increases at Slowest Pace in 2 Years. *New York Times.* Retrieved on July 3, 2013, from http://www.nytimes.com/2012/07/06/business/economy/positive-reports-on-us-jobs.html.

Services. (2010). India Brand Equity Foundation. Retrieved on August 29, 2010, from http://ibef.org/economy/services.aspx.

Shachaf, P. (2008). Cultural Diversity and Information and Communication Technology Impacts on Global Virtual Teams: An exploratory study. *Information and Management, 45,* 131–142.

Shaughnessy, H. (2012, September 7). Who Are the Happiest Workers in America (And Who Is Getting Happier)? *Forbes.* Retrieved on June 1, 2013, from http://www.forbes.com/sites/haydnshaughnessy/2012/09/07/who-are-the-happiest-workers-in-america-and-who-is-getting-happier/.

Sheer, V. C. & Chen, L. (2004). Improving Media Richness Theory: A Study of Interaction Goals, Message Valence, and Task Complexity in Manager-Subordinate Communication. *Management*

Communication Quarterly, 18, 76–93.

Shekhar, S. (2006). Understanding the Virtuality of Virtual Organizations. *Leadership & Organization Development Journal, 27,* 465–483.

Sheppard, L. & Aquino, K. (2012). Two Sides of the Same Story: A Conceptualization of the Nature of Conflict Among Professional Women and Observers' (Biased?) Perceptions of Conflict Among Professional Women. *Academy of Management Perspectives, 27*(1), 52–62.

Shinn, M. (1982). Methodological Issues: Evaluating and Using Information. In W. S. Paine (ed.), *Job Stress and Burnout: Research, Theory and Intervention Perspectives* (pp. 61–79). Beverly Hills, CA: Sage.

Shockley-Zalabak, P. (2002). Protean Places: Teams Across Time and Space. *Journal of Applied Communication Research, 3,* 231–250.

Shockley-Zalabak, P. & Morley, D. D. (1994). Creating a Culture: A Longitudinal Examination of the Influence of Management and Employee Values on Communication Rule Stability and Emergence. *Human Communication Research, 20,* 334–355.

Shore, L. M., Chung-Herrera, B. G., Dean, M. A., Ehrhart, K. H., Jung, D. I., Randel, A. E. & Singh, G. (2009). Diversity in Organizations: Where Are We Now and Where Are We Going? *Human Resource Management Review, 19,* 117–133.

Short, J., Williams, E. & Christie, B. (1976). *The Social Psychology of Telecommunications.* New York: Wiley.

Shuler, S. & Sypher, B. D. (2000). Seeking Emotional Labor: When Managing the Heart Enhances the Work Experience. *Management Communication Quarterly, 14,* 50–89.

Shultz, K. S., Morton, K. R. & Weckerle, J. R. (1998). The Influence of Push and Pull Factors on Voluntary and Involuntary Early

Retirees' Retirement Decision and Adjustment. *Journal of Vocational Behavior, 53,* 45–58.

Shumate, M. (2012). The Evolution of the HIV/AIDS NGO Hyperlink Network. *Journal of Computer-Mediated Communication, 17,* 120–134.

Shumate, M. & Contractor, N. (2013, Forthcoming). Organizational Communication and Social Networks. In L. L. Putnam & D. K. Mumby (eds.), *The SAGE Handbook of Organizational Communication,* 3rd ed., Thousand Oaks, CA: Sage.

Shumate, M., Fulk, J. & Monge, P. (2005). Predictors of the International HIV-AIDS INGO Network Over Time. *Human Communication Research, 31,* 482–510.

Sias, P. & Jablin, F. (1995). Differential Superior-Subordinate Relations, Perceptions of Fairness, and Coworker Communication. *Human Communication Research, 22,* 5–38.

Sias, P. M., Pedersen, H., Gallagher, E. B. & Kopaneva, I. (2012). Workplace Friendship in the Electronically Connected Organization. *Human Communication Research, 38,* 253–279.

Siegel, D. S. (2009). Green Management Matters Only If It Yields More Green: An Economic/Strategic Perspective. *Academy of Management Perspectives, 23*(3), 5–16.

Silverman, R. E. (2013, February 22). Office Conflict: Women and the 'Catty' Trap. *The Wall Street Journal.* Retrieved on June 1, 2013, from http://blogs.wsj.com/atwork/2013/02/22/conflict-at-the-office-women-and-the-catty-trap/.

Silverman, R. E. & Weber, L. (2013, April 9). The New Résumé: It's 140 Characters. *The Wall Street Journal.* Retrieved on June 1, 2013, from http://online.wsj.com/article/SB10001424127887323820304578412741852687994.html.

Silverstein, K. (2012, October 27). Are Utilities Ready for Hurricane Sandy?

Forbes. Retrieved on June 1, 2013, from http://www.forbes.com/sites/kensilverstein/2012/10/27/are-utilities-ready-for-hurricane-sandy/.

Simon, H. A. (1960). *Administrative Behavior,* 2nd ed., New York: Macmillan.

_____. (1987). Making Management Decisions: The Role of Intuition and Emotion. *Academy of Management Executive, 1,* 57–64.

Sitkin, S. B., Sutcliffe, K. M. & Barrios-Choplin, J. R. (1992). A Dual-Capacity Model of Communication Media Choice in Organizations. *Human Communication Research, 18,* 563–598.

Sloan, A. (2002, January 21). Who Killed Enron? *Newsweek,* pp. 18–24.

Smart, B. (ed.) (1999). *Resisting McDonaldization.* London: Sage.

Smith, F. L. M. & Dougherty, D. S. (2012). Revealing a Master Narrative: Discourses of Retirement Throughout the Working Life Cycle. *Management Communication Quarterly, 26,* 453–478.

Smith, F. L. & Keyton, J. (2001). Organizational Storytelling: Metaphors for Relational Power and Identity Struggles. *Management Communication Quarterly, 15,* 149–182.

Smith, R. C. & Eisenberg, E. M. (1987). Conflict at Disneyland: A Root Metaphor Analysis. *Communication Monographs, 54,* 367–380.

Snyder, J. L. (2012). Extending the Empathic Communication Model of Burnout: Incorporating Individual Differences to Learn More About Workplace Emotion, Communicative Responsiveness, and Burnout. *Communication Quarterly, 60,* 122–142.

Solomon, M. (2012). *High-Tech, High-Touch Customer Service.* New York: AMACOM.

Soukup, E. (2003, September 22). CEOs: That's What That Is. *Newsweek,* p. 10.

Springen, K. (2008, May 12). Cutting Back Your Hours. *Newsweek,* p. 60.

Sproull, L. & Kiesler, S. (1986). Reducing Social Context Cues: The Case of Electronic Mail. *Management Science, 32,* 1492–1512.

Stage, C. W. (1999). Negotiating Organizational Communication Cultures in American Subsidiaries Doing Business in Thailand. *Management Communication Quarterly, 13,* 245–280.

Standifer, R. L., Lester, S. W., Schultz, N. J. & Windsor, J. M. (2013). How Age Similarity Preference, Uncertainty, and Workplace Challenges Affect Conflict. *Human Relations,* online version downloaded June 25, 2013.

Statistics on Aging. (2007). Administration on Aging. Retrieved on September 14, 2007, from http://www.aoa.gov/prof/Statistics/statistics.asp.

Steinberg, R. J. & Figart, D. M. (1999). Emotional Labor Since The Managed Heart. *Annals of the American Academy of Political and Social Science, 561,* 8–26.

Stephens, K. K., Barrett, A. K. & Mahometa, M. J. (2013). Organizational Communication in Emergencies: Using Multiple Channels and Sources to Combat Noise and Capture Attention. *Human Communication Research, 39,* 230–251.

Stephens, K. K. & Dailey, S. L. (2012). Situated Organizational Identification in Newcomers: Impacts of Preentry Organizational Exposure. *Management Communication Quarterly, 26,* 404–422.

Stephens, K. K. & Davis, J. (2009). The Social Influences on Electronic Multitasking in Organizational Meetings. *Management Communication Quarterly, 23,* 63–83.

Stern, L. (2007, September 17). Care from Afar. *Newsweek,* p. E18.

Stiff, J. B., Dillard, J. P., Somera, L., Kim, H. & Sleight, C. (1988). Empathy, Communication, and Prosocial Behavior. *Communication Monographs, 55,* 198–213.

Stiglitz, J. E. (2002). *Globalization and Its Discontents.* New York: Norton.

_____. (2006). *Making Globalization Work.* New York: Norton.

Stohl, C. (1986). The Role of Memorable Messages in the Process of Organizational Socialization. *Communication Quarterly, 34,* 231–249.

_____. (2001). Globalizing Organizational Communication. In F. M. Jablin & L. L. Putnam (eds.), *The New Handbook of Organizational Communication: Advances in Theory, Research, and Methods* (pp. 323–375). Thousand Oaks, CA: Sage.

Stohl, C. & Cheney, G. (2001). Participatory Processes/Paradoxical Practices: Communication and the Dilemmas of Organizational Democracy. *Management Communication Quarterly, 14,* 349–407.

Stohl, C. & Stohl, M. (2007). Networks of Terror: Theoretical Assumptions and Pragmatic Consequences. *Communication Theory, 17,* 93–124.

_____. (2011). Secret Agencies: The Communicative Constitution of a Clandestine Organization. *Organization Studies, 32,* 1197–1215.

Stone, B. (2003, November 24). Soaking in Spam. *Newsweek,* pp. 66–69.

_____. (2004, April 19). Should I Stay or Should I Go? *Newsweek,* pp. 52–54.

Summers, N. (2010, April 1). Chaos Theory: The New Rules of Management for People Who Hate Rules and Management. *Newsweek,* pp. 46–47.

Surber, J. P. (1998). *Culture and Critique: An Introduction to the Critical Discourses of Cultural Studies.* Boulder, CO: Westview Press.

Sutton, R. I. (2007). *The No Asshole Rule: Building a Civilized Workplace and Surviving One That Isn't.* New York: Warner Business Books.

Swift, M. (2010, May 9). Social Media Ease into Workplace. Retrieved on August 23, 2010, from http://www.newsobserver.com/2010/05/09/472466/social-media-ease-into-the-workplace.html.

Tao, D. (2013, March 22). Why the Gym Is Becoming the New Center for Business. *Forbes*. Retrieved on June 1, 2013, from http://www.forbes.com/sites/davidtao/2013/03/22/why-the-gym-is-becoming-the-new-center-for-business/.

Tavernise, S. (2011, May 26). Married Couples Are No Longer a Majority, Census Finds. *New York Times*. Retrieved on June 5, 2013, from http://www.nytimes.com/2011/05/26/us/26marry.html?_r=0.

Taylor, B. & Conrad, C. (1992). Narratives of Sexual Harassment: Organizational Dimensions. *Journal of Applied Communication Research, 20*, 401–418.

Taylor, F. W. (1911). *The Principles of Scientific Management*. New York: Harper & Row.

Taylor, M. & Doerfel, M. L. (2003). Building Interorganizational Relationships That Build Nations. *Human Communication Research, 29*, 153–181.

Taylor, P. & Cohn, D. (2012, November 7). A Milestone En Route to a Majority Minority Nation. Retrieved on June 5, 2013, from http://www.pewsocialtrends.org/2012/11/07/a-milestone-en-route-to-a-majority-minority-nation/.

Teboul, J. C. B. (1995). Determinants of New Hire Information-Seeking During Organizational Encounter. *Western Journal of Communication, 59*, 305–325.

Teboul, J. C. B. & Cole, T. (2005). Relationship Development and Workplace Integration: An Evolutionary Perspective. *Communication Theory, 15*, 389–413.

Temin, D. (2013, May 13). How a CEO Can Wreck a Brand in One Interview: Lessons from Abercrombie & Fitch vs. Dove. *Forbes*. Retrieved on June 1, 2013, from http://www.forbes.com/sites/daviatemin/2013/05/13/abercrombie-and-fitch-v-dove-or-how-a-ceo-can-wreck-a-brand-in-1-interview-7-years-ago/.

Tengler, C. D. & Jablin, F. M. (1983). Effects of Question Type, Orientation, and Sequencing in the Employment Screening Interview. *Communication Monographs, 50*, 243–263.

The American Workforce: 2004–14. (2007). Retrieved on November 24, 2007, from http://careers.stateuniversity.com/pages/838/American-Workforce-2004-14.html.

Therborn, G. (1980). *The Ideology of Power and the Power of Ideology*. London: Verso.

Thomas, D. (1993). Racial Dynamics in Cross-Race Developmental Relationships. *Administrative Science Quarterly, 38*, 169–194.

Thomas, K. W. (1976). Conflict and Conflict Management. In M. Dunnette (ed.), *Handbook of Industrial and Organizational Psychology* (pp. 889–936). Chicago: Rand McNally.

Timmerman, C. E. (2003). Media Selection During the Implementation of Planned Organizational Change: A Predictive Framework Based on Implementation Approach and Phase. *Management Communication Quarterly, 16*, 301–340.

Tjosvold, D. (2008). The Conflict-Positive Organization: It Depends on Us. *Journal of Organizational Behavior, 29*, 19–28.

Tjosvold, D. & Tjosvold, M. M. (1991). *Leading the Team Organization*. New York: Lexington Books.

Tobin, D. R. (1998). *The Knowledge-Enabled Organization*. New York: AMACOM.

Tomlinson, J. (1997). Cultural Globalization and Cultural Imperialism. In A. Mohammadi (ed.), *International Communication and Globalization* (pp. 170–190). Thousand Oaks, CA: Sage.

Tompkins, P. K. & Cheney, G. (1985). Communication and Unobtrusive Control in Contemporary Organizations. In R. D. McPhee & P. K. Tompkins (eds.), *Organizational Communication: Traditional Themes and New Directions* (pp. 179–210). Beverly Hills, CA: Sage.

Tracy, S. J. (2000). Becoming a Character for Commerce: Emotional Labor, Self-Subordination, and Discursive Construction of Identity in a Total Institution. *Management Communication Quarterly, 14*, 90–128.

_____. (2005). Locking Up Emotion: Moving Beyond Dissonance for Understanding Emotion Labor Discomfort. *Communication Monographs, 72*, 261–283.

Tracy, S. J. & Rivera, K. D. (2010). Endorsing Equity and Applauding Stay-at-Home Moms: How Male Voices on Work-Life Reveal Aversive Sexism and Flickers of Transformation. *Management Communication Quarterly, 24*, 3–43.

Treem, J. W. (2012). Communicating Expertise: Knowledge Performances in Professional-Service Firms. *Communication Monographs, 79*, 23–47.

Trethewey, A. (1999). Disciplined Bodies: Women's Embodied Identities at Work. *Organization Studies, 20*, 423–450.

_____. (2000). Revisioning Control: A Feminist Critique of Disciplined Bodies. In P. M. Buzzanell (ed.), *Rethinking Organizational and Managerial Communication from Feminist Perspectives* (pp. 107–127). Thousand Oaks, CA: Sage.

Tretheway, A. & Ashcraft, K. L. (2004). Practicing Disorganization: The Development of Applied Perspectives on Living with Tension. *Journal of Applied Communication Research, 32*, 81–88.

Trethewey, A., Scott, C. & LeGreco, M. (2006). Constructing Embodied Organizational Identities: Commodifying, Securing, and Servicing Professional Bodies. In B. Dow & J. T. Wood (Eds.), *Handbook of Gender and Communication* (pp. 123–141). Thousand Oaks, CA: Sage.

Trevino, L. K., Lengel, R. H. & Daft, R. L. (1987). Media Symbolism, Media Richness, and Media Choice in Organizations: A Symbolic Interactionist Perspective. *Communication Research, 14*, 553–574.

Tsoukas, H. (2010). Foreward: Representation, Signification, Improvisation—A Three-Dimensional View of Organizational Knowledge. In H.E. Canary & R. D. McPhee (Eds.), *Communication and Organizational Knowledge: Contemporary Issues for Theory and Practice* (pp. x–xix). New York: Routledge.

Turnage, J. J. (1990). The Challenge of New Workplace Technology for Psychology. *American Psychologist, 45*, 171–178.

Turner, L. H. & Henzl, S. A. (1987). Influence Attempts in Organizational Conflict: The Effects of Biological Sex, Psychological Gender, and Power Position. *Management Communication Quarterly, 1*, 32–57.

Turner, L. H. & Shuter, R. (2004). African American and European American Women's Visions of Workplace Conflict: A Metaphorical Analysis. *Howard Journal of Communications, 15*, 169–183.

Turner, P. K. (2003). Paradox of Ordering Change: I Insist That We Work as a Team. *Management Communication Quarterly, 16*, 434–439.

Tyler, K. (2008). Treat Contingent Workers with Care: Consider Both Your Company's and Workers' Needs in Contingent Workforce Planning. *HR Magazine*. Retrieved on August 24, 2010, from http://findarticles.com/p/articles/mi_m3495/is_3_53/ai_n24946741.

Ulmer, R. R., Sellnow, T. L. & Seeger, M. W. (2010). *Effective Crisis Communication: Moving From Crisis to Opportunity*, 2nd ed., Thousand Oaks, CA: Sage.

Van Camp, J. (2013, May 6). Galaxy S4 Ad Says Samsung Is for College Grads and Cool Dads, iPhone Is for Old Folks. Retrieved on July 3, 2013, from http://www.digitaltrends.com/mobile/galaxy-s4-commercials-college-grad-iphone-old-folks/.

van Knippenberg, D. & Schippers, M. C. (2007). Work Group Diversity. *Annual Review of Psychology, 58*, 515–541.

Van Maanen, J. (1975). Breaking In: Socialization to Work. In R. Dubin (ed.), *Handbook of Work, Organization and Society* (pp. 67–120). Chicago: Rand McNally.

Van Maanen, J. & Schein, E. H. (1979). Toward a Theory of Organizational Socialization. In B. M. Staw & L. L. Cummings (eds.), *Research in Organizational Behavior, Vol. 1* (pp. 209–264). Greenwich, CT: JAI Press.

Veil, S. R., Sellnow, T. L. & Petrun, E. L. (2012). Hoaxes and the Paradoxical Challenges of Restoring Legitimacy: Dominos' Response to Its YouTube Crisis. *Management Communication Quarterly, 26*, 322–345.

Volkema, R. J., Bergmann, T. J. & Farquhar, K. (1997). Use and Impact of Informal Third-Party Discussions in Interpersonal Conflicts at Work. *Management Communication Quarterly, 11*, 185–216.

Wagner, C. & Schroeder, A. (2010). Capabilities and Roles of Enterprise Wikis in Organizational Communication. *Technical Communication, 57*, 68–89.

Wagner, J. A. (1994). Participation's Effect on Performance and Satisfaction: A Reconsideration of Research Evidence. *Academy of Management Review, 19*, 312–330.

Waldron, V. R. (2000). Relational Experiences and Emotion at Work. In S. Fineman (ed.), *Emotion in Organizations*, 2nd ed. (pp. 64–82). London: Sage.

_____. (2012). *Communicating Emotion at Work*. Cambridge: Polity Press.

Walker, K. L. & Stohl, C. (2012). Communicating in a Collaborating Group: A Longitudinal Network Analysis. *Communication Monographs, 79*, 448–474.

Walther, J. P. & Bunz, U. (2005). The Rules of Virtual Groups: Trust, Liking, and Performance in Computer-Mediated Communication. *Journal of Communication, 55*, 828–846.

Wanous, J. P. (1992). *Organizational Entry: Recruitment, Selection, Orientation, and Socialization of Newcomers*, 2nd ed., Reading, MA: Addison-Wesley.

Wanous, J. P. & Colella, A. (1989). Organizational Entry Research: Current Status and Future Directions. In K. M. Rowland & G. R. Ferris (eds.), *Research in Personnel and Human Resource Management, Vol. 7* (pp. 59–120). Greenwich, CT: JAI Press.

Wanous, J. P., Poland, T. D., Premack, S. L. & Davis, K. S. (1992). The Effects of Met Expectations on Newcomer Attitudes and Behaviors: A Review and Meta-Analysis. *Journal of Applied Psychology, 77*, 288–297.

Watson, W. E., Kumar, K. & Michaelsen, L. K. (1993). Cultural Diversity's Impact on Interaction Progress and Performance: Comparing Homogeneous and Diverse Task Groups. *Academy of Management Journal, 36*, 590–602.

Way, D. & Tracy, S. J. (2012). Conceptualizing Compassion as Recognizing, Relating and (Re)acting: A Qualitative Study of Compassionate Communication at Hospice. *Communication Monographs, 79*, 292–315.

Weaver, V. J. (1999, May/June). If Your Organization Values Diversity, Why Are They Leaving? *Mosaics, 4*.

Weber, M. (1946). *From Max Weber: Essays in Sociology*, H. H. Gerth & C. Wright Mills, trans, and eds. New York: Oxford University Press.

_____. (1947). *Max Weber: The Theory of Social and Economic Organization*, T. Parsons & A. M. Henderson, trans, and eds. New York: Free Press.

_____. (1968). *Economy and Society*, G. Roth & C. Wittich, trans, and eds. New York: Bedminster.

Weick, K. E. (1969). *The Social Psychology of Organizing*. Reading, MA: Addison-Wesley.

_____. (1979). *The Social Psychology of Organizing*, 2nd ed., Reading, MA: Addison-Wesley.

_____. (1995). *Sensemaking in Organizations*. Newbury Park, CA: Sage.

_____. (1998). Enacted Sensemaking in Crisis Situations. *Journal of Management Studies, 25*, 305–317.

Weissman, J. (2013, April). The Ever-Shrinking Role of Tenured College Professors (In 1 Chart). *The Atlantic.* Retrieved on July 2, 2013, from http://www.theatlantic.com/business/archive/2013/04/the-ever-shrinking-role-of-tenured-college-professors-in-1-chart/274849/.

Wendt, R. (1994). Learning to "Walk the Talk": A Critical Tale of the Micropolitics at a Total Quality Management University. *Management Communication Quarterly, 8*, 5–45.

Wendt, R. F. (1998). The Sound of One Hand Clapping: Counterintuitive Lessons Extracted from Paradoxes and Double Binds in Participative Organizations. *Management Communication Quarterly, 11*, 323–371.

Whitley, R. (2009). U.S. Capitalism: A Tarnished Model? *Academy of Management Perspectives, 23*(2), 11–22.

Why Do We Need E-Race? (2007, July 17). U.S. Equal Employment Opportunity Commission. Retrieved on November 24, 2007, from http://www.eeoc.gov/initiatives/e-race/why_e-race.html.

Whyte, W. H. (1956). *The Organization Man.* Garden City, NY: Doubleday.

Williamson, A. P. (1994). Executive Commentary to "Getting Anointed for Advancement: The Case of Executive Women." *Academy of Management Executive, 8*(2), 64–66.

Wood, V. F. & Bell, P. A. (2008). Predicting Interpersonal Conflict Resolution Styles from Personality Characteristics. *Personality and Individual Difference, 45*, 126–131.

Work Groups Make Telecommute a Social Affair. (2007, September 12). *Morning Edition,* National Public Radio.

Wright, K. B., Banas, J. A., Bessarabova, E. & Bernard, D. R. (2010). A Communication Competence Approach to Examining Health Care Social Support, Stress, and Job Burnout. *Health Communication, 25*, 375–382.

Yates, J. & Orlikowski, W. J. (1992). Genres of Organizational Communication: A Structurational Approach to Studying Communication and Media. *Academy of Management Review, 17*, 299–326.

Yoon, D., Choi, S. M. & Sohn, D. (2008). Building Customer Relationships in an Electronic Age: The Role of Interactivity of E-Commerce Web Sites. *Psychology & Marketing, 25*, 602–618.

Zahra, S. A. (1999). The Changing Rules of Global Competitiveness in the 21st Century. *Academy of Management Executive, 13*(1), 36–42.

Zeidner, M., Matthews, G. & Roberts, R. D. (2004). Emotional Intelligence in the Workplace: A Critical Review. *Applied Psychology: An International Review, 53*, 371–399.

Zey, M. (1991). *The Mentor Connection.* Homewood, IL: Dow Jones-Irwin.

Zoller, H. M. (2003). Health on the Line: Identity and Disciplinary Control in Employee Occupational Health and Safety Discourse. *Journal of Applied Communication Research, 31*, 118–139.

Zorn, T. E., Flanagin, A. J. & Shoham, M. D. (2011). Institutional and Noninstitutional Influences on Information and Communication Technology Adoption and Use Among Nonprofit Organizations. *Human Communication Research, 37*, 1–33.

Zorn, T. E., Page, D. J. & Cheney, G. (2000). Nuts About Change: Multiple Perspectives on Change-Oriented Communication in a Public Sector Organization. *Management Communication Quarterly, 13*, 515–566.

Name Index

Subject Index

Page numbers followed by *f* indicate figures; those followed by *t* indicate tables